The German Minority in Interwar Poland

The German Minority in Interwar Poland analyzes what happened when Germans from three different empires – the Russian, Habsburg, and German – were forced to live together in one new state. After the First World War, German national activists made regional distinctions among these Germans and German-speakers in Poland, with preference initially for those who had once lived in the German Empire. Rather than becoming more cohesive over time, Poland's ethnic Germans remained divided and did not unite within a single representative organization. Polish repressive policies and unequal subsidies from the German state exacerbated these differences, while National Socialism created new hierarchies and unleashed bitter intra-ethnic conflict among German minority leaders. Winson Chu challenges prevailing interpretations that German nationalism in the twentieth century viewed "Germans" as a single homogeneous group of people. His revealing study shows that nationalist agitation could divide as well as unite an embattled ethnicity.

Winson Chu is an assistant professor at the University of Wisconsin-Milwaukee. He has received awards and fellowships from the American Council of Learned Societies; the United States Holocaust Memorial Museum; the German Historical Institute in Warsaw; the Friends of the German Historical Institute in Washington, D.C.; and the American Council on Germany.

Recent books in the series

The German Minority in Interwar Poland

WINSON CHU

University of Wisconsin-Milwaukee

GERMAN HISTORICAL INSTITUTE

Washington, D.C.

and

CAMBRIDGE
UNIVERSITY PRESS

CAMBRIDGE UNIVERSITY PRESS
Cambridge, New York, Melbourne, Madrid, Cape Town,
Singapore, São Paulo, Delhi, Mexico City

Cambridge University Press
32 Avenue of the Americas, New York, NY 10013-2473, USA

www.cambridge.org
Information on this title: www.cambridge.org/9781107008304

First published 2012

Printed in the United States of America

A catalog record for this publication is available from the British Library.

Library of Congress Cataloging in Publication Data
Chu, Winson.
The German minority in interwar Poland / Winson Chu.
p.   cm. – (Publications of the German Historical Institute)
Includes bibliographical references and index.
ISBN 978-1-107-00830-4
1. Germans – Poland – History – 20th century.   2. Poland – Ethnic relations – Political aspects.
3. Poland – Politics and government – 1918-1945.   4. Poland – Foreign relations – Germany.
5. Germany – Foreign relations – Poland.   I. Title.   II. Series.
DK4121.5.G4C48   2012
305.83′10438–dc23   2011031554

ISBN 978-1-107-00830-4 Hardback

For Karolina

Contents

Figures

Tables

Acknowledgments

This work owes its completion to many more people than can be recounted here in full. My thanks go to Margaret Lavinia Anderson, John Connelly, David Frick, and Andrew Janos for their friendship and advice over the years. As I worked through the revisions of the manuscript, I often thought of Gerald Feldman, who inspired me with his dedication to the profession. I would also like to thank the history department at the University of California, Berkeley, for giving me the 2007 James H. Kettner award. Likewise, I am indebted to the Friends of the German Historical Institute, its president, David Blackbourn, and the 2007 Fritz Stern Prize committee, headed by Norman Goda.

The University of Wisconsin-Milwaukee, with its encouraging atmosphere for research and teaching, made it possible to complete this book. I am especially grateful to my colleagues in the history department and elsewhere for their advice. Besides the support of the German Historical Institute in Warsaw, including its directors Eduard Mühle and Klaus Ziemer, I would also like to acknowledge the past and continuing support of Arnd Bauerkämper, Jürgen Kocka, and Philipp Ther from the Center (and Berlin School) for Comparative European History (ZVGE/BKVGE) at the Free University in Berlin. The helpful staffs of the many Polish and German archives I visited have been indispensable. I would also like to thank the City and Regional Library in Łódź and the State Archive there, especially Adam Lajdenfrost. At the Federal Archives in Berlin, Sven Devantier was helpful in locating relevant records. It would be fair to say that largest share of this book was written at my home away from home, the legendary Staatsbibliothek on Potsdamer Straße in Berlin.

Over the years, various scholars have offered their suggestions and critiques for my research, and I am especially grateful to Richard Blanke, Jochen Böhler, Astrid Eckert, Eike Eckert, Ingo Eser, Lidia Jurek, Jesse

Kauffman, Jerzy Kochanowski, Kristin Kopp, Andreas Kossert, Andrea Löw, Michael Meng, Jan Musekamp, and Bernhard Struck. This undertaking also would not have been possible without the exchanges (and deadlines) of several conferences, presentations, and publications. I would like to thank the organizers and collaborators as well as those who shared their work with me and gave me generous professional advice: Eliza J. Ablovatski, Doris Bergen, Monica Black, Hans-Jürgen Bömelburg, Chad Bryant, Elizabeth Morrow Clark, Stefan Dyroff, Astrid Eckert, Geoff Eley, Catherine Epstein, Michael Fahlbusch, Moritz Föllmer, Rüdiger Graf, Neil Gregor, Ingo Haar, Jennifer Jenkins, Wolfgang Kessler, Albert Kotowski, Ingrid Kleespies, Daniel Kronenfeld, Markus Krzoska, Eric Kurlander, Torsten Lorenz, Brian McCook, Robert Nelson, Conor O'Dwyer, David Pendas, Brian Porter-Szűcs, Krystyna Radziszewska, Cornelia Rauh, Nils Roemer, Mark Roseman, Isabel Röskau-Rydel, Annemarie Sammartino, Karl Schlögel, Detlef Schmiechen-Ackermann, James Sheehan, Edith Sheffer, Helmut Walser Smith, Roland Spickermann, Claus-Christian Szejnmann, David Tompkins, T. Hunt Tooley, Maiken Umbach, Max Vögler, Lisa Walker, Tobias Weger, Eric Weitz, Gerhard Wolf, Daniel Ziblatt, and Lisa Zwicker. A special thank you goes out to the many more friends and scholars to whom I am indebted and unable to list here.

My parents and siblings have understood if not forgiven all the missed birthdays and holidays over the past years. Above all, I would like to thank Karolina May-Chu, who has helped me give sense and purpose to this work through countless conversations. This book is dedicated to her.

The editorial staff at Cambridge University Press has been an enormous source of help. Eric Crahan and Abigail Zorbaugh have shown exemplary patience in handling my many questions about the publishing process. My thanks also go to the two anonymous readers for their insightful suggestions regarding revisions. David Lazar provided advice about the German Historical Institute series and gave the manuscript a judicious reading. Finally, some of the findings in this work on the Germans in interwar Poland have appeared in the following volumes and journals. I appreciate the permission of the publishers to reproduce them in modified form:

"The Geography of Germanness: Recentering German History in Interwar Poland." *Bulletin of the German Historical Institute*, no. 42 (Spring 2008): 95–104.

"'*Volksgemeinschaften unter sich*': German Minorities and Regionalism in Poland, 1918–39." In *German History from the Margins*, edited by Neil Gregor, Nils Roemer, and Mark Roseman, 104–126. Bloomington: Indiana University Press, 2006.

"Metropole der Minderheit: Die Deutschen in Lodz und Mittelpolen, 1918–1939." In *Die "Volksdeutschen" in Polen, Frankreich, Ungarn und der Tschechoslowakei. Mythos und Realität,* edited by Jerzy Kochanowski and Maike Sach, 95–111. Osnabrück: Fibre Verlag, 2006.

"Ostforschung im Wandel: Die deutsche Minderheit in Polen, 1918–1945." In "Raumkonstruktionen und Bevölkerungspolitik im Nationalsozialismus." Special issue, *Historische Sozialkunde,* no. 2 (2005): 32–40.

"'Das ganze Deutschtum soll es sein!' Regionalismus und die Jungdeutsche Partei in Polen 1921–1939." *Inter Finitimos. Wissenschaftlicher Informationsdienst Deutsch-Polnische Beziehungen,* nos. 19/20 (2001): 43–51.

Note on Translations, Place Names, and Concepts

All translations of Polish and German sources (primary and secondary) are mine, unless indicated otherwise. As in many histories of Central Europe, place names have different spellings, and the choice of language often appears serendipitous. In this book, English place names will be used whenever possible, for example Warsaw, Cracow, but also the regions of Pomerelia, Poznania, Volhynia, and Teschen Silesia. For certain cities in interwar Poland that do not have a commonly used English equivalent, the Polish name will be used across time and regimes for consistency. For example, local Germans and Reich Germans before the war often wrote the name of Łódź simply as Lodz (but pronounced it as "Lodsch"). After the conquest of Poland in September 1939 but before the renaming to Litzmannstadt in April 1940, German occupation authorities spelled out the city's name as Lodsch. After the war, the German spelling went back to Lodz. To keep in line with Polish sources from the main period of this study, however, this book uses Łódź (as well as Poznań, Bydgoszcz, Cieszyn) whenever there is a general reference to the city. In the names of organizations, publication information, and quotations from German and English, the spellings as they appear in the source text, such as "Lodz," "Lodsch," or "Litzmannstadt" will be kept. Moreover, I will also use the German forms "Lodzer," "Posener," "Bielitzer," and so forth when it appears in the original German or when the emphasis on Germanness and place is important.

Among the trickiest concepts are collective terms for religious, national, or ethnic affiliations. German, Poles, and Jews often appear in the sources as ascribed categories, but these labels fail to convey multiple or countervailing affiliations. Although this book will use these terms conventionally to group very disparate peoples, it will also clarify these when necessary. Finally, usage of the term Volk, and especially in associated terms such as Volksdeutsche (ethnic German) or völkisch, should be understood only in the context of ethno-national claims and not the essential nature of groups or individuals.

Abbreviations and Acronyms

BBWR	Bezpartyjny Blok Współpracy z Rządem (Nonpartisan Bloc of Cooperation with the Government)
BDP	Bund der Deutschen Polens (also Bund der Deutschen in Polen; League of the Germans in Poland, 1920–1924)
BDP	Bürgerliche Deutsche Partei (Civic German Party, mid-1920s)
BDP	Bund der Deutschen in Polen (League of the Germans in Poland, proposed 1938–1939, never founded)
BdV	Bund der Vertriebenen (League of Expellees)
DAI	Deutsches Ausland-Institut (German Foreign Institute)
DAP	Deutsche Arbeitspartei Polens (German Labor Party of Poland)
DKuWB	Deutscher Kultur- und Wirtschaftsbund (German Culture and Economic League)
DKVP	Deutsche Katholische Volkspartei (German Catholic People's Party)
DNVP	Deutschnationale Volkspartei (German National People's Party, Germany)
DP	Deutsche Partei (German Party, proposed 1920, never founded)
DP	Deutsche Partei (German Party, Upper Silesia)
DSAP	Deutsche Sozialistische Arbeitspartei Polens (German Socialist Labor Party in Poland, 1925–1939)
DSP	Deutsche Sozialdemokratische Partei Polens (German Social Democratic Party in Poland, Bydgoszcz)
DtB	Deutschtumsbund zur Wahrung der Minderheitenrechte (Germandom League for the Protection of Minority Rights, 1921–1923)

DV, also DViSuS   Deutsche Vereinigung im Sejm und Senat (German Union
                  in Sejm and Senate, 1923–1934)
DV, also DVW   Deutsche Vereinigung in Westpolen (German Union in
                  Western Poland, 1934–1939)
DVP   Deutsche Volkspartei (German People's Party, Germany)
DVV   Deutscher Volksverband (German People's Union,
                  1924–1939)
EWZ   Einwandererzentrale (Immigration Central Office)
JDP   Jungdeutsche Partei für Polen (Young German Party for
                  Poland, Bielsko, 1929–1939)
LWW   Landsmannschaft Weichsel-Warthe (postwar expellee
                  organization for Germans from interwar Poland)
NSDAP   Nationalsozialistische Deutsche Arbeiterpartei (National
                  Socialist German Workers' Party; Nazi Party, Germany)
PPS   Polska Partia Socjalistyczna (Polish Socialist Party)
RDP   Rat der Deutschen in Polen (Council of the Germans in
                  Poland)
VB   Volksbund (People's League, Upper Silesia, 1922–1939)
VDA   Verein für das Deutschtum im Ausland (Association for
                  Germans Abroad); after 1934, Volksbund für das Deutschtum
                  im Ausland (People's League for Germans Abroad)
VDR   Volksdeutscher Rat (Ethnic German Council, Germany)
VoMi   Volksdeutsche Mittelstelle (Ethnic German Liaison Office)
ZAG   Zentral-Arbeits-Gemeinschaft (also
                  Zentralarbeitsgemeinschaft; Central Labor Community)
ZOKZ   Związek Obrony Kresów Zachodnich (Union for the
                  Defense of the Western Borderlands); after 1934, Polski
                  Związek Zachodni (Polish Western Union; PZZ)

Introduction

On a winter afternoon in 1936 in the Polish city of Łódź, well over a thousand people gathered in the hall of the men's choral society on the city's main thoroughfare, Piotrkowska Street. They were there for a rally held by a German minority organization, the German People's Union (DVV). Among the attendees, however, were numerous members of a rival group, the Young German Party (JDP). When the local leader of the Young Germans entered the hall, someone called out the command "Achtung, Young Germans!" and the room thundered to the shouts of "Heil." When the youth leader for the German People's Union arrived in the crowded building, however, someone else from the balcony likewise called out "Achtung, Young Germans!" Several of the disoriented Young Germans, not knowing that they were cheering their opponent, began to applaud and yell "Heil." After realizing their error, the enraged Young German intruders attacked the balcony, cleared it of the troublesome members of the German People's Union, and occupied it. The meeting, which was a German People's Union event after all, went downhill from there.

The gathering came to order with great difficulty. The first speaker of the German People's Union emphasized that the Germans in Poland, as part of the greater national community of Germans led by Adolf Hitler, did not need a political party but sought unity in a national organization instead. This seemingly minor nuance angered the Young Germans, who were likewise supporters of Hitler but who wanted a unified political party for all Germans in Poland. Having taken up the front rows, the Young Germans attacked the stage and were only beaten back with great difficulty. Several fights broke out in the audience, and the catcalls and jeering by the Young Germans forced the first speaker to leave. The next speaker likewise complained about the goals of the Young German party. The Young Germans again felt provoked and had to be fought back once more.

1

The third speaker also criticized the idea of a German party in Poland, saying the Germans should work for the good of the national community instead. At this moment, the Young Germans rushed the stage, grabbed and ripped apart the host party's banner, and a melee ensued. The meeting's organizers from the German People's Union called the city police, and order was briefly restored after the arrest of three Young Germans. However, another wave of fighting led to the breakup of the meeting altogether, and the Polish police were needed once again to forcibly evacuate those stubborn Young Germans who still refused to leave.[1]

This example was just one in a long conflict among various German parties within interwar Poland. In this case, both of these German parties claimed to be National Socialist, and both espoused a similar rhetoric of unity, especially regarding the national community, or *Volksgemeinschaft*. Not only could they not agree on what this unity meant in practical terms, but they and other German nationalist groups fought rhetorically and physically in public spaces before Polish observers over its interpretation. Despite the widespread view of the Polish state as the primary enemy of the German minority, it was not unusual for Poles to mediate in this internecine German conflict. Indeed, German minority leaders often denounced one another to Polish authorities, who were themselves confused by how the idea of German national unity could cause these deep divisions. One Polish police official who tried to keep order at the rowdy meeting in Łódź shamed the Germans by reminding them that they were "civilized people" after all.[2]

Yet this strife between German rival parties also had a spatial dimension that can be traced to the aftermath of the virtually unexpected collapse of three Central European empires in 1918. The victorious Allied coalition hammered out a series of new states on the principle of national self-determination. These states, although having a titular nationality, were hardly nation-states in reality. Each state had significant ethnic minorities, many of which harbored bitter resentment against the loss of their right to national self-determination. Among these minorities were the Germans, who were found in settlements throughout East Central Europe. Owing to

1 Voivodeship of Łódź (Vice-Voivode A. Potocki) to Nationalities Department of the Interior Ministry in Warsaw, January 8, 1936, copy as attachment sent by Skarbek, Interior Ministry to Polish Foreign Ministry (Wydział Ustrojów Międzynarodowych), January 14, 1936, in AAN, MSZ, folder 2238, 1–3.
2 Annotated accounts that minimized Young German criticisms and were skewed favorably toward the German People's Union include the following newspaper articles: "Kundgebungen des Deutschen Volksverbandes. Vormarsch der volksdeutschen Front gegen Terror und Haßpropaganda. Organisierter Überfall jungdeutscher Sprengtrupps auf die Redner. – Die wahre Art der jungdeutschen 'Erneuerung,'" *Freie Presse*, January 7, 1936, 1–2; "Brief an uns. Ein Unparteiischer über dieVorfälle," (letter by Gustav Schumann, dated January 10, 1936), in *Freie Presse*, January 12, 1936, 6.

the still powerful position of a defeated Germany, these German minorities had disproportionate influence on domestic and foreign affairs. Both Weimar and Nazi claims to take care of German compatriots abroad made the treatment of German minorities in Eastern Europe a flashpoint of international tensions, leading toward the Second World War. In the 1938 Munich Agreement, the European powers dismembered Czechoslovakia so that the Sudeten German minority could join its putative fatherland. In Poland, the situation proved to be more intractable. The instrumentalization of the German minority for foreign policy goals reached its apex in 1939, when reports of Polish abuses against Germans were used to legitimate Hitler's invasion of Poland. Although postwar Polish and German historians have disagreed over whether the German minority served as a fifth column, they do agree that Polish repression and National Socialism led to the minority's growing unity. Behind this façade of *völkisch* (ethnic) unity, however, lurked serious divisions that undercut the political cohesion of this minority. Despite the efforts of Reich officials and the National Socialist fervor of the German minority leaders, these Germans were never unified into a comprehensive party along the lines of Konrad Henlein's Sudetendeutsche Heimatfront. Rather, the Germans in Poland remained fractured among several regional organizations.

These divisions can be understood by examining the problems of national cohesion and regional particularism. Unlike Czechoslovakia, where a great majority of the Germans came from Austrian Bohemia, interwar Poland inherited Germans from all three shattered Central European empires. The Germans of Western Poland, living on lands formerly of the German Empire, had enjoyed political and social domination prior to 1918. The conversion from *Staatsvolk* – people of the state – to *Volksdeutsche* – ethnic Germans – was a particularly hard blow for them.[3] Most of these Germans found it difficult to come to terms with Polish rule, and Germany's claims on the ceded territories only reinforced their negative attitude toward Poland. The German speakers in Central and Eastern Poland, which included the former Congress Kingdom and other lands freed from Russian rule, had already experienced life in a state where Germans rarely belonged to the political elite and where German language had been increasingly suppressed. Many German activists here initially viewed the new Polish state with great hope, for they believed that the Poles would be more hospitable to their own national minorities than the former Russian masters. Likewise, German-speakers in the formerly Austrian lands of southeastern Poland were

---

3 *Staatsvolk* can also be translated here as "titular nationality."

accustomed to local rule by Poles. Especially the peasant populations in formerly Austrian Galicia and formerly Russian Volhynia were rarely pre-occupied with issues concerning Germany or Germanness.

That these German-speaking groups had substantial historical differences is nothing new. Yet this book tells a different story from the standard narrative of these "three minorities" becoming one over time.[4] Throughout the interwar period, there were several attempts to forge these heterogeneous elements politically, but all these attempts at "minority building" failed.[5] Over time, in fact, the Germans in interwar Poland were increasingly splintered along regional lines. This book examines how German leaders in Poland proclaimed unity in word while undermining it in deed. In short, it focuses on the limits of national solidarity within the German minority in Poland.

THE HISTORIES OF THE GERMANS IN POLAND

The instrumentalization of the minority in the war's outbreak has meant that the literature devoted to the minority is fairly broad. Yet little attention has been paid to the question of cross-cutting loyalties within the minority itself. Rather, both Poles and Germans have emphasized the nationality struggle, or *Volkstumskampf*, between the minority and the Polish state. Much of the Polish and German literature consists of short contributions collected in edited volumes; monographs of book length make up only a small fraction. Many of the authors are part of the *Erlebnisgeneration* (those who experienced the events first hand), which often led to insufficient detachment and analysis: indeed, the majority of German works can be classified as sentimental memoirs or *Heimatliteratur* (homeland literature).[6] Especially the debates about whether the minority was a fifth column or who was to blame for the *Bromberger Blutsonntag* (the massacre of several hundred people in Bromberg on the first Sunday after the German invasion of Poland in 1939) has overshadowed the many fruitful questions that an

---

4 On the unification of the "three minorities," see Marian Wojciechowski, "Die deutsche Minderheit in Polen (1920–1939)," in *Deutsche und Polen zwischen den Kriegen. Minderheitenstatus und "Volkstumskampf" im Grenzgebiet. Amtliche Berichterstattung aus beiden Ländern, 1920–1939*, ed. Rudolf Jaworski et al., vol. 1, 1–26 (Munich: Sauer, 1997), here 4.

5 On minority building, see Ingo Eser, *"Volk, Staat, Gott!" Die deutsche Minderheit in Polen und ihr Schulwesen 1918–1939* (Wiesbaden: Harrassowitz, 2010), 34.

6 In one example, the German historian Sabine Bamberger-Stemmann notes that as much as 95% of the existing literature for Polish Upper Silesia can be labeled as "Heimatliteratur." Markus Krzoska, "Tagungsbericht: Die Erforschung der Geschichte der Deutschen in Polen. Stand und Zukunftsperspektiven," Conference of the Kommission für die Geschichte der Deutschen in Polen e.V. from May 29 to 31, 1999, in Mainz, report dated November 1, 1999, accessed August 10, 2006, http://hsozkult.geschichte.hu-berlin.de/BEITRAG/TAGBER/polen.htm.

examination of the German minority in Poland poses. Moreover, the issue of the loyalty of the interwar German minority is intrinsically tied to the question of the expulsions of the Germans from the eastern territories lost after the Second World War. This emotionally laden topic of viewing the Germans and the German nation as victims of the Second World War was revived in the late 1990s and especially in discussions about establishing a Center Against Expulsions, planned by the Bund der Vertriebenen (BdV) with support from Christian Democrats and several Social Democrats. Many works are accusatory in nature, and even more scholarly (and lengthy) attempts to provide documentation of the other nation's crimes only reveal how politically charged this topic was and remains – despite the recent thaw in German-Polish relations. Nationalized positions have not necessarily declined after 1989 – indeed, they have often reinvented themselves.

By focusing on majority-minority conflict that is integral to the Volks-tumskampf narrative, the scholarly literature has tended to attribute the same experience to *all* Germans living in the Polish state, thus underplaying the depth of political conflict within the minority. Instead, they reproduce a narrative in which the Germans in Poland slowly overcame the legacies of the partitions to become one national community. Indeed, the very vocabulary used to describe the minority suggests harmony among the Germans. As Rogers Brubaker notes, the word "national minority" connotes "internally unified, externally sharply bounded groups."[7] Although the word *Minderheit* (minority) was in common usage in the interwar period, many used the term *Volksgruppe* (ethnic or national group) instead. There is no equivalent for Volksgruppe in the English language, and it also has ambiguous meanings in German. In its narrow sense, the contemporary usage of Volksgruppe referred to specific regional settlements within a minority; thus a minority could be made up of several Volksgruppen. However, in its broader, more common usage, Volksgruppe referred to an entire minority community within a state.[8] Whereas Minderheit and Volksgruppe were often used interchangeably, the latter became increasingly loaded and politicized with a normative claim of ethnic cohesion. Not surprisingly, contemporary German nationalists preferred Volksgruppe precisely because it invoked the connection of the Reich with Germans living abroad.[9] The concept of

---

7 Rogers Brubaker, *Nationalism Reframed. Nationhood and the National Question in the New Europe* (Cambridge/New York: Cambridge University Press, 1996), 62.
8 Valdis O. Lumans, *Himmler's Auxiliaries: The Volksdeutsche Mittelstelle and the German National Minorities of Europe, 1933–1945* (Chapel Hill: University of North Carolina Press, 1993), 22–23.
9 See Horand Horsa Schacht, *Du mußt volksdeutsch sein!* (Dortmund: Crüwell, 1935), 9. Max Hildebert Boehm, a Volkstum theorist, refused to use the word *Minderheit* (minority) because of its foreign nature and because it failed to express the diversity of German experience abroad. Moreover, he believed

Volksgruppe became a positivistic, teleological category that emphasized spiritual and biological unity while concealing the dissonance and power conflicts between the Germans in Poland. It implied not just growth and evolution but also a collective will toward unity.

This book refers to the master narrative of "Volksgruppe-in-becoming" as the "Volksgruppe paradigm."[10] Works by German and Polish historians have repeated the thesis that the uniform experience of repression, the struggle for minority rights, and a National Socialist renewal had transformed the loose and heterogeneous German minority into a tightly bound and homogeneous Volksgruppe.[11] Even if these works state that a Volksgruppe never fully evolved due to lack of time and other obstacles, they still maintain that the minority was on this trajectory of growing unity, hence confusing program with action.[12] Substantial differences are downplayed, and there is the danger of reifying the concept of Volksdeutsche by reaffirming the premises and wishful thinking of German nationalists. The fact that former German minority members dominated the scholarship on the Germans in interwar Poland into the 1980s only made the task of breaking this paradigm more difficult. Many German and Polish historians still fall into this Volksgruppe paradigm, even as they simultaneously argue for a more differentiated view of the minority.[13] One study, for example, called for using the term Volksgruppe as an analytical category that is different from simple minority status.[14] Yet as we have seen, the very concept of Volksgruppe is itself loaded, and its constructed nature needs to be analyzed.

that the use of the term would give recognition to Poland as a nation-state. See *Grenzdeutsch – Großdeutsch. Vortrag anläßlich der Hauptausschußtagung des V.D.A. im November 1924* (Dresden: Verein für das Deutschtum im Ausland, 1925), 1–2; Max Hildebert Boehm, *Die deutschen Grenzlande* (Berlin: Reimar Hobbing, 1925), 198–199.

10 On the "Volksgruppe paradigm," see Ingo Haar, "Vom 'Volksgruppen-Paradigma' bis zum 'Recht auf Heimat': Exklusion und Inklusion als Deutungsmuster in den Diskursen über Zwangsmigrationen vor und nach 1945," in *Die "Volksdeutschen" in Polen, Frankreich, Ungarn und der Tschechoslowakei. Mythos und Realität*, ed. Jerzy Kochanowski and Maike Sach, 17–39 (Osnabrück: Fibre, 2006).

11 One of the most notable proponents of the thesis that the German minority had transformed into a Volksgruppe was Richard Breyer, who grew up in Central Poland and became director of the Herder-Institut in Marburg. See Richard Breyer, *Das Deutsche Reich und Polen, 1932–1937. Außenpolitik und Volksgruppenfragen* (Würzburg: Holzner, 1955), especially 49–51, 227–236, 255–256. See also another work by a German from Central Poland: Theodor Bierschenk, *Die deutsche Volksgruppe in Polen, 1934–1939* (Würzburg: Holzner, 1954).

12 See Joachim Rogall, "Einheit in Vielfalt der Deutschen aus Polen," in *Archive und Sammlungen der Deutschen aus Polen. Erlebte Geschichte, bewahrtes Kulturgut*, ed. Peter E. Nasarski, 13–18 (Berlin/Bonn: Landsmannschaft Weichsel-Warthe, 1992); Wilfried Gerke, "Auf dem Wege zur Einheit. Die Deutschen in Polen zwischen den Weltkriegen," *Germano-Polonica. Mitteilung zur Geschichte der Deutschen in Polen und der deutsch-polnischen Beziehungen* 2 (2002/2003): 10–17.

13 For recent examples, see Wojciechowski, "Die Deutsche Minderheit in Polen (1920–1939)," 4; Jörg K. Hoensch, *Geschichte Polens* (Stuttgart: Eugen Ulmer, 1998), 274–275.

14 Carsten Eichenberger, *Die Deutschen in Polen. Von der verleugneten Minderheit zur anerkannten Volksgruppe* (Augsburg: Bukowina-Institut, 1994), 18–22.

The remarkable resiliency of the Volksgruppe paradigm reveals not only how well this concept fit into German and Polish political agendas but also into broader conceptions of modernization that underplay the problem of regionality and regionalism. As the American historian Richard Blanke has noted, the postwar historiography has acknowledged regional differences within the minority, yet they have not made them into a "primary consideration."[15] The question of how regions are translated into political factors within the minority is ignored, and regionality is reduced to anecdotal and folkloric characterizations.[16] Indeed, this view of the region as somehow backward and even reactionary merely reinforces the Volksgruppe-in-becoming interpretation of nationalism as a positive, modernizing force. The stubbornness of this thesis is due in part to its ideological proximity to national grand narratives elsewhere, where the success of the national project is commensurate to the steady reduction of regionalism. Such normative language is not unique to the Germans in Poland, of course, but is apparent in many other narratives of national awakening and unity. It is comparable to the traditional Jewish historiography on the Jews in Poland, whereby two approaches have emerged: to reveal the anti-Semitic nature of Polish state and society on the one hand and the flourishing of Jewish cultural life and the vibrancy of the struggle against this anti-Semitism on the other. Other strands of Jewish life that do not fit this mold, such as the assimilationists, are often downplayed or criticized.[17]

The scholarly preoccupation with the Volkstumskampf in the formerly Prussian territories of Poznania/Great Poland (Poznań/Posen), Pomerelia (Pomorze/Pommerellen), and Upper Silesia has only strengthened the Volksgruppe narrative. By focusing on the heightened nationality conflict in these areas, such works have set not only the tone but also the terms of debate in examining the German minority in Poland. During the interwar period, the territories lost by Prussia became the subject of an incessant propaganda war between Germany and Poland. German spokesmen criticized Polish nationalist policies for the dramatic decline of the Germans in Western Poland after 1918.[18] Polish journalists and scholars refuted these

15 Richard Blanke, *Orphans of Versailles: The Germans in Western Poland, 1918–1939* (Lexington: University Press of Kentucky, 1993), 3–4.
16 See especially Gotthold Rhode, "Lodzer Deutsche – Posener Deutsche. Keine wissenschaftliche Untersuchung, sondern eine Plauderei," in *Suche die Meinung. Karl Dedecius, dem Übersetzer und Mittler zum 65. Geburtstag*, ed. Elvira Grözinger and Andreas Lawaty, 237–256 (Wiesbaden: Harrassowitz, 1986), here 254–256.
17 Ezra Mendelsohn, "Jewish Historiography on Polish Jewry," *Polin: Studies in Polish Jewry* 8 (1994): 3–13, here 4–6.
18 See especially Ernst Hansen, *Polens Drang nach dem Westen* (Berlin: Koehler, 1927); Hermann Rauschning, *Die Entdeutschung Westpreußens und Posens. Zehn Jahre polnischer Politik* (Berlin: Reimar Hobbing, 1930); Richard Kammel [Gottfried Martin, pseud.], *"Brennende Wunden." Tatsachenbericht*

accusations by claiming that the emigration of Germans was tied to their overwhelming dependence on the state for civil service jobs and subsidies. To them, the Germans had illegitimately established their presence through an aggressive *Drang nach Osten* (drive to the east) and the historical crime of the Polish partitions.[19]

After the Second World War, national partisanship politicized the minority issue even more. Historians supporting Poland's right to westward expansion accused ethnic German Polish citizens (especially in Pomerelia and eastern Upper Silesia) of disloyalty to the Second Polish Republic, using this charge of treason to justify Poland's postwar expulsion of several million Germans from the so-called recovered territories. For Mirosław Cygański, a postwar Łódź historian, this annexation was an act of historical justice.[20] German historians, however, have emphasized the injustice done by Versailles as well as the loyalty of the German minority to the Polish state.[21] In their view, the behavior of the German minority was a reaction to Poland's repressive policies in the interwar period, thus making their postwar loss (and the expulsion of other German groups elsewhere) unwarranted. The

über die Notlage der evangelischen Deutschen in Polen (Berlin: Eckart, 1931); Richard Bahr, *Volk jenseits der Grenzen* (Hamburg: Hanseatische Verlagsanstalt, 1933); Friedrich Heidelck, *Die deutschen Ansied-lungen in Westpreußen und Posen in den ersten zwölf Jahren der polnischen Herrschaft* (Breslau: Priebatsch, 1934); Viktor Kauder, *Das Deutschtum in Posen und Pommerellen*, vol. 3 of *Das Deutschtum in Polen. Ein Bildband*, edited by Viktor Kauder (Leipzig: Hirzel, 1937).

19 Karol Gostyński, "Zarys historii politycznej niemców w województwach zachodnich po wojnie," in "Problem niemiecki na Ziemiach Zachodnich," special issue, *Strażnica Zachodnia* 12, nos. 1–2 (1933): 45–81; Karol Gostyński, "Przewrót hitlerowski w Niemczech i Niemcy w Polsce (Część pierwsza)," *Sprawy Narodowościowe* 10, nos. 1–2 (1936): 22–39; Karol Gostyński, "Przewrót hitlerowski w Niemczech i Niemcy w Polsce (Dokończenie)," *Sprawy Narodowościowe* 10, no. 3 (1936): 197–222; Edmund Męclewski, *Walka graniczna trwa* (Poznań: Gospodarka Zachodnia, 1939); Józef Winiewicz, *Mobilizacja sił niemieckich w Polsce* (Warsaw: Polityka, 1939).

20 Mirosław Cygański: *Mniejszość niemiecka w Polsce centralnej w latach 1919–1939* (Łódź: Wydawnictwo Łódzkie, 1962), 149–150. See also Andrzej Leśniewski, ed., *Irredentism and Provocation: A Contribution to the History of the German Minority in Poland* (Poznań: Wydawnictwo Zachodnie, 1960); Karol Grünberg, *Niemcy i ich organizacje polityczne w Polsce międzywojennej* (Warsaw: Wiedza Powszechna, 1970); Marian Drożdowski, "The National Minorities in Poland 1918–1939," *Acta Poloniae historica* 22 (1970): 226–251; Edward Wynot, "The Polish Germans, 1919–1939: National Minority in a Multinational State," *The Polish Review* 17, no. 1 (Winter 1972): 23–64.

21 See especially Friedrich Swart, *Diesseits und jenseits der Grenze. Das deutsche Genossenschaftswesen im Posener Land und das deutsch-polnische Verhältnis bis zum Ende des Zweiten Weltkrieges* (Leer: Rautenberg & Möckel, 1954); Christian Höltje, *Die Weimarer Republik und das Ostlocarno-Problem, 1919–1934. Revision oder Garantie der deutschen Ostgrenze von 1919* (Würzburg: Holzner, 1958); Friedrich Swart and Richard Breyer, "Die deutsche Volksgruppe im polnischen Staat," in *Das östliche Deutschland. Ein Handbuch*, ed. Göttinger Arbeitskreis (Würzburg: Holzner, 1959), 477–526; Erich Keyser, "Der Deutschtumsverlust in Westpreußen 1918–1939," *Ostdeutsche Wissenschaft* 8 (1961): 63–79; Gotthold Rhode, "Das Deutschtum in Posen und Pommerellen in der Zeit der Weimarer Republik," in *Die deutschen Ostgebiete zur Zeit der Weimarer Republik*, ed. Erwin Hölzle, 88–132 (Cologne/Graz: Böhlau, 1966); Walther Threde and Peter E. Nasarski, eds., *Polen und sein preußischer Streifen, 1919–1939. Die deutsche Volksgruppe in Posen und Pommerellen* (Berlin/Bonn: Westkreuz, 1983); Hugo Rasmus, *Pommerellen-Westpreußen 1919–1939* (Munich: Herbig, 1989).

Polish mistreatment of the minority, especially in the first days of the war, and the expulsion of the Germans from Polish territory are legitimate topics of study, but they still tend to give disproportional weight to the minority's victimization and reproduce the terms of a Manichean Volkstumskampf. In contrast, the literature on the central and southeastern areas of Poland remains sparse.[22] By embedding the history of the Central and Eastern Polish Germans into the narrative of their Western Polish counterparts, these authors have downplayed the role of political particularisms within the minority; and willingly or not, they have historically constructed the Volksgruppe that did not exist in the interwar period.

Since 1989, several new developments in the historiography have become apparent. For example, improved relations between Germany and Poland have led to a presentist tendency. Some Polish historians have attempted to make good for overly nationalistic judgments in the past by reevaluating the myth of the German fifth column and overcoming the distortions of the Polish government both in the interwar and communist periods. Pleading for German-Polish reconciliation, these authors use the history of the interwar German minority as a lesson for neighborly coexistence in a post-national European Union and for the better treatment of the sizeable German/Upper Silesian minority in Poland today.[23] Other works attempt to contextualize the Germans in Poland in a broader East Central European perspective or in the analytic framework of borderlands. In *Orphans of Versailles*, for example, Richard Blanke examines the nationalism of a "fallen people," and Rogers Brubaker is interested in understanding the interaction of homeland, host state, and minority nationalisms.[24]

Several historians have also studied peripheral groups within the minority. Pia Nordblom's study of Eduard Pant's German Catholic Party and Petra Blachetta-Madajczyk's work on the German Socialists in Poland have given new recognition to anti-Nazi movements within the minority.[25] Several

22 Krzysztof Woźniak, "Forschungsstand und Forschungsdesiderata zur Geschichte der Deutschen in Mittelpolen," *Nordost-Archiv* 9, no. 2 (2000): 413–427.
23 See for example Dariusz Matelski, *Niemcy w Polsce w XX wieku* (Warsaw/Poznań: Wydawnictwo Naukowe PWN, 1999), 343. Several Polish sociologists have examined post-communist Upper Silesia and the German and Silesian groups there. See Zbigniew Kurcz, *Mniejszość niemiecka w Polsce* (Wrocław: Wydawnictwo Uniwersytetu Wrocławskiego, 1995); Krzysztof Frysztacki, ed., *Polacy, Ślązacy, Niemcy. Studia nad stosunkami społeczno-kulturowymi na Śląsku Opolskim* (Cracow: Universitas, 1998); Maria Szmeja, *Niemcy? Polacy? Ślązacy! Rodzimi mieszkańcy Opolszczyzny w świetle analiz socjologicznych* (Cracow: Universitas, 2000).
24 Blanke, *Orphans of Versailles*, 4–5, Brubaker, *Nationalism Reframed*, 58.
25 Petra Blachetta-Madajczyk, *Klassenkampf oder Nation? Deutsche Sozialdemokratie in Polen 1918–1939* (Düsseldorf: Droste, 1997); Pia Nordblom, *Für Glaube und Volkstum. Die katholische Wochenzeitung "Der Deutsche in Polen" (1919–1939) in der Auseinandersetzung mit dem Nationalsozialismus* (Paderborn: Ferdinand Schöningh, 2000).

works have used the German minority in Poland to examine the interwar minority treaties and Germany's foreign policy during the Weimar period.[26] In particular, Christian Raitz von Frentz has strongly criticized the Minorities Protection Treaty that had been mandated by the Treaty of Versailles, condemning the treaty's exacerbation of the nationality conflict.[27] The tendency to draw forgotten lessons from the German minority in Poland is due partially to the growing concern for the rights of ethnic minorities: the shocking brutalities in campaigns of ethnic cleansing and genocide that have occurred in the last two decades have shown that such problems can be as intractable now as they were at the beginning of the twentieth century.

Scholars from Germany have also followed the wider trend of everyday history (*Alltagsgeschichte*) and have used case studies to examine daily life "from below."[28] In localized contexts, nationality itself appears as only one of many competing loyalties, for both "Germans" and "Poles" were heterogeneous collectivities that were ridden with internal conflict.[29] As Mathias Niendorf suggests, a glance at the local sections of newspapers offers a very different view of ethnic relations than what is presented in the political section.[30] Putting nationality conflict in the background thus opens a window on daily inter-ethnic cooperation, which was – in light of the increasing nationalist claims – a variation of *Eigensinn* (having one's own mind), to use Alf Lüdtke's usage of the term.[31] Moreover, Alltagsgeschichte offers the possibility of comparative study of minorities along a common border as well as examinations that transcend conventional periodizations.

---

26 Helmut Pieper, *Die Minderheitenfrage und das Deutsche Reich 1919–1933/34* (Hamburg: Institut für Internationale Angelegenheiten der Universität Hamburg, 1974); John W. Hiden, "The Weimar Republic and the Problem of the Auslandsdeutsche," *Journal of Contemporary History* 12 (1977): 273–289; Bastiaan Schot, *Nation oder Staat? Deutschland und der Minderheitenschutz. Zur Völkerbundspolitik der Stresemann-Ära* (Marburg/Lahn: Johann-Gottfried-Herder-Institut, 1988); see also various works by Carole Fink: "Defender of Minorities: Germany in the League of Nations, 1926–1933," *Central European History* 5, no. 4 (1972): 330–357; "Stresemann's Minority Policies, 1924–29," *Journal of Contemporary History* 14, no. 3 (1979): 403–422; "The Weimar Republic and its Minderheitenpolitik: Challenge to a Democracy," *German Politics and Society* 14, no. 1 (Spring 1996): 80–95.

27 Christian Raitz von Frentz, *A Lesson Forgotten. Minority Protection Under the League of Nations: The Case of the German Minority in Poland, 1920–1934* (New York: Lit, 1999).

28 Mathias Niendorf, "Deutsche und Polen in Pommerellen von 1920 bis 1945. Rollenerwartungen und Realität," *Nordost-Archiv* 6, no. 2 (1997): 687–728; Mathias Niendorf, *Minderheiten an der Grenze. Deutsche und Polen in den Kreisen Flatow (Złotów) und Zempelburg (Sępolno Krajeńskie) 1900–1939* (Wiesbaden: Harrassowitz, 1997); Torsten Lorenz, *Von Birnbaum nach Międzychód. Bürgergesellschaft und Nationalitätenkampf in Großpolen bis zum Zweiten Weltkrieg* (Berlin: Berliner Wissenschafts-Verlag, 2005).

29 Niendorf, "Deutsche und Polen in Pommerellen," 714.

30 Niendorf, "Deutsche und Polen in Pommerellen," 705–706.

31 See Alf Lüdtke, ed., *Alltagsgeschichte. Zur Rekonstruktion historischer Erfahrungen und Lebensweisen* (Frankfurt/Main: Campus, 1989); Alf Lüdtke, *Eigen-Sinn. Fabrikalltag, Arbeitererfahrungen und Politik vom Kaiserreich bis in den Faschismus* (Hamburg: Ergebnisse-Verlag, 1993).

By focusing on both ethnic groups, such local studies also avoid the oft-voiced criticism of being overly fixated on just one nationality.[32] They challenge the neat dualistic framework of nationality struggle and show that the allegiances of German minority nationalists were less than clear as they navigated between Berlin's demands, economic considerations, völkisch ideals, familial and social obligations, as well as their own interests as citizens of the Polish state.

There is, however, the danger of throwing out the baby with the bathwater. By equating minority politics with the conflict between German leaders and Polish authorities, microstudies either limit politics to Volkstumskampf or ignore political activity altogether. There are still many aspects of German political life in Poland, such as regionalization, that are associated with the so-called nationality struggle in indirect but important ways.[33] Two recent works reveal the differentiated politics within German institutions in interwar Poland. Ingo Eser has examined the German minority school system to show the limits of integration in a nationalizing state.[34] Beata Lakeberg's study of the German minority press reveals political and regional differences in the Germans' self-image and stereotypes of other nationalities.[35] At the same time, there needs to be a better understanding of how these regional differences were not simply legacies but constructed over time through political competition.

SUBJECTS OF ENQUIRY, METHODS, AND AIMS

The study of nationalism has long been preoccupied with the division between primordialist and instrumentalist/constructivist views. The two differ on how nationalism arises and national identity spreads, but they both emphasize its ability to politically unite people who share certain (i.e., ethnic) traits. There is a great need, however, to examine in greater depth how nationalisms evolve once a common sense of nationhood has been established among activists. This book examines the apparent paradox: Why

---

32 Niendorf, *Minderheiten an der Grenze*, 10.
33 Mathias Niendorf is a particularly strong proponent of the approach "from below." Niendorf, *Minderheiten an der Grenze*, 15; see also Niendorf, "Deutsche und Polen in Pommerellen," 688–689nn6, 8, where he criticizes one recent work for its "neglect of the regional problem to the benefit of pan-state aspects."
34 Eser, *Volk, Staat, Gott*.
35 Beata Lakeberg, *Die deutsche Minderheitenpresse in Polen 1918–1939 und ihr Polen- und Judenbild* (Frankfurt/Main: Peter Lang, 2010). See also Beata Lakeberg, "Identitätsfragen in der deutschen Minderheitenpresse während der ersten Jahre der Zweiten Polnischen Republik," in *Grenzdiskurse. Zeitungen deutschsprachiger Minderheiten und ihr Feuilleton in Mitteleuropa bis 1939*, ed. Sibylle Schönborn, 81–93 (Essen: Klartext, 2009).

and how did an increasing nationalization of political life in the minority widen regional divisions? Although much has been written on the appeal and integrative nature of nationalism (and National Socialism), the potential of nationalism to *create* conflict within a national group is still largely understudied.[36] Nationalist German leaders in Poland, seeing themselves as part of an embattled minority, were largely in consensus about what their cultural goals were. Yet their different historical development and the region-specific policies of Poland and Germany meant that minority leaders had different ideas regarding the shape of the German national community in Poland. How did regional German leaders protect their particular interests through nationalist ideology and rhetoric, and how did their appeals to the nation undermine the status quo and foster disunity? How did nationalism, and especially National Socialism, catalyze latent cleavages and create new conflicts that had not existed previously? In short, what are the limits of national integration?

A reframing of the problem from inter-ethnic to intra-ethnic conflict – and especially between region and nation – offers new perspectives on the dynamics of minority mobilization. Among these is the question of agency. Studies of national minorities often portray minority leaders as passive actors by concentrating on the policies of the ethnic motherland and/or the host nation-state. This view thus reduces the minorities themselves to peripheral objects that merely react to decisions determined at the metropoles.[37] Instead of nationalism bridging regionalism, this book examines how a common ideology could divide as much as it unites. It focuses on how German activists perceived one another in light of regional variations and how they constructed and politically instrumentalized notions of difference. Indeed, regional cleavages between Germans were growing more salient over time. It suggests that such attempts to build a "we" community in Poland exacerbated regional conflict and undercut the project of unity.

Much has been made of nations as "imagined communities," but it is rarely asked what happens when these members of the imagined community actually meet and have to cooperate. How does the imagination stretch to encompass diversity?[38] In German history especially, the study of regions

36 For recent works that examine this problem, see Helmut Walser Smith, *German Nationalism and Religious Conflict: Culture, Ideology, and Politics, 1870–1914* (Princeton: Princeton University Press, 1995); Sven Oliver Müller, "Die umstrittene nationale Gemeinschaft. Nationalismus als Konfliktphänomen," in *Politische Kollektive. Die Konstruktion nationaler, rassischer und ethnischer Gemeinschaften*, ed. Ulrike Jureit, 122–143 (Münster: Westfälisches Dampfboot, 2001); Moritz Föllmer, "The Problem of National Solidarity in Interwar Germany," *German History* 23, no. 2 (2005): 202–231.

37 Niendorf, *Minderheiten an der Grenze*, 12.

38 On "imagined communities," see Benedict Anderson, *Imagined Communities: Reflections on the Origins and Spread of Nationalism* (London/New York: Verso, 2006).

has enjoyed a long pedigree from the *Kleinstaaterei* (multitude of small states) of the Holy Roman Empire to reunified Germany. Allan Mitchell notes that regional particularism in Germany is the "subject that will not go away."[39] Still, only recently has regionality been taken seriously.[40] If nationalism is a term fraught with many meanings, however, regionalism can be even more elusive. Previous works on regionalism have tended to see regional identity as a form of community that is somehow more primary than national identity or at least a factor mitigating national loyalty. Yet as one sociologist has argued, "It is important not to view 'the community' as a given natural unit. Collectivities and 'communities' are to some extent ideological and material constructions, and their boundaries, structures and norms are a result of constant processes of struggles and negotiations."[41] The collectivity of region is no different, and it is not the purpose of this study to reify regional identities or to show that they are more essential than nations. Rather, this study examines the dynamic relation between regional and national forms of belonging, their shifting meanings, and their mutual reinforcement of one another. It will examine how region came to be imagined as a significant point of self-reference, especially in the way minority elites used region-building for nation-building – and vice versa.

Many studies of regionalism describe in actuality a type of nationalist separatism (e.g., Basque regionalism) or supranational cooperation (Baltic regionalism). Indeed, the former seems to be a particularly common case, thus many works on regionalism are really studies of separatist movements with the goal of establishing a nation-state – or at least autonomy.[42] On the other hand, other regions are often seen as failed nations. In a 1999 forum in *American Historical Review*, Celia Applegate argues that "[r]egions should not be understood only as would-be nations; from that perspective, it takes only one small step to return to the notion that regionalism is therefore backward, archaic, and, above all, transitional."[43] In concurrence with Applegate, Eric

---

39 Quoted in Celia Applegate, "A Europe of Regions," in AHR Forum: "Bringing Regionalism back to History," *American Historical Review* 104, no. 4 (October 1999): 1156–1220, here 1167.

40 Recent works on Imperial Germany, for example, tend to see a regionalization, not nationalization, of politics: Thomas Kühne, "Historische Wahlforschung in der Erweiterung," in *Modernisierung und Region im wilhelminischen Deutschland. Wahlen, Wahlrecht und Politische Kultur*, ed. Simone Lässig, Karl Heinrich Pohl, and James N. Retallack, 39–67 (Bielefeld: Verlag für Regionalgeschichte, 1995).

41 Nira Yuval-Davis, "Women, Citizenship and Difference," *Feminist Review* 57 (Autumn 1997), 4–21, here 8.

42 A recent work argues for the similarity of regional and national movements in their claims, language, and organization: Heinz-Gerhard Haupt, Michael G. Müller, and Stuart Woolf, "Introduction," in *Regional and National Identities in Europe in the XIXth and XXth Centuries = Les identités régionales et nationales en Europe aux XIXe et XXe siècles*, ed. Heinz-Gerhard Haupt, Michael G. Müller, and Stuart Woolf, 1–21 (The Hague/London/Boston: Kluwer Law, 1998), here 10–14.

43 Applegate, "A Europe of Regions," 1171.

Storm notes that research on regionalism remains dominated by traditional nation-state narratives, whereby regional distinctions are often considered backward anomalies that have managed to resist the national idea.[44] Thus, both Applegate and Storm are in line with recent works that have shown that national and regional imaginings are not necessarily in competition with each other but are both modern creations that complement each other.[45]

Applegate also makes the distinction between "resistant" and "accommodating" regionalisms: whereas the former is usually an autonomous or separatist movement centered around a claim to nationhood, the latter "emphasize[s] a distinctiveness that can reinforce national markers of difference – in effect, performing variations on a common national theme."[46] Although her categories are helpful conceptually, there is no way to pigeonhole the subjects of this study. The development of regional cleavages among those who understood themselves as German – in short, within a collectivity that is already nationally bounded – exemplifies the accommodating form of regionalism. Because perceptions of regional inequality complicated the cohesiveness of this collectivity, causing Germans to put forth competing notions of Germanness to assert their national self-worth and claims to power, this book is also a study of the resistant type of regional particularism.

A related theme concerns the role of marginality and nation building. As Peter Sahlins' study of the French-Spanish borderlands shows, an examination of the territorial margins allows new insight into the process of region building and national identity.[47] Nation building is not merely a project brought from the metropoles to the peripheries, but it can occur in the opposite direction. Moreover, border studies also demonstrate that the dissolution of a political border can lead to the discovery of new differences and

44 Eric Storm, "Regionalism in History, 1890–1945: The Cultural Approach," *European History Quarterly* 33, no. 2 (2003): 251–265, esp. 252–255, 261.

45 Celia Applegate, *A Nation of Provincials. The German Idea of Heimat* (Berkeley: University of California Press, 1990); Charlotte Tacke, *Denkmal im sozialen Raum. Nationale Symbole in Deutschland und Frankreich im 19. Jahrhundert* (Göttingen: Vandenhoeck & Ruprecht, 1995); Alon Confino, *The Nation as a Local Metaphor: Württemberg, Imperial Germany, and National Memory, 1871–1918* (Chapel Hill: University of North Carolina Press, 1997); Abigail Green, *Fatherlands: State-Building and Nationhood in Nineteenth-Century Germany* (Cambridge/New York: Cambridge University Press, 2001); Nancy R. Reagin, "Recent Work on German National Identity: Regional? Imperial? Gendered? Imaginary?" *Central European History* 37, no. 2 (2004): 273–289; Siegfried Weichlein, *Nation und Region. Integrationsprozesse im Bismarckreich* (Düsseldorf: Droste, 2004); Michael B. Klein, *Zwischen Reich und Region. Identitätsstrukturen im Deutschen Kaiserreich (1871–1918)* (Stuttgart: Franz Steiner, 2005).

46 Applegate, "A Europe of Regions," 1179.

47 Peter Sahlins, *Boundaries. The Making of France and Spain in the Pyrenees* (Berkeley: University of California Press, 1989).

the construction of a territorial–cultural identity.[48] This study goes one step further and examines the margins of an already peripheral group, that is, a national minority. By exploring the perception of differences and their hierarchical arrangement within the German minority, the relationship between power and territoriality can be better understood: regionalization, after all, went hand in hand with exclusionary politics. The national project to build a German minority in Poland created peripheries that were marginalized and also malleable. Indeed, in times of hypernationalism, former pariahs were not just rehabilitated but even became a national model for Germans in Poland and in the Reich.

This book examines not just the (re)construction of regional homelands but also the politicization of these regional cleavages. The focus is hence less on identities than identity politics. Whereas recent *Heimat* studies have shown that local identities are instrumental in mediating and furthering national feeling, the emphasis here will be to investigate the converse of this relationship and analyze how attempts to create a national community contributed to a regionalization of the minority. The self-identification of many Germans in Poland as "Poznanian-Pomerelians," "Galician Germans," or "Germans in Central Poland" was a phenomenon that had not existed widely or at all before 1918. The very attempts by national activists to turn similarity into community also meant the creation of new marginal groups among the Germans in Poland. A similar process can be seen in the case of today's unified Germany, where Germans living apart for forty years now share the same state. The initially high expectations of national brotherhood have given way to the disappointing perception of unequal treatment and political marginalization, allowing a common sense of East Germanness to reinvent itself and even to be much stronger than in the early 1990s.

Whereas this study focuses on German minority activity in Poland, it also contributes to the understanding of the German state, German nationalism, and National Socialism. Much emphasis has been placed on the breakthrough of völkisch ideology after the First World War, thus suggesting the continuity of minority policies between Nazi and Weimar Germany, and even with the Imperial period.[49] These examinations have converged

---

48 Daphne Berdahl, *Where the World Ended: Re-Unification and Identity in the German Borderland* (Berkeley: University of California Press, 1999).

49 Kurt Sontheimer, *Antidemokratisches Denken in der Weimarer Republik. Die politischen Ideen des deutschen Nationalismus zwischen 1918 und 1933* (Munich: Nymphenburger Verlagshandlung, 1962); Peter Schöttler, ed., *Geschichtsschreibung als Legitimationswissenschaft 1918–1945* (Frankfurt/Main: Suhrkamp Taschenbuch, 1999); Ingo Haar and Michael Fahlbusch, eds., *German Scholars and Ethnic Cleansing, 1919–1945* (New York: Berghahn Books, 2005); Elizabeth A. Drummond, "From 'verloren gehen' to 'verloren bleiben': Changing German Discourses on Nation and Nationalism in

with several recent works on German constructions of Eastern Europe.[50] Together, this research has shown that the First World War, Germany's defeat, and its territorial losses were crucial elements in a paradigmatic shift, what Gregor Thum has called a "völkisch turn," in Germany's relationship with Eastern Europe.[51] Yet as this book argues, the concern of the Weimar government for its former citizens in Poland reveals the limits of völkisch ideology on Weimar Germany's minority policies. By carefully examining the conflicting agendas and motives of different national activists, this book questions if völkisch ideology had widely penetrated the German population as a whole and if it was decisive in the policy making of Weimar and Nazi officials. Völkisch thought was certainly not homogenous, and it often divided as much as it united Germans.

More broadly, this book also expands the notion of Germany as a subject for historical inquiry. In 1981, James J. Sheehan asked "What is German History?" in the *Journal of Modern History*. In his article, Sheehan argued that history writing on Germany should not just serve as proof of the success of nation building but that it should also serve as "a case study of the nation's limitations, both as a historical force and as a historiographical category."[52] He added that "If we shift the picture of the German past just slightly, its pieces fall together in a different way." For too long, Prussia and the Bismarckian Reich have served as the prism for understanding German history. Germany's postwar division likewise created new teleological narratives. Before German reunification in 1989, there was the tendency to project West German states back on to the past.[53] This study will try to

Poznania," in *The Germans and the East*, ed. Charles W. Ingrao and Franz A.J. Szabo (West Lafayette: Purdue University Press, 2008), 226–240; Annemarie Sammartino, *The Impossible Border: Germany and the East, 1914–1922* (Ithaca: Cornell University Press, 2010), 106–107, 119.

50 Guntram Henrik Herb, *Under the Map of Germany: Nationalism and Propaganda 1918–1945* (London/ New York: Routledge, 1997); Michael Burleigh, *Germany Turns Eastwards: A Study of Ostforschung in the Third Reich* (Cambridge/New York: Cambridge University Press, 1988); Vejas Gabriel Liulevicius, *War Land on the Eastern Front. Culture, National Identity and German Occupation in World War I* (Cambridge/New York: Cambridge University Press, 2000); Gregor Thum, ed., *Traumland Osten. Deutsche Bilder vom östlichen Europa im 20. Jahrhundert* (Göttingen: Vandenhoeck & Ruprecht, 2006); Wolfgang Wippermann, *Die Deutschen und der Osten. Feindbild und Traumland* (Darmstadt: Primus, 2007); Charles W. Ingrao and Franz A.J. Szabo, eds., *The Germans and the East* (West Lafayette: Purdue University Press, 2008); Vejas Gabriel Liulevicius, *The German Myth of the East: 1800 to the Present* (Oxford: Oxford University Press, 2009); Robert L. Nelson, ed., *Germans, Poland, and Colonial Expansion to the East* (New York: Palgrave Macmillan, 2009).

51 Gregor Thum, "Mythische Landschaften. Das Bild vom 'deutschen Osten' und die Zäsuren des 20. Jahrhunderts," in *Traumland Osten. Deutsche Bilder vom östlichen Europa im 20. Jahrhundert*, ed. Gregor Thum, 181–211 (Göttingen: Vandenhoeck & Ruprecht, 2006), 190–191.

52 James J. Sheehan, "What is German History?" *Journal of Modern History* 53, no. 1 (March 1981): 1–23, here 4.

53 Hartmut Boockmann, "Deutsche Geschichte ist mehr als rhein-donauländische Heimatkunde. Die ostdeutsche Geschichte wird in der Bundesrepublik zuwenig erforscht," *Frankfurter Allgemeine Zeitung*, May 22, 1989, 12.

escape such determinism by showing the limits of nationalism. It will look beyond the state in analyzing national activism, and at the same time explain how many German nationalists remained fixated on the Reich in a time of broad völkisch-ideological upheaval.

While expanding German history geographically, however, many scholars have become wary of reading too much of Germany and Germanness into the past. Not surprisingly, scholars of the Habsburg lands have provided much of the impetus in decentering the state. An increasing body of work in Central Europe has noted the importance of national indifference and is skeptical of the way many scholars of nationalism have ethnicized the past in a deterministic way that has established the nation as the telos.[54] Scholars in this field include Tara Zahra and Pieter Judson on Bohemia and Czechoslovakia as well as James Bjork on Upper Silesia.[55] Whereas Central Europe before the First World War was dominated by dynastic and local loyalties, the interesting point for these scholars is not how certain ethnic groups inevitably belong to or become one national group, but how nationalist activists constructed and politicized the threat of national indifference in contested lands. As the historian Jeremy King put it, we as historians have to avoid "ethnicism" or risk becoming "closet primordialists."[56]

Finally, this study reveals how the interwar Polish state and society functioned within a multiethnic reality, for the Poles also faced the problem of post-partition integration.[57] A major point here is that Polish authorities offered more leeway than suggested by German contemporaries and

54 On national indifference, see Tara Zahra, "Imagined Non-Communities: National Indifference as a Category of Analysis," *Slavic Review* 69 (Spring 2010): 93–119.

55 Pieter Judson, *Guardians of the Nation: Activists on the Language Frontiers of Imperial Austria* (Cambridge: Harvard University Press, 2006); Tara Zahra, *Kidnapped Souls: National Indifference and the Battle for Children in the Bohemian Lands, 1900–1948* (Ithaca: Cornell University Press, 2008); James E. Bjork, *Neither German nor Pole: Catholicism and National Indifference in a Central European Borderland* (Ann Arbor: University of Michigan Press, 2009). See also Jeremy King, *Budweisers into Czechs and Germans: A Local History of Bohemian Politics, 1848–1948* (Princeton: Princeton University Press, 2002); Chad Bryant, "Either German or Czech: Fixing Nationality in Bohemia and Moravia, 1939–1946," *Slavic Review* 61, no. 4 (Winter 2002): 683–706; Chad Bryant, *Prague in Black: Nazi Rule and Czech Nationalism* (Cambridge: Harvard University Press, 2007).

56 Jeremy King, "The Nationalization of East Central Europe: Ethnicism, Ethnicity, and Beyond," in *Staging the Past: The Politics of Commemoration in Habsburg Central Europe, 1848 to the Present*, ed. Maria Bucur and Nancy M. Wingfield, 112–152 (Lafayette: Purdue University Press, 2001), here 125. For a similar critique, see Pieter Judson, "When Is a Diaspora Not a Diaspora? Rethinking Nation-Centered Narratives about Germans in Habsburg East Central Europe," in *The Heimat Abroad: The Boundaries of Germanness*, ed. Krista O'Donnell, Renate Bridenthal, and Nancy Reagin, 219–247 (Ann Arbor: University of Michigan Press, 2005).

57 See Barbara Wysocka, *Regionalizm wielkopolski w II Rzeczypospolitej 1919–1939* (Poznań: Uniwersytet im. Adama Mickiewicza, 1981); Thomas Serrier, "'Deutsche Kulturarbeit in der Ostmark.' Der Mythos vom deutschen Vorrang und die Grenzproblematik in der Provinz Posen (1871–1914)," in *Die Nationalisierung von Grenzen. Zur Konstruktion nationaler Identität in sprachlich gemischten Grenzregionen*, ed. Michael G. Müller and Rolf Petri, 13–33 (Marburg: Verlag Herder-Institut, 2002).

historians. The weak central government in Warsaw resulted in varying local conditions. The particularly strong presence of the Polish National Democrats in Western Poland, a legacy of fumbled Prussian policies, also meant that the German leaders there were more hard line than their counterparts in Central and Eastern Poland. Another point is that the Germans in Poland were not merely a parallel society in the Polish state, and internal conflict within the minority often meant German leaders turned to Polish authorities for assistance. Indeed, one important reason for the Germans' own weak impulse to unify was the very success of the German regional parties in the Polish parliamentary system in the 1920s, in which Germans were over-represented in the Sejm. The participation of the Germans in Polish institutions in the 1920s and even 1930s was not necessarily subversive, but in many ways it helped to stabilize the new Polish state.

SCOPE AND ORGANIZATION

The main actors of this story are the German leaders of the various regional political organizations: Deutsche Vereinigung in Western Poland (i.e., Poznania and Pomerelia), the Deutscher Volksverband in Central Poland, and the Volksbund in the semiautonomous voivodeship of Silesia. After 1933, the Jungdeutsche Partei from formerly Austrian Silesia became a major factor in minority politics and attempted to expand to all of Poland. Not all German minority organizations were officially registered as parties. This technicality was used in order to deflect the unwanted scrutiny of Polish authorities. However, even these self-avowedly non-political groups were political in their goals, principles, organization, and activity. For example, the Deutsche Vereinigung, officially just a network of German representatives in the two houses of the Polish parliament, served as the most important focal point for minority mobilization within Western Poland.[58] Because of this fact and for the sake of convenience, the term "political organization" and "party" will be used interchangeably. Although the primary subjects of this study are German political organizations and their leaders, this study is not an organizational history. Nor does it focus on the parliamentary activity of the German minority leaders, although this subject still requires further investigation.[59] Rather, the study focuses on the conflicts for power

---

58 Przemysław Hauser, *Mniejszość niemiecka na Pomorzu w okresie międzywojennym* (Poznań: Wydawnictwo Naukowe UAM, 1998), 94.

59 The only monograph devoted exclusively to the role of the German activity in the Sejm and Senate appeared only recently: Janusz Fałowski, *Parlamentarzyści mniejszości niemieckiej w Drugiej Rzeczypospolitej* (Częstochowa: Wydawnictwo Wyższej Szkoły Pedagogicznej w Częstochowie, 2000).

and influence between the various actors within a framework of regional organizations, and how these actors used national and regional arguments to legitimate their power and to achieve their goals. Other actors examined in this book include German officials in the Reich and in Poland, especially those who sought to monitor or manipulate these leaders, as well as Polish authorities who sought to do the same.

The focus on German nationalist political organizations and leaders reduces the ambiguities about the Germanness of the subjects here. The experiences of the German minority were necessarily vast and varied, and it is difficult to demarcate the boundaries of the term "Germans in Poland." Many Germans lived in areas where coexistence with their Slavic neighbors had been the rule for centuries. A large number had been assimilated ("Polonized") and/or were largely unconcerned with their nationality. Yet the subjects of this study will be those who not only thought of themselves as Germans but also took upon themselves the task of preparing others to think and act that way as well. These activists may not have represented all, or even most, Germans in Poland, but their claims to speak to and for them were generally recognized by Polish and German authorities. Although it is extremely difficult to describe how most Germans in Poland felt about these activists, the increasingly nationalized atmosphere decreased the opportunities for exercising subjective nationality. People who were described as German were given "their" leaders whether they liked it or not, and the nebulous silent majority accepted events and action in their name passively.[60] Some Germans may have opposed these leaders actively, but their opposition was often couched in terms of what was truly "German" or, later, "National Socialist."

The organization of the book follows a chronological and thematic format. After the introduction are six main chapters following important phases grouped around seminal events for the minority. It does not have a strictly comparative approach and does not exhaustively examine each region in each chapter. Rather, it takes on political events, demographic developments, and personal ambitions as they come in order to reveal the regionally fractured nature of minority politics. The time frame of the study is limited to the period in which Germans lived under the authority of the Polish state. Due to the contested nature of Poland's borders, Polish rule had various beginning dates: 1918 in Central Poland, 1920 in most western areas, and 1922 in Upper Silesia. Due to its status as a free city and a separate citizenship during the interwar period, this study does not include the city

60 Lumans, *Himmler's Auxiliaries*, 28.

of Gdańsk (Danzig). The primary period of investigation ends in 1939, with the beginning of the Second World War and the collapse of the Second Polish Republic.

The first half of the book investigates the establishment of a center in the minority's western half. Chapter 1 examines the impact of the lost war on German institutions and nationalism, especially in light of the Versailles Treaty. It pays special attention to how Reich politics privileged the recovery of the lost territories and the Germans living there. Chapter 2 evaluates the impact of German revisionist policies on former Reich citizens in Western Poland and how German activists there deployed a sense of Reichness vis-à-vis other Polish Germans. An analysis of an expedition in 1926 to Eastern Poland to discover the Germans there reveals this hierarchical relationship. Chapter 3 allows for a deeper examination of power dynamics within the minority by examining the city of Łódź in Central Poland. Here, Poland's largest concentration of German-speakers became a negative other that was personified in the stereotype of the anational *lodzermensch*. It also examines how Łódź German pacifists and socialists contributed to this regional distinctiveness.

The second half of the book explains how factors in the Reich and Poland undermined the established hierarchy of Germanness. Chapter 4 examines the role of National Socialism in this trend, in part through the thaw between Germany and Poland that culminated in the non-aggression pact of January 1934. In particular, it explores how attempts at *Gleichschaltung* did not necessarily turn the Germans against Poland, nor did it unify them, as the increasing regionalization triggered by the upstart Young German Party (JDP) reveals. Relatively little has been written on the Young Germans, and this book is one of the first analyses of the roots, methods, and impact of the JDP. Moreover, the bitter conflict and denunciations among rival nationalist groups has made it possible for the historian to gain insight into the workings of intra-minority politics, which were often conducted covertly. Chapter 5 examines how demographics and racial-völkisch ideology resulted in the easternization of the minority. The upgrading of Germans in Eastern Poland from national pariahs to völkisch vanguards elucidates the tortuous dynamics of nationalization. Chapter 6 goes beyond the interwar period and covers the ostensible return of Polish Germans to the German Empire. It pays attention to how new hierarchies created both tensions and opportunities for ethnic cleansing. This chapter also outlines the legacy of interwar regionalism within the milieu of expellee organizations in Germany's postwar period.

1

Phantom Germans

Weimar Revisionism and Poland (1918–1933)

The close of the First World War brought momentous changes throughout East Central Europe, especially for Poland and Germany. On October 7, 1918, 123 years after the Third Partition of Poland, the Regent Council in Warsaw proclaimed the Polish Republic.[1] For many Polish nationalists, this tumultuous event represented the fulfillment of a lifelong dream. Many Poles saw their state as the continuation of the "Republic of Nobles" that disappeared at the end of the eighteenth century. Others, including the Pope, saw in the resurrection of Poland the chance for the country to resume its historical mission as Christianity's eastern bulwark.[2] Yet Poland in late 1918 existed more in name than in reality.[3] This problem was exacerbated in the following years, as not just Poland's borders but also its very existence was contested. The state expanded its borders several times and steadily increased its population – Polish and otherwise. By July 1922, Poland encompassed more than 388,000 square kilometers and had a population of 27 million, of which only approximately 19 million were ethnically Polish.[4] About one million inhabitants of the new state were considered to be German and were distributed throughout Poland as shown in Figure 1.1.

Because Hitler justified his invasion of Poland with allegations of abuse against the German minority there, this ethnic group commonly represents the intractable nationality problems that interwar Poland faced. Rather

1 Rudolf Jaworski, Christian Lübke, and Michael G. Müller, *Eine kleine Geschichte Polens* (Frankfurt/Main: Suhrkamp, 2000), 302; Jörg K. Hoensch, *Geschichte Polens* (Stuttgart: Eugen Ulmer, 1998), 250–251.
2 Neal Pease, *Rome's Most Faithful Daughter: The Catholic Church and Independent Poland, 1914–1939* (Athens: Ohio University Press, 2009), 19.
3 Margaret Macmillan, *Paris 1919: Six Months That Changed The World* (New York: Random House, 2003), 208, 210.
4 Hoensch, *Geschichte Polens*, 257.

Country and regional names have been translated into English, city and town names as well as rivers have been generally left as spelled in the source map.

Figure 1.1. German settlements in Poland between the wars. Map adapted from Richard Breyer and Paul Nasarski, *Erfahrung und Zeugnis der Deutschen aus Polen* (Berlin/Bonn: Westkreuz-Verlag, 1987), 10. Map reprinted with permission of Westkreuz-Verlag Berlin/Bonn GmbH.

Figure 1.1 (*continued*)

than reducing German–Polish relations to matters concerning this minority, however, this chapter examines how the loss of citizens *and* territories to Poland influenced Reich politics and society. This cross-border approach allows for a better understanding of the spatial hierarchy of Germanness within the minority. The territories that Germany ceded to the new Polish state comprised three distinct regions: Pomerelia, Poznania, and eastern Upper Silesia. The loss of each of these territories and their German inhabitants was a blow to many Germans – nationalist or not – and significantly influenced Reich politics toward Poland.

Despite their historical differences and certain regional antagonisms, Poznania and Pomerelia (formerly West Prussia; the "Polish Corridor") were often grouped together due to their historical and geographical proximity to Germany and to each other. Together, these regions made up 11 percent of the Polish state's territory and had a combined population of 2.9 million.[5] After Upper Silesia was divided in 1922, Poland had acquired a sizable portion of Prussia, but these territories were hardly homogenous and had several centers. Whereas Poznań city was the focus of Germans in central and southern Poznania, Bydgoszcz in the northern Poznanian Voivodeship (the Noteć/Netze region) became the center of minority activity in the former West Prussian districts. Despite rivalry between minority leaders in Poznań and Bydgoszcz, their common past in Imperial Germany and their common desire for a border revision fostered the formation of a collective identity among the German activists there. This community building, which crosscut the larger project of making a "Germandom in Poland," was in part due to the tendency of the Polish and the German governments to group the regions Poznania and Pomerelia as an integral unit. As later chapters will show, German nationalists in these Western Polish territories began to refer to themselves as "Posen-Pommereller," a construct that had not existed in Imperial Germany. Upper Silesia, which was subject to different laws and a different administration, stood distinctly apart from the other ceded Prussian territories. Politics, ethnic makeup, and geography would make Katowice a competing center within the minority; and regional tensions flickered between Poznania-Pomerelia and the Upper Silesian Germans throughout the interwar period.

As Alexander B. Murphy has argued, political and social ideologies play an important role in territorialization.[6] Likewise, space and place maintained a functional significance among the Polish Germans because they affected

5 Hoensch, *Geschichte Polens,* 258.
6 Alexander B. Murphy, "Regions as Social Constructs: The Gap Between Theory and Practice," *Progress in Human Geography* 15, no. 1 (1991): 23–36, here 28–29.

their "paths and projects." Hence, it is still possible to speak of Germany's ceded territories together as a category of analysis. The legacy of Imperial Germany fostered a commonality among the Germans living there. Weimar policies, as will be shown, continued to construct a distinctive Western Polish region that enjoyed privileges largely denied Germans elsewhere in Poland. The German press propagated these regional differences, and material and political limits underscored these borders. By utilizing these boundaries to further their own interests, German leaders contributed to the construction of discrete German home regions in Poland. Western Poland existed as a political region within the minority, for the Germans there had different goals and life chances than Germans elsewhere in Poland. This evolving sense of distinction meant that differences within Western Poland were less salient than they were vis-à-vis the non-Prussian territories. Even the Reich's administrative makeup was supposed to remind the Germans in Germany and in Poland of the so-called bleeding borders, as shown by the formation of miniature provinces. The border province of Posen and West Prussia (Provinz Grenzmark Posen-Westpreußen) was erected to underscore the ties to the lost territories, even though the province consisted of only one district (Regierungsbezirk Schneidemühle). Likewise, the creation of the rump province of Upper Silesia following the partition revealed the government's unwillingness to accept the loss of eastern Upper Silesia.[7]

The Polish government also contributed to regional distinctiveness among German activists. The formerly Prussian territories in Poland remained in voivodeships that largely reflected their prewar provincial boundaries, and these regions were not mixed with territories from the formerly Austrian or Russian partitions. There was one major exception: the voivodeship of Silesia incorporated not just eastern Upper Silesia but also the formerly Austrian Teschen Silesian region centered around the cities of Bielsko and Cieszyn. The population there had not been allowed to vote in the Upper Silesian plebiscite: indeed, many Teschen Silesian Germans had hoped that all of Upper Silesia would remain with Germany, which might have then increased their own chances for joining the German state. Yet the fact that eastern Upper Silesia remained in Polish hands meant that adjacent Teschen Silesia remained Polish as well. The 40,000 Germans in Bielsko – the only German-majority city in Poland – would form yet another subcenter, competing for leadership in the Silesian province and in the minority as a whole. The binding of formerly Prussian and Austrian Silesia in a Polish

---

7 Elizabeth R. Harvey, *Women and the Nazi East: Agents and Witnesses of Germanization* (New Haven/London: Yale University Press, 2003), here 25.

voivodeship sharpened resentments between supposed haves and have-nots within the minority and later fostered the first National Socialist movement among the Germans in Poland.

GERMANS WITHOUT BORDERS? REEXAMINING HOMELAND NATIONALISM

The matter of the ceded Prussian territories now turns to the question of how nationalism played itself out between the German Reich, Poland, and German minority actors. As Rogers Brubaker states, Germany experienced a "völkisch reorientation of nationalism" in the Weimar period.[8] His work and that of Dieter Gosewinkel have examined the role of citizenship beyond its mere institutional and legal forms. They have focused on the interplay between citizenship and nationhood and analyzed how the growing concern for German minorities abroad in the early twentieth century gave German citizenship a strong ethno-cultural inflection.[9]

Indeed, contemporaries often saw the First World War as the source of a new form of nationalism.[10] Interwar observers themselves constructed ideas of pan-German belonging by describing how German armies and administrators discovered German minorities in the East.[11] Another development seen to be crucial in the rise of ethnonational thinking was Germany's defeat in the First World War and the subsequent territorial losses.[12] The Versailles Treaty stranded more than a million former fellow citizens abroad, and this fact is thought to have driven many Reich Germans to imagine the nation less in terms of state borders and more in ethnic categories.[13] Whereas Germans had lived beyond Germany's borders prior to 1914, the new groups of "minorities of fate" or "unreal" minorities gave new impetus to nationalist conceptions that reached beyond Germany's

8 Rogers Brubaker, *Nationalism Reframed: Nationhood and the National Question in the New Europe* (Cambridge/New York: Cambridge University Press, 1996), 118.
9 Dieter Gosewinkel, *Einbürgern und Ausschließen. Die Nationalisierung der Staatsangehörigkeit vom Deutschen Bund bis zur Bundesrepublik Deutschland* (Göttingen: Vandenhoeck & Ruprecht, 1991).
10 Kurt Sontheimer, *Antidemokratisches Denken in der Weimarer Republik. Die politischen Ideen des deutschen Nationalismus zwischen 1918 und 1933* (Munich: Nymphenburger Verlagshandlung, 1962), 125–132.
11 For recent examples supporting this thesis, see Gosewinkel, *Einbürgern und Ausschließen*, 400; Rainer Münz and Rainer Ohliger, "Auslandsdeutsche," in *Deutsche Erinnerungsorte I*, ed. Etienne François and Hagen Schulze, 370–388 (Munich: Beck, 2001), here 373–375; Vejas Gabriel Liulevicius, *War Land on the Eastern Front: Culture, National Identity and German Occupation in World War I* (Cambridge/New York: Cambridge University Press, 2000).
12 Ingo Eser, "*Volk, Staat, Gott!*" *Die deutsche Minderheit in Polen und ihr Schulwesen 1918–1939* (Wiesbaden: Harrassowitz, 2010), 147.
13 Fritz Karge, "Die Geschichte des deutschen Ostraums im Unterricht der Mittelstufe. Eine Längsschnittdarstellung," *Vergangenheit und Gegenwart* 28, no. 2 (1938): 79–94, here 91.

borders.[14] A common saying among völkisch thinkers was that "the war had to be lost in order for Germandom to be won."[15]

Overall, the Weimar Republic experienced a hyperinflation of the term *Volk* and its variants.[16] Such expressions, of course, not only fostered the belief that the First World War had served as a catalyst for Germany's awareness of Germans abroad, but they were themselves attempts to give meaning to national loss and trauma. As Rüdiger Graf and Moritz Föllmer have demonstrated, political radicals constructed visions of crisis to delegitimate the Weimar Republic and legitimate their own views.[17] The perceived divisiveness of Weimar politics and society facilitated the longing for the unified Volk that could serve as a solution to the ostensible crisis. Some elites saw in völkisch ideals the key for creating an authoritarian, corporate state that would restore Germany's power.[18] In her recent study of efforts to help Polish German immigrants to the Reich during the German "crisis of sovereignty" after the First World War, Annemarie Sammartino has noted that "in the laws and policies of the national and Prussian states as well as the Red Cross, ethnicity trumped both current and former citizenship as the salient category for apportioning aid."[19] She argues that a deterritorialization of German identity after the First World War fostered Weimar policies toward ethnic Germans abroad that "were driven by a völkisch logic."[20] Although not always successful in its implementation, Prussian and Reich officials had "embraced a völkisch definition of German identity."[21]

Although völkisch concerns may have applied to policies for Polish Germans who moved to the Reich, it is important not to overethnicize Weimar support to Germans in Poland. There is a need to investigate further how widespread the "völkisch turn" was and to question in particular the causality between inflated völkisch rhetoric and Weimar political practice. An initial examination of Reich policies toward Germans in formerly Prussian territories, for example, can easily lead to a conflation of revisionist form with völkisch content. Yet Reich and Prussian government officials were motivated by a mix of concerns, including a sense of obligation to

---

14 Brubaker, *Nationalism Reframed*, 118; Rudolf Jaworski, "Der auslandsdeutsche Gedanke in der Weimarer Republik," *Annali dell'Istituto storico italo-germanico in Trento* 4 (1978): 369–386, 373.

15 Jaworski, "Der auslandsdeutsche Gedanke in der Weimarer Republik," 378.

16 Sontheimer, *Antidemokratisches Denken in der Weimarer Republik*, 308.

17 Moritz Föllmer and Rüdiger Graf, eds. *Die "Krise" der Weimarer Republik. Zur Kritik eines Deutungsmusters* (Frankfurt/Main: Campus, 2005). See especially the introduction for their analysis of "crisis" as an interpretative model in the historiography of the Weimar Republic. The editors refer to "crisis" as a "magical concept" that historians have too often used when explanation fails (21).

18 Sontheimer, *Antidemokratisches Denken in der Weimarer Republik*, 308–309.

19 Annemarie Sammartino, *The Impossible Border: Germany and the East, 1914–1922* (Ithaca: Cornell University Press, 2010), 106–107.

20 Sammartino, *Impossible Border*, 119.   21 Sammartino, *Impossible Border*, 119.

former citizens stranded in Poland. Prewar membership in clubs, pensions, and unions continued to create ties and mutual obligations with people and institutions in Germany. Although it was important that these former citizens were somehow "German," Weimar revisionist policies had little to do with the currents of völkisch thought that saw the minorities as important for their intrinsic ethnic or racial qualities. Rather, these policies were more in tune with etatist thinking that sought to instrumentalize the minorities for territorial-revisionist aims. Supporting Germans in Poland was thus not an end in itself, but also served the goal of recovering the lost territories. Past boundaries continued to act as "phantom borders," whereby the past exerted its weight on the present.[22]

Ethnic irredentism and territorial revisionism tend to overlap in their goals and methods. Both concern the fate of conational minorities abroad and their relationship to the homeland and to the host state. Both support a change in the current political and international order, with military force often held as an option to achieve these goals. Although ethnic irredentism and revisionism blended and reinforced one another, they were not interchangeable, and it is useful to separate actors and organizations into these two categories. By analyzing how revisionists and irredentists conceived the role of territory and how the nation-state should treat German minorities abroad, it is possible to delineate them more clearly. Making such distinctions also avoids mislabeling a variety of activities as völkisch, and thus avoids suggesting a political telos between the Weimar period and National Socialism.[23]

REVISIONISM

Revisionism was an important political force in interwar Germany.[24] Michael Salewski even speaks of a "revisionism syndrome" that acted as

22 The concept of "phantom borders" is the thematic focus of an interdisciplinary research network begun in 2011 that investigates how historical borders in East Central Europe have continued to influence spatial dimensions in the region. Béatrice von Hirschhausen of the Centre Marc Bloch in Berlin heads the network, which includes several institutions in Germany and is supported by the German Federal Ministry of Education and Research (BMBF). See "Phantomgrenzen in Ostmitteleuropa," Centre Marc Bloch, accessed March 11, 2012, http://phantomgrenzen.eu. Philipp Ther has noted that Germany experienced phantom pain in relation to the colonies and territories it lost after the First World War but that nationalists concentrated on restoring the Reich to its 1914 borders. See Philipp Ther, "Deutsche Geschichte als imperiale Geschichte. Polen, slawophone Minderheiten und das Kaiserreich als kontinentales Empire," in *Das Kaiserreich transnational. Deutschland in der Welt 1871–1914*, ed. Sebastian Conrad and Jürgen Osterhammel, 129–158 (Göttingen: Vandenhoeck & Ruprecht, 2004), here 145–146.

23 For an example of this telos, see Norbert Friedrich Krekeler, *Revisionsanspruch und geheime Ostpolitik der Weimarer Republik. Die Subventionierung der deutschen Minderheit in Polen* (Stuttgart: Deutsche Verlags-Anstalt, 1973), 148, 150.

24 Hagen Schulze, "Versailles," in *Deutsche Erinnerungsorte I*, 407–421, here 417.

the durable "glue of the state" in an otherwise divisive Weimar Republic.[25] Revisionism is, however, a murky concept, and it is not helpful that it is often conflated with irredentism. Quite simply, revisionists wanted to restore Germany's great power status. According to Andreas Hillgruber, revisionists in the Weimar period had three main goals: (1) the end of reparations; (2) the lifting of military limitations; and (3) the reacquisition of territory, namely Danzig, the so-called Polish Corridor, and eastern Upper Silesia, in that order.[26] The privileging of any one of these points may have varied according to interest group and time period. Many Germans were outraged by the "debt slavery" that would last for generations to come.[27] According to Margaret Macmillan, reparations became the "preeminent symbol" for those who saw the Versailles Treaty as a "vindictive, shortsighted and poisonous document."[28] It is arguable, however, that territorial corrections remained the most popular and durable of the three goals that Hillgruber lists. As Hartmut Boockmann points out, the loss of territories united all parties in Germany in their rejection of the Treaty of Versailles.[29] Limiting revisionism to its territorial component also allows us a firmer grasp on an otherwise very slippery subject. As Salewski notes, revisionism was a backward-looking ideology, a flight from the present and a return to the past.[30] In territorial terms, it is likely that this position meant at the very least a return to some semblance of Germany's 1914 borders. Many German nationalists saw the intrinsic connection between inner and outer revision; territorial expansion abroad could also be used to roll back the hated Weimar system at home.[31]

There were, of course, those in the Weimar Republic who wanted more than a simple return to the past. Communists and Nationals Socialists especially worked instead for a political breakthrough.[32] Salewski calls the nationalist revisionism that sought more than mere territorial restoration or compensation "super revisionism," and this current gained momentum toward the end of the Weimar Republic.[33] These super revisionists were preoccupied with ideas of a German-controlled Eastern European empire

25 Michael Salewski, "Das Weimarer Revisionssyndrom," *Aus Politik und Zeitgeschichte* 30 (1980): 14–25, here 15.
26 Andreas Hillgruber, "'Revisionismus' – Kontinuität und Wandel in der Außenpolitik der Weimarer Republik," *Historische Zeitschrift* 237 (1983): 597–621, here 604.
27 Detlev Peukert, *Weimar Republic: The Crisis of Classical Modernity*, trans. Richard Deveson (New York: Hill and Wang, 1993), 53.
28 Macmillan, *Paris 1919*, 181.
29 Hartmut Boockmann, *Ostpreußen und Westpreußen. Deutsche Geschichte im Osten Europas* (Berlin: Siedler, 1992), 396.
30 Salewski, "Das Weimarer Revisionssyndrom," 18–19.
31 Salewski, "Das Weimarer Revisionssyndrom," 18.
32 Salewski, "Das Weimarer Revisionssyndrom," 18.
33 Salewski, "Das Weimarer Revisionssyndrom," 23.

that had briefly become reality with the Ober-Ost military occupation of the eastern territories in 1917–1918. For them, a restoration of the 1914 borders would serve as a springboard for wider territorial gains in Eastern Europe.

Yet such super revisionists were not necessarily irredentists, but rather state-oriented nationalists who saw German hegemony in Eastern Europe as a precondition for Germany to regain its world-power status.[34] They wanted to make Germany into an economic powerhouse that would be largely self-sufficient in the next war. Such annexations would include territories that did not have a predominately German population. A Germanization process might have been planned, but not in a radical, genocidal fashion. For both revisionists and super revisionists, the power of the state – not the inclusion of purported conationals – was the end. Although revisionists of all colors were willing to use the language of national self-determination when it suited their needs, it was not necessarily their main concern.

IRREDENTISM

The term irredentism is derived from the Italian word *irredenta*, meaning "unredeemed." It appeared as a political term in the latter half of the nineteenth century, when Italian nationalists demanded that the regions of Trent, Trieste, Istria, Dalmatia, and South Tirol be annexed to the newly created Italian nation-state. The concept of irredentism can be quite expansive and encompasses many movements for territorial expansion, including those using geographical-historical arguments.[35] Much of the theoretical literature on irredentism, however, focuses on its ethnic component.[36] Thomas Ambrosio, for example, writes that "[i]rredentism . . . is a state-based, but not necessarily government-backed, movement that seeks to retrieve an external minority together with the territory the latter inhabits across an existing border, i.e., to add territory as well as population to an existing state."[37] As an ideal type, then, irredentism has less to do with territory for its

---

34 Hillgruber, "'Revisionismus' – Kontinuität und Wandel in der Außenpolitik der Weimarer Republik," 612.

35 Naomi Chazan, "Introduction," in *Irredentism and International Politics*, ed. Naomi Chazan, 1–8 (Boulder: Lynne Rienner Publishers, 1991), 1.

36 Stefan Wolff, *Disputed Territories: The Transnational Dynamics of Ethnic Conflict Settlement* (New York/Oxford: Berghahn Books, 2003), 22. Another example of focusing on the ethnic component of irredentism is Donald L. Horowitz, *Ethnic Groups in Conflict* (Berkeley: University of California Press, 1985), 280.

37 Thomas Ambrosio, "Irredentism: Self-Determination and Interstate War," in *International Law and the Rise of Nations. The State System and the Challenge of Ethnic Groups*, ed. Robert J. Beck and Thomas Ambrosio, 284–312 (New York/London: Chatham House, 2002), 284.

own sake than with purported co-nationals who remained "unredeemed" as long as they were not living in the borders of "their" nation-state. Irredentism thus has its roots in the perception of an unfair application of the nationality principle.

After the First World War, it was widely believed in Germany that the principle of national self-determination had been grossly skewed toward the interests of the victorious powers. Max Hildebert Boehm, a prominent specialist on Eastern Europe (*Ostforscher*) originally from Russian Latvia, served as the director of the Institut für Grenz- und Auslandsstudien and of the Deutschtumsseminar at the Hochschule für Politik in Berlin.[38] He called for a new Reich that would include the lost territories as well as Austria and the Baltic countries.[39] Boehm claimed that the unjust fate of the Austrian Germans was instrumental in developing irredentist ideas in Germany.[40] Boehm couched irredentism as a symptom of a broader, unhealthy state of international affairs. As he suggested in 1923 in *Europa Irredenta*, the internecine conflict over borders would have larger world historical consequences by ultimately undermining Europe's role on the world stage.[41]

Among German nationalists, the restoration-revisionists and ethnic irredentists differed not necessarily on the extent of their territorial demands but on how these claims were to be legitimated. Whereas revisionists did not necessarily go as far as irredentists in their demands to include all ethnic brethren in the nation-state, irredentists in principle were willing to forgo ethnically foreign territories. For irredentists, territorial acquisition was still crucial, but it was a means, not an end. Expansion was subordinated to the ethnic imperative of including as many putative conationals as possible, even where they did not necessarily form a majority. The inclusion of ethnic Germans living abroad in a geographically reasonable and feasible nation-state was the sine qua non for German irredentists. Given the complex nationality picture in Eastern Europe, other ethnic groups would be incorporated as a sort of by-catch. They would have to be assimilated, de-voiced, or expelled at some point.

38 Guntram Henrik Herb, *Under the Map of Germany: Nationalism and Propaganda 1918–1945* (London/New York: Routledge, 1997), 58.
39 Ingo Haar, *Historiker im Nationalsozialismus. Deutsche Geschichtswissenschaft und der "Volkstumskampf" im Osten* (Göttingen: Vandenhoeck & Ruprecht, 2000), 35. See also Max Hildebert Boehm, *Grenzdeutsch – Großdeutsch. Vortrag anläßlich der Hauptausschußtagung des V.D.A. im November 1924* (Dresden: Verein für das Deutschtum im Ausland, 1925), 5.
40 Boehm, *Grenzdeutsch – Großdeutsch*, 2.
41 Max Hildebert Boehm, *Europa Irredenta. Eine Einführung in das Nationalitätenproblem der Gegenwart* (Berlin: Reimar Hobbing, 1923), 9–10, 323–325.

In practice, of course, there was considerable room for revisionism and irredentism to overlap and to piggyback on one another. Revisionists, after all, used the principle of national determination to support their territorial claims. Irredentists instrumentalized the general desire to return to the borders of 1914 to support a more comprehensive project of ethnic inclusion. Expansion beyond ethnic borders was more than acceptable to irredentists if it was seen as necessary in strengthening the ethnic homeland. At the same time, irredentists could also forgo territory occupied by purported ethnic conationals when it suited grander strategic goals. Principled irredentism was often hard to find. In issues like the Austrian and Sudeten German annexation, *großdeutsch* (Greater German) nationalism was derived from a sense of a common history mingled with more modern ethno-national concepts.

One more distinction needs to be made here. In the German case, irredentism is often conflated with völkisch thinking, but they were often at odds. Although völkisch activists sought to awaken and activate putative ethnic cohorts in foreign states, their motives were not necessarily aggressive or territorially expansionist, for völkisch claims did not necessarily entail a border change. By reformulating and essentializing community in ethno-national rather than in political-state terms, völkisch thought was a way for a core national state to acknowledge its possession of putative national cohorts in other countries. In this cross-border community, the Volk encompassed not just those Germans within the Reich but also some 40 million Germans who lived abroad, thus giving rise to the claim of the Germans being a people of 100 million. Hans Steinacher, the leader of the Volksbund für das Deutschtum im Ausland in the 1930s, was aware of the complications that irredentism could cause for an active völkisch program. He equated ethnic-based border change with etatist thinking, whereas völkisch thinking sought to connect with Germans abroad in ways besides irredentism.[42] The demand to "redeem" these Germans could be placated by uniting them with Germany on the cultural level. Put another way, this form of transnational bonding could be seen as a kind of soft irredentism. As long as the international situation made a border change unlikely or inopportune, these ideas of connecting with ethnic brothers abroad often remained benign. The overlap of territorial revisionist claims with völkisch ideology, however, could result in the hard irredentism that justified expansionist claims based on ethno-national principles.

---

42 Hans-Adolf Jacobsen, ed., *Hans Steinacher. Bundesleiter des VDA 1933–1937. Erinnerungen und Doku-mente* (Boppard am Rhein: Boldt, 1970), xxxi.

CIVIL SOCIETY AND HOMELAND NATIONALISM

An examination of homeland nationalism in the Weimar Republic must look not only at the role of the state but also at that of German civil society. The Weimar Republic appeared divided and polarized, and the search to overcome this divisiveness was intense. It was, however, this splintering that makes an examination of the limits of nationalism so challenging and fruitful. Civil society nationalists were often much more virulent in tone than official nationalists. Groups such as the Pan-German League (Alldeutscher Verband) and the Association for Germandom Abroad (Verein für das Deutschtum im Ausland) had advocated the care of Germans living in other countries, but they had still been limited in their reach. A radical-right fringe demanding a greater world role for Germany and the need to combat the perceived Slavic threat had grown in Germany, especially in the 1890s. However, the Pan-German League had been more concerned with questions of Germany's global influence than with the care of the Germans themselves. For other German nationalists, Bismarck's legacy was less a unification of Germany than its division.[43] Still, expansionist and völkisch nationalism had attained only a small following before the First World War. Germans before the First World War had little knowledge about the situation of German-speakers living abroad. Rather, German citizens had become etatist in their thinking and had largely come to associate Germany with the German state. As John Breuilly notes, "[B]y 1914 few German speakers in the German Empire thought of Germany as anything other than the territory of that Empire."[44]

The First World War did not fundamentally undermine prewar German imaginations of how the German state should look, and it can be argued that many, if not most, Germans continued to think of a right-sized Germany to essentially be the one in its 1914 borders. Many in interwar Germany denounced the Treaty of Versailles and especially the Reich's new borders.[45] Despite this wide consensus, revisionism, even when limited to claims on territory, could have several potentially conflicting meanings. Precisely this lack of clarity allowed revisionism to speak to the various resentments and

---

43 John Breuilly, "The National Idea in Modern German History," in *The State of Germany: The National Idea in the Making, Unmaking, and Remaking of a Modern Nation-State*, ed. John Breuilly, 1–28 (New York: Longman, 1992), 12. See also Lawrence Birken, "Völkisch Nationalism in Perspective," *The History Teacher* 27, no. 2 (1994): 133–143, here 137.

44 Breuilly, "The National Idea in Modern German History," 14. Also quoted in Herb, *Under the Map of Germany*, 11n26, notes on p. 188.

45 Peter Fischer, *Die deutsche Publizistik als Faktor der deutsch-polnischen Beziehungen 1919–1939* (Wiesbaden: Harrassowitz, 1991), 11.

longings of so many Germans.[46] Still, it is important here to differentiate the often competing strands of nationalist thought. Concern for Germans abroad was not tantamount to the hard irredentism mentioned previously. Many völkisch professionals were wary of expansionist solutions and preferred cultural autonomy for minorities abroad.

The Austrian question was trickier. As Stanley Suval has argued, much of public opinion in the Weimar period had a predilection for Greater German ideas and favored unification with Austria.[47] Yet this desire to unite with Austria was not necessarily anchored in ethnic irredentist thought, and it is difficult to determine how decisive such desires were and where they ranked among other concerns. Nor should the specific Austrian question be conflated with a radical großdeutsch revisionism that called for the outright annexation of Austria, the Sudetenland, and the Baltic countries, as well as establishing German influence over East Central Europe in a reprise of plans in the First World War for creating a German-dominated Mitteleuropa.[48]

Revisionism tended to reaffirm rather than undermine the borders of 1914, which suggests the successful imprint of the German Empire in the minds of many Germans. Although Boehm emphasized the importance of the border question and the lost Germans in reawakening the Greater German question, even he noted that the enthusiasm for unification with Austria was waning.[49] He complained that the "mechanical memory" that sought a return to the statehoods of the prewar period was not comparable to großdeutsch thinking.[50] As Salewski suggests, the prewar experience retained an important cognitive role as an imprint for revisionist desires.[51] Territorial restoration to some semblance of the 1914 borders was the lowest common denominator in Weimar revisionism. As Rogers Brubaker has noted, maximal demands varied widely, but the return of the Danzig, Upper

---

46 Works that differentiate the meanings of revisionism in the Weimar period include: Krekeler, *Revisionsanspruch und geheime Ostpolitik*; Klaus Megerle, "Danzig, Korridor und Oberschlesien. Zur deutschen Revisionspolitik gegenüber Polen in der Locarnodiplomatie," *Jahrbuch für die Geschichte Mittel- und Ostdeutschlands* 25 (1976): 145–178; Salewski, "Das Weimarer Revisionssyndrom," especially 616–620; Manfred Joachim Enssle, *Stresemann's Territorial Revisionism. Germany, Belgium, and the Eupen-Malmédy Question, 1919–1929* (Wiesbaden: Steiner, 1980); Hillgruber, "'Revisionismus' – Kontinuität und Wandel in der Außenpolitik der Weimarer Republik," especially 604–605, 619–621.

47 Stanley Suval, "Overcoming Kleindeutschland: Historical Mythmaking in the Weimar Republic," *Central European History* 2, no. 4 (December 1969): 312–330, here 328. A recent work that also emphasizes the important role of großdeutsch nationalism among republicans in both Germany and Austria is Erin Regina Hochman, "Staging the Nation, Staging Democracy: The Politics of Commemoration in Germany and Austria, 1918-1933/34," (PhD dissertation, University of Toronto, 2010), 278.

48 Max Hildebert Boehm was one such supporter of the "Großdeutschland-Begriff," as were Karl Haushofer and Karl C. von Loesch. See Haar, *Historiker im Nationalsozialismus*, 35, 45–50.

49 Boehm, *Grenzdeutsch – Großdeutsch*, 2–5.   50 Boehm, *Grenzdeutsch – Großdeutsch*, 10.

51 Salewski, "Das Weimarer Revisionssyndrom," 18, 25.

Silesia, and the Polish Corridor remained "universal minimum demands" for Weimar Germany, making up a revisionist consensus.[52] It is likely that territorial ambitions broader than the 1914 borders would have generated less support and created tensions. After all, it was easy to mobilize people around the loss-minimizing and lower-risk agenda of recouping land that had belonged to Germany just a few years before. It would have been more difficult to convince people of the need to acquire territories whose relationship to Germany was considerably more abstract or tenuous, especially given the higher risks involved. The possibility of another (failed) war for a fantastic Empire in the East, especially so shortly after the World War, was hence less popular. Although restorationists relied on historical, ethnic, economic, and humanitarian arguments for the return of the lost territories, these arguments were largely counterproductive when claiming territory beyond the 1914 borders. Moreover, sweeping claims could be detrimental to more focused and better justified cases, thus increasing the risk of getting nothing altogether. Especially ethnic claims were a double-edged sword when dealing with contested lands.

The violation of the prewar borders, the trauma of loss, and the longing for restoration helps explain why the calls for a return of these territories and people were so virulent, informing and shaping politics. In many ways, these popular conceptions of nationalism generally reflected the official nationalism in that they remained etatist and focused on the political-territorial notion of the nation-state. Undoubtedly, official nationalism played a role in shaping people's expectations, and most people adopted the positions and formulations of those in power. Many continued to see citizenship and nationality as one and the same, albeit the problem of lost citizens who found themselves stranded abroad posed a special problem.

It is not surprising then that pan-German nationalists feared that the majority of Germans – far from becoming more völkisch in their orientation – was actually adjusting to the postwar borders. After all, one of the more common complaints of nationalists was the persistence of etatist conceptions among German politicians and population at large. The young Walter Kuhn, a nationalities scholar and later professor in Breslau, remarked in an article that the average German in the Reich understood only the people within the borders of the German state to be German. According to Kuhn, their definition of Germanness excluded Austrians and ethnic Germans abroad, but it included the Wends, the Poles, and the Masurians.[53] As in the period before 1914, nationalist activists were worried that the

---

52 Brubaker, *Nationalism Reframed*, 140n92.
53 Walter Kuhn, "Versuch einer Naturgeschichte der deutschen Sprachinsel," *Deutsche Blätter in Polen* 3, no. 2 (February 1926): 65–140, here 139.

new Germany would forget and exclude those Germans living outside the postwar borders. Although radical politics grew in its virulence, it is important to see that these unofficial forms of nationalism were not necessarily widespread. The exhortations of völkisch advocates to think outside state borders reveal less the embrace of völkisch thought in German politics and society than the limited headway these ideas made during the Weimar period. Nevertheless, many Germans who were influential in shaping public opinion did share these beliefs and agitated for a new form of nationalism.

A multitude of organizations flourished during the Weimar Republic with the professed goal of supporting Germans abroad. Such groups had existed during the Imperial era, and they were able to piggyback on broader revisionist desires after the war. These civil society organizations became an important political lobby. They were not state institutions, but they were also not completely private: they received funds from government sources and private donations, and they often undertook mass-based fundraisers and lobbying drives. Although these organizations are often touted as völkisch and grouped together, a closer examination shows that they were quite heterogeneous. Their concern for Germans abroad differed in their means and ends, thus hindering a more unified agenda in approaching the Germans abroad in general and the Germans in Poland in particular.

The Verein für das Deutschtum im Ausland (VDA; Association for Germandom Abroad) was the largest of these organizations devoted to supporting Germandom during the Weimar period. Founded originally in 1881 as the Allgemeiner Schulverein (General School Association), it changed its name in 1908. The VDA used membership dues and state subsidies to fund schools, youth programs, and cultural groups for various German minorities. In the Weimar period, the organization received between 165,000 and 195,000 Reichsmark (RM) from the government annually.[54] After the First World War, the organization grew quickly. Among groups devoted to ethnic Germans in other countries, the VDA stood out for its deeply conservative, even reactionary attitudes.[55] It continued to propagate knowledge about the Germans abroad and to send money to German minorities, but this aid and the motives behind it were not necessarily irredentist. Indeed, many considered the VDA too traditional to be an effective organization to bring together the varied völkisch and nationalist strands in

---

54 Richard Blanke, *Orphans of Versailles: The Germans in Western Poland, 1918–1939* (Lexington: University Press of Kentucky, 1993), 151.
55 Blanke, *Orphans of Versailles*, 150.

Germany.[56] The role of the VDA in supplying money to minorities abroad remained minimal and largely restricted to educational needs. The Foreign Ministry and the affiliated Deutsche Stiftung felt the VDA functioned more like a "book and school" society.[57] In the case of aid to Germans in Poland, the VDA complemented the role of the Deutsche Stiftung. The latter focused on the formerly Prussian regions, whereas the former kept contact with German activists in the so-called "old abroad." Like many mass organizations, the VDA soon came to serve primarily itself. Constantly running out of money, the VDA found it even harder to raise funds during the Great Depression, and it resorted to shaming potential donors. At its meetings, the VDA harped on the fear that the Germans abroad were holding on by a thread, while Reich Germans were allegedly losing interest in the Germans abroad.[58] Likewise, the VDA organized excursions to Germany's "bleeding borders." Such activities designed to promote the so-called German East provided an outlet especially for German women to express their national engagement.[59]

Like the VDA, the Pan-German League had its origins in Imperial Germany. Alfred Hugenberg proposed a nationalist organization to promote colonization following the uproar over the Helgoland-Zanzibar Treaty of 1890, and after some reorganization, the group was founded in 1894 under the name Alldeutscher Verband.[60] In 1903, the Pan-German League adopted a policy of national opposition, but its agitation against the Reich government diminished its influence. In 1914, the number of members in the Pan-German League was about 18,000, and membership rose to 36,677 by 1918. In 1922, there were some 52,000 members, but membership sank steadily thereafter. By 1932, the Pan-German League had only around 8,000 members.[61]

Despite its name, the Pan-German League was not devoted primarily to supporting ethnic Germans abroad, and the pan-German aspects in its agenda remained incoherent. Roger Chickering's study reveals that a

---

56 Krekeler, *Revisionsanspruch und geheime Ostpolitik*, 30: Krekeler uses the term "Kristallisationspunkt" to describe Germany's role as an ethnic homeland. See also Brubaker, *Nationalism Reframed*, 119–120.

57 Krekeler, *Revisionsanspruch und geheime Ostpolitik*, 47–48.

58 "Weniger Interesse fürs Auslandsdeutschtum?" *Vossische Zeitung*, November 11, 1930, in GStA, I HA, Rep. 77, Tit. 856, folder 317, p. 35.

59 Elizabeth R. Harvey, "Pilgrimages to the 'Bleeding Border': Gender and Rituals of Nationalist Protest in Germany, 1919–39," *Women's History Review* 9, no. 2 (2000): 201–229.

60 Rainer Hering, *Konstruierte Nation. Der Alldeutsche Verband 1890 bis 1939* (Hamburg: Christians, 2003), here 110–118.

61 Michael Peters, "Alldeutscher Verband (ADV) (1891–1939)," *Historisches Lexikon Bayerns*, accessed August 10, 2006, http://www.historisches-lexikon-bayerns.de/artikel/artikel_44184.

broader vision of *Pan-Germanismus*, which supported the Germanic community that could encompass Scandinavians and Anglo-Saxons, was less
appealing to the Pan-German League than ideas of a more restrictive
Alldeutschtum.[62] As Chickering points out, the Pan-Germans saw *Volk*
and state as the "closest approximation to political perfection."[63] They
denounced the Bismarckian nation-state as incomplete and claimed that
the *Volk* was more precious than the state. At the same time, the state's
practice of power always came first for the Pan-Germans. The League's
main interest of making Germany a major player on the world stage meant
building a fleet and acquiring colonies, and these concerns often overshadowed if not conflicted with the issue of Germans abroad. Practical
considerations also hindered the prewar pan-German vision of an evolutionary Central European empire, especially the lack of support within the
lands to be incorporated, including Austria.[64]

During the war, the League followed an expansionist program that
demanded a Central European sphere of influence for the Reich; ideas
of ethnically cleansing the region were already pronounced.[65] Although
the Pan-German League was a relatively small organization, it was loud
and was thus considered influential, especially in spreading anti-Semitic
resentments. Despite its maximalist statements and goals during the war,
however, the Pan-German League's postwar territorial claims on Poland
remained minimal, for it sought to restore rather than to expand. In its
Bamberg Declaration of February 16, 1919 – 300,000 copies of which
were distributed as inserts in major newspapers – the League made a rather
vague call for a "unification of all of Central European Germandom."[66]
In the new statutes passed on August 31, 1919, the territorial demands
were clearer: the recovery of the territories lost to Poland as well as the
old Pan-German goal of annexing Austria. There was no call, however, for
annexing additional Polish territory beyond the 1914 borders.

The stance of the Pan-German League toward the Germans in Poland
beyond the 1914 border also fell within the general call for support of
Germandom abroad.[67] Irredentist claims were surely a consideration for

62 Roger Chickering, *We Men Who Feel Most German: A Cultural Study of the Pan-German League,
    1886–1914* (Boston: Allen & Unwin, 1984), 78.
63 Chickering, *We Men Who Feel Most German*, 77.
64 Chickering, *We Men Who Feel Most German*, 78.
65 Hering, *Konstruierte Nation*, 133–138; Fritz Fischer, *Griff nach der Weltmacht. Die Kriegszielpolitik des
    kaiserlichen Deutschland 1914/18* (Düsseldorf: Droste, 1967), here 87–108.
66 Hering, *Konstruierte Nation*, 143.
67 Alfred Kruck, *Geschichte des Alldeutschen Verbandes 1890–1939* (Wiesbaden: Steiner, 1954), 129–130.

some Pan-Germans, but the promotion of Germans abroad competed with geopolitical concerns that were often more salient. This continuing focus on the state was frustrating to völkisch thinkers at the time. Boehm complained that the prewar Pan-German League understood "all-German" to mean imperialism guided by economic questions and power.[68] Although Rainer Hering's recent work on the Pan-German League outlines its increasing militant nationalism in the Weimar Republic, it remains questionable how these ideas were translated into policies. Given the League's small size and the constraints imposed on the government by foreign policy, it is likely that its pan-German ideas had little influence in shaping actual Reich policies in the period after the First World War.

An umbrella organization for various organizations devoted to Germans abroad was the Deutscher Schutzbund für das Grenz- und Auslands-deutschtum (German Protective League for Germandom in Borderlands and Abroad), which was founded in January 1922.[69] Two of its founding leaders, Karl Christian von Loesch and Max Hildebert Boehm, both came from the prewar nationalist circle around Arthur Moeller van den Bruck.[70] Given this background, it is not surprising that the organization harbored ethnic irredentist as well as super revisionist ideas. In the beginning, the Deutscher Schutzbund was supposed to compete against the Verein für das Deutschtum im Ausland, which was considered by many to be obsolete.[71] Gradually, however, the Deutscher Schutzbund became more of a "private counter-organization" to the semi-governmental Deutsche Stiftung.[72] The Deutscher Schutzbund also published books on the Germans abroad, including Karl Christian von Loesch's influential *Volk unter Völkern* (1925).[73] For all its oppositional stance, a 1929 survey reveals that it received about RM 50,000 a year from government sources, although that year it lost all funding temporarily because of financial irregularities.[74] Not surprisingly, men dominated the makeup of such societies. Else Frobenius, a Latvian

---

68 Boehm, *Grenzdeutsch – Großdeutsch*, 2.
69 Jörg Hackmann, "Deutsche Ostforschung und Geschichtswissenschaft," in *Deutsche Ostforschung und Polnische Westforschung im Spannungsfeld von Wissenschaft und Politik. Disziplinen im Vergleich*, ed. Jan M. Piskorski, Jörg Hackmann, and Rudolf Jaworski, 25–45 (Osnabrück: Fibre, 2002), 34.
70 Sontheimer, *Antidemokratisches Denken in der Weimarer Republik*, 310–311.
71 Blanke, *Orphans of Versailles*, 150–151.
72 Jens Boysen, "Der Geist des Grenzlands. Ideologische Positionen deutscher und polnischer Meinungsführer in Posen und Westpreußen vor und nach dem Ersten Weltkrieg," in *Die Geschichte Polens und Deutschlands im 19. und 20. Jahrhundert. Ausgewählte Beiträge*, ed. Markus Krzoska and Peter Tokarski, 104–123 (Osnabrück: Fibre, 1998), 119.
73 Michael Burleigh, *Germany Turns Eastwards: A Study of Ostforschung in the Third Reich* (Cambridge/New York: Cambridge University Press, 1988), 25.
74 Blanke, *Orphans of Versailles*, 151–152.

German, was the only woman present at the founding of the Deutscher Schutzbund.[75]

The members of the Deutscher Schutzbund's constituent organizations were mostly immigrants from German communities in Eastern Europe, and they tended to be more concerned with their own refugee interests than with the well-being of the Germans abroad.[76] German organizations in Poland and these refugee organizations in Germany, in fact, had opposing interests; both wanted to increase their membership base and influence within their respective states. For example, German leaders in Poland accused the German Eastern Association (Deutscher Ostbund) of encouraging the Germans to leave Poland and agitating for the generous compensation of refugees. Besides the problems the population drain would have for the German leaders in Poland, there was the fear that the heightened expectations created by the Ostbund would lead to demands for higher indemnification and to greater dissatisfaction in refugee camps in the Reich.[77]

The discussion of civil society nationalism shows that the drawing of new political borders after the First World War had created a paradoxical situation. On the one hand, the fact that former fellow citizens now found themselves living abroad increased the general awareness for the plight of Germans in other countries. On the other hand, the example of Poland shows that there were very real limits to this kind of pan–German thinking, for concern for ethnic brethren varied in degree and priority. Not necessarily all of these Germans mattered in the same way, and the Germans in the lost borderlands received much, if not most, of the attention. The Reich borders of 1914 continued to exert themselves in many German minds in the 1920s. Certain academic and journalist circles, however, increasingly encouraged the need to think beyond these phantom borders in Poland: those boundaries between the old partitioned territories that could not be seen but continued to be felt.

OSTFORSCHUNG

Given the importance of proving ethnic claims on the lost territories, scholarship was soon enlisted to bolster the politics of revision. *Ostforschung*, or the

---

75 Harvey, *Women and the Nazi East*, 28–29.   76 Blanke, *Orphans of Versailles*, 150–151.
77 Consulate General in Poznań (Stobbe) to German Foreign Ministry, May 31, 1922, in PAAA, Pol IV, Politik 25 Polen, vol. 10, R82190, 115–118; Copy of unsigned and undated report by "German circles in Poland," sent by Prussian Ministry for Agriculture, Estates, and Forests (Ramm) to German Foreign Ministry, July 3, 1922, in PAAA, Pol IV, Politik 25 Polen, vol. 11, R82191, 112–115, here 115.

German study of the East, has become a classic example of how scholarship merged with political activism in interwar Germany.[78] Involving scholars from various fields such as history, geography, ethnography, economics, and philology, Ostforschung mixed politics and research to prove the inherent Germanness of Eastern Europe and to buttress German claims to territory or influence there.[79] After the Second World War, the role of many German academics in Ostforschung had been largely suppressed or ignored. Historians such as Theodor Schieder and Werner Conze enjoyed distinguished careers in West Germany, and their previous work on ethnic history was regarded by many in the postwar period not just as benign but also as a forerunner of modern social historical methods.[80] Despite early attempts in East and West Germany to uncover the connections between Ostforschung and Nazi racial selection and resettlement schemes, it was not until 1988, when Michael Burleigh published *Germany Turns Eastward*, that a new wave of interest in the subject arose.[81] At the annual congress of German historians (Historikertag) in Frankfurt/Main in 1998, the role of German historians in the Third Reich was examined. The ensuing debate was widely publicized and revealed a generational shift in the German historical landscape.

Ostforschung was a product of the profound changes caused during and after the First World War. This generation of German academics, of course, represented an interesting mix of official and civil society nationalism. Eduard Mühle has argued that the mental maps of the Ostforscher reflected mainstream German perceptions of the East.[82] In turn, the Ostforscher informed and shaped foreign policy while simultaneously fostering the fear of a Slavic threat. In practice, the Ostforscher sought to prove the legitimacy of German claims with pseudo-scientific methods involving dubious data collections, one-sided interpretations, and exaggerated historical conclusions. Yet contrary to the homogeneity that the term implies,

---

78 Burleigh, *Germany Turns Eastwards*, 39.
79 Kristin Leigh Kopp, "Contesting Borders: German Colonial Discourse and the Polish Eastern Territories" (Ph.D. dissertation, University of California, Berkeley, 2001), 191; Hackmann, "Deutsche Ostforschung und Geschichtswissenschaft," 31, 41.
80 For two views on this subject, see Götz Aly, "Rückwärtsgewandte Propheten – Bemerkungen in eigener Sache," in *Macht – Geist – Wahn. Kontinuitäten deutschen Denkens*, 153–183 (Berlin: Argon, 1997) and Hans-Ulrich Wehler, "Nationalsozialismus und Historiker," in *Deutsche Historiker im Nationalsozialismus*, ed. Winfried Schulze and Otto Gerhard Oexle, 306–339 (Frankfurt/Main: Fischer Taschenbuch, 1999). For an overview of debates in the historical profession in the postwar Federal Republic of Germany, see Klaus Große Kracht, *Die zankende Zunft. Historische Kontroversen in Deutschland nach 1945* (Göttingen: Vandenhoeck & Ruprecht, 2005).
81 Georg G. Iggers, "Foreword," in *German Scholars and Ethnic Cleansing, 1919–1945*, ed. Ingo Haar and Michael Fahlbusch, vii–xviii (New York: Berghahn Books, 2005), viii.
82 Eduard Mühle, "The Mental Map of German Ostforschung," in *Germany and the European East in the Twentieth Century*, ed. Eduard Mühle, 107–130 (Oxford/New York: Berg, 2003), here 109–110.

Ostforschung was hardly a monolithic project, nor was it necessarily coherent in its aims. Its subjection to the politics of the day meant that the relation between two crucial components, race and space, remained in flux. Especially the changing position of the Ostforscher regarding the Germans in Poland reveals the malleability and opportunism of their völkisch views and the inherent conflicts within them. The twists and turns in Ostforschung vis-à-vis the Germans in Poland show especially how kleindeutsch (Little German, i.e., Germany in its Bismarckian form) and großdeutsch concepts often conflicted. A closer look at these tensions allows for a reassessment of the meanings and limits of revisionism.

Although not widely used before the Second World War, the term Ostforschung began to appear in correspondence around 1928.[83] Although scholarly interest in Germandom beyond Germany's eastern border had existed before 1918, its institutionalization in the First World War was decisive for its development. Research centers were founded across Germany, including the Institut für ostdeutsche Wirtschaft (Institute for Eastern German Economy) in Königsberg. In 1918, the Osteuropa-Institut (Eastern Europe Institute) in Breslau was created to examine the areas ceded by Russia in the Treaty of Brest-Litovsk.[84] Initially, these institutes were supposed to examine general questions about the territories that had come under German occupation. After the First World War, however, it seemed that the centuries-old process of German colonization in the East had suddenly been thrown in reverse. Although the German migration from the eastern territories had been going on for almost half a century, the new political realities accelerated this process. The danger of a "space without people" – or at least without the right kind of people – was becoming apparent. Many blamed Polish repression for causing Germans to give up land that had been hard-won in the past. Calls to remedy this situation became louder. In autumn of 1923, the Mittelstelle für zwischeneuropäische Fragen (Liaison Office for Inter-European Issues) was founded in Leipzig.[85] This institution is generally considered the first true expression of Ostforschung. In 1925, the center was renamed the Deutsche Mittelstelle für Volks- und Kulturbodenforschung (German Liaison Office for Research on Ethnic and Cultural Territory). On October 30, 1926, it once again changed names and became the Stiftung für deutsche Volks- und Kulturbodenforschung (Foundation for Research on German Ethnic and Cultural Territory).

83 Hackmann, "Deutsche Ostforschung und Geschichtswissenschaft," 28.
84 Burleigh, *Germany Turns Eastwards*, 24–25.
85 Haar, *Historiker im Nationalsozialismus*, 26, 38, 51.

According to Michael Burleigh, the reorganization of the Mittelstelle in 1926 represented the shift in Ostforschung from the study of Eastern European economies and societies to the exclusive focus on the settlement of Germans in Eastern Europe. As Burleigh states, "the institute's name reflected the considerable influence that ethnocentric geo-political and cultural-geographical concepts were to have upon Ostforschung thereafter."[86] In 1926, the Stiftung's director, Wilhelm Volz, published an essay volume called *Der ostdeutsche Volksboden*, an influential work that was a manifesto of sorts for the new direction in Ostforschung.[87] The Volks- und Kulturboden concept allowed Ostforschung to involve several different fields related to East Central Europe. Albert Penck outlined this conceptual duality in his "Deutscher Volks- und Kulturboden," an essay in *Volk unter Völkern*.[88] For Penck, Volksboden referred to the areas where Germans could still be found and the German language heard. Penck's concept of Kulturboden, which he drew from Friedrich Ratzel's prewar theories of Kulturlandschaft,[89] was the more innovative part.[90] Penck reranked, even privileged, cultural work in evaluating how German a certain space was.[91] According to Kulturboden arguments, if Germans were no longer or only weakly present, their lingering influence could still be discerned in the higher standards of living and productivity of the local population as well as architectural and urban development. Given the massive migration of Germans from the ceded territories, such an argument was opportune to say the least, for it could encompass those regions denuded of any German persons, however defined.[92] As Michael Burleigh notes, this definition was highly subjective and thus made German claims to Kulturboden "practically limitless."[93]

Despite its revolutionary interdisciplinarity, Ostforschung in practice had a narrow thematic focus and facilitated a völkisch slant in German academia. Ostforschung operated on the assumption that the Germans and Germany

---

86 Burleigh, *Germany Turns Eastwards*, 25–26. On page 70, Burleigh notes that the Reich Interior Ministry founded the Stiftung für deutsche Volks- und Kulturbodenforschung in 1921.

87 Burleigh, *Germany Turns Eastwards*, 28–32; Wilhelm Volz, ed., *Der ostdeutsche Volksboden. Aufsätze zu den Fragen des Ostens* (Breslau: Hirt, 1926).

88 Burleigh, *Germany Turns Eastwards*, 25–26; Albrecht Penck, "Deutscher Volks- und Kulturboden," in *Volk unter Völkern*, ed. Karl C. von Loesch and A. Hillen Ziegfeld, 62–73 (Breslau: Hirt, 1925).

89 Kopp, "Contesting Borders," 182–183.

90 On the innovation of Penck's maps, see Michael Fahlbusch, *Wissenschaft im Dienst der nationalsozialistischen Politik? Die "Volksdeutschen Forschungsgemeinschaften" von 1931–1945* (Baden-Baden: Nomos Verlagsgesellschaft, 1999), 229. According to Guntram H. Herb, Penck actually invented the concept of "Kulturboden" in Ostforschung (Herb, *Under the Map of Germany*, 56).

91 Kopp, "Contesting Borders," 179. 92 Kopp, "Contesting Borders," 180.

93 Burleigh, *Germany Turns Eastwards*, 26.

were culturally superior to the Poles and the Polish state.[94] Indeed, its purpose was to give greater proof to this claim, and the terms of inquiry were already preloaded with stereotypes and self-conceptions of German superiority. Prussian historiography had long portrayed the Poles as unable to rule themselves, and the Germans could play upon catch phrases such as "Polish economy" to suggest chaos or incompetence.[95] As ostensible carriers of culture in this narrative, the Germans assumed the role of a "cultural fertilizer" in an otherwise barren eastern landscape.[96] By revealing the essential Germanness of a region, scholars could underscore the special right of Germans to rule or to reacquire various territories. With this new focus, the Stiftung für deutsche Volks- und Kulturbodenforschung became a point of coordination for various projects examining the Germandom abroad. This think tank also supported exchange between the government and those organizations promoting Germans abroad.[97] The institute published *Deutsche Hefte für Volks- und Kulturbodenforschung* and began work on the *Handwörterbuch des Grenz- und Auslanddeutschtums*.[98] Polish scholars, in turn, saw interwar German expansionist and revisionist designs as an updated edition of the *Drang nach Osten*, which served as a homogeneous and dehistoricized portrayal of German colonization in Eastern Europe.[99]

Like the concept of Volks- und Kulturboden, the coining of the phrase "Border Germans and Germans Abroad" also represented a conceptual breakthrough. It tied together those putatively unreal German minorities along the borders, including those who had been lost recently at Versailles, with those Germans who had been living for centuries in foreign

94 Fischer, *Die deutsche Publizistik*, 13–14. See also Harry K. Rosenthal, *German and Pole: National Conflict and Modern Myth* (Gainesville: University Presses of Florida, 1976).
95 Hubert Orłowski, "'Polnische Wirtschaft': The History and Function of the Stereotype," *Polish Western Affairs* 32, no. 2 (1991): 107–128; Hubert Orłowski, "'Polnische Wirtschaft,'" in *Deutsche und Polen. Hundert Schlüsselbegriffe*, ed. Ewa Kobylińska, Andreas Lawaty, and Rüdiger Stephan, 515–522 (Munich: Piper, 1992); Hubert Orłowski, *"Polnische Wirtschaft": Zum deutschen Polendiskurs der Neuzeit* (Wiesbaden: Harrassowitz, 1996).
96 Chickering, *We Men Who Feel Most German*, 88; Haar, *Historiker im Nationalsozialismus*, 8n61; Eduard Kneifel, "Adolf Eichler – Ein Leben im Dienste des Deutschtums," in *Deutschtum im Aufbruch. Vom Volkstumskampf der Deutschen im östlichen Wartheland*, ed. Adolf Kargel and Eduard Kneifel, 11–32 (Leipzig: Hirzel, 1942), here 16.
97 Fahlbusch, *Wissenschaft im Dienst der nationalsozialistischen Politik*, 231.
98 Hackmann, "Deutsche Ostforschung und Geschichtswissenschaft," 34.
99 See Wolfgang Wippermann, *Der "deutsche Drang nach Osten." Ideologie und Wirklichkeit eines politischen Schlagwortes* (Darmstadt: Wissenschaftliche Buchgesellschaft, 1981); Benedykt Zientara, "Zum Problem des geschichtlichen Terminus 'Drang nach Osten,'" in *Preußen, Deutschland, Polen im Urteil polnischer Historiker. Millenium Germano-Polonicum*, ed. Lothar Dralle, 171–181 (Berlin: Historische Kommission zu Berlin, 1983); Wojciech Wrzesiński, *Sąsiad, czy wróg? Ze studiów nad kształtowaniem obrazu Niemca w Polsce w latach 1795–1939* (Wrocław: Wydawnictwo Uniwersytetu Wrocławskiego, 1992); Henry Cord Meyer, *Drang nach Osten: Fortunes of a Slogan-Concept in German-Slavic Relations, 1849–1990* (Bern: Peter Lang, 1996).

environments. As Rudolf Jaworski notes, the term "Border Germans and Germans Abroad" was often deployed in such a way that the differences in the motives behind the support of these groups faded.[100] By squaring this circle, the idea was crucial in the later project of creating a more egalitarian view of Germans abroad: the move toward seeing all Germans in foreign countries (without German citizenship) as part of the German Volk. Although the new research was German-centric, the Volksboden definition of Germandom remained inclusive enough to encompass apparently disparate groups. In *Der ostdeutsche Volksboden*, Volz argued that even those who did not speak German could still belong to the Volk:

Race does not determine ethnicity – is the Sorb physically different from the Saxon? The "wasserpolnisch" speaking Upper Silesian [different] from the German speaker? – but the will and consciousness of ethnicity. Therefore the problems in the East are quite different from those in the West: the language frontier is not the ethnic frontier! The eastern German "*Volksboden*" encompasses the peripheral intermediate peoples of the German nation.[101]

In this interpretation, different ethnicities could exist within the same (German) race. Völkisch thought, both as a discipline and in its broader reception, was flexible, and who belonged to the Volk remained contested. Such conceptual openness was not always undesirable, however, for it could facilitate German demands abroad.

Ostforscher in the interwar period often claimed that their efforts were a reaction to Polish attempts to legitimate their claims to the German East. Some Polish writers advocated not just keeping the territories already ceded by Germany but also annexing other historically Slavic lands, in some cases as far west as the Elbe River.[102] Although such claims remained marginal in Polish government and society, German scholars exaggerated their influence in order to bring more money and attention to their own work. Albert Brackmann, who became director of the Prussian State Archives in 1929 and oversaw the founding of the Publikationsstelle Dahlem in 1931, was concerned with this Polish "onrush," which included the Baltic Institute, founded in Toruń in 1925.[103] The activities of other Polish nationalist organizations, such as the Union for the Defense of the Western Borderlands (Związek Obrony Kresów Zachodnich) and the Overseas and Colonial League (Liga Morska i Kolonjalna) only

---

100 Jaworski, "Der auslandsdeutsche Gedanke in der Weimarer Republik," 383.
101 Translated quotation from Burleigh, *Germany Turns Eastwards*, 28.
102 For an example of a Polish propaganda poster, see Mühle, "The Mental Map of German Ostforschung," 114.
103 Burleigh, *Germany Turns Eastwards*, 49–50.

encouraged such doomsaying. Brackmann was especially worried about Germany inadvertently helping such Polish claims. He believed that German archives were recklessly granting access to Polish historians who were working under the auspices of the Polish government. German scholars, on the other hand, were not getting the resources they needed to defend German interests. Nonetheless, Polish "Westforschung" was hardly institutionalized in the way German Ostforschung was, and it remained more of a chimera than a real threat.[104]

Although many Ostforscher adhered to the Greater German idea in the 1920s, they also had to make compromises. Up until 1931, Wilhem Volz, the director of the Stiftung für Volks- und Kulturbodenforschung, recognized the limits of revisionism and supported Stresemann's kleindeutsch policies.[105] Much of the Stiftung's work focused on the area of the German state in its 1914 borders. These topics included the economic plight of East Prussia resulting from the loss of Poznania and West Prussia (Pomerelia) and the importance of inner colonization to stop the Slavic threat from within. Yet not all were satisfied with these limitations. As mentioned earlier, Max Hildebert Boehm pushed for the founding of a new Reich beyond the 1914 borders, which he rejected as "formalism."[106] Starting with Foreign Minister Gustav Stresemann's death in 1929, Ostforschung freed itself of its Little German straitjacket: no longer was the German minority merely to serve the recovery of lost territory. Rather, territory was now supposed to support the needs of the Volk. In 1931, geographers such as Albrecht Penck and Friedrich Metz campaigned against Volz and forced the Reich Interior Ministry to dissolve the Stiftung in 1931.[107]

This tension between restorationist revisionism and expansionist irredentism could even be seen in Ostforschung maps. Several recent studies on the growth of German geopolitical thought after the First World War have focused on the role of cartography.[108] As Kristin Kopp has pointed out, cartography in Germany – as elsewhere – was taken as a serious science, and maps were seen as the "mirror of nature."[109] Maps had an inordinate

---

104 Burleigh, *Germany Turns Eastwards*, 43–45; Jan M. Piskorski, "Polish *myśl zachodnia* and German *Ostforschung*: An Attempt at a Comparison," in *German Scholars and Ethnic Cleansing, 1919–1945* (see note 81), 260–271, here 266–268. See also the following works: Wojciech Wrzesiński, *Twórcy polskiej myśli zachodniej* (Olsztyn: Ośrodek Badań Naukowych, 1996); Jan M. Piskorski, Jörg Hackmann, and Rudolf Jaworski, eds., *Deutsche Ostforschung und Polnische Westforschung im Spannungsfeld von Wissenschaft und Politik. Disziplinen im Vergleich* (Osnabrück: Fibre, 2002).
105 Haar, *Historiker im Nationalsozialismus*, 61.
106 Haar, *Historiker im Nationalsozialismus*, 35; see also Boehm, *Grenzdeutsch – Großdeutsch*, 5.
107 Herb, *Under the Map of Germany*, 74; Haar, *Historiker im Nationalsozialismus*, 52, 61–69.
108 David Thomas Murphy, *The Heroic Earth: Geopolitical Thought in Weimar Germany, 1918–1933* (Kent/London: The Kent State University Press, 1997), 248–249.
109 Kopp, "Contesting Borders," 173.

power of suggestion and provided vivid proof of the injustice done by Versailles. A common tool of suggestive cartography was the geo-organic portrayal of the state as a living organism. The lost eastern territories were shown as being brutally ripped from the body of the German Reich, thus reinforcing political catchphrases such as "bleeding borders."[110] In one example, Kopp's analysis reveals how the name of Germany that stretched from west to east was spliced by the Polish Corridor. The map visualized an amputated Germany as "Deutsches Rei...ch."[111] Other, more völkisch-oriented Ostforscher focused on the distribution and influence of ethnic German settlement. For these German scholars, state borders would always be secondary to nationality borders.[112] Such geo-organic maps delegitimated Weimar Germany's territorial form as unnatural and may have opened the idea to an even more expansive Germany.

Yet geopolitical and ethnographic maps could be read in different, even contradictory ways, as seen in Figure 1.2. With the caption "Poland's Triumph over Wilson: The Incorporation of Pomerelia into Poland," it is not surprising that it focused on the lost German territories. The heavy lines suggested the sanctity of the prewar borders and hardly the acquisition of additional territory, which themselves would delegitimate the 1914 borders. Notably, the Central Polish city of Łódź did not appear despite its large German-speaking population, even though a few smaller cities appear.[113] The geographer Guntram Herb has analyzed these tensions between these depictions of Germany and explained the development from revisionist to expansionist maps.[114] Yet maps that showed German claims in Poland reflected the conflicting concepts of revisionism in nationalist politics and in Ostforschung. This precarious balance of competing claims reveals a crooked path rather than a linear one in the relationship between race and space in determining territorial revisions.

The Ostforscher and Germandom organizations played an important role in advocating what they thought were ethnic German concerns. Book series, newspaper articles, and public lectures took up the cause of the

110 Fischer, *Die deutsche Publizistik*, 43. Fischer notes the use of "terminological tools" (Begriffswerkzeuge) that played on this imagery. See also Karol Fiedor, "'Blutende Grenze' – Haslem pruskiego nacjonalizmu," in *Górny Śląsk po podziale w 1922 roku. Co Polska, a co Niemcy dały mieszkańcom tej ziemi?*, vol. 2, ed. Maria Wanatowicz, 103–121 (Bytom: Uniwerstytet Śląski w Katowicach, 1997); Harvey, "Pilgrimages to the 'Bleeding Border,'" 211.
111 Kopp, "Contesting Borders," 196.
112 Herb, *Under the Map of Germany*, 62.
113 Map in Friedrich Heiss and A. Hillen Ziegfeld, *Deutschland und der Korridor* (Berlin: Volk und Reich Verlag, 1933), 282.
114 Guntram Henrik Herb, "Von der Grenzrevision zur Expansion. Territorialkonzepte in der Weimarer Republik," in *Welt-Räume. Geschichte, Geographie und Globalisierung seit 1900*, ed. Iris Schröder and Sabine Höhler, 175–203 (Frankfurt/Main: Campus, 2005).

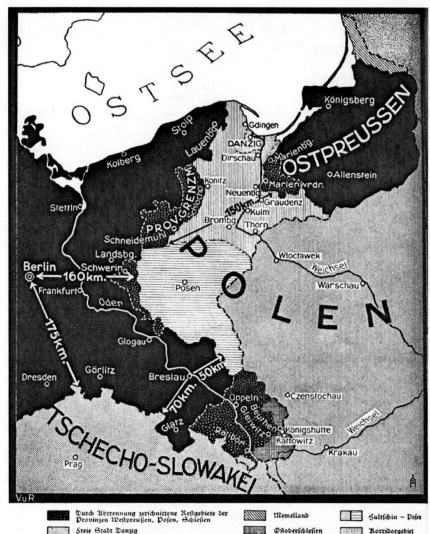

Figure 1.2. Interwar depiction of Germany's lost regions. Note the absence of Łódź. Translation: "Poland's Triumph over Wilson: The Incorporation of Pomerelia in Poland."
Source: Friedrich Heiss and A. Hillen Ziegfeld, *Deutschland und der Korridor* (Berlin: Volk und Reich Verlag, 1933), 282.

Germans abroad. Not surprisingly, the various "host states" rarely came out in a good light. Such propaganda helped to create a hardened, maximalist attitude vis-à-vis Germany's eastern neighbors. Peter Fischer has examined how German children often absorbed the ill will of their environment. A survey published in 1932 asked schoolchildren between eleven and fourteen years of age in Germany's eastern borderlands about their attitude toward Poland. Of those surveyed, 92 percent said they hated the Poles, 6 percent said they loved the Poles, and 2 percent did not care. Many saw Poland as "our enemy in the East" that Germany needed to destroy. Such were the attitudes of the generation that would bear arms against Poland in 1939.[115]

THE TIES THAT BIND: OFFICIAL HOMELAND NATIONALISM

It is likewise important to make the distinction between official nationalism and civil society nationalism. Despite their personal opinions or public pronouncements of what Germany's ultimate goals should be, German political leaders confined their actions to the possible and practical. In the case of territorial revision, a return to the 1914 borders was seen by most statesmen as the maximum of what Germany could realistically achieve. During the peace treaty proceedings at Versailles, the German delegates were more worried about the likely loss of existing Reich territory than the improbable acquisition of new ones. For this reason, the representatives only mentioned the Sudeten Germans once in their written comments.[116] The delegates were also not overly engrossed with Austria,[117] probably because they anticipated that the Allies would forbid a union with Germany. Subsequent Weimar German policy worked toward ameliorating the conditions imposed by the Versailles Treaty, which virtually precluded the possibility of asking for any territory that had not previously belonged to the prewar German Reich.

Although the Weimar German government strove for a return of the territories lost at Versailles, the motivation of the actors involved varied. Many adhered to a form of Greater German nationalism. In March 1926, Carl-Heinrich von Stülpnagel of the Defense Ministry gave his view of what needed to be done. They were in order of importance: the remilitarization of the Rhineland and the Saarland, the reincorporation of the Polish Corridor and Upper Silesia, the annexation of Austria, and the elimination of the

115 Fischer, *Die deutsche Publizistik*, 16–17.   116 Macmillan, *Paris 1919*, 237.
117 Macmillan, *Paris 1919*, 252.

demilitarized zone.[118] Some super revisionists wanted to destroy the Polish "Saisonstaat" (seasonal, i.e., temporary, state) entirely. Hans von Seeckt, the chief of the Army Command, declared that "Poland's existence is unbearable, incompatible with Germany's vital needs. She must disappear and will disappear, through her own internal weakness and through Russia, with our help."[119] Accompanying this visceral hatred for Poland was the desire to extend German dominance deep into Eastern Europe. Yet as we have seen, these fantasies were not necessarily ethnic irredentist in their motive.

Germany's limits were well recognized by Gustav Stresemann, who was briefly German chancellor in 1923 and then served as foreign minister from 1923 until his death in 1929. As a member of the National Liberal Party, he had been an advocate of annexationist policies during the war. After the war he helped to found the German People's Party (Deutsche Volkspartei, DVP). As foreign minister, Stresemann foresaw some kind of territorial revision as Germany's main goal in the middle term, and he wanted to prepare the international stage for this possibility. His cooperation with the Western powers led to the Treaty of Locarno on December 1, 1925, for which he and French Premier Aristide Briand received the Nobel Peace Prize in 1926. Still, his efforts earned him much scorn at home for his policy of fulfilling the terms of the Versailles settlement, and especially the National Socialists detested him. The publication of documents shortly after his death also led to a reassessment in the 1930s. He was condemned for having been dishonest with the world community, and later his revisionist ambitions were regarded as an important link between Wilhelmine and Nazi expansionist policies. Recent research, however, has portrayed him as a realpolitiker who was truly devoted to the concept of collective security.[120]

In the latter half of the 1920s, Foreign Minister Stresemann worked toward a revision of the Versailles Treaty that would restore the lost Reich territories.[121] His policies embodied what will be termed here "official

---

118 "Oberst von Stülpnagel (Reichswehrministerium) an Vortragenden Legationsrat von Bülow," March 6, 1926, in *ADAP*, ser. B, vol. 1, part 1, document no. 144, pp. 341–350; Hillgruber, "'Revisionismus' – Kontinuität und Wandel in der Außenpolitik der Weimarer Republik," 612.

119 Quotation from Blanke, *Orphans of Versailles*, 123; Hoensch, *Geschichte Polens*, 262.

120 Books on Gustav Stresemann include Enssle, *Stresemann's Territorial Revisionism*; Peter Krüger, *Die Außenpolitik der Republik von Weimar* (Darmstadt: Wissenschaftliche Buchgesellschaft, 1985); Christian Baechler, *Gustave Stresemann (1878–1929). De l'impérialisme à la sécurité collective* (Strasbourg: Presses Universitaires de Strasbourg, 1996); Georg Arnold, *Gustav Stresemann und die Problematik der deutschen Ostgrenzen* (Frankfurt/Main: Peter Lang, 2000); Karl Heinrich Pohl, ed., *Politiker und Bürger. Gustav Stresemann und seine Zeit* (Göttingen: Vandenhoeck & Ruprecht, 2002); Eberhard Kolb, *Gustav Stresemann* (Munich: C.H. Beck, 2003); Jonathan Wright, *Gustav Stresemann: Weimar's Greatest Statesman* (Oxford: Oxford University Press, 2004).

121 Haar, *Historiker im Nationalsozialismus*, 51.

kleindeutsch revisionism." He expressed this view in various speeches and documents that reveal his desire to regain the ceded territories. In a January 1925 memo, he stated that the immediate goal of German foreign politics would be the revision of the politically and economically untenable borders resulting from the peace treaty, whereby he explicitly included the Polish Corridor and Upper Silesia.[122] In 1925, Stresemann assured Karl Christian von Loesch, who was leading a delegation of the Bund deutscher Ostverbände, that Germany would support the German minority in the ceded territories with "the most effective means at its disposal."[123]

Stresemann's preoccupation with the lost territories, and especially the eastern borders with Poland, can be contrasted to his views on annexing Austria. The *Anschluß* (annexation) question remained a vexing problem for a generation of politicians and for historians who had grown up with both the kleindeutsch school of Prussian-German history and großdeutsch nationalism. Although initially großdeutsch in his political leanings, Stresemann was no principled ethnic irredentist. Stresemann had an uncanny sense of what his audience wanted to hear, and his continuing use of the Austrian annexation question catered to his listeners as well as to his own wishes. Stresemann ranked großdeutsch nationalist goals behind the territorial restoration of the prewar German Empire, however, and it is likely that a mix of realism and emotional attachment determined this hierarchy. The desire for Austrian annexation was tempered by his own private reservations about the Austrian people in general and the political and social stress that unification would entail.[124] Moreover, the issue of annexing Austria required great caution, for it would open up a range of other international questions in postwar Central Europe.[125] By 1926, Stresemann privately doubted the feasibility and desirability of an Austrian annexation altogether.[126]

In contrast to Stresemann's ambivalent position toward Austria and Czechoslovakia, the desire to solve the Eastern Question regarding Germany's border with Poland remained a consistent priority. In a passage of a

122 Stresemann memorandum on "die außenpolitische Notwendigkeit einer den Bedürfnissen der deutschen Minderheit in Europa entsprechenden Regelung des Minderheitenrechts innerhalb des Reiches," January 13, 1925, quoted in Megerle, "Danzig, Korridor und Oberschlesien," 162.

123 Bastiaan Schot, *Nation oder Staat? Deutschland und der Minderheitenschutz. Zur Völkerbundspolitik der Stresemann-Ära* (Marburg/Lahn: Johann-Gottfried-Herder-Institut, 1988), 150; "Aufzeichnung des Vortragenden Legationsrats von Dirksen. Aufzeichnung über den Empfang des Bundes der Deutschen Ostverbände durch den Herrn Reichsminister," December 28, 1925, in *ADAP*, ser. B, vol. 2, part 1, document no. 19, pp. 63–65.

124 Suval, "Overcoming Kleindeutschland," 320–321.

125 Peter Krüger, "The European East and Weimar Germany," in *Germany and the European East in the Twentieth Century*, ed. Eduard Mühle, 7–27 (Oxford/New York: Berg, 2003), 12.

126 Wright, *Gustav Stresemann*, 268, 326, 361, 400.

speech at a meeting of the DVP in Hannover, Stresemann stated the need to go forward "one step at a time": the eastern border first, later Austria, and finally the colonies.[127] The primary focus on the *lost* territories is also apparent in his much-publicized letters to former Crown Prince Wilhelm of September 7, 1925, in which Stresemann outlined his long-term plans.[128] The correspondence has been used to show the expansive nature of Weimar German revisionist policies,[129] but the historian Peter Krüger has countered that the letters have often been taken out of context.[130] Indeed, Stresemann's correspondence actually underlines the limited nature of his proposals. Although Stresemann's "third great task" mentioned the Anschluß with Austria, it was almost in passing. His immediate territorial claims remained within Germany's 1914 borders. In another letter to Crown Prince Wilhelm, he listed the disadvantages of an Anschluß. He mentioned the growing clerical and socialist influence and the possibility of Austria and Bavaria ganging up on Prussia within an enlarged Reich.[131] Nor did Stresemann press for a change of the Czechoslovak-German border.[132] On other issues as well, Stresemann's goals seemed to be more restoration-revisionist rather than ethnic irredentist. In a circular dated January 13, 1925, Stresemann stated that an annexation of "compact" German settlements in Central Europe could only be a distant goal of German hope, while Germany's immediate goals should be the reacquisition of the Corridor and Upper Silesia.[133]

Above all, Pomerelia (the Polish Corridor) remained a sore point for Germany. The German Foreign Ministry believed that a border revision was feasible, but it was willing to wait until an opportune moment.[134] Stresemann expressed this line of thinking in a circular in June 1925, in which he stated that propaganda regarding the Corridor should be scaled down without ever giving up claims on it. Stresemann showed a willingness to make territorial concessions to the Poles, and he proposed in a circular that Germany could give up its claim to the city of Poznań and most of what had been the southern Province of Posen in exchange for the bulk

---

127 Arnold, *Gustav Stresemann*, 116.

128 Salewski, "Das Weimarer Revisionssyndrom," 17.

129 Karl Heinrich Pohl, "Der 'Kronprinzenbrief' Gustav Stresemanns vom September 1925 – Ein Beispiel für wissenschaftliche Quelleninterpretation auf der Oberstufe des Gymnasiums," *Geschichtsdidaktik* 8 (1983): 152–163.

130 Krüger, *Die Außenpolitik der Republik von Weimar*, 207–208n1.

131 Wright, *Gustav Stresemann*, 326; Hillgruber, "'Revisionismus' – Kontinuität und Wandel in der Außenpolitik der Weimarer Republik," 609–610.

132 Wright, *Gustav Stresemann*, 361; Arnold, *Gustav Stresemann*, 9.

133 Megerle, "Danzig, Korridor und Oberschlesien," 162; cf. Eser, *Volk, Staat, Gott*, 144.

134 Megerle, "Danzig, Korridor und Oberschlesien," 149–150.

of the Corridor.[135] According to Christian Baechler, there were rumors after 1926 that Stresemann was even willing to give up Upper Silesia.[136] Carl Ulitzka, a member of the Upper Silesian Center Party, attacked Stresemann for focusing too much on the Corridor question and not enough elsewhere.[137] Jonathan Wright, however, points out that Stresemann never gave up Germany's claim to Upper Silesia.[138] Although Stresemann's tactics changed, his overall restorationist strategy did not. During Poland's growing internal crisis at the beginning of 1926, Stresemann hoped that economic and political turmoil would make Poland bend to Germany's will.[139] Yet Józef Piłsudski's coup in May 1926 reestablished political stability in Poland and ended German hopes for taking advantage of Polish weaknesses. In late 1928, Stresemann stated that both a German–Polish border revision and the annexation of Austria were not "within the domain of practical politics,"[140] but it is likely that the former remained a higher priority.

Bastiaan Schot has argued that Stresemann was less interested in revisionism itself than in using the issue to keep different nationalist organizations behind him.[141] Despite the controversy about Stresemann's final goals, however, what is relevant here are the actions he took and how these were influenced by politics and public opinion. The fact that he felt compelled to keep the eastern borders question on the stove, switching between front and back burners, is important. These self-imposed limitations reflected and structured governmental policies and public discourse. Despite the dissatisfaction of many nationalists with Bismarck's Little Germany, it was not so easy to overcome as the central point of reference after it had existed for four decades.

The idea that Poland should at some point return the Corridor became even more urgent after Stresemann's death. The troubles of Weimar democracy contributed to this process, in which polarization in domestic politics heightened tensions with Poland. In response to the agitated appeal of minority leaders, Chancellor Heinrich Brüning acknowledged that his government had a "moral obligation" to the German landowners in Western

---

135 Megerle, "Danzig, Korridor und Oberschlesien," 156–157. See also "Runderlaß des Reichministers des Auswärtigen Stresemann," June 30, 1925, in *ADAP*, ser. A, vol. 13, document no. 177, pp. 473–483, here 473. The Reich Foreign Ministry excluded the counties of Strasburg und Löbau from the Corridor question due to their overwhelmingly Polish population. See attachment to the circular: ibid., here 476.
136 Jonathan Wright, review of *Gustave Stresemann (1878–1929). De l'impérialisme à la sécurité collective*, by Christian Baechler, *German History* 16, no. 1 (1998): 107–108.
137 Wright, *Gustav Stresemann*, 411.   138 Wright, *Gustav Stresemann*, 411.
139 "Der Reichsminister des Auswärtigen Stresemann an die Botschaft in London," April 19, 1926, in *ADAP*, ser. B, vol. 2, part 1, document no. 150, pp. 363–376, here 363.
140 Citation from Krüger, "The European East and Weimar Germany," 25.
141 Schot, *Nation oder Staat*, 150.

Poland and that a subcommittee should explore all options to "encourage Germans in Pomerelia to persevere in their difficult situation."[142] Stresemann's successor as foreign minister, Julius Curtius, had remained fixated on the same Polish territories: the Corridor, the Noteć region, and eastern Upper Silesia. Like his predecessor, Curtius sometimes had an ambivalent, even enigmatic stance. He stated his willingness to give up Poznania for the Corridor, but he was also opposed to any compromise solutions.[143] Although Curtius had said in 1931 that the time had not yet come for a territorial revision,[144] he stated the following year that the eastern border remained crucial in Germany's foreign policy: "without the return of the 'Polish Corridor' to Germany, a solution of the German–Polish problem is not possible or conceivable."[145] Still, the continuity in tone throughout the period of the Weimar Republic is remarkable. The possibility of revising Germany's eastern borders was an issue that no politician could afford to ignore.

The border problem was all the more urgent because Germans were leaving Poznania-Pomerelia in large numbers. The reports of German emigration from these areas set off alarms even before the regions were officially ceded in 1920. Not only were the formerly German territories now under Polish rule, but the population was becoming overwhelmingly Polish as well. By the end of 1921, emigration from Poznania and Pomerelia may have been as high as 592,000 Germans.[146] Most, but not all, went to Germany. A 1925 census established that about 470,000 residents in the Reich had lived in the ceded territories of Poznania and Pomerelia in 1914.[147] The high number of emigrants severely altered the nationality balance in the ceded territories, thus compromising Germany's chances of later using the nationality principle to reclaim these lands. Public opinion, of course, exerted pressure on the government to act. Calling for greater support for the Germans remaining in the Polish Corridor, Max Hildebert Boehm wrote that these besieged homesteaders were fulfilling their "German duty" simply by holding their ground.[148]

---

142 Blanke, *Orphans of Versailles*, 157.
143 "Der Reichsminister des Auswärtigen Curtius an den Botschafter in London Freiherr von Neurath," March 17, 1931, in *ADAP*, ser. B, vol. 17, document no. 18, pp. 54–61, here 55.
144 Hillgruber, "'Revisionismus' – Kontinuität und Wandel in der Außenpolitik der Weimarer Republik," 616; "Der Reichsminister des Auswärtigen Curtius an den Botschafter in London Freiherr von Neurath," March 17, 1931, in *ADAP*, ser. B, vol. 17, document no. 18, pp. 54–61, here 54.
145 Blanke, *Orphans of Versailles*, 127.   146 Blanke, *Orphans of Versailles*, 32.
147 Gotthold Rhode, "Das Deutschtum in Posen und Pommerellen in der Zeit der Weimarer Republik," in *Die deutschen Ostgebiete zur Zeit der Weimarer Republik*, ed. Erwin Hölzle, 88–132 (Cologne/Graz: Böhlau, 1966), 99.
148 Max Hildebert Boehm, *Die deutschen Grenzlande* (Berlin: Reimar Hobbing, 1925), 205.

Yet revisionism was not the only factor driving a Germandom policy designed to keep the Germans in Poland and to stem the tide of migrants. Their upkeep and integration in the Reich were not only a financial burden on the state's budget, but there were serious social costs as well. This stream of refugees competed with locals and demobilized soldiers for scarce low-income housing.[149] The German migrants from Western Poland, many of whom lingered in refugee camps, fostered growing conflict at home and increasingly tested the limits of national solidarity.[150] The camps often were the sites of potential disruption: nationalists tried to mobilize discontented campmates against Poland, while socialists threatened to turn on these nationalists.[151] Moreover, favorable exchange rates meant that sending money to Germans in Poland was considerably cheaper than providing for German refugees in Germany.[152] Especially the compensation of German immigrants who had left property behind in Poland was seen as a big mistake. In the 1920s, Dr. Carl Georg Bruns, an advocate for German minority issues in Poznania and Pomerelia, advised against generous indemnification for repatriates, seeing this practice as a reward for those who had given up the nationality struggle all too easily. Rather, he called for policies to foster self-help at the grassroots in the same way that Polish activists had worked under Prussian-German rule.[153] Because humanitarian reasons excluded the possibility of stopping aid to repatriates altogether, however, the need to persuade minority members to stay in Poland became all the greater. Thus, the double burden of emigration – the reduced chances of regaining the lost territories and the increased financial, social, and political costs at home – encouraged efforts to keep the Germans in Poland where they were.

Yet the policies of the German Foreign Ministry were not motivated by völkisch or irredentist concerns per se, but by concerns over maintaining claims on former subjects and lands of the German Empire. Ulrich Rauscher, the German ambassador in Warsaw, warned that the "building of an irredenta" would make the German minority more difficult to control.[154] Instead, the Foreign Ministry desired a weak, passive minority that would

---

149 Richard Bessel, *Germany after the First World War* (Oxford: Clarendon Press, 1993), 180, 190.
150 Moritz Föllmer, "The Problem of National Solidarity in Interwar Germany," *German History* 23, no. 2 (2005): 202–231, here 208–209. See also Annemarie Sammartino, "Culture, Belonging, and the Law: Naturalization in the Weimar Republic," in *Citizenship and National Identity in Twentieth-Century Germany*, ed. Geoff Eley and Jan Palmowski, 57–72 (Stanford: Stanford University Press, 2008).
151 Regierungspräsident Schneidemühl to Prussian Interior Minister, "Bestrebungen der Posener Flüchtlinge," August 21, 1920, in GStA, I HA, Rep. 77, Tit. 856, folder 31, p. 326.
152 Krekeler, *Revisionsanspruch und geheime Ostpolitik*, 50; Burleigh, *Germany Turns Eastwards*, 100.
153 Schot, *Nation oder Staat*, 100.
154 Krekeler, *Revisionsanspruch und geheime Ostpolitik*, 45.

do its bidding. Excesses on the part of minority leaders might have complicated the international situation and narrowed the Reich's diplomatic room
to maneuver.[155] In other words, to keep revisionist hopes alive, the German
minority had to be kept from acting in an irredentist manner. Thus, the
dilemma was born: How could the Foreign Ministry continue to make
Germans in Poland believe that the Reich would one day reclaim them,
and thus encourage them to stay in place, but without stoking the fires too
much so that minority members would actively work toward this goal by
themselves?

THE "NEW ABROAD": OFFICIAL HOMELAND NATIONALISM IN ACTION

As a result of these pressures, the Prussian and Reich governments implemented a policy of what Norbert Krekeler calls "preemptive refugee
care."[156] Over the decade and a half of its existence, the Weimar Republic
spent millions of marks in trying to keep the Germans from leaving Poland.
Yet much of this money came from disparate sources that appeared incoherent, and the confusion over the status of the Polish Germans created considerable bureaucratic infighting and inter-ministerial competition. Especially
the complicated lines of jurisdiction between Prussia and the Reich troubled Germany's relationship with German minority leaders abroad. The
Prussian government and the Reich Ministry of the Interior maintained
responsibility for the to-be-ceded territories until 1920, when the Treaty
of Versailles took effect.

After the cession of the territories, Prussian authorities continued to feel
responsible for these Prussian Germans. The large archival collections of
the Prussian Interior Ministry, rarely drawn upon for studies of the German
minority in Poland, as well as the ministry's frequent correspondence with
the Foreign Ministry on minority issues, attest to this official interest in the
Germans in Western Poland as very much a domestic problem. In 1919,
for example, the Prussian finance minister stressed that Prussian revenue-
gathering and expenditures would continue in the previous manner even
after the hand-over of the territories to Poland. This situation would last
until there was a "proper" handover of these financial matters to Polish
authorities.[157] In other words, Prussian authorities had decided on their
own terms if and how they would continue their relationship with Germans

---

155 Krekeler, *Revisionsanspruch und geheime Ostpolitik*, 35, 44–45.
156 Krekeler, *Revisionsanspruch und geheime Ostpolitik*, 48, 63.
157 Preußischer Finanzminister to Regierungspräsident in Danzig, August 2, 1919, in GStA, I HA,
      Rep. 77, Tit. 856, folder 253.

in another country – and hence stepped on the toes not just of the Polish government but also of the Reich Foreign Ministry, which likewise claimed responsibility for Germans in the ceded territories. Importantly, the parties distinguished between this "new abroad" and the "old abroad" (outside the borders of 1914).[158]

Since 1920, the Foreign Ministry had been supporting the Germans in Western Poland with the help of a semi-independent organization, the Deutsche Stiftung.[159] In May 1922, the plans of the Foreign Ministry to centralize the coordination of minority support organizations provoked the reaction of Dr. Adolf Köster, the Reich interior minister. Köster attempted to reassert control by claiming that in the matter of the ceded territories it was not possible to separate "in-border" matters from those of the "out-border." Köster, who was from the Social Democratic Party, was especially afraid that the Foreign Ministry's plan would concentrate power in rightist circles at home and abroad and thereby have a detrimental impact on projects for Germans abroad. Moreover, Köster asserted that the Foreign Ministry should be grateful for not having to deal with potentially irredentist matters, which would be embarrassing and harm diplomatic relations.[160]

The Foreign Ministry countered this last claim by stating that it was in a better position to conceal the flow of support for the Germans abroad. Although Reich Chancellor Joseph Wirth, on the left wing of the Catholic Center Party, sided with the Foreign Ministry in October 1922, the conflict was not settled until November 1922, when a new Reich Cabinet with a new Reich interior minister, Dr. Rudolf Oeser, took office. Oeser was more amenable to the claims of the Foreign Ministry, now under Frederic-Hans von Rosenberg. In January 1923, an agreement was reached between the two ministries: the Foreign Ministry was to give up its centralization plans, but it would continue to play the leading role in German minority affairs in the ceded territories.[161] Although the Foreign Ministry was to direct activities for Germans in both the "new abroad" and the "old abroad," the phantom border between them would continue to play an increasing role in German minority life in the next two decades.

It was of course an open secret in the interwar period that the Weimar Republic was providing substantial support, both politically and financially, to the German minority. Still, The German Foreign Ministry was understandably afraid that its efforts in Western Poland would be seen as

---

158 Krekeler, *Revisionsanspruch und geheime Ostpolitik*, 47.
159 Krekeler, *Revisionsanspruch und geheime Ostpolitik*, 16–17.
160 Krekeler, *Revisionsanspruch und geheime Ostpolitik*, 41–42.
161 Krekeler, *Revisionsanspruch und geheime Ostpolitik*, 43–47.

"irredentism."[162] Wary of a possible diplomatic backlash, it sought to hide any glaring connections to the German government. Whereas the subsidies in themselves were not illegal, Polish intervention or international outcry could disrupt the smooth transfer of subsidies.[163] Moreover, the details of how the payments were made or who received them had to be kept covert. The Foreign Ministry thus required a network of putatively private organizations to organize the support for the Germans in Poland.

The most important of these semi-official organizations was the aforementioned Deutsche Stiftung, which was founded in November 1920 and was headed by Erich Krahmer-Möllenberg. The Deutsche Stiftung grew from the Inter-Party Eastern Committee, which had been established in 1919 by the National Assembly to monitor the Germans in what was to become Poland and to provide aid to them. It was funded by the Reich and Prussian governments and was formally under the German Foreign Ministry. Krahmer-Möllenberg himself had been a civil servant in the Prussian Interior Ministry and an authority on eastern affairs.[164] After the inflation of 1923 created financial difficulties for the Deutsche Stiftung, the organization tightened its ties with the Foreign Ministry, which began to provide most of its operating funds. The Deutsche Stiftung also supported think tanks such as the Deutsches Ausland-Institut in Stuttgart.[165] Affiliated organizations included the Konkordia Literarische Gesellschaft, founded in 1920. Headed by Max Winkler, it supported newspapers and cultural organizations abroad.[166]

It appears that the leading figures in the Foreign Ministry saw money as the best way to solve the problems facing the minority.[167] Millions went to German institutions and organizations in Poland. The Deutsche Stiftung gave money not just to build schools, but it also supplemented teacher salaries and supplied textbooks. It also ensured that cultural activities for Germans would flourish. For Upper Silesia, the Deutsche Stiftung budget from 1929 to 1930 shows that RM 45,000 were allocated to a theater in Katowice; RM 10,000 for a choral society; RM 33,600 for a German coal miners' union; RM 8,000 for school construction; and RM 4,000 for a German retail union. It also paid various benefits to former citizens in Poland. Between 1926 and 1933, Germany provided RM 60 to 70 million *annually* in unemployment benefit supplements to Germans in

162 Krekeler, *Revisionsanspruch und geheime Ostpolitik*, 44. Krekeler's quotes a document from the German Foreign Ministry to embassies in Copenhagen, Warsaw, Vienna, and Prague, September 29, 1922.
163 Blanke, *Orphans of Versailles*, 148–149.   164 Blanke, *Orphans of Versailles*, 143.
165 Blanke, *Orphans of Versailles*, 145.   166 Burleigh, *Germany Turns Eastwards*, 100.
167 Krekeler, *Revisionsanspruch und geheime Ostpolitik*, 45.

Poland.[168] The government targeted large firms and estates with its aid. It made payments of RM 10,000 per day in subsidies to German firms in Polish Silesia, and it had special import quotas for firms that employed Germans.[169] The Deutsche Stiftung also helped to offset legal costs from suits filed by German individuals and minority organizations against the Polish government.[170] Besides grants and payments, other forms of subventions included affordable loans, especially after 1924–1925.[171] Using banks and other credit institutions, especially those based in Danzig, the Deutsche Stiftung gave German farmers and businessmen the opportunity to acquire loans at rates lower than those in the Reich. The German government also helped German farmers in Poland by purchasing agricultural products such as butter and grain at favorable tariffs.[172]

In 1926, Germany's Foreign Minister Gustav Stresemann supported Krahmer-Möllenberg's plan to distribute RM 30 million in direct grants and credits to support German ownership of land and businesses abroad. The plan earmarked RM 21.5 million for the Germans in Poland.[173] Another organization called the Ossa Vermittlungs- und Handelsgesellschaft (also called Ossa-Konzern after its reorganization in 1928[174]) was founded to distribute these funds and was headed by a steering committee including Krahmer-Möllenberg, Max Winkler, and eight others. Outwardly independent, Ossa was in fact controlled by the Foreign Ministry and the Deutsche Stiftung.[175] Ossa in turn operated a series of institutions that channeled money to the minority. The largest of these was the Hollandsche Buitenland Bank, which was set up in 1925 with an initial budget of RM 11.8 million. Although it had Dutch officers, it remained subject to an all-German committee that included Krahmer-Möllenberg.[176] These substantial sums at a time when the German economy was still reeling from the war and hyperinflation show that support for the Germans in Poland was a priority for the Reich government. Because political motives outweighed economic

---

168 Blanke, *Orphans of Versailles*, 145.   169 Blanke, *Orphans of Versailles*, 145.

170 Blanke, *Orphans of Versailles*, 144–145.

171 Przemysław Hauser, "Die deutsche Minderheit in den Wojewodschaften Posen und Pommerellen 1919–1939," in *Deutsche und Polen zwischen den Kriegen. Minderheitenstatus und "Volkstumskampf" im Grenzgebiet. Amtliche Berichterstattung aus beiden Ländern, 1920–1939*, vol. 1, ed. Rudolf Jaworski et al., 273–282 (Munich: Saur, 1997), 278.

172 Blanke, *Orphans of Versailles*, 146–147, 158; Hauser, "Die Deutsche Minderheit in den Wojewodschaften Posen und Pommerellen 1919–1939," 278 (Hauser uses the example of the Danziger Raiffeisen bank).

173 My calculations are according to Krekeler, *Revisionsanspruch und geheime Ostpolitik*, 93. Blanke comes to a different calculation and notes that "16.5 million were to go to the Polish Germans" in 1926. See Blanke, *Orphans of Versailles*, 147.

174 Krekeler, *Revisionsanspruch und geheime Ostpolitik*, 93.

175 Blanke, *Orphans of Versailles*, 147.   176 Blanke, *Orphans of Versailles*, 146–147.

feasibility in granting loans, it was clear that defaults would be high.[177] Unsurprisingly, Ossa's operating expenses grew quickly. The initial RM 30 million for all its operations soon ran out, and more funds were granted. By 1931, Ossa had distributed RM 37.5 million in credits to Germans in Poznania and Pomerelia alone, with an additional RM 8 million planned for 1932. Upper Silesia had received RM 5.5 million between 1926 and 1931, with another million marks slated for 1932.[178]

The considerable sums for Germandom policy might give the appearance that official nationalism had taken a völkisch turn, but the "völkisch logic" of German authorities tended to be scattered rather than coherent.[179] The wrangling between ministries was more than a political or bureaucratic conflict. It was an attempt to redefine the Reich's relationship to its former citizens and territories: should these areas be treated as if they were still part of the Reich, and who would still be entitled to government benefits? The solution was complicated by the fact that Poland included territories that were both "new abroad" (prewar Prussian lands) and the "old abroad" (prewar Austrian and Russian lands). Both of these spheres had substantial German minorities. Yet there was a remarkable convergence among competing authorities in the Prussian government, the Reich Interior Ministry, and the Foreign Ministry on the special role of the Germans in Western Poland. Just as Germany treated the ceded regions as residual territories that were never fully lost, the Weimar-era governments approached the Germans in Western Poland not just as abstract members of a national community based on their ethnicity but rather as residual citizens who continued to enjoy certain membership rights. The existence of phantom borders, it seems, shaped the thinking of the different institutions in Germany even when they disagreed about methods.

Norbert Krekeler has argued that the financial support from Germany bound the Germans closer to Reich institutions, both emotionally and materially.[180] At the same time, the great bulk of the subsidies went to the Germans in the ceded territories. More attention needs to be paid to how the asymmetrical distribution of this money affected self-perception and political solidarity within the minority. The subsidies may have made the minority dependent on Germany and thus vulnerable to Reich machinations when the Nazis came to power, but they also fostered bitterness and

177 Krekeler, *Revisionsanspruch und geheime Ostpolitik*, 86–87.
178 Blanke, *Orphans of Versailles*, 148.
179 On this "völkisch logic," see Sammartino, *Impossible Border*, 119.
180 Krekeler, *Revisionsanspruch und geheime Ostpolitik*, 56.

incalcitrance on the part of those minority activists who felt excluded. The next chapter will explore how subsidies reflected and fostered a hierarchy of Germanness within the minority. Reich policies toward the phantom Germans in Western Poland were in practice more divisive than inclusive for the minority as a whole.

2

Residual Citizens

German Minority Politics in Western Poland (1918–1933)

According to the official Polish census for 1921, there were 1,059,154 Germans in Poland, or 3.9 percent of the total population.[1] With the formal inclusion of the eastern Upper Silesian territories in July 1922, an additional 330,000 German-speakers were added. This figure of roughly 1.4 million Germans sank drastically in the first few years of the 1920s as tens of thousands of German-speakers emigrated from Western Poland and Silesia to Germany. Yet more than a half million of these "German" Prussians remained in Poland, exchanging German for Polish citizenship. No longer members of the titular nationality, many German-speakers found it difficult to come to terms with their new minority status.

This chapter focuses on the situation of German national activists in interwar Western Poland in the first half of the interwar period. It examines how the loss of formal forms of belonging to the Reich affected their sense of Germanness and their political activities. It asks, for example, how the legacy of German citizenship constructed boundaries of inclusion and exclusion within the German minority in Poland after 1918. How did past borders become revived as regional interests were formulated and articulated? This chapter shows how a sense of residual Reichness in Western Poland hindered the solidarity of German activists. Indeed, the early attempts to cooperate with German activists in other regions not only failed in politically unifying the minority but also deepened regional cleavages.

GERMAN MIGRATION AND POLISH NATIONALITY POLICY

As Rogers Brubaker has argued, Poland was a "nationalizing state" in the interwar period. The attempts to create a homogenous nation-state are often

---

1 Richard Blanke, *Orphans of Versailles: The Germans in Western Poland, 1918–1939* (Lexington: University Press of Kentucky, 1993), 32.

referred to as Polonization. Yet the term is not precise enough to include the contradictory aims inherent in Polish nationalizing policies. According to Brubaker, the Poles followed two very different approaches: an assimilationist nationalism that attempted to eliminate differences, and a disassimilationist nationalism that presupposed differences to be "axiomatic and foundational" and thus attempted to separate groups and treat them differently.[2] In the eastern areas, where the Poles deemed the Belarusian and Ukrainian populations to be culturally and nationally similar but underdeveloped,[3] attempts were made to assimilate these groups. In Western Poland, however, Germans were considered to be already nationally developed, and the hardened German–Polish antagonisms in Western Poland also discouraged Germans from assimilating into Polish society. Brubaker argues that any attempt to cultivate the political loyalty of German-speaking Polish citizens would have "presupposed (1) an understanding of Germans' political loyalty and identity as open and contingent, and (2) an understanding of the Polish state as the state of and for all its citizens, not merely the state of and for Poles. But neither was forthcoming."[4] Few actually believed that these Germans could one day become Poles. Nationalist projects in Western Poland therefore foresaw the Polonization of the land, but Polish authorities did not attempt to win over the German population. Rather, they took a disassimilationist approach that encouraged the German population, however defined, to leave.

The peacemakers at Versailles had already foreseen the potential for nationality conflict in the coming postwar order. During the conference, David Lloyd George expressed his exasperation with the Polish delegates and his concern with where Poland was heading: "It fills me with despair the way in which I have seen small nations before they have hardly leaped into the light of freedom, beginning to oppress other races than their own."[5] Because of the potential for the abuse of minorities, the peacemakers forced the Polish delegates to sign the Minorities Protection Treaty, also known as the Little Versailles Treaty, on June 28, 1919 – the day Germany signed the main treaty. Therefore, Polish statesmen were usually careful in their public pronouncements and swore to fulfill international obligations. Some even claimed the Poles went beyond the letter of the Minority Treaty in terms of offering minority-language schools. Yet the danger of being outflanked

2 Rogers Brubaker, *Nationalism Reframed. Nationhood and the National Question in the New Europe* (Cambridge/New York: Cambridge University Press, 1996), 88.
3 Blanke, *Orphans of Versailles*, 63; Brubaker, *Nationalism Reframed*, 97–103.
4 Brubaker, *Nationalism Reframed*, 89.
5 Margaret Macmillan, *Paris 1919: Six Months That Changed the World* (New York: Random House, 2003), 226.

by the political right weighed heavily on Polish officials and statesmen, and nationalist statements for domestic consumption were common. Stanisław Grabski, the chairman of the Sejm's foreign affairs committee and later education minister who leaned toward the right-wing National Democratic camp, announced his views on ethnic minorities in a speech in October 1919: "We want to base our relationships on love, but there is one kind of love for countrymen and another for aliens. Their percentage among us is definitely too high; Poznania can show us the way by which the percentage can be brought from 14 percent or even 20 percent down to 1.5 percent. The foreign element will have to consider whether it will not be better off elsewhere; Polish lands for the Poles!"[6]

Given such attitudes, many Germans did not wait to test the new state and left before the territories were formally ceded in 1920.[7] The dramatic drop in the number of Germans in the Western Polish regions – what Richard Blanke calls the "great exodus"[8] – continued unabated after January 1920. The reasons for this emigration were varied. Already suffering from the consequences of Germany's military defeat, the Prussian Germans were the least satisfied of all ethnic Germans with their new status in Poland. A significant factor, although not the only one, was status anxiety. After all, the previous ethno-social and political hierarchy had been turned on its head. Prussian Germans, accustomed to being the Staatsvolk, may well have felt declassed overnight. German civil servants and professionals especially could not find work within the Polish administrative and legal systems because of unfamiliarity with the new regulations and with the Polish language. The desire to gain the necessary qualifications to earn a living in Poland was dampened by the prospect of lower wages and an overall decline in material standards.[9] Not wanting to learn Polish or to send their children to Polish schools, many Germans found resettlement in Germany a better prospect.[10]

For others, the trauma of national reversal only intensified the hatred toward the upstart Polish nation. In 1927, the conservative *Deutsche Allgemeine Zeitung* printed a letter from an embittered German in Poland, who complained that goods from Germany now had Polish labels, a practice he found to be a "slap in the face." He added that Polish customers would mistake these German goods for being inferior Polish products and reject them. He claimed that even Polish firms used German labels, for German

---

6 Quotation from Blanke, *Orphans of Versailles*, 63.
7 Gotthold Rhode, "Das Deutschtum in Posen und Pommerellen in der Zeit der Weimarer Republik," in *Die deutschen Ostgebiete zur Zeit der Weimarer Republik*, ed. Erwin Hölzle, 88–132 (Cologne/Graz: Böhlau, 1966), 99–100, 101.
8 Blanke, *Orphans of Versailles*, 32.   9 Blanke, *Orphans of Versailles*, 38.
10 Blanke, *Orphans of Versailles*, 47.

was naturally the language spoken by any "serious" businessman.[11] Whereas Michael Salewski has argued that businesses in the Reich tended not to be openly revisionist in order not to hurt business relations,[12] the anguished German perceived the advent of Polish-language labels on products made in the Reich as a threat to his nationality and even as a reversal of Germany's civilizing mission in Eastern Europe.

Polish authorities made life extremely difficult for the Germans, offering not only few positive inducements to stay but also a wide array of measures to make them leave.[13] An effort was made to deny Polish citizenship to Germans, for as non-nationals they would then be easier to expel.[14] Yet under the Versailles Treaty's Article 91, German nationals (*Reichsangehörige*) in the areas to be ceded to Poland were to become Polish citizens ipso facto. There was one significant exception. Those Germans who became residents after January 1, 1908 (the year that the Prussian Expropriation Law took effect) as well as their descendants would need permission from Polish authorities to become Polish citizens. After the treaty came into force, Germans over eighteen years of age had two years (i.e., until January 1922) to opt for German citizenship. Similar option provisions for German citizenship were also made for Poles residing in Germany.

Still, the devil was in the details, and confusion over the particulars of the option was widespread. The consequences for those who chose German citizenship but wanted to stay in Poland, or of the property of those who left for Germany, remained a matter of bitter dispute between Germany and Poland. According to some accounts, Polish administrators deliberately misinformed Germans, telling them that choosing German citizenship would entail neither deportation nor expropriation. Germans who opted for Reich citizenship were subsequently informed that they had to leave.[15] On the other hand, German authorities did not want to encourage the Germans to leave Poland, and one Reichstag deputy suspected that the lack of information coming from the German side was the source of numerous complaints about the option.[16] In the end, more than 140,000 Germans from Western Poland and Silesia ended up taking German citizenship and leaving Poland,

---

11 "Deutsche Reklame in polnischer Sprache," *Deutsche Allgemeine Zeitung*, July 16, 1927, in GStA, I HA, Rep 77, Tit. 856, folder 33, 100.
12 Michael Salewski, "Das Weimarer Revisionssyndrom," *Aus Politik und Zeitgeschichte* 30 (1980): 14–25, here 24.
13 Brubaker, *Nationalism Reframed*, 88.   14 Blanke, *Orphans of Versailles*, 66.
15 The Polish position was that Germans who opted for German citizenship had until 1924 to resettle in Germany.
16 Schultz-Bromberg (M.d.R.) to German Foreign Ministry, February 4, 1922, in PAAA, Pol IV, Politik 25 Polen, vol. 9, R82189, 4.

willingly or not.[17] Only in 1924 could a settlement of the option issue be reached.[18]

The German "exodus" (Richard Blanke) may have been as high as 592,000 people from Poznania and Pomerelia by the end of 1921.[19] Contemporaries often portrayed the development in even more drastic terms. The Danzig politician Hermann Rauschning, originally from West Prussia and sympathetic to National Socialism but who would later become famous for denouncing Hitler's expansionist plans, claimed that 800,000 people, or as much as 85 percent of the German population, had left Pomerelia and Poznania by 1926.[20] More conservative estimates by Gotthold Rhode suggest that only 575,000 people had left Poznania and Pomerelia by 1925.[21] Others have put the figure at 750,000 emigrants by 1939.[22] Towns accounted for much of this loss, and the rump German minority in Western Poland became overwhelmingly rural, although Rhode says that the losses in towns might not have been as severe as once thought, for many Germans could assimilate more readily in the more anonymous urban environment. Because Jews in Western Poland were usually considered "German" rather than "Polish," their departure also affected these statistics.[23] With tens of thousands more leaving those parts of Upper Silesia ceded to Poland, the German migration seemed to have reached catastrophic proportions.

German historians have pointed to the numerical drop in the German population to argue that the government indeed ruthlessly pursued a policy of Polonization that was unjustified and inhumane. The widespread closings of German schools and businesses, due in large part to the declining German population, reinforced the common belief that the Polish government was leading a determined effort to de-Germanize the country, arguably a soft form of ethnic cleansing.[24] Still, it is hard to speak of a centralized Polish nationality policy, especially in the early years.[25] Polish attitudes and action toward national minorities, and especially the Germans, were often ambivalent, leading to a contradiction between official statements of reconciliation and the rapid decline of the German population. Polish leaders

17 Blanke, *Orphans of Versailles*, 34–37.   18 Blanke, *Orphans of Versailles*, 66.
19 Blanke, *Orphans of Versailles*, 32.
20 Hermann Rauschning, *Die Entdeutschung Westpreußens und Posens. Zehn Jahre polnischer Politik* (Berlin: Reimar Hobbing, 1930).
21 Rhode, "Das Deutschtum in Posen und Pommerellen in der Zeit der Weimarer Republik," 99–100.
22 Jörg K. Hoensch, *Geschichte Polens* (Stuttgart: Eugen Ulmer, 1998), 264.
23 Rhode, "Das Deutschtum in Posen und Pommerellen in der Zeit der Weimarer Republik," 99–100.
24 See for example, Torsten Lorenz, "Międzychód optiert. Behördenpolitik, Migration und Wandel in einem westpolnischen Landkreis," in *Preußens Osten – Polens Westen. Das Zerbrechen einer Nachbarschaft*, ed. Helga Schultz, 145–181 (Berlin: Berlin Verlag Arno Spitz, 2001).
25 Albert S. Kotowski, *Polens Politik gegenüber seiner deutschen Minderheit, 1919–1939* (Wiesbaden: Harrassowitz, 1998), 116–118, 137–138.

often had to walk a tightrope, taking both international opinion and radical Polish nationalists into consideration. Whereas the former mandated tolerance of minorities, the latter accused the government of being too soft on minorities.

For many in the new Poland, past injustices were to excuse new ones. Polish nationalists and authorities defended the necessity of anti-German policies by pointing to the over-representation of Germans in business, trade, and land ownership. They especially saw the repressive Prussian policies in the late Imperial period as the cause for the allegedly wrong ethnic makeup in Western Poland. Polish nationalists often criticized the Polish government for having done too little to displace this overly privileged minority. The perception of a minority *problem* fostered the mindset that the German question had to be solved somehow.

Reasons of security often justified attempts to expel the Germans, especially in the ceded regions that Germany wanted to recover. The result was a security dilemma: Polish nationalizing policies intended to deprive Germany of a demographic base for its revisionist claims in Western Poland exacerbated negative public opinion in Germany and fueled revisionism there. Loud protests in the Reich to protect German compatriots abroad from Polish machinations in turn only increased the pressure on Polish authorities to solve the German problem. The quest for national security was greatest in the Polish Corridor, where German revisionist strivings were loudest. Yet even there, Polish authorities made sure that their discriminatory policies would appear to have ostensibly objective reasons. In a plan reminiscent of Prussian settlement policies, the voivode of Pomerelia proposed settling a nationally conscious Polish population in the region, using land reform as a cover. Heavier taxes on the Germans would induce them to leave. Moreover, a ten-kilometer border strip and the land surrounding Toruń, the capital of the voivodeship of Pomerelia, were also to be Polonized.[26] Government policies continued to favor titular Polish nationals within the overall citizenry, thus pursuing an ethnic-based political community that largely excluded the German minority.

But were Polonizing policies successful in breaking the back of German political life in the former Eastern Marches? As we have seen, the number of "Germans" in interwar Poland is difficult to determine. The statistics do not always reflect the number of people who were bilingual or felt themselves to be German. More importantly, numbers tell little about the *kind* of German community that remained. In Western Poland in particular,

26 Blanke, *Orphans of Versailles*, 113–114.

the German communities had shrunk to a hard core of rural conservatives.[27] Despite the loss of many German leaders, new ones sprang up to take their place, and the minority's political situation was not as hopeless as they had often claimed.

GERMAN POLITICAL ORGANIZATIONS IN THE POLISH POLITICAL SYSTEM

Perhaps the most obvious way for Germans to improve their condition was to participate in the Polish political system, especially in the parliamentary system. The Polish parliament had two houses, the upper-house Senate and the lower-house Sejm, the latter being considerably more powerful. Between 1922 and 1935, there were 111 seats in the Senate and 444 in the Sejm. The composition of the Sejm was determined by a proportional representation system, which in theory allowed even very small parties to gain seats. In practice, however, the division of districts and the distribution of mandates were designed to hinder the number of seats won by parties representing ethnic minorities. As representatives of a relatively small minority, German leaders needed to form coalitions with other political or minority groups if they were to enter parliament. By participating in the Minorities Bloc, German parties were in fact very successful in sending representatives to the Sejm and Senate in the 1920s.

The first step was to consolidate and mobilize the German minority itself. German political parties, as minority organizations, depended on a constituency that consciously identified itself as German. Increasing this constituency itself became the virtual platform of almost all German political organizations, and the parties' exhortations to be more German became an institutionalized ritual. As Russell Hardin has noted, "[O]ne of the peculiarities of identity talk is the tendency to suppose that the mere *fact* of an identity makes certain actions *right*. This popular move is an instance of the derivation of a moral from a descriptive fact, of an 'ought' from an 'is.'"[28] The drive for a larger self-identified German constituency, intended as a means to a political end (e.g., protection of German cultural institutions or, in the case of the socialists, mobilization of the working class), became an end in itself.

Not surprisingly, the German leaders' greatest fear concerned widespread indifference to nationality, which could mean decreased involvement with

---

27 Rhode, "Das Deutschtum in Posen und Pommerellen in der Zeit der Weimarer Republik," 102.
28 Russell Hardin, *One for All: The Logic of Group Conflict* (Princeton: Princeton University Press, 1995), 8. Emphasis in the original.

German political parties. Such national indifference was, according to various accounts, especially marked in Central Poland. Lack of support for German parties often spurred pessimism about the future of German nationality in Poland, although playing on such cultural despair could in turn serve the political interests of German leaders. German conservative-nationalist and German socialist parties alike faced the task of mobilizing the German vote, and an effective way to attain a high degree of German political consciousness was to focus on the minority's victimization. Violations of private property rights, lack of employment opportunities, and legal disadvantages undoubtedly colored the view of many Germans and prompted political engagement in some cases. Yet the most widely discussed issue in the interwar period concerned the restriction and even loss of German cultural institutions, namely schools and churches. It is not surprising, then, that in their political battles with Polish parties and with one another, German leaders relentlessly kept cultural issues at the forefront. Throughout Poland, attempts to preserve these institutions marked German political life from beginning to end.

GERMAN CONSERVATIVE-NATIONALIST PARTIES

Germans and Poles alike associated the struggle for Germandom most strongly with the conservative-nationalist parties. The majority of politically active Germans in Poland participated in at least one of these organizations, each bound to specific territories that corresponded to the prewar partition borders. These political organizations never amalgamated because of two factors. First, the Polish government was wary of any German minority party that would extend over all of Poland and in the early 1920s had restricted organizations with such aspirations.[29] The second, and more significant, factor was the regional particularism of the various German parties, especially of those with a conservative-national program. Given their varied experiences in partitioned Poland and their different weight in foreign political calculations during the interwar period, it is not surprising that these parties remained split along regional lines. These regional conservative-nationalist political organizations did cooperate during electoral campaigns for parliament, but between elections they largely ignored or even worked against one another.

In Western Poland, German conservatism adhered strongly to ideas of the old Staatsvolk, and a territorial revisionism flavored the political rhetoric in

---

29 Blanke, *Orphans of Versailles*, 56.

this region. Conservative interests, notably those of German agrarians, had a long tradition of dominating West Prussian politics.[30] Roland Spickermann has argued that these local leaders had already undergone a metamorphosis during the Imperial German period, as the National Liberals gained influence and the conservatives adapted to the politics of democracy.[31] Yet with the hemorrhaging of the urban German population after 1918, the prewar basis for liberals largely disappeared. Not surprisingly, the chief minority functionaries were almost all agrarian conservatives.[32] Old style Honoratienpolitik – deference to local notables in political matters – thus survived longer within German communities in Poland. The clubby nature of the minority organizations and the frequent need for secrecy meant that German leaders were often self-appointed or at most elected in small circles. They were hardly accountable to the Germans they claimed to represent. Because the Weimar government relied on the network of elites to pass on money and to communicate with the minority in a discreet manner, however, its policies too strengthened the hand of the German local notables. The reversal of the German-Polish hierarchy in the old Prussian East made the claims of local German elites appear especially urgent, and they adeptly conflated their private and particular needs with the national interest.

The Deutsche Vereinigung, the main German minority organization in Western Poland, originated from the fusion of two competing Pomerelian groups on May 8, 1921.[33] It ended up taking the name Deutschtumsbund zur Wahrung der Minderheitenrechte; and despite the fusion of some moderate elements, the new organization remained conservative-nationalist in its character and leadership.[34] Many of its important functionaries were estate owners, including Erwin Hasbach and Alfred Hintze.[35] Eugen Naumann from Poznania became head of the main committee, and Kurt Graebe from Bydgoszcz acted as its executive director. Although this arrangement ensured that Poznania and Pomerelia would both be represented in the top leadership in Western Poland, it did not always prevent conflict from

30 Szczepan Wierzchosławski, "Społeczeństwo Prus Zachodnich wobec administracji Pruskiej (1815–1914)," in *Toruń i Pomorze pod władzą pruską. Materiały konferencji z 10–11 grudnia 1993 r. w Toruniu*, ed. Szczepan Wierzchosławski, 63–76 (Toruń: Towarzystwo Naukowe w Toruniu, 1995), here 65.

31 Roland Spickermann, "The Elections Cartel in Regierungsbezirk Bromberg (Bydgoszcz), 1898–1903: Ethnic Rivalry, Agrarianism, and 'Practicing Democracy,'" *Central European History* 37, no. 1 (2004): 91–114.

32 Norbert Friedrich Krekeler, *Revisionsanspruch und geheime Ostpolitik der Weimarer Republik. Die Subventionierung der deutschen Minderheit in Polen* (Stuttgart: Deutsche Verlags-Anstalt, 1973), 36–37.

33 Dariusz Matelski, *Mniejszość niemiecka w Wielkopolsce w latach 1919–1939* (Poznań: Wydawnictwo Naukowe UAM, 1997), 77.

34 Krekeler, *Revisionsanspruch und geheime Ostpolitik*, 28; Blanke, *Orphans of Versailles*, 55.

35 Matelski, *Mniejszość niemiecka w Wielkopolsce*, 79; Blanke, *Orphans of Versailles*, 55.

breaking out between Graebe and Naumann. The double leadership in Western Poland would persist until the mid-1930s.

The Deutschtumsbund was not officially a political party, but rather a "united front."[36] There were four groups representing formerly Prussian regions: northern Pomerelia, southern Pomerelia, Noteć (Netze) District, and Poznania.[37] The Reich Foreign Ministry stressed that the organization should not be perceived as a political community.[38] It served as a coordination center for various organizations, including educational organizations (Gustav-Adolf-Verein, Lehrerverein), a women's club (Frauenverein), occupational groups (Bauernverein and Handwerkerverband), a theater group (Deutsche Bühne), as well as sports groups.[39] Because cultural and educational issues could not be easily separated from political issues, and because there was no other organizational framework available, the Deutschtumsbund essentially served as the political party for the Germans in Western Poland in the 1920s.

German leaders in Western Poland, of course, entertained the idea of spreading their influence to other territories, especially in the former Congress Kingdom, where hundreds of thousands of Germans lived. In 1920, there was a plan to create a statewide Deutsche Partei,[40] but nothing came of it. The first significant impulse to create a nationwide German minority organization occurred with a meeting of top minority leaders on August 16, 1921, in Warsaw. The German embassy in Warsaw reported that Łódź would function as the seat for the new organization, although a handwritten comment by a Foreign Ministry official indicated that this choice would probably not lead to a merger of the different organizations.[41] The meeting took place with thirty-six participants from throughout the Polish state. There were no members from Upper Silesia because the plebiscite issue there had not yet been resolved, but there were representatives from

---

36 Blanke, *Orphans of Versailles*, 56.
37 Der Deutsche Bevollmächtigte to the Prussian Interior Ministry, Marienwerder, June 17, 1921, copy sent by Prussian Interior Ministry to Krahmer-Möllenberg, June 26, 1921, in GStA, I HA, Rep. 77, Tit. 856, folder 31, 493; same report also sent to German Foreign Ministry, in PAAA, Pol IV, Politik 25 Polen, vol. 5, R82185, 30–31.
38 German Foreign Ministry (Referat Polen) to Prussian Interior Ministry, "Anschauungen und Wünsche der Vertreter des Deutschtums im ehemals Preußischen Gebiete (Zusammengestellt auf Grund einer Besprechung in Posen am 28.4.1920 nachmittags, mit führenden Männern der verschiedensten Berufsarten und bisherigen Parteirichtungen)," May 3, 1920, in GStA, I HA, Rep. 77, Tit. 856, folder 31, 282–292, here 289–290.
39 Matelski, *Mniejszość niemiecka w Wielkopolsce*, 78.
40 "Gründung der Deutschen Partei in Posen," *Tägliche Rundschau* (Berlin), July 10, 1920, in GStA, I HA, Rep. 77, Tit. 856, folder 31, 306.
41 German Embassy in Warsaw (Dirksen) to German Foreign Ministry, July 30, 1921, in PAAA, Pol IV, Politik 25 Polen, vol. 6, R82186, 174.

formerly Austrian Teschen Silesia. The "lively exchange" at the meeting resulted in the establishment of the Hauptvorstand der Deutschtumsbünde Polens (Main Board of Germandom Organizations in Poland), which included the four existing regional suborganizations within the Western Polish Deutschtumsbund as well as the German organizations representing Congress Poland, Galicia, and Teschen Silesia.[42] Eugen Naumann, from Poznań and already leader of the Deutschtumsbund, became the head of the Hauptvorstand, and Ludwig Wolff (the elder) from Łódź became the deputy leader.[43] One of the purposes of the Hauptvorstand was to maintain a "certain control" over the eight German deputies in the Sejm, for there had been complaints about their lack of activity.[44]

With members from all over Poland, the Hauptvorstand der Deutschtumsbünde Polens appeared to represent consolidation and reconciliation within the minority, and its leaders could claim with some justification to speak for the entire German minority in Poland. Yet the Hauptvorstand helped instead to harden regional lines between the German political organizations by institutionalizing their territorial boundaries. Whereas the Deutschtumsbund served formerly Prussian territories in Western Poland, German nationalists in the former Congress Kingdom had their own organization, the Łódź-based Bund der Deutschen Polens (BDP, also referred to as Bund der Deutschen in Polen, not to be confused with the various plans later to create an organization with the same name). There had been great reservations on the part of the Western Polish Germans about the attitude and character of Behrens, the leader of the BDP. Still, the German embassy's report noted that the most salient problem within the minority, the gulf between the Poznań and Łódź Germans, was indeed subsiding as the former were slowly overcoming their distrust of Behrens and coming to recognize what he had done for the Germans in Łódź. It was telling, however, that Behrens was not a member of the umbrella committee, the Hauptvorstand.[45]

Moreover, another report ("from Bromberg") of the August 1921 meeting in Warsaw showed that this mistrust toward the Łódź Germans was not

42 German Embassy in Warsaw (Schoen) to German Foreign Ministry, August 17, 1921, in PAAA, Pol IV, Politik 25 Polen, vol. 6, R82186, 225–233.
43 Copy of memo, unsigned and undated, in PAAA, Pol IV, Politik 25 Polen, vol. 6, R82186, 246.
44 German Embassy in Warsaw (Schoen) to German Foreign Ministry, August 17, 1921, in PAAA, Pol IV, Politik 25 Polen, vol. 6, R82186, 225–233; also copy of memorandum (unsigned and undated), sent by Bruns to Kessler, August 24, 1921, ibid., 245–246; Prussian Interior Ministry (Loehrs) to German Foreign Ministry, September 5, 1921, ibid., vol. 7, R82187, 16–18.
45 German Embassy in Warsaw (Schoen) to German Foreign Ministry, August 17, 1921, in PAAA, Pol IV, Politik 25 Polen, vol. 6, R82186, 225–233.

fading away. Indeed, there seemed to have been concerns in the Foreign Ministry that the BDP could become too influential in pan-minority politics. Listing the results from the meeting, the report mentioned first the explicit limitation of the BDP to the formerly Russian territories, a restriction that the organization was to carry in its name.[46] Significantly, there was no further mention of Łódź as the future seat of the Hauptvorstand. On the face of things, representation in the Hauptvorstand was equitable, with the Germans in the Western Polish regions having exactly half of the sixteen seats. Given their shared history and relatively cohesive interests, however, the Western Polish German votes could rely on having more voice within the Hauptvorstand than the other regions. Perhaps more importantly, this political calculus also ensured that the Western Polish Germans could not be dominated by the other regions. Despite − or because of − the Hauptvorstand's supraregional pretensions, German leaders, especially those in Western Poland, did not take it seriously, as subsequent events will show.

The meeting that created the Hauptvorstand also planned a general convention to underline the fledgling expressions of political unity within the minority. The first Congress of the Germans in Poland took place in Łódź on September 10–11, 1921, with a reported 3,000 participants.[47] Yet hopes for a unified stance of minority leaders proved to be too optimistic. The meeting started out with trouble flaring up between Łódź German leaders and other Polish Germans. During the board meetings at the beginning of the congress, the Łódź German representatives unanimously demanded that the delegates send a declaration of loyalty to the Polish president and premier, whereas the German activists from elsewhere wanted to submit a complaint to the League of Nations instead. Only when Eugen Naumann threatened to pull out all the organizations he represented (i.e., those in Western Poland) did the Łódź Germans yield and give up the telegram proposal. The whole meeting had almost fallen apart over this issue. The head of Germany's Passport Agency in Łódź, Paul Drubba, first complained about the poor logistical organization of the conference and was then taken aback by how "the tensions exploded instantaneously so that the success of the conference was put in question." It is just as difficult to accept, however,

---

46 Copy of memorandum (unsigned and undated), sent by Bruns to Kessler, August 24, 1921, in PAAA, Pol IV, Politik 25 Polen, vol. 6, R82186, 245–246.

47 "Die 1. Deutsche Tagung. Die Entschließungen," *Lodzer Freie Presse*, September 12, 1921, sent as attachment 2 to following document, German Passport Agency in Łódź (Drubba) to German Foreign Ministry, September 14, 1921, in PAAA, Pol IV, Politik 25 Polen, vol. 7, R82187, 38–44.

that Drubba believed that the "fundamentally different outlooks" could not have been predicted.[48]

The participants agreed to settle their disagreements after the meeting in order to keep the congress going. In his report, Drubba gave the obligatory remark that the congress should be booked as a success, and that the "possibility and need for a closer union" was gaining ground.[49] However, these differences would soon explode again. A mere two months after the congress, Drubba complained about continuing differences within the Hauptvorstand, which "lacked common principles and close cooperation of any kind." He advocated greater intervention on the part of the Reich in order to bring about this cooperation – leaving the issue to the minority alone, he feared, would lead to even greater divisions. He proposed that he himself should travel to Poznań to talk to German minority leaders there. It is likely that Drubba had wanted to explain to the German minority leaders in Western Poland that it was in their interest to treat the Łódź Germans with "caution and tactfulness." Despite his sympathy for the Łódź Germans and his desire for a unified minority, however, Drubba had made it clear that the formerly Prussian German leaders should take the leading role in the minority.[50]

Drubba eventually planned such a meeting for early December 1921, before German leaders in Western Poland were to travel to Warsaw for a meeting with other regional German leaders about the impending Sejm elections. It seems, however, that his intentions had been misunderstood by his colleagues and by the German leaders in Western Poland. The German consul in Poznań, Georg Stobbe, had consulted with the minority leader in his district, Eugen Naumann. Stobbe was disturbed by Drubba's interference and his advocacy in the unification question, and he suggested to the German Foreign Ministry that it would not be opportune for Drubba to travel to Poznań. Stobbe claimed that the decision to unify should be left to the minority leaders on the one hand, and that Reich official involvement could compromise the minority on the other.[51] It appears that both Drubba and Stobbe took positions that reflected the interests of their respective German minority leaders, and both officials argued that if their own

---

48 German Passport Agency in Łódź (Drubba) to German Foreign Ministry, September 14, 1921, in PAAA, Pol IV, Politik 25 Polen, vol. 7, R82187, 38–44.
49 German Passport Agency in Łódź (Drubba) to German Foreign Ministry, September 14, 1921, in PAAA, Pol IV, Politik 25 Polen, vol. 7, R82187, 38–44.
50 German Passport Agency in Łódź (Drubba) to German Foreign Ministry, November 12, 1921, in PAAA, Pol IV, Politik 25 Polen, vol. 8, R82188, 17.
51 Consulate General in Poznań (Stobbe) to German Foreign Ministry, December 5, 1921, in PAAA, Pol IV, Politik 25 Polen, vol. 8, R82188, 179.

suggestions were not followed, the interests and existence of Germandom in Poland would be endangered.

Stobbe later sent a telegraph to Drubba and asked him to postpone his trip, which in effect canceled the meeting. Expressing his disappointment, Drubba argued that he expected the upcoming conference of German minority leaders in Warsaw to be stormy and that he had simply wanted to "even the terrain" before the meeting. He stated that the Łódź German leaders had become embittered by the German leaders in Western Poland, who had recently submitted a complaint to the League of Nations in the name of the entire German minority. According to Drubba, the Łódź German leaders had agreed in principle with the complaint, but they wished that they had been consulted first. Drubba noted that the Łódź German wanted to be treated as equals, but they felt that they were becoming mere "appendages" who need not be considered. Concerned with the future development of the German minority, Drubba summed up the dilemma: either German leaders in Western Poland should decide to go on their own and ignore the Central Polish Germans altogether – and hope that the tensions do not worsen; or the German leaders in Western Poland could work for more unity with the Łódź Germans. The latter choice would require the "Posener and Bromberger gentlemen" to stop their "autocratic behavior" and show some "tact and political understanding."[52]

German leaders in Western Poland, it appears, opted for the former path and eschewed consulting their eastern cohorts during the 1920s. Despite events and issues during which German leaders from east and west showed public solidarity, this unity seldom went beyond lofty words in speeches and academic publications. Tensions over goals and methods were unmistakable, and they could break out at any time. The lack of significant inter-regional cooperation was in part due to the Deutschtumsbund's own preoccupations: the deep dissatisfaction with the Polish state and the hope for a return of their territory to the German state were specific to the Western Polish Germans. Despite the real and perceived decline in prosperity, the higher economic status of the minority in Western Poland vis-à-vis the Germans in the other regions also facilitated a sense of distinction. As Richard Blanke notes, 60 percent of all registered automobiles in Poland in 1939 were in the regions of Poznania, Pomerelia, and Upper Silesia.[53] Moreover, the Prussian-agrarian background of the Western Polish regions did not mesh well with the needs of Germans in other regions, especially in the urban

52 German Passport Agency in Łódź (Drubba) to German Foreign Ministry, December 7, 1921, in PAAA, Pol IV, Politik 25 Polen, vol. 8, R82188, 189–193.
53 Blanke, *Orphans of Versailles*, 115.

milieu of Łódź. As a privileged group, the Germans in Western Poland focused on their own hardships and barely noticed the advantages they held relative to the other German groups in Poland. As Drubba had remarked in his reports, the haughty and often disparaging attitude of the Western Polish German leaders toward the Germans in the East remained a source of complaint.[54] Probably because of the bitter experience between the Germans in Łódź and Western Poland in the late summer and fall of 1921, there was never again a statewide meeting to follow the first Congress of Germans in Poland.

LOOKING TO THE REICH

Instead of building bridges with the Germans elsewhere in Poland, the Deutschtumsbund strengthened the close ties between Reich authorities and Western Polish leaders. The Reich Foreign Ministry likewise used the Deutschtumsbund to gather information about Germans in Western Poland, especially concerning the value of assets lost. The headquarters in Bydgoszcz employed twenty-seven people in its staff.[55] Citing its expansion and growing needs, the Deutschtumsbund asked Krahmer-Möllenberg's Deutsche Stiftung in June 1922 for 2.4 million marks as a partial compensation for its expenses during the current year. Deutschtumsbund leaders pointed out that they were helping to save the social peace in the Reich and preventing other problems by sorting through potential refugees and giving them proper information about what they could have compensated.[56] The arguments seemed convincing enough. In September 1922, the Foreign Ministry transferred the entire sum directly to the Deutschtumsbund to pay for its services. The German General Consulate received an additional 600,000 marks earmarked for the Deutschtumsbund.[57]

For many Poles, the Deutschtumsbund in Western Poland embodied the aggressive irredentism of the German minority. Because the Deutschtumsbund was the largest and best-organized minority organization and because Polish authorities suspected its close ties with Reich authorities,

---

54 See also Richard Breyer, *Das Deutsche Reich und Polen, 1932–1937. Außenpolitik und Volksgruppenfragen* (Würzburg: Holzner, 1955), 232.

55 Matelski, *Mniejszość niemiecka w Wielkopolsce*, 78. Władysław Grabski, economist and prime minister from December 1923 to December 1925, replaced the Polish Mark with the Złoty as the official currency in April 1924 (Hoensch, *Geschichte Polens*, 261).

56 Consulate General in Poznań (Stobbe) to German Foreign Ministry, "Finanzielle Unterstützung des Deutschtumsbundes," June 9, 1922, with memorandum from Deutschtumsbund, June 2, 1922, in PAAA, Pol IV, Politik 25 Polen, vol. 11, R82191, 2–5.

57 Memorandum dated September 1922, in PAAA, Pol IV, Politik 25 Polen, vol. 11, R82191, 185; Blanke, *Orphans of Versailles*, 73–74.

the border danger overshadowed all other issues concerning the German minority.[58] German leaders put pressure on the Polish government by cataloging abuses in citizenship rights as well as in school and cultural issues. They then reported these violations to the Mixed Commission of the League of Nations, which enforced the Minorities Protection Treaty. The Deutschtumsbund, for example, started and won a trial at the World Court against Poland. Altogether, representatives of the German minority submitted the most complaints of any minority group in Poland. The Germans in Polish Upper Silesia, which possessed semi-autonomous status, sent 9,942 petitions to the Mixed Commission during the interwar period, although the League of Nations felt that only 43 of the cases were worth further investigation.[59] The reports to international bodies especially incensed the Polish government, which blamed the German government for agitating the minority. Not surprisingly, Polish authorities rarely complied with the decisions made by the Mixed Commission.

THE DEUTSCHE VEREINIGUNG

Irritated by the Deutschtumsbund's activities, Polish authorities had long contemplated a crackdown on it. Already in March 1922, the German Foreign Ministry was alarmed about an impending move against the Deutschtumsbund. The Polish government finally decided to dissolve the organization on April 25, 1923, but it waited until foreign political circumstances were more opportune to act. On August 6, 1923, Polish authorities raided the offices of the Deutschtumsbund and disbanded it on charges of espionage and treason.[60] German scholars have often portrayed the dissolution of the Deutschtumsbund as a major setback for the German minority and as evidence of Poland's repressive policies. Polish intentions of disrupting the minority's political activity were clear, but the dissolution of the Deutschtumsbund did little to hinder German activity in Western Poland. The old Deutschtumsbund leaders and functionaries soon formed the Deutsche Vereinigung im Sejm und Senat für Posen, Netzegau und Pommerellen, also known simply as the Deutsche Vereinigung (DV). Notably, the DV's full name expressed the lack of pretension in becoming a Poland-wide organization. Like its predecessor, the DV was not officially a political

---

58 Blanke, *Orphans of Versailles*, 63.
59 Anthony Tihamer Komjathy and Rebecca Stockwell, *German Minorities and the Third Reich: Ethnic Germans of East Central Europe Between the Wars* (New York: Holmes & Meier, 1980), 68.
60 Matelski, *Mniejszość niemiecka w Wielkopolsce*, 82; Harald von Riekhoff, *German-Polish Relations, 1918–1933* (Baltimore: Johns Hopkins Press, 1971), 208.

organization. Rather, it was formally a network of the offices kept by German parliamentarians, but the organization functioned as a German party in Western Poland. The Naumann–Graebe leadership constellation remained the same as in the Deutschtumsbund, and even the headquarters stayed in the same building in Bydgoszcz. The DV continued to represent the conservative-nationalist interests of the bulk of its members. Its major newspaper organs included the *Deutsche Rundschau* (based in Bydgoszcz, circulation 25,000), the *Posener Tageblatt* (circulation 15,000), and the *Pommereller Tageblatt* (circulation 3,500).[61] Newspapers played an important role in transmitting the DV's values for German-speakers in Poland. When compared to the estimated number of potential readers, German language newspapers were above average in both the number of daily newspapers in circulation per person (12.7 copies per 100) as well as in newspaper titles (1 title for every 7,100).[62]

As with the Deutschtumsbund, the Polish government suspected the DV of treasonous activity and used various means to keep the organization in check. Moreover, the Weimar Republic's so-called minority offensive in the late 1920s did much to mobilize the anti-German National Democrats, who were particularly strong in Western Poland. The National Democrats spoke often of the national minorities as a danger to the existence of the Polish state, and in their view these were first and foremost the Germans.[63] Anti-German sentiment often accompanied anti-Semitism, and those making ethnic slurs and epithets often did not bother with distinctions.[64] Gotthold Rhode recalled that as a schoolchild in Poznań, passersby often called him "Jew boy" (*żydek*) when he wore his blue German school cap.[65]

In Upper Silesia, the region's semi-autonomous status allowed the main conservative-nationalist party there, the Deutsche Partei, to escape restrictive measures. Like the Deutschtumsbund/DV further north, members of the Deutsche Partei came from a conservative, nationalist, and liberal spectrum that corresponded to the Deutschnationale Volkspartei (DNVP), the Deutsche Volkpartei (DVP), and Deutsche Demokratische Partei (DDP) in

---

61 Riekhoff, *German-Polish Relations*, 208–209.

62 Maria Gierlak, "Deutsche Presse in Polen 1919–1939. Forschungsstand, -postulate und -desiderate," in *Grenzdiskurse. Zeitungen deutschsprachiger Minderheiten und ihr Feuilleton in Mitteleuropa bis 1939*, ed. Sibylle Schönborn, 67–80 (Essen: Klartext, 2009), 70–71.

63 Albert S. Kotowski, *Hitlers Bewegung im Urteil der polnischen Nationaldemokratie* (Harrassowitz: Wiesbaden, 2000), 165, 167.

64 See copies of telegram by Consulate General in Poznań (Vice Consul Ziemke) to German Foreign Ministry, June 22, 1921, in PAAA, Pol IV, Politik 25 Polen, vol. 5, R82185, 74, 204.

65 Gotthold Rhode, "Lodzer Deutsche – Posener Deutsche. Keine wissenschaftliche Untersuchung, sondern eine Plauderei," in *Suche die Meinung. Karl Dedecius, dem Übersetzer und Mittler zum 65. Geburtstag*, ed. Elvira Grözinger and Andreas Lawaty, 237–256 (Wiesbaden: Harrassowitz, 1986), here 245.

Weimar Germany.[66] In this region, however, political Catholicism remained a significant factor. The former Center Party became the Katholische Volkspartei, which reorganized once again in 1927 into the Deutsche Katholische Volkspartei (DKVP). Under Eduard Pant's leadership, the DKVP took a less nationalist and more centrist position than the Deutsche Partei. In order to present a united front, these two parties cooperated loosely in the Volksbund, which was directed by Otto Ulitz. The Volksbund had about 35,000 members.[67]

By the early 1920s, German leaders had effectively abandoned their efforts to create a centralized organization for all Germans in Poland, but this development was not necessarily a reversal for minority leaders. Rather, it likely fostered German interests by reducing the considerable potential for infighting within a larger organization. After all, the most serious points of contention within the German minority were the questions of organizational cooperation and centralization. Relieved of divisive leadership struggles inherent in the unification project, regional German leaders could focus their activities on the practical issues at hand while presenting a united front vis-à-vis the Polish government when the need arose. Especially during elections, German activists sought to portray themselves as a German community above private or particular – and especially regional – interests.

GERMAN ELECTORAL SUCCESSES

Overall, German leaders adapted to the Polish parliamentary system in the 1920s, and the conservatives-nationalist in the western provinces did especially well. In the 1919 elections, eight Germans came into the Sejm. Six were from the district of Grudziądz in Pomerelia, and two came from Łódź. Officially, the German delegates from Pomerelia did not sit in the Sejm until the territories came under Polish rule on January 10, 1920.[68] Germans from Poznania boycotted the elections altogether. The parliamentary elections of 1922 were the first to include the participation of all of the ceded Prussian territories (including Upper Silesia). German cooperation within the Minorities Bloc in the 1920s proved enormously fruitful. The German

---

66 Przemysław Hauser, "The German Minority in Poland in the Years 1918–1939. Reflections in the State of Research and Interpretation, Proposals for Further Research," *Polish Western Affairs* 32, no. 2 (1991): 13–38, here 23.

67 Blanke, *Orphans of Versailles*, 57. Eduard Pant also led the Verein deutscher Katholiken in Polen (Association of German Catholics in Poland), which claimed some 25,000 members and published the largest German newspaper in Poland, the *Oberschlesischer Kurier* (Blanke, *Orphans of Versailles*, 56).

68 Marian Wojciechowski, "Die deutsche Minderheit in Polen (1920–1939)," in *Deutsche und Polen zwischen den Kriegen. Minderheitenstatus und "Volkstumskampf" im Grenzgebiet. Amtliche Berichterstattung aus beiden Ländern, 1920–1939*, ed. Rudolf Jaworski et al., vol. 1, 1–26 (Munich: Saur, 1997), here 7.

Table 2.1. *1928 Sejm Elections in Poland (select parties)*

BBWR (government party)	2,399,032 votes	(125 seats)
PPS (with DSAP)	1,481,279 votes	(64 seats)
Minorities Bloc	1,438,725 votes	(55 seats)
National Democrats	925,744 votes	(38 seats)
Communists	217,298 votes	(5 seats)
Bund	80,219 votes	(0 seats)[69]

parties gained seventeen seats in the Sejm.[70] Of the 111 senators, 5 were Germans. The 1928 Sejm elections showed a clear shift to the left in the overall Polish political scene. In the Sejm elections, the votes and initial seat distribution broke down as shown in Table 2.1.

In addition to the seats shown in the table, more seats were distributed according to the state lists, giving German conservative-nationalist parties within the Minorities Bloc a total of eighteen seats. The German socialists in Western Poland, who broke away from the other Polish German socialists and worked with the conservative-nationalist German parties, also won one seat, resulting in a total of nineteen German seats in the Sejm won through the Minorities Bloc. In the Senate elections one week later, the German parties again received five seats.[71] In addition to these German mandates within the Minorities Bloc, the German socialists gained two Sejm seats and no seats in the Senate.

The twenty-one seats won by German organizations in total (nineteen seats within the Minorities Bloc and two from German socialist participation with the Polish Socialist Party, PPS) represented 4.8 percent of all Sejm seats (444 total). The number of German senators remained stable at five, or 4.5 percent of the total (111 seats).[72] Thus, the German representation in both Sejm elections in the 1920s remained slightly overproportional to the estimated German population, even when the more generous German population statistics are considered. The successes of German and other minority leaders ended in 1930, however, when the general political crackdown and a heightened nationalist atmosphere led to a reduced number of seats for all minority parties. The German parties could only claim five Sejm deputies and three Senators that year.

Significantly, the gap in minority representation between the formerly Prussian regions and the rest of Poland widened during the 1920s despite

69 Petra Blachetta-Madajczyk, *Klassenkampf oder Nation? Deutsche Sozialdemokratie in Polen 1918–1939* (Düsseldorf: Droste, 1997), 167.
70 Zygmunt Stoliński, *Die deutsche Minderheit in Polen* (Warsaw: Instytut Badań Spraw Narodowościowych, 1928), 41.
71 Hauser, "The German Minority in Poland," 28.
72 Stoliński, *Die deutsche Minderheit in Polen*, 40.

the demographic decline in the western regions. In 1922, ten of the seventeen (59 percent) German Sejm deputies were from the formerly Prussian regions.[73] In 1928, German organizations in Western Poland, including Upper Silesia, accounted for sixteen of the twenty-one seats (76 percent). In the latter elections, the nationalist German organization in Central Poland, the Deutscher Volksverband (German People's Union, or DVV), won only three Sejm seats (9.5 percent of the German total) and one Senate seat (20 percent).[74] Looking at just the German socialists, however, the distribution was reversed. The Western Polish German socialists, who cooperated with the conservative-nationalist Germans in the Minorities Bloc, received just one mandate. The main group of socialists represented by the Deutsche Sozialistische Arbeitspartei Polens (DSAP; German Socialist Labor Party in Poland) gained two seats, both in the Central Polish city of Łódź. In light of the poor showing of the German nationalists there, socialism within the German minority increasingly became an eastern phenomenon.

That the German activists in the former Prussian areas fared much better than their counterparts in Central and Eastern Poland is not surprising. In part, the success of the formerly Prussian Germans was due to their experience of "practicing democracy" in Imperial Germany.[75] Germans in the Russian Empire and in the Habsburg Monarchy could not draw upon the same experience of political mobilization. The Germans in Western Poland also lived in fairly compact areas, which facilitated the attainment of direct mandates because the greater likelihood of acquiring a seat was itself a motivational factor in electoral turnout. The clearer delineation of Germanness and Polishness in Western Poland also meant that few "German" votes were lost to parties not explicitly German. This problem for German activists was apparent in other regions where German-speakers often voted for Polish mainstream parties, including the Polish Socialist Party. Finally, the fixed idea of a lost homeland and a possible return was crucial for the mobilization of the Germans in Western Poland.

RESIDUAL REICHNESS AND THE CONSTRUCTION OF WESTERN
POLISH GERMANDOM

William Hagen has written that the Eastern Marches lacked a collective identity in Imperial Germany.[76] Historical and socioeconomic differences

73 Stoliński, *Die deutsche Minderheit in Polen*, 41.   74 Stoliński, *Die deutsche Minderheit in Polen*, 43.
75 Margaret Lavinia Anderson, *Practicing Democracy: Elections and Political Culture in Imperial Germany* (Princeton: Princeton University Press, 2000).
76 William W. Hagen, *Germans, Poles, and Jews: The Nationality Conflict in the Prussian East, 1772–1914* (Chicago: University of Chicago Press, 1980), 270.

accounted for this lack of commonality among the Germans in the region, and they would persist, albeit in diminishing form, in the Polish state. As will be shown here, however, a common "groupness"[77] began to take shape after these areas were lost to Poland. Despite lingering differences between Poznania and Pomerelia, the identification and self-identification of these Germans as a distinct group grew. Especially the relative political success of German organizations in Western Poland exacerbated the cleavage between the formerly Prussian regions and the non-Prussian territories. There were of course intra-regional tensions between German leaders in the Western Polish towns of Poznań and Bydgoszcz.[78] Still, the DV served as a network that (re)connected the former Reich possessions of Pomerelia and Poznania, turning them into a particular Western Polish region within the minority landscape. Despite their claim to represent all the Germans in Poland, the DV occupied itself first and foremost with the affairs of Western Polish Germans.[79] These leaders began to perceive themselves and the Germans they claimed to represent as a uniform group, especially vis-à-vis the other Germans in Poland, and there was a certain distinction to being a Western Polish German, or "Posen-Pommereller." Embittered by the loss of their Staatsvolk status and more prone to revanchist sentiments, the DV members' mental maps remained firmly centered on the Reich.

As former Reich Germans, the German minority in Western Poland continued to enjoy a kind of informal, residual Reich citizenship. They accepted it as natural that the Reich should continue to care for its former citizens. Whereas politics, history, and geography played an important role, the predisposition to help the Germans in Western Poland was compounded by the fact that the large landowners in Western Poland often came from the same social background as the political and administrative class in Germany.[80] Not surprisingly, virtually all the minority leaders in Western Poland had been in *deutschnational* circles in the prewar period.[81] An important exception was Kurt Graebe, who was closer to the DVP line

---

77 For a discussion of "groupness" and "groupism" as problems of scholarly analysis, see various works by Rogers Brubaker, especially Rogers Brubaker and Frederick Cooper, "Beyond Identity," *Theory and Society* 29 (2000): 1–47, here 31–32.

78 Joachim Rogall, *Die Deutschen im Posener Land und in Mittelpolen* (Munich: Langen Müller, 1993), 134.

79 Blanke, *Orphans of Versailles*, 56, 74.

80 Michael Burleigh, *Germany Turns Eastwards: A Study of Ostforschung in the Third Reich* (Cambridge/New York: Cambridge University Press, 1988), 99–100.

81 Krekeler, *Revisionsanspruch und geheime Ostpolitik*, 36. These upper-class men included the Poznanian district administrator Eugen Naumann, the manor owner Witzleben in the Noteć (Netze) region, the manor owner Koerber in southern Pomerelia, and the estate owner Dr. Zabel in northern Pomerelia. See Der Deutsche Bevollmächtigte to the Prussian Interior Ministry, Marienwerder, June 17, 1921, copy sent by Prussian Interior Ministry to Krahmer-Möllenberg, June 26, 1921, in GStA, I HA, Rep. 77, Tit. 856, folder 31, 493.

of Gustav Stresemann, a onetime National Liberal.[82] German local notables in Western Poland exploited old networks with influential people in the Reich, whereas Germans in non-Prussian regions largely lacked these connections. Geographically and financially, Germans in Western Poland were also better able to travel to Berlin, Danzig, and Breslau to press their cases. These Western Polish Germans were often quite successful in instrumentalizing the national issue in their personal favor and taking advantage of Reich coffers, especially when they could emphasize their importance in keeping in place those Germans who would otherwise emigrate to Germany and live from state help there.[83] The Prince of Pless in Upper Silesia, for example, received a loan of RM 3 million in 1925 and another loan of RM 5 million three years later. The West Prussian estate in Runowo, which belonged to the nephew of former Imperial Chancellor Bethmann-Hollweg, was to receive a loan of RM 400,000.[84] Although these funds were provided as loans, they were in effect grants due to the unlikely ability of the landowners to pay back these enormous sums. Bethmann, for example, became indebted and had to sell his estate.[85] Thus, the money from the Reich often proved ineffective or even counterproductive in maintaining Germandom in the ceded territories.

More importantly, such examples reveal not just the endurance of political and social bonds across new state borders. German authorities privileged and nurtured old connections and networks. For German and Polish observers alike, the Germans in Western Poland appeared to be more advanced economically, culturally, and nationally than the Germans in the formerly Russian and Austrian regions. Not surprisingly, the bulk of news reports and scholarly studies in the 1920s ignored these eastern areas and focused instead on the Corridor and on Upper Silesia.[86] Indeed, with their material and political support from Germany, their higher standard of living, and a livelier organizational and cultural life, these Germans were very much the center of the German minority.

Even if a collective identity was not yet widespread among most Western Polish German-speakers in the 1920s, their leaders acted along regional alignments. On the political stage, these German activists often formulated their claims in terms of the significance of the ceded territories; or as the example of the petition to the League of Nations in 1921 has shown,

82 Blanke, *Orphans of Versailles*, 56.   83 Blanke, *Orphans of Versailles*, 154–155.

84 Burleigh, *Germany Turns Eastwards*, 100; Krekeler, *Revisionsanspruch und geheime Ostpolitik*, 88.

85 Krekeler, *Revisionsanspruch und geheime Ostpolitik*, 88–89.

86 Wolfgang Kessler, "Die 'Ostforschung' und die Deutschen in Polen," *Nordost-Archiv* 9, no. 2 (2000): 379–411, here 394.

they claimed to speak for the whole minority on matters that referred almost exclusively to the Western Polish situation. The German leaders from Western Poland could trust one another in their new projects because they had a shared political experience in the Imperial period. Yet the new sense of belonging rested less on past affectations than on the ways the current situation made them look at their past. Their groupness, in other words, intensified after the territories had been lost to Poland. The traumatic loss of their Staatsvolk status played a role in fostering status anxiety, a siege mentality, and feelings of injustice. Repression, both real and alleged, encouraged local German leaders to prove their value to Germandom and to extol the virtues of holding out as part of Germany's struggle against Slavdom.

In many ways, state-centered thinking persisted in new permutations among the Germans in Western Poland. They had inherited etatist models of Germanness from the German Empire, and this approach was supported by the revisionist politics of the Weimar period. In their current situation, Germanness had a largely voluntary and political definition. German language and culture remained important, but it was more significant if the person in question could help support the German cause in Poland. True, Polish-speaking persons who had been German citizens were now largely excluded, but those who felt German were not rejected outright from this version of the German national community. When it came to counting the number of Germans in Poland, nationally minded statisticians deemed people from purportedly mixed ethnicities such as Upper Silesians or Kashubians (most of whom had been German citizens before the war), or even Polish-speaking persons, as "German." German Jews, although few in number in Poznania and Pomerelia, served in the Volksbund in Upper Silesia.[87] On the other hand, the apparent precariousness of the minority's situation also led to an even starker hierarchization of Germanness: "good" Germans were eligible for (German) state support, but "bad" Germans who disagreed with or even worked against German government goals were excluded altogether.

As discussed previously, recent scholarship has indicated a transformation in German self-understanding after 1918. The cases shown here, however, qualify the narrative of a völkisch turn. Germans in Western Poland maintained their distinct status (and their material claims) largely based on their residual connections to the Reich. A sense of difference from the other Germans in the East was implicit. Reich and minority leaders considered

---

87 Blanke, *Orphans of Versailles*, 166.

the Germans in Western Poland to be borderland (*Grenzland*) Germans who were categorically different from the German settlements further east, for which German journalists used the terms diaspora and scattered settlement (*Streusiedlung*).[88] Yet in many ways the Germans in Western Poland were initially more diasporan in their outlook and activity than the supposedly less-national brethren elsewhere. William Safran argues that one of the important qualities of a diaspora is that "they continue to relate, personally or vicariously, to that homeland in one way or another, and their ethnocommunal consciousness and solidarity are importantly defined by the existence of such a relationship."[89] The relationship to the mother country, and especially the desire for a return, was strong among the Western Polish Germans right from the start, and it was only later that such a relationship would grow among the putatively real diaspora Germans in Central and Eastern Poland. At the same time, Western Polish German ethnocommunal consciousness was itself primarily focused on the nation-state, and only secondarily on contact with other German diasporan communities elsewhere in Poland and Eastern Europe.

Rogers Brubaker notes that Germany had crystallized into such a homeland for ethnic Germans abroad in the interwar period. This reorientation was the case even for Sudeten Germans, who had looked toward Vienna rather than Berlin before the war.[90] But Germans in Western Poland had a special relationship with Germany. Their homeland was not just close geographically but experientially as well. Germany may have served as a mythic or imaginary homeland for the German-speakers in the other Polish regions and in other countries, but the Western Polish Germans had grown up in a German nation-state and lived in it up until 1920. The continuing centrality of the German nation-state (as opposed to Germandom in general) could be seen in the following letter by a German in Toruń, which was copied and sent to the Deutsche Stiftung in 1919: "The government has sacrificed us to bring you in the Reich the blessings of the peace more quickly and hence to give you peace, security, and order."[91] Another Reich German official reported that the Germans in Western Poland still felt that it was their duty to hold out and act as a protective wall for their "old

---

88 For examples of the term "diaspora," see Kuhn, *Das Deutschtum Kongreßpolens*, 71; "Wie eine deutsche Gesandtschaft Auslandsdeutsche 'betreut,'" *Völkischer Beobachter*, July 29, 1930, in GStA, I HA, Rep. 77, Tit. 856, folder 610, 34.

89 William Safran, "Diasporas in Modern Societies: Myth of Homeland and Return," *Diaspora* 1, no. 1 (1991): 83–99.

90 Brubaker, *Nationalism Reframed*, 117.

91 Südgau der Deutschen Volksräte der Provinz Westpreußen, July 7, 1919, copy in GStA, I HA, Rep. 77, Tit. 856, folder 31, 105–106.

Fatherland."[92] Such reports may have well reflected the wishful thinking of Reich authorities, but the rhetoric of Volkstumskampf, the glorification of the German mission in the East, and the emphasis on holding on to the homestead had left their impact on the Germans' self-perception. The apparent sacrifice of these lost citizens, in turn, exacerbated the sense of obligation among officials in Germany. These close ties with the Reich meant that a basic problem of the Western Polish German organizations – their dependence on Reich funds and a persisting culture of dependency – could not be readily solved.

SUBVENTION MENTALITY

As residual citizens, the German leaders could claim and expect to receive subsidies from the Reich, and the sense of entitlement and over-reliance on subventions appeared to grow with time. Undoubtedly, many Germans truly believed that they were fulfilling Germany's national mission simply by staying put, and they expected to be justly compensated, even rewarded, for this sacrifice.[93] With the considerable sums flowing from the Reich into Western Poland, many feared that a "subvention mentality" was starting to take hold: German political, economic, and social life was becoming dependent on Reich finances.[94] The eastern regions of Prussia, after all, had enjoyed various subsidies during the Imperial period. As Kristin Kopp has noted, the politics of the Eastern Marches were revived after the First World War, albeit in different form.[95] The Germans in Western Poland skillfully manipulated the rhetoric of self-sacrifice and conflated their private welfare with that of the German nation in order to underline their claims. The subsidies took on considerable dimensions as the scope of the projects expanded, seemingly without end. The cost explosion for the Deutsche Stiftung prompted German officials from different ministries to consider alternative forms of help besides cash payments.[96] Moreover,

---

92 Der Deutsche Bevollmächtigte to the Prussian Interior Ministry, Marienwerder, June 17, 1921, copy sent by Prussian Interior Ministry to Krahmer-Möllenberg, June 26, 1921, in GStA, I HA, Rep. 77, Tit. 856, folder 31, 493; same report also sent to German Foreign Ministry, in PAAA, Pol IV, Politik 25 Polen, vol. 5, R82185, 30–31.

93 Consulate General in Poznań (Stobbe) to German Foreign Ministry, report "Finanzielle Unterstützung des Deutschtumsbundes," June 9, 1922, with memorandum from Deutschtumsbund, June 2, 1922, in PAAA, Pol IV, Politik 25 Polen, vol. 11, R82191, 2–5.

94 Blanke, *Orphans of Versailles*, 155.

95 Kristin Leigh Kopp, "Contesting Borders: German Colonial Discourse and the Polish Eastern Territories" (Ph.D. diss., University of California, Berkeley, 2001), 147.

96 Reich Interior Minister (Oeser) to German Foreign Ministry, January 4, 1923, and German Foreign Ministry to Reich Interior Ministry (draft), February 28, 1923, in PAAA, Pol IV, Politik 25 Polen, vol. 13, R82193, 10–11, 13.

German Foreign Ministry authorities wanted to keep the Germans who stayed in Poland from feeling disadvantaged vis-à-vis those Germans who left Poland for Germany.[97]

The demands for more money embittered the German Foreign Ministry, where the impression grew that minority leaders were abusing the situation for personal gain. Bernhard Wilhelm von Bülow, state secretary of the German Foreign Office, stated: "If some Pomorze [Pomerelian] landowners take the position that the Reich is obliged to preserve them as state pensioners and relieve them of every material worry, then this sort of attitude must be resisted with all necessary bluntness."[98] There was the feeling that these Germans, long accustomed to support from the state, were leaving Poland because they had never learned to be self-sufficient.[99] Max Hildebert Boehm hence complained that the Eastern Marches policies had backfired by spoiling the Germans there. The "enemy peoples" were ahead of the Germans in the struggle.[100] Many Poles, but also many Germans, believed that the local Germans had no real attachment to land.[101] Reich caretakers and minority leaders thus called for more self-help within the minority.[102]

It is important to emphasize, however, that the subvention mentality afflicted not just German minority leaders, but their caretakers in the Reich as well. Whereas many authorities privately doubted that money alone could keep the Germans in Poland, they simply had no other viable alternatives to this system of support; and thus Reich authorities were complicit in continuing the prewar program of Eastern Aid (*Osthilfe*). This approach was exemplified by Stresemann himself, who vainly hoped that the subsidies would encourage self-help among the Germans in Poland.[103] Rather than weaning them from aid, Reich officials in the Weimar period tried to meet the demands of the minority leaders within reason. In a 1927 memo, the Committee of Five, which was the highest council for minority affairs in

---

97 German Foreign Ministry to Schultz-Bromberg (M.d.R.), February 13, 1922, in PAAA, Pol IV, Politik 25 Polen, vol. 9, R82189, 5–6.

98 Translated quotation cited in Blanke, *Orphans of Versailles*, 158.

99 Boockmann, *Ostpreußen und Westpreußen*, 401.

100 Max Hildebert Boehm, *Grenzdeutsch–Großdeutsch. Vortrag anläßlich der Hauptausschußtagung des V.D.A. im November 1924* (Dresden: Verein für das Deutschtum im Ausland, 1925), 9. Interestingly, in the same year this lecture was published, Boehm published another book that claimed that the Germans in Western Poland had undergone this change with "remarkable discipline and self-control [Selbstüberwindung]." See Max Hildebert Boehm, *Die deutschen Grenzlande* (Berlin: Reimar Hobbing, 1925), 198.

101 Blanke, *Orphans of Versailles*, 46–47.

102 Jens Boysen, "Der Geist des Grenzlands. Ideologische Positionen deutscher und polnischer Meinungsführer in Posen und Westpreußen vor und nach dem Ersten Weltkrieg," in *Die Geschichte Polens und Deutschlands im 19. und 20. Jahrhundert. Ausgewählte Beiträge*, ed. Markus Krzoska and Peter Tokarski, 104–123 (Osnabrück: Fibre, 1998), 113.

103 Krekeler, *Revisionsanspruch und geheime Ostpolitik*, 92.

Western Poland, asked for RM 120,000 as a one-time payment in the first year, and then RM 157,000 annually thereafter. The Foreign Ministry saw these sums as maximal demands, and approved the full one-time payment of RM 120,000 but reduced the annual payment to RM 47,000 and 51,600 Złoty (approximately RM 25,000).[104]

The lack of transparency in the subsidies had long led to murmurings of cronyism and corruption. Those who felt left out accused the Weimar government and German minority leaders of favoring big industry and large landowners.[105] Even the Deutsche Stiftungs's Krahmer-Möllenberg doubted the representative nature of German minority organizations, and he saw a danger in the fusion of economic and political positions within the minority. The Committee of Five was chosen by the forty-five members of the Main Committee, which represented various rural and urban economic organizations. The Deutsche Stiftung insisted on proof that the forty-five voting members had been freely sent by their respective organizations and had not themselves been chosen by the Committee of Five, as complaints had indicated.[106] Yet these problems were difficult to eradicate because it appeared that a web of mutual dependency had developed between Reich authorities and minority leaders. One Foreign Ministry official attributed the frequent complaints to the "especially close relationships between here and there."[107] In 1929–1930, tensions between Graebe and Naumann led to the addition of four more members into the Committee of Five (making it the Committee of Nine) in the hope of giving more representation to those groups that felt excluded.[108]

Yet the culture of dependency continued. Indeed, the assiduous pleas by minority activists for more money were often thinly veiled attempts at blackmail that threatened a renewed wave of refugees if their requests remained unfulfilled.[109] Kurt Graebe was not beyond playing this game and underlined in 1930 how precarious the situation was for the Germans in Poland, binding their fate to the whole of Germandom.[110] One of his letters claimed that if the Reich did not send more funds immediately,

---

104 "Aufzeichnungen des Konsuls Freiherr von Hahn," February 22, 1927, in *ADAP*, ser. B, vol. 4, document no. 175, pp. 380–381, here 380n2.
105 Przemysław Hauser, "Die deutsche Minderheit in den Wojewodschaften Posen und Pommerellen 1919–1939," in *Deutsche und Polen zwischen den Kriegen*, 273–282, here 278.
106 Krekeler, *Revisionsanspruch und geheime Ostpolitik*, 27–29, 70–73, 109–110.
107 "Aufzeichnungen des Konsuls Freiherr von Hahn," February 22, 1927, in *ADAP*, ser. B, vol. 4, document no. 175, pp. 380–381, here 380.
108 Blanke, *Orphans of Versailles*, 89.
109 Blanke, *Orphans of Versailles*, 156–157, 159. This situation was not unlike the "Wende" in 1989/1990, when East Germans threatened to come to West Germany if the government of the Federal Republic did not introduce the D-Mark to East Germany.
110 Blanke, *Orphans of Versailles*, 155.

the situation of the minority would become "embarrassing," and minority leaders would resign collectively.[111] The danger of over-reliance on the Reich became apparent during the depression of the 1930s, when several smaller German clubs and economic organizations in Poland faced a crisis due to the lack of funds.[112] At the same time, it seems that the Germans in Western Poland had not been fully "orphaned" by Versailles.[113] Germany may have lost custody over its metaphorical "children," but it remained an active "parent" that paid considerable support and sought to regain the lost home in Western Poland. German authorities spoke openly of the special obligations to the Germans in the ceded territories, and with the hope that they would one day be reunited. These responsibilities to its residual citizens were quite stark when compared to the situation of German groups elsewhere in Poland.

SUBSIDIES AND HIERARCHY

Richard Blanke has noted that "many of the Reich's programs aided Germans all over Poland, whether or not they had ever been Reich citizens." German projects were conceived primarily as humanitarian aid for individual conationals who might leave Poland and not primarily as support for territorial revisionist goals.[114] Looking at subsidies for the German minority as a whole, however, reveals a focus on the territories within Germany's 1914 borders, for the main beneficiaries of Reich aid were those Germans in Western Poland, including Upper Silesia. In the 1926 loan program proposed by Krahmer-Möllenberg and supported by Stresemann, Ossa was to distribute RM 21.5 million to the Germans in Western Poland. Of this amount, RM 14 million in loans were to go to Poznania and Pomerelia, and relatively tiny Polish Upper Silesia was to receive RM 6.5 million. Central Poland, Galicia, and Volhynia, regions that contained roughly 40 percent of the estimated minority at the time, were allotted together only RM 1 million, or less than 5 percent of what was proposed for the formerly Prussian territories.[115] In comparison, North Schleswig, a territory ceded to Denmark, received RM 5 million. An Ossa report from June 28, 1927,

---

111 "Undatierte Aufzeichnung ohne Unterschrift," cited as Document K 197/K 038 646–48 in "Vortragender Legationsrat von Dirksen (z.Zt. in Genf) an Vortragenden Legationsrat Zechlin," September 20, 1927, in *ADAP*, ser. B, vol. 6, document no. 218, pp. 476–478, here 477.
112 Hauser, "Die deutsche Minderheit in den Wojewodschaften Posen und Pommerellen 1919–1939," 278.
113 Blanke, *Orphans of Versailles*.   114 Blanke, *Orphans of Versailles*, 161.
115 Krekeler, *Revisionsanspruch und geheime Ostpolitik*, 93.

Table 2.2. *Distribution of Ossa Funds to the German Minority in Poland by Region until 1927*

(a)	Poznania-Pomerelia	14,579,000
(b)	Upper Silesia	5,193,000
(c)	Congress Poland and Galicia	548,000
Total	RM	20,320,000[116]

summarizing the aid given to date is yet more revealing, for the discrepancy between regions was even greater (see Table 2.2).

In contrast to Upper Silesia and Poznania-Pomerelia, the formerly Russian and Austrian regions received only 2.7 percent of the total amount distributed by Ossa, even though a German estimate for Congress Poland and Galicia in 1921 had put the number of Germans there to be 365,000, or about 28 percent of the entire minority.[117] Moreover, the RM 548,000 given to Congress Poland and Galicia combined paled in comparison to the RM 7,194,000 that some 166,000 Germans in North Schleswig received at the same time.[118]

The selective and asymmetrical distribution of subsidies from the Reich strengthened these bonds of residual citizenship in Western Poland by increasing the German minority's dependency and contributing to a sense of regional groupness among its leaders. Although the actual sums may have been disappointing to minority leaders in Western Poland, they amounted to tens of millions of marks annually. Proportions mattered, and German activists elsewhere in Poland rarely saw a fraction of this money. Even more significant than the actual distribution of funds, however, was the *perception* that the Germans in Western Poland received lavish subsidies, which exacerbated the sense of haves and have-nots. Exclusion was a powerful force in fostering regional alignments, and the unfair distribution of Reich funds and the question of territorial revision complicated political cooperation with German organizations outside of Western Poland.

Scholars have emphasized how Polish-German antagonisms have structured German identity, especially in the way these reflected and formulated notions of German superiority over the Poles.[119] For Germans in Poland

---

116 "Ossa Vermittlungs- und Handelsgesellschaft mbH an das Auswärtige Amt," June 28, 1927, in *ADAP*, ser. B, vol. 5, document no. 263, pp. 614–616.

117 Dariusz Matelski, *Niemcy w Polsce w XX wieku* (Warsaw/Poznań: Wydawnictwo Naukowe PWN, 1999), 44.

118 "Ossa Vermittlungs- und Handelsgesellschaft mbH an das Auswärtige Amt," June 28, 1927, in *ADAP*, ser. B, vol. 5, document no. 263, pp. 614–616.

119 Peter Fischer, *Die deutsche Publizistik als Faktor der deutsch-polnischen Beziehungen 1919–1939* (Wiesbaden: Harrassowitz, 1991), 26; Thomas Serrier, "'Deutsche Kulturarbeit in der Ostmark.' Der

especially, ethnic entrepreneurs attempted to use potential and real conflict with the Polish state and society to mobilize the German minority and to create the sense of an embattled community. As a normative concept in ethnopolitical practice, for example, the term *Volksgruppe* served to reframe the Germans in Poland from a "category" into a "group."[120] Yet the focus on these ethnic dichotomies in identity formation also runs the danger of reifying the construct of "German" as well as "Polish." Especially the expectations (and disappointments) vis-à-vis a border change informed a particular Western Polish German groupness. Unhappy with their status as a "fallen people,"[121] Prussian Germans in Poland were especially adamant in their desire to return to the German Reich, be it through emigration or territorial revision.

THE QUESTION OF MINORITY IRREDENTISM

Contemporary observers, both German and Polish, often saw the German minority as a national irredenta. For example, the *Vossische Zeitung* in 1925 proclaimed that it was "undeniable" that elements of the borderland Germans in Poland were irredentist.[122] Indeed, many if not most German-speakers in Western Poland looked to the Reich to relieve them of their predicament. Yet were the political convictions of German activists in Western Poland driven by a general belief in bringing as many Germans as possible together in one state? Many harbored territorial-revisionist sympathies; but as discussed previously, this position should not be confused with irredentism, even if contemporaries themselves often used the terms interchangeably. Because their claims often sounded similar, German and Polish observers alike failed to see the difference between a restoration-revisionism inspired by territorial concerns and an irredentism driven by ethnic inclusiveness.

German activists in Western Poland were irredentist in the sense that they desired a political-geographical return to the homeland, that is, their region should be brought back under German rule. In general, however,

Mythos vom deutschen Vorrang und die Grenzproblematik in der Provinz Posen (1871–1914)," in *Die Nationalisierung von Grenzen. Zur Konstruktion nationaler Identität in sprachlich gemischten Grenzregionen*, ed. Michael G. Müller and Rolf Petri, 13–33 (Marburg: Verlag Herder-Institut, 2002), 24–28.

120 For a discussion of "category" versus "group," see Rogers Brubaker, "Ethnicity Without Groups," *Archives européennes de sociologie* 43, no. 2 (2002): 163–189, esp. 166–168; Rogers Brubaker, "Neither Individualism nor 'Groupism': A Reply to Craig Calhoun," *Ethnicities* 3(2003): 553–557, here 554.

121 Blanke, *Orphans of Versailles*, 4–5,

122 "Notwendige Klärung. Auslandsdeutsche und Grenzdeutsche," *Vossische Zeitung*, September 5, 1925, in GStA, I HA, Rep. 77, Tit. 4032, folder 15, 15.

the limits of this German irredentism ran along the 1914 borders. Like their official caretakers in the Reich described in the previous chapter, Western Polish Germans were not irredentists in principle. A principled irredentist stance would have encompassed a large number of Germans beyond the 1914 borders. Short of going to war, however, such a solution would have jeopardized the revisionist project altogether. Moreover, Western Polish German irredentist claims were based not just on some understanding of a shared ethnicity but also on historical argument and the notion of cultural superiority toward the Poles. The events of the early 1920s, when Poland faced great economic and political instability, contributed to the hope that these Germans could soon return to the Reich. The initially high expectations, however, led to deep disappointment as German leaders in Western Poland recognized that a border revision would not happen in the near future. The disenchantment with the efforts of the Reich to bring the Germans home was all the more real for those who had been imbued with the rhetoric of nationality struggle and the importance of the Germans to hold out in Poland for a future revision. There was a growing feeling of despair among the Germans in Poland, many of whom felt abandoned not by the Versailles settlement but by Germany.

By the mid-1920s, German leaders in Western Poland were forced to recognize that they would be in Poland for the long run, and they would have to find some sort of accommodation with the Polish state and society. The stabilization of Poland's precarious domestic situation hastened this process. In May 1926, Marshal Józef Piłsudski, who had done much to carve modern Poland's border on the battlefield, overthrew Poland's shaky democratic government in a coup d'etat and set up his own authoritarian regime.[123] Poland's political situation stabilized, and the Polish economy also began to recover. The Piłsudski coup in fact diminished the influence of the virulently anti-German National Democrats and gave German leaders new hope for better treatment by Polish authorities.[124] Even hardened national activists and the most embittered opponents of Poland started to take a more moderate line, at least in word if not deed. In Toruń in 1925, a group of German leaders submitted a lengthy report called "The Political Task of the German Minority in Poland" to the German consul. The memo stated that the Germans in Pomerelia were ready to move beyond revanchism and renounced the goal of a political reunification with Germany. According to the authors, the Pomerelian Germans were now to work with the other Germans in Poland for cultural autonomy within the Polish state.[125]

The denunciation of irredentism and revisionism by many German minority leaders in their speeches and correspondence should not be seen as a final position growing out of conviction. As countless documents attest, revisionist hopes within the Reich and among many Germans in Poland were never given up entirely. German minority activists believed that their situation would only be temporary. Calls for greater cooperation were rarely due to any newly discovered love for Poland. Rather, they represented a tactical retreat in light of the facts on the ground. Openly disloyal statements and acts, after all, would make a revision more difficult. Carl Meissner, a functionary in the Deutscher Kulturausschuss in Polen, called for a conciliatory approach because Germans in the old Eastern Marches lacked the necessary "civil courage" and were not fit for the "inner battle." Only by giving up an openly revisionist stance would it be possible to maintain the cultural work that would conserve and build up the "national strength" needed for a future border revision.[126] Minority leaders in Western Poland put revisionist demands on the back burner, but these claims could become salient again if tensions ran high and/or if a border change somehow appeared more likely.

This stance was not collaboration or even attentism, but a kind of "tethered revisionism."[127] German minority leaders may have continued to hope for a border revision, but they did not necessarily act in a subversive manner. In the meantime, German activists traded demands for "exit" in exchange for "voice" in the political system.[128] German parties in the Sejm did take an active position on minority issues, and they introduced 245 interpellations between 1922 and 1928.[129] As the historian Paweł Korzec has argued,

---

125 Consulate General in Poznań (Mackeben) to Hahn, April 17, 1925, with attachment "Die politische Aufgabe der deutschen Minderheit in Polen 11.IV.1925," in PAAA, Pol IV, Politik 25 Polen, vol. 19, R.82199, 158–180. Also cited in Blanke, *Orphans of Versailles*, 87n77.

126 Carl Meissner, Geschäftsführer des Deutschen Kultur-Ausschusses in Polen, undated letter sent as attachment by Krahmer Möllenberg to Ministerialdirektor Dr. Lohrs, Prussian Interior Ministry, "Arbeitsvermächtnis des Kulturausschusses in Polen," January 18, 1921, in GStA, I HA, Rep. 77, Tit. 856, folder 31, 459, 460–464. Meissner, a poet, would head the cultural affairs section of the Deutschtumsbund and later served in the Deutsche Vereinigung in Sejm and Senat and in the Deutsche Vereinigung in Westpolen (Matelski, *Mniejszość niemiecka w Wielkopolsce*, 277–279).

127 I am adapting Charles Maier's term "tethered consciousness," which he used to describe how many East Germans found accommodation with the German Democratic Republic. See Charles Maier, *Dissolution: The Crisis of Communism and the End of East Germany* (Princeton: Princeton University Press, 1997).

128 See Albert O. Hirschman, *Exit, Voice, and Loyalty: Responses to Decline in Firms, Organizations, and States* (Cambridge: Harvard University Press, 1970).

129 Breyer, *Das Deutsche Reich und Polen*, 45.

however, minority participation in the political system was not an attempt to undermine the state but actually had a stabilizing effect.[130] By integrating themselves into Polish politics and society, German leaders invariably became involved in promoting Poland's well-being.[131]

IRREDENTISM AND MINORITY COHESION

Faced with new political realities, German leaders in Western Poland were encouraged to redefine their role in other ways as well. Whereas the ultimate goal for many German leaders in the immediate borderlands remained the return to the Reich, many also saw that cooperating with the Germans from the other Polish areas could only strengthen their political clout. These two modes of thinking, however, were ultimately not compatible. The sociologist and nationalism scholar Michael Hechter has suggested two ideal types of nationalist movements: "irredenta nationalism" and "unification nationalism." Irredentist nationalism demands an exit from the state, whereas unification nationalism seeks to unify different territories.[132] With some modification, Hechter's model could be applied to the Germans in Poland, where differing interpretations of unification also ran along regional alignments. Western Polish German revisionism fed off the belief that an eventual border change was not just desired but also likely. Many non-Prussian Germans may have wanted out of the Polish state as well, but the foreign political context meant that a territorial revisionism that would include them appeared remote. One German newspaper from formerly Austrian Galicia made clear that "we in Galicia [Kleinpolen] are not an irredenta and have virtually no hope to change our political situation."[133] The underlying assumption in such statements, however, was that Germans elsewhere – that is, Western Poland – did indeed behave as an irredenta and could reasonably hope that the political situation would change in their favor. Indeed, the attempts by German activists in Western Poland at unification only exacerbated tensions. As the disappointment with the Hauptvorstand der Deutschtumsbünde showed, the Western Polish German version of unification

---

130 Paweł Korzec, "Der Zweite Block der Nationalen Minderheiten im Parlamentarismus Polens 1927–1928," *Zeitschrift für Ostforschung* 26, no. 1 (1977): 76–116, here 113; see also Paweł Korzec, "Der Block der Nationalen Minderheiten im Parlamentarismus Polens des Jahres 1922," *Zeitschrift für Ostforschung* 24, no. 2 (1975): 193–220.

131 Janusz Fałowski, *Parlamentarzyści mniejszości niemieckiej w Drugiej Rzeczypospolitej* (Częstochowa: Wydawnictwo Wyższej Szkoły Pedagogicznej w Częstochowie, 2000), 402.

132 Michael Hechter, *Containing Nationalism* (Oxford: Oxford University Press, 2000), 15–17. For a discussion of both types of nationalism in nineteenth-century Europe, see John Breuilly, *Nationalism and the State* (Manchester: Manchester University Press, 1993), 96–148.

133 "Advent. Deutsches Volk in Zerstreuung," *Ostdeutsches Volksblatt*, November 27, 1927.

nationalism meant the subordination of the Germans in Central and Eastern Poland, and in turn this domineering attitude undermined the dignity and cooperation of those Germans in Central and Eastern Poland who may have desired closer unification. In other words, irredenta-nationalist tendencies specific to Western Poland weakened the unification-nationalist commitment to build a single party for the entire minority.

Donald L. Horowitz has outlined the intra-minority conflict that irredentism can cause between potential "rump" and "secessionist" regions.[134] Any secessionist solution short of the elimination of Poland altogether (as happened in 1939) would have left a substantial number of German-speakers – perhaps even the majority – in a rump Poland. Yet German nationalists in Western Poland who favored a secession must have realized that their chances for being reannexed were conversely related to the size of Germany's demand on Polish territory. As former Reich citizens settled compactly along the border, they believed they had the best and strongest claim, and in order to increase their own chances they were more than willing to limit revisionist claims to themselves only. Asking for more, after all, might have ruined the chances for any revision whatsoever. There were still about a half-million people who could be claimed as ethnic Germans in the Polish territories further east, but they constituted too small a share of the overall population for using the principle of national self-determination. As long as the Germans in Western Poland had one foot out the door, their interest in an equal cooperation with the Germans elsewhere with little revisionist hopes could only be limited.

Because it would have involved new exclusions, a border revision risked creating new losers. The non-Prussian German activists may have been less interested in territorial revisionism, but they did not necessarily feel themselves to be any less German. They were just as adamant about protecting their own German interests, which the secessionist agenda of the Western Polish German leadership appeared to endanger. For the Germans in the potential rump territories, then, the scenario of being part of an even smaller minority exposed to the wrath of a vengeful Polish populace must have been frightening indeed. They would have encountered further political disadvantages as a smaller minority, both in absolute and in proportional terms. Moreover, those remaining in Poland could have well expected even less attention from Germany once it had regained its coveted lost territories. Hence, it was hardly in the interest of the Germans in Central and Eastern

---

134 Donald L. Horowitz, *Ethnic Groups in Conflict* (Berkeley: University of California Press, 1985), 266–267.

Poland to support the revisionist tendencies of the secessionist Germans in Western Poland.

Contemporary nationality scholars also saw how differential possibilities for a border revision had the potential to divide minorities. In his *Europa Irredenta*, Max Hildebert Boehm argued that East Central Europe's postwar borders had caused an unhealthy environment for international politics through the creation of irredentist movements.[135] Boehm believed, for example, that the unjust fate of the Austrian Germans had been instrumental in driving irredentist ideas in Germany.[136] In order to correct this situation, Boehm believed that minorities abroad had an important role to play. For example, he stated that German minorities should segregate themselves into irredenta pockets that would eventually destabilize their host states and allow Germany to claim them.[137] At the same time, Boehm recognized that such scenarios were not possible everywhere in Europe or even in one country. Indeed, his völkisch activist principles of strengthening German culture abroad could clash with irredentist goals in the new East Central European political landscape:

The großdeutsche mission in the East should be seen as the following: Germandom abroad, which is becoming increasingly united spiritually, must go beyond its own role and become closely connected with the whole of Germandom. In this process we must be conscious of the fact that the long-term interests of the Germans in East Central Europe are not in agreement in themselves. If we do not want to rehash the sources of inner German alienation after 1866, then we must soberly recall the inner split in this Eastern Germandom. As part of a future Reich, the irredenta regions have different long-term interests than the permanent settlements abroad. And the border between the two groups often goes right through the middle of the German nationalities in the new, artificial states. When Hungarian Germans who had succumbed to the idea of the Hungarian state worked against ceding the Burgenland to Austria, they were nationally right in a certain way with their claim that the entirety of Hungarian Germandom would be weakened by the loss of Western Hungary. The irredenta's loss is thus in many cases an advantage for the permanent settlements abroad.[138]

Boehm's line of reasoning followed Horowitz's framework of rump and secession regions: a border change would likely leave some Germans in what was left of the host state, creating new losers who, as part of an even smaller

---

135 Max Hildebert Boehm, *Europa Irredenta. Eine Einführung in das Nationalitätenproblem der Gegenwart* (Berlin: Reimar Hobbing, 1923), 312.
136 Boehm, *Grenzdeutsch–Großdeutsch*, 2.
137 Ingo Haar, "German Ostforschung and Anti-Semitism," in *German Scholars and Ethnic Cleansing, 1919–1945*, ed. Ingo Haar and Michael Fahlbusch, 1–27 (New York: Berghahn Books, 2005), here 3.
138 Boehm, *Grenzdeutsch–Großdeutsch*, 8–9.

minority, would be more vulnerable than before. Hence, an irredentist-inspired annexation to "redeem" Germans in a foreign country would actually endanger Germany's völkisch connection with those Germans who remained there. Given this possibility, Boehm acknowledged that Germany might need to refrain from well-founded ethnic claims in some cases, at least in the short term. Likewise, Germans in certain so-called irredenta regions would have to come to terms with their situation for the time being, and even assume a role as mentors for German diaspora settlements further east.[139] Although Boehm does not suggest it here, it seems that only a more radically expansionist policy of expulsions and Germanization could resolve this apparently irreconcilable conflict of interests within minority groups.

The potential of a border revision hence complicated long-term political cooperation between German nationalists in interwar Poland because the structural problems in the relationship between potential rump and secession regions among German organizations in interwar Poland were never solved. Regardless of whether they were from the borderlands or from deep within Poland, however, the minority leaders needed each other during election periods to increase the German vote. They largely promoted a "unification nationalist" position in public, with loud pronouncements of closer cooperation. Because of the differences in their long-term interests, however, there was a tendency to stick to loose coalitions of regional organizations that reflected a geographical hierarchy of Germanness in Poland.

REINVENTING REICHNESS AND WESTERN POLISH GERMAN DOMINANCE

As Dieter Gosewinkel points out, citizenship is not just a legal definition but can also convey great symbolic value for its holder. Conversely, the loss of citizenship also has tremendous social and psychological implications, as the Nazi attempt to stigmatize German Jews through denaturalization shows.[140] The traumatic loss of their titular nation status likewise destabilized the self-perception of the Western Polish Germans, who continued to feel neither at home nor abroad. Their most tangible anchor in Germanness, their experience in the Reich, was rapidly fading. Increasingly, German leaders certainly saw the need to come to terms with being Auslandsdeutsche (Germans living outside of Germany) in general and being Germans in

---

139 Boehm, *Die deutschen Grenzlande*, 273.
140 Dieter Gosewinkel, *Einbürgern und Ausschließen. Die Nationalisierung der Staatsangehörigkeit vom Deutschen Bund bis zur Bundesrepublik Deutschland* (Göttingen: Vandenhoeck & Ruprecht, 1991), 373, 379.

Poland in particular. The humiliation that accompanied their perception of being second-rate Germans could be compensated with the new goal of raising and cultivating the ethnic cohorts in the East. Boehm, for example, suggested that the mission of the "ceded German borderlands" was to act as a magnet for the scattered German settlements throughout Central Europe. The Germans in Western Poland could play an important role as middleman, mentor, and role model for other German minorities.[141]

German leaders in Western Poland were thinking along the same lines. In the already mentioned 1925 memo "The Political Task of the German Minority in Poland," they attempted to form a political program for the German minority. Despite the title, it dealt essentially with the role of the Germans in Western Poland. From this perspective, the memo also followed established views in presenting the essential problems facing the minority. It noted that the Germans in Congress Poland, Galicia, and Volhynia were numerically much greater, but clearly far behind in their Volk conscious-ness, than their German counterparts in Western Poland. The memo then posed the following question, which reflected the tensions of unification nationalism and irredentism nationalism: Should the Germans in Western Poland suppress their Prussianness and try to win the other Germans to a border German (grenzdeutsch) position; or should the Germans in Western Poland be less border German and hence more auslandsdeutsch in order to lend their cultural energy to the nationally weaker Germans in the East? The authors stated that the first path would permanently drive away the "Congress Polish" Germans, who already had a "weakened German con-sciousness" and who already were living in self-exclusion, allegedly because they had little affinity for the "unconscious border German" thinking of the Germans in Western Poland. Although the decision would be very difficult, the only choice for creating the largest possible conglomeration of Germans in Poland was for all German activists to commit to the aus-landsdeutsch direction. In the opinion of the authors, this path should be followed even if not all the Germans in Western Poland could be won over, for it was the only way that the minority would stay German in the long run. Although the Germans in Western Poland would then recenter their cultural world in the East and not in Germany, ties with the Reich would not be cut completely; its culture would continue to sustain the minority as "milk from mother to child." Such a change was necessary, too, because the authors noted that the border German position had a tendency to run

---

141 Boehm, *Die deutschen Grenzlande*, 273.

into "political irredentism," which the Polish state would not permit.[142] While the proposal seems to signal a shift in minority politics, this call actually reveals the deepening divides within the minority and how difficult the cutting of ties with the Reich would be for the Germans in Western Poland. It is significant that the authors of the program also assumed the natural superiority and continuing leadership of the Western Polish Germans. These would simply have to reinvent their Reich legacy with the new tools at their disposal. Rather than taking völkisch-sounding statements about a growing unity of Germans in Poland at face value, it is necessary to see how regional minority leaders used the rhetoric of the common good to gain more funds and influence for particular ends.

In December 1926, minority leaders wrote up another memo called "The Preservation of Germandom in Poznania and Pomerelia." As the title of the thirty-four-page memo suggests, it was mainly concerned with the current situation and the future of the 360,000 Germans in Western Poland, but it also emphasized that the fate of the Germans there was tied to their mission to raise the national consciousness of Germans elsewhere in Poland. Already on the first page, the report stressed that the Germans in Poznania and Pomerelia had a "very special meaning" for the Germandom in Poland due to their greater national resolve and their ability to moderate party political and confessional conflict. Indeed, the authors highlighted the importance of the Germans in Western Poland for the Reich and criticized the generous compensation for Germans who left Western Poland, stating that the resulting drain on Reich finances would ultimately weaken those Germans who remained in Poland. The authors stated that the Germans in Western Poland would not be able to hold out on their own – the need for more money was apparent. Most cynically, however, the leaders said that they were not interested in just maintaining the Germans in Poznania and Pomerelia, that is, thinking of themselves, but that they were acting "in the interest of the Germans in Poland and ultimately all of Germandom." They assumed the task of culturally and economically awakening the Germans in Volhynia and Central Poland, a task they could accomplish if only the "Poznanian-Pomerelian German population had more means at its disposal." Thus, the Germans in Western Poland emphasized their own hardship but also their selflessness in accepting the burden of enlightening their purportedly needy compatriots in the East. At the same time, this

---

142 Consulate General in Poznań (Mackeben) to German Foreign Ministry (Hahn), April 17, 1925, with attachment "Die Politische Aufgabe der Deutschen Minderheit in Polen 11.IV.1925," in PAAA, Pol IV, Politik 25 Polen, vol. 19, R82199, 158–180.

mission justified additional funds. That relatively little money would actually go to the Germans in the eastern regions was clear. The authors stated
that there were some 440,000 counted Germans in Central Poland and
Volhynia, but the total could be as high as 750,000 (probably increased gen-
erously to inflate their need). Still, they proposed that the money for books
and libraries in the eastern areas would require only about RM 30,000
annually, which was about half the amount received by the potentially far
fewer Germans in Poznania and Pomerelia.[143]

The claim to build a German national community in Poland was not
just an important financial resource but also a significant identity resource
for the German leaders in Western Poland. The continued maintenance
of the Germans in Poznania and Pomerelia, after all, required them to
change their image as victims of Polish repression and as dependents living
on handouts from the Reich. Instead, German activists in Western Poland
now had the opportunity to take up a more positive, active role based on
their residual citizenship. This reconfigured and compensatory Reichness
allowed the Western Polish Germans to enjoy a relative improvement in
their status from the prewar period. From a backwater periphery of the
German Reich, Poznania-Pomerelia had become the political, cultural,
and communications center for German national activists in Poland.

Indeed, the prewar mission to Germanize the eastern territories of the
Reich was now directed within the minority and could be seen as inner
colonization, or even internal orientalism.[144] By reclaiming their Reichness,
the German nationalists in the prewar Eastern Marches could resume their
role as bearers of civilization, but not so much to civilize the Slavs as to
civilize the other Germans in Poland. With the special burden of being the
most perfect of the Germans in Poland, however, Western Polish German
leaders invented the Germans in the other regions as a negative other that
needed help. The East remained a terra incognita that could be won. In
her analysis of English travel literature about the Balkans, Maria Todorova
notes, "Obviously, geographical discovery was going hand in hand with
a simultaneous invention of the region and the two processes are, in fact,

---

143 Graf Podewils (Abteilung VI) to Hahn (Abteilung IV), memorandum date stamped December
   30, 1926, in PAAA, Pol IV-Geheimakten, Politik 25 Polen, vol. 2, R30861. The folder contains
   various copies of the report "Die Erhaltung des Deutschtums in Posen und Pommerellen"; see also
   Krekeler, *Revisionsanspruch und geheime Ostpolitik*, 106–109.
144 Tara Zahra examines the postcolonial aspects of the Nazi mission to civilize Sudeten Germans
   who had been purportedly damaged while living under Czech oslovakian rule: *Kidnapped Souls:
   National Indifference and the Battle for Children in the Bohemian Lands, 1900–1948* (Ithaca: Cornell
   University Press, 2008), 177–182.

inseparable."[145] Similarly, the Western Polish Germans could claim their right to lead the Germans elsewhere in Poland.

THE VOLHYNIAN GERMANS AND INTERNAL COLONIALISM

One of the best documented examples of this inner colonization of the German minority was the Volhynia Expedition in 1926. In August of that year, twelve men from the Reich, Western Poland, and Teschen Silesia traveled to Eastern Poland to study the German settlements there. Financed by various agencies in Germany, the voyage of discovery was the first publicized encounter of the minority with its eastern margins. There was a separate trip made by Kurt Lück from Poznań in October of that year, in effect making him the thirteenth man of the expedition. The results from both trips were published that same year in a special issue of the minority journal *Deutsche Blätter in Polen*.

The ostensible purpose of the expedition was to find out more about German settlements. Instead, as historian Michael Burleigh has pointed out, it served mainly to reinforce the young adventurers' notions of German superiority vis-à-vis the Poles. According to Burleigh, these Germans saw themselves as "bearers of civilization" who sought any evidence of ethnic consciousness.[146] Shortly before the trip, Walter Kuhn (later professor in Breslau) published an article in *Deutsche Blätter in Polen* on the objectives of "eastern German Heimat research." Kuhn noted that the purpose was "to transform the instinctive feeling of superiority and pride toward the surrounding peoples that characterises the colonists into a true national consciousness that is not based solely upon feelings, but also upon the knowledge of the strength and beauty of the German Volkstum. That is the fundamental task of national education in the eastern lands."[147] Similarly, Wolfgang Kessler reaffirms that the expedition's discovery of the Volhynian Germans was crucial to the nationalizing project of building a Volksgruppe in Poland.[148] Previous examinations of the 1926 expedition have

145 Maria Todorova, "The Balkans: From Discovery to Invention," *Slavic Review* 53, no. 2 (1994): 453–482, here 461.

146 Burleigh, *Germany Turns Eastwards*, 107.

147 Translated quotation from Burleigh, *Germany Turns Eastwards*, 107, his translation. Burleigh quotes Hans Freiherr von Rosen, *Wolhynienfahrt 1926* (Siegen: Selbstverlag der J.G. Herder-Bibliothek Siegerland e.V., 1982), 43. Rosen in turn cites Walter Kuhn, "Wege und Ziele ostlanddeutscher Heimatforschung," *Deutsche Blätter in Polen* 3, no. 7 (1926): 368–380, here 379.

148 Wolfgang Kessler, "Die Deutschen im polnischen Westwolhynien (1921–1939/40) in der historischen Forschung," *Nordost-Archiv* 9, no. 2 (2000): 449–457, here 451.

thus emphasized how German nationalists used the Volhynian Germans to construct a "master race" ideology.[149]

A close reading, however, reveals how the Western Polish Germans betrayed a domineering, even colonial, attitude toward their eastern co-brethren. It also shows tensions between the actors. Of the twelve members in the main group, about half were from the Reich, and half were members of the minority in Poland. Two of the Polish German participants were from Poznań: Hans Freiherr von Rosen and Erich Jaensch. Walter Kuhn, Alfred Karasek, and Walter Lanz were from Bielsko (Bielitz), a German-speaking "language island" in Teschen Silesia. There was one Upper Silesian, Otto Breuler, but it remains unclear whether he came from the Polish or German zone. Heinz Heckel was an Austrian German from the Bukovina who had moved to Lwów (Lemberg) before the First World War. Although Rosen calls him the "spiritus rector" of the expedition, the accounts barely mention him, and he himself remains largely silent in the ensuing publications.[150] Although this expedition appeared to encompass Germans from throughout Poland, including those from Prussian and non-Prussian areas, it is notable that no representatives from Volhynia or elsewhere in formerly Russian Poland were themselves part of the expedition.

The main expedition in August 1926 split into subgroups once they arrived in Volhynia. The amateurism of the travelers and ideological preju-dices came across in several episodes. In one incident, Erich Jaensch from Poznań came upon two children, whom he considered too good-looking to be anything but members of the local German minority. Indeed, he was so sure that they were German that he swore to eat his socks if they were not, and he was of course astounded when they proclaimed – in German – that they were Jewish. Fortunately for Jaensch, his companions did not hold him to his promise. In his postwar recollections, Rosen pondered the background of these Jewish children and the reasons for this apparent ethnic anomaly – notably, Rosen did not waste a single word about their possible fate during the war.[151]

The expedition was also supposed to gather statistics, and questionnaires were created for this purpose. Yet the Germans gave up any pretense of working methodologically and largely ignored the surveys.[152] Rosen notes

149 For an example of this argument, see Wilhelm Fielitz, *Das Stereotyp des wolhyniendeutschen Umsiedlers. Popularisierungen zwischen Sprachinselforschung und nationalsozialistischer Propaganda* (Marburg: N.G. Elwert, 2000), 280.
150 Heinz Heckel did have at least one publication: "Die Deutschen in Wolhynien," *Der Auslanddeutsche* (undated clipping) in PAAA, Pol IV, Politik 25 Polen, vol. 22, R82202, 66–67.
151 Rosen, *Wolhynienfahrt 1926*, 41.
152 Fielitz, *Das Stereotyp des wolhyniendeutschen Umsiedlers*, 53.

their lax attitude toward the survey, but he tries to downplay the significance of the resulting discrepancies.[153] Rather, the participants of the Volhynia expedition were more interested in listening to the stories and sorrows of the Volhynian Germans. They were, of course, selective in what they thought important. The German researchers assiduously recorded the complaints of Volhynian Germans regarding their treatment as "Russians" by Reich authorities during the First World War. The denigration of those Volhynian Germans brought to the Reich as manual laborers included their being placed under Polish supervision.[154] In the conclusion to the special issue of *Deutsche Blätter in Polen*, Kuhn quoted the following from an unnamed woman about her wartime experience in Germany: "The Russians did not treat us so shabbily like the Germans in this time, we left Germany again with a thousand cheers. And we were despised everywhere as Russians. The people behaved as if we were not German. Of course we were just as good Germans as they were, and we also have the German confession. Only because we were Russian citizens, but how was that our fault?"[155] The anonymity of the person telling the story is revealing. The Western Polish and Bielsko Germans literally spoke for the Volhynian Germans, and it is more than likely that they were putting words in their mouths. The Volhynian Germans were, after all, the objects of the study, and as such they had no voice.

German scholarship's belated discovery of the Germans in the East encouraged the perception that these poorer brethren needed help.[156] The expedition's overall impression was that the Volhynian Germandom comprised a rural underclass with a low cultural level.[157] For them, the fact that many of the Volhynians lived in earthen huts was a tangible expression of their backward condition. The expedition members attributed this hardship to the dislocation, damage, and poor economic situation caused by the world war.[158] Yet this sympathy was often mixed with a certain contempt for their backwardness. This disparaging attitude was often reformulated and expressed in terms of the Volhynian Germans being in national danger, for poverty and ethnic mish-mash appeared to go hand in hand. The consensus

---

153 Rosen, *Wolhynienfahrt 1926*, 42.   154 Rosen, *Wolhynienfahrt 1926*, 57–58.

155 Walter Kuhn, "Schlusswort," *Deutsche Blätter in Polen* 3, nos. 11–12 (1926): 629–634, 632.

156 Wolfgang Kessler, "Volksgeschichte oder Regionalgeschichte? Grundlinien der deutschen historischen und heimatkundlichen Forschung über Zentralpolen," in *Polska Środkowa w niemieckich badaniach wschodnich. Historia i współczesność*, ed. Lucjan Meissner, 7–20 (Łódź: Ibidem, 1999), here 8.

157 Fielitz, *Das Stereotyp des wolhyniendeutschen Umsiedlers*, 57, 59.

158 Fielitz, *Das Stereotyp des wolhyniendeutschen Umsiedlers*, 58.

of the generally low cultural and intellectual development of the Volhy-nian Germans was reinforced by various anecdotes. Rosen recalled that the group's Wandervogel-style outfits led one Volhynian German woman to mistake the visitors for envoys from the League of Nations. As Michael Burleigh notes, these expedition members might have well been from the moon.[159] Rosen also states that the Volhynian Germans lived in a world where nationality was still confused with confession: "The average colonist could not imagine at all that a German could be Catholic. Kuhn was once told, 'A lot of Poles live in Austria, but they all speak German, they don't understand Polish at all.'"[160]

Such portrayals did not just infantilize the Germans in Volhynia but also set them up as unspoiled "noble savages." As such, the Volhynian Germans served as a mirror to reveal problems in the observer's society. It was often claimed, for example, that the more developed Germans in the western regions could learn from these more easterly Polish Germans. Still, these assertions often came across as empty formulations, and more concrete were the claims of the Western Polish Germans to raise the other Germans in Poland so they could fulfill their mission in the East better. The irony of this project was that German activists had failed miserably in the so-called nationality struggle in both the prewar Eastern Marches and in postwar Western Poland, whereas the Polish Germans further east had long enjoyed a reputation as successful colonizers among the local Poles.[161]

Especially the complaints of the Volhynian Germans that Reich Germans associated Germanness with state borders seemed to have touched a raw nerve among the Polish German researchers. Unaware of the patronizing undertones in their own portrayal of the Volhynian Germans, the various authors of the expedition sought to defend the honor of their eastern brethren. Kuhn, the German from formerly Austrian Bielsko, wrote:

The unholy Reich German superstitiousness has led to a terrible sin here in the belief that only someone within the Reich German borders can be a real and full-fledged German. A great and strong German tribe can only look back at its sojourn in the "mother country" with great bitterness because the Germans at home do not want to and cannot comprehend that there are still Germans beyond the border posts. . . . This sentimental and mushy way of regarding issues concerning Germans abroad stems from the outrageous overestimation of the meaning of the

159 Burleigh, *Germany Turns Eastwards*, 108.
160 Rosen, *Wolhynienfahrt 1926*, 55.
161 Przemysław Hauser, "Kolonista niemiecki na ziemiach polskich w okresie rozbiorów (Uwagi i refleksje na temat funkcjonowania mitu oraz rzeczywistości)," in *Niemieccy osadnicy w Królestwie Polskim 1815–1915*, ed. Wiesław Caban, 225–242 (Kielce: Wyższa Szkoła Pedagogiczna, 1999).

state, which leads to the opinion that ethnic comrades living outside of the state's borders are only half Germans.[162]

According to several accounts, including another article by Kuhn, this etatist thinking continued in the interwar period.[163] Rosen, a Posener and former Reich citizen, espoused a similar view in his postwar account of the expedition: "It is unfortunately a widespread disposition of the domestic Germans [*Binnendeutsche*] to look down arrogantly upon the Germans abroad and to see them as 'not really German anymore,' merely because they live among other peoples and know how to get along there. In reality the Germans abroad were often the much better Germans!"[164] The lamenting over this injustice was surely influenced by the fact that these authors were Polish citizens and had themselves probably encountered discrimination in the Reich as "not really German anymore." For example, there were repeated complaints that Germans from Poland were disadvantaged when it came to things such as university placement in Germany.[165] Germans from Poland who traveled in the Reich often had to pay a foreigner tax at hotels, museums, castles, and theaters.[166] Yet such complaints reveal that these Germans felt that they had a right to be treated as if they were still living in Germany. Thus, the German expedition members echoed the idea that Germanness should be decoupled from formal citizenship. In effect, the German scholars from Bielsko and Poznań agitated less for the recognition of the Volhynian Germans and more for reasserting their own self-worth.

Although the post-trip reports made much of the brotherhood of all Germans and denounced state-oriented thinking, statements on the völkisch equality of all Germans did not necessarily show a growing unification of the Germans in Poland. Their egalitarian proclamations did not preclude the expedition members from harboring their own condescending prejudices. As former Reich Germans, the Germans in Western Poland were prone to treat the eastern cousins poorly. In one memoir by Herbert

162 Kuhn, "Schlusswort," 633.
163 Walter Kuhn, "Versuch einer Naturgeschichte der deutschen Sprachinsel," *Deutsche Blätter in Polen* 3, no. 2 (February 1926): 65–140, here 139.
164 Rosen, *Wolhynienfahrt 1926*, 58. This passage by Rosen is also cited in Burleigh, *Germany Turns Eastwards*, 108.
165 Carl Georg Bruns to Prussian Interior Ministry, March 3, 1932, in GStA, I HA, Rep. 77, Tit. 856, folder 32, 209.
166 Reich Interior Minister to German Foreign Ministry, "Pflege enger Beziehungen der Grenz- und Auslandsdeutschen zum Mutterlande," copy sent by Reich Interior Ministry (Oeser) to all Land governments, Prussian Interior Ministry, Bavarian Foreign Ministry, January 18, 1923, in PAAA, Pol IV, Politik 25 Polen, vol. 13, R82193, 23–24; German Foreign Ministry to German embassy in Warsaw, consulates in Poznań, Danzig, Memel, Katowice, Toruń, Cracow, January 31, 1923, in ibid., 25; Prussian Interior Ministry (Loehrs) to German Foreign Ministry, April 11, 1923, in PAAA, Pol IV, Politik 25 Polen, vol. 14, R82194, 35–38.

Henke, a Volhynian German, the author recalled how as a child he had attended a German school in Poznań. The German classmates called him "Russian" (*russki*) or the "Russian" (*Russe*). Perhaps eager not to emphasize the differences, however, Henke notes that after the initial confrontation, he was accepted by the others as a real German.[167] Yet the construction of the Volhynian Germans as a praised but backward subgroup played an important role in identity politics and resource mobilization within the minority. Although the expedition members generally believed themselves to be culturally more developed than the Volhynian Germans, they drew very different conclusions from the latter's backwardness, thereby revealing the regional tensions within the German minority in Poland.

The intra-German debate over the qualities of the Volhynian Germans was intricately related to Volkstumskampf, or nationality struggle, and the role of the German state. Both Poseners and Bielitzers in the expedition denounced the persistence of thinking in terms of state borders, but they had different motivations. The Western Polish Germans, having been once part of the Reich, desired being treated equally with current Reich Germans. To them, it was an unfair accident that they had been stranded outside the Reich. Although they claimed to have become introspective and questioned the role of borders and nationality, it seems that they never seriously doubted their own essential Reichness nor the role of the nation-state. Indeed, their attempts to be considered equal to Reich Germans or to return to the Reich only underlined the dominance of etatist ideas in their definition of Germanness. This internalized distinction accounts for the repeated complaints that the Germans in Western Poland had never learned to become Auslandsdeutsche.

As former Reich Germans, the Poseners took a pessimistic view of the Volhynian Germans that revealed their inability to think beyond etatist lines. The historian Wilhelm Fielitz notes that Kurt Lück had a view markedly different from the Bielitzers.[168] Although Kurt Lück did not travel with the main group, he was the only Posener to contribute to the special issue on the Volhynian Germans in *Deutsche Blätter in Poland*, which was published only a few months after the excursion. According to Fielitz, Lück's report was "crass, agitative, and pessimistic." Lück's concern with Germandom was determined by a national-political standpoint in which ethnic markers such as language were important.[169] Based on these assumptions, Lück drew the

---

167 Herbert Henke, "Heimat in Topcza – Familienschicksal und Lebenslauf," in *Heimat Wolhynien*, vol. 2, ed. Alfred Cammann (Marburg/Lahn: N.G. Elwert, 1988), 65–102.
168 Fielitz, *Das Stereotyp des wolhyniendeutschen Umsiedlers*, 63–67.
169 Fielitz, *Das Stereotyp des wolhyniendeutschen Umsiedlers*, 55, 63.

conclusion that the Volhynian Germans were in desperate need: "This must be said with all severity: Germandom is not up to the competitive struggle that is beginning and will lose more and more ground unless it takes up a self-conscious stand against these dangers and is supported vigorously in this by the other German regions in Poland."[170] Notably, Lück mentions three times in his introduction that the Germans in the "other Polish territories" were obliged to help the Volhynian Germans. It is likely that he expected that this help would come almost entirely, if not exclusively, from the formerly Prussian territories and perhaps formerly Austrian Bielsko.

Western Polish German leaders, of course, could then parlay this call for help into new positions and influence. Kurt Lück himself had the opportunity to practice what he preached. In 1926 he settled in the Volhynian town of Łuck, where he started Kredit Lutzk, a branch of the Genossenschaftsbank in Poznań.[171] He ended up staying in Volhynia for several years. This involvement was hardly altruistic, for it provided not just employment for him but also placed relatively large sums of money at his disposal. This position provided considerable influence not just over many Volhynian Germans but also among other German leaders in Poland. As a relatively younger German (he was born in 1890) and not a member of the landowning class, there were few other alternatives for him besides creating a position for himself. His ethnic entrepreneurial career in poor rural Volhynia resembled that of a carpetbagger. Yet such hardship posts in the East gave ample opportunity for a younger generation of aspiring minority leaders to prove their credentials in Volkstum matters. He eventually became not just the minority's expert on the Volhynian Germans but also their mouthpiece.

OUTSIDERS AS INSIDERS

The Bielitzers in the expedition were markedly more optimistic than their Western Polish colleagues about the prospects of making Volhynian Germans into full-fledged members of the Volksgemeinschaft. Having experienced Volkstumskampf before the war in Austria Silesia, they had different ideas about minority accommodation and nationality struggle. Indeed, the Bielsko Germans were actually proud of their lack of formal training in ethnology, which Alfred Karasek thought to be too focused on the

---

170 Kurt Lück, "Das Deutschtum innerhalb der Bevölkerung Wolhyniens," *Deutsche Blätter in Polen* 3, nos. 11–12, special issue: Vom Deutschtum in Wolhynien (November–December 1926): 521–529, here 523. The text is also reprinted in Rosen, *Wolhynienfahrt 1926*, 59 and Fielitz, *Das Stereotyp des wolhyniendeutschen Umsiedlers*, 63n111. Translation from: Burleigh, *Germany Turns Eastwards*, 108.
171 Burleigh, *Germany Turns Eastwards*, 108.

mythical. Karasek believed the Bielitzers' engineering backgrounds would give them greater distance and objectivity.[172] For the Bielitzers, the Volhynian Germans were living proof of Germandom's biological superiority. Alfred Karasek placed the situation of the Volhynian Germans in a continuum of stages in cultural development.[173] Because all groups moved forward along this continuum, it was only a matter of time before the Volhynian Germans would converge with the other Germans in Poland. The Bielitzers' avid interest in biological-völkisch explanations led Walter Kuhn to downplay many of the alleged faults of the Volhynian Germans noted by Lück as mere teething pains that were common to young language islands.[174] Kuhn, who contributed five of the eight essays in the 1926 special volume of *Deutsche Blätter in Polen*, believed that the natural strengths should be allowed to develop without outside interference. He made only one reference to help from other Germans in Poland, and he strongly suggested that Volhynian Germans be given the opportunity to develop on their own. It is significant that Kuhn merely refers to the "more mature language islands" as the source of guidance – in the Polish context he probably meant his hometown, Bielsko.[175] Because the Germans in the formerly Prussian territories had never experienced the struggle of living in language islands, it seems that they were less relevant to this leadership role in the Bielitzer's view.

Kuhn and Karasek's rush to defend the dignity and worth of the Volhynian Germans was probably informed by the fact that the Bielitzers themselves came from a non-Prussian region, making them sensitive to any insinuations of backwardness. Playing the Volhynian Germans' advocate, the Bielitzers could use the Volhynian Germans as a foil to express their own frustration with the arrogant attitude of the Reich Germans, who continued to show a dismissive ignorance of Germans outside of the Reich's borders.[176] Kuhn's call to view the Germans in Volhynia more fairly was hence a simultaneous plea to appreciate the non-Prussian regions in Poland, including the Bielsko region itself. Their biological-völkisch arguments were subversive in that they showed the Volhynian Germans as up and coming, that is, becoming more like the Germans in Western Poland and Bielsko. Yet the Volhynian

172 Alexander Pinwinkler, "Walter Kuhn (1903–1983) und der Bielitzer 'Wandervogel e.V.' Historisch-volkskundliche 'Sprachinselforschung' zwischen völkischem Pathos und politischer Indienstnahme," *Zeitschrift für Volkskunde* 105 (2009): 29–52, here 33.
173 Fielitz, *Das Stereotyp des wolhyniendeutschen Umsiedlers*, 55, 62.
174 Walter Kuhn, "Kirche und Schule," *Deutsche Blätter in Polen* 3, nos. 11–12 (1926): 613–629, here 628–629; also cited in Fielitz, *Das Stereotyp des wolhyniendeutschen Umsiedlers*, 64.
175 Kuhn, "Kirche und Schule," 613–629, 628.
176 Kuhn, "Schlusswort," 633.

Germans and other allegedly backward groups could prove to be a source of vitality and dynamism for the entire minority. Hence, the Bielitzers revealed the potential of peripheral groups to challenge the Western Polish Germans for leadership in the minority. Although the political implications of these ideas were not yet drawn, the lines of conflict in the next decade were already starting to form.

The Germans from formerly Austrian Bielsko introduced their own völkisch ideas about the basic equality of Germans that was independent of any association with a German nation-state. By going further to decouple Reichness and Germanness, the Germans from Bielsko thus played a much more active role in teaching cultural self-help. In perhaps typical Austrian fashion, they could play the better, truer Germans who did not need a nation-state to be German. The Bielitzers traversed the line between the Western Polish and the eastern diaspora Germans, and they maintained a certain authority among both. Max Hildebert Boehm, himself from the Baltic region originally, stated that the formerly Prussian *ostmärkische* Germans could stimulate the Germans in the other regions in many aspects; but he also emphasized the special role of the Austrian Germans, who were supposed to "fertilize" the Germans of the old Eastern Marches.[177] Such language went beyond the common platitudes of simply learning from the colonists further east.

In the end, German activists from semi-peripheral Bielsko themselves participated in the self-essentializing discourse of German hierarchies and western superiority when it came to raising – in all senses of the word – the Volhynian Germans. At the time of the Volhynian expedition, Walter Kuhn claimed that the young language islands in Central and Eastern Poland, around Łódź, and in other parts of Eastern Europe were "historyless in the Western sense."[178] In a 1931 essay, Kuhn sounded the national alarm as he described how Ukrainians were surpassing the Volhynian Germans on a cultural level. Still, he noted that things were improving since the western territories in Poland (he probably assumed Bielsko to be part of this construction) had brought help.[179] Other Bielitzers also revealed a patronizing tone toward the Volhynian Germans. Viktor Kauder was born in Łódź but

---

177 Boehm, *Die deutschen Grenzlande*, 202–203.

178 Walter Kuhn, "Wege und Ziele ostlanddeutscher Heimatforschung," *Deutsche Blätter in Polen* 3, no. 7 (1926): 368–380, here 368–369. See also Hans-Werner Rautenberg, "Geschichte und Gegenwart Mittelpolens in der Forschung des Herder-Instituts," in *Polska Środkowa w niemieckich badaniach wschodnich*, 71–89, here 76.

179 Walter Kuhn, "Statistik der Volksbildung bei den Deutschen Wolhyniens," in *Die deutschen Siedlungen in Wolhynien. Geschichte, Volkskunde, Lebensfragen*, ed. Alfred Karasek and Kurt Lück, 32–41 (Leipzig: Hirzel, 1931), here 41.

grew up in Bielsko and became part of the Bielitzer Kreis around Kuhn and Karasek. He served as director of the Deutscher Kulturbund für Oberschlesien and was a prodigious writer and publisher. In the foreword to a collection of essays published in 1931 by Alfred Karasek and Kurt Lück, Kauder wrote that the Volhynian Germans were indeed one of Germandom's sturdiest offshoots, but that the Germans in the western regions of Poland must continue to be aware of their "obligations" toward these Germans and to offer "cultural assistance."[180] The inbetweenness of the Bielsko Germans and their ability to navigate their role as insiders and outsiders in the minority contributed to the minority infighting in the 1930s. As will be shown later, the desire of Bielitzers to prove themselves the better Germans would foster a strong support for National Socialism, which reshuffled the deck in the game of Germanness.

Rereading the 1926 Volhynian excursion not just as an exercise in Herrenmensch ideology but also as an expression of inner-minority cleavages opens up new perspectives on the German political experience in Poland. The Volhynian Germans served as a convenient foil for various issues related to status and power among their would-be benefactors and fulfilled a double function. On the one hand, they provided living proof of Germanic superiority over their Slavic neighbors. By proving ethnic stereotypes, they were to reveal the unity and equality of Germans abroad with the Reich Germans. On the other hand, the discursive treatment of the Volhynian Germans expressed the true relations of power within the minority and facilitated the ranking of regional groups within the minority. The attitude of the Western Polish Germans and also of the Bielsko Germans toward the Volhynian Germans reveals a hierarchical, even colonial, relationship within the minority. The purported weakness of the Germans in the East confirmed the prerogative of German minority leaders in Western Poland to lead and manage the other Germans. The process allowed the Western Polish Germans to reinvent their Reichness by establishing themselves at the top of the hierarchy of Germanness. The Western Polish German position did less to foster the völkisch togetherness of all Germans than to reassert residual Staatsvolk privileges. This civilizing mission, however, could also be usurped by the semi-peripheral Bielsko Germans, who could claim to have had more experience with völkisch struggle abroad.

---

180 Viktor Kauder, "Vorwort," in *Die deutschen Siedlungen in Wolhynien* (see note 179), v. Also quoted in Kessler, "Die Deutschen im polnischen Westwolhynien (1921–1939/40) in der historischen Forschung," 451.

These purported hardships allowed German nationalist leaders throughout Poland to make further claims and to mobilize the German minority around issues of the common welfare. For example, a frequent activity for German minority organizations in Western Poland was the collection of money for destitute Germans in Poland (known as the *Winterhilfe*, or winter relief). While German national activists raised money and touted their cross-regional solidarity, their calls for compassion also drew upon tropes of eastern backwardness and neediness. The slogan for one winter relief campaign in the 1930s asked in a shaming manner, "Do you know your brother in the East?"[181] Although these German activists claimed the need to make their poorer eastern brethren more ethnically conscious, they were in fact recentering and reethnicizing themselves as the better Germans. Western Polish Germans could cleanse themselves of the stain of cultural and national weakness associated with the loss of their Staatsvolk status by contrasting their own situation with those less-fortunate Germans in the East.

Thus, the mobilization of Germans in Poland in the 1920s also saw a process of hierarchization within the minority. Even in later discussions of their future, the Volhynian Germans themselves continued to say little. In the twenty or so contributions to the aforementioned 1931 volume on Volhynia edited by Karasek and Lück, it is significant that only one was written by a Volhynian, Leopold Platenik – and he was originally from the Reich. Another essay in a volume published by Lück in 1940 also did not bother using the names of Volhynian Germans.[182] As before, Germans from other regions found it more suitable to speak for them. This patronage often took grotesque forms. For example, Lück stressed the need to purify the Volhynian German language of Polish and Russian expressions.[183] When he and Karasek ascertained that the Volhynian Germans did not have enough suitable folk songs, they scoured existing texts, modifying them to eliminate foreign words and inconvenient religious content. They pepped up the songs by adding the accompaniment of musical instruments. Their resulting song book, named *Singendes Volk*, was a clear example of the invention of tradition.[184]

181 Breyer, *Das Deutsche Reich und Polen*, 256.
182 See note 179; Ingo Eser, *"Volk, Staat, Gott!" Die deutsche Minderheit in Polen und ihr Schulwesen 1918–1939* (Wiesbaden: Harrassowitz, 2010), 153–154; "Von Wolhynien nach Bereza Kartuska. Erzählt von wolhynischen Kolonisten," in *Marsch der Deutschen in Polen. Deutsche Volksgenossen im ehemaligen Polen berichten über Erlebnisse in den Septembertagen 1939*, ed. Kurt Lück, 103–106 (Berlin: Grenze und Ausland, 1940).
183 Kurt Lück, "Um die Reinheit unserer Muttersprache," in *Die deutschen Siedlungen in Wolhynien*, 45–48, here 47; Burleigh, *Germany Turns Eastwards*, 108–109.
184 Wilhelm Fielitz, "Volkslied und Volksliedsammlung zwischen den Weltkriegen in Wolhynien," *Germano-Polonica. Mitteilungen zur Geschichte der Deutschen in Polen und der deutsch-polnischen Beziehungen* 3 (2003): 17–24.

Thus, the Germans in the eastern regions of Poland became an exoticized and feminized Orient within the minority, one that needed the guidance of the masculinized Germans from Western Poland. Yet this internal Orient was also a threat. Todd Kontje's analysis of Gustav Freytag's *Soll und Haben* shows the double nature of the German relationship to the East: "While Freytag never suggests that Wohlfart has Polish ancestors, Anton's vehement reaction suggests that the Poles function not only as an external enemy to the German way of life, but also as an internal threat to his sense of self: the Poles are both that which he is not and that which he fears he might become."[185] Volhynian Germans could much serve the same role within the Volksgemeinschaft in Poland. Yet there was yet another Orient within the minority that was less subservient and more dangerous to the German national project in Poland. The purportedly renegade Germans in Central Poland would be crucial in defining the limits of Germanness in Poland. The perceived threat of the Germans in Łódź lay less in their economic and cultural backwardness than in their embodiment of the ills of modernity.

185 Todd Kontje, *German Orientalisms* (Ann Arbor: University of Michigan Press, 2004), 199.

3

On the Margins of the Minority

Germans in Łódź (1900–1933)

The previous chapter described how the former Reich Germans in the Western Polish regions held on to their residual citizenship and reinvented their Reich Germanness. Their attempts to discover the other Germans elsewhere in Poland also reflected and reinforced their dominant position within the minority. Things were different on the minority's periphery, and the Germans in the eastern regions of Poland formed what could be termed the minority's underclass. Although they were themselves very heterogeneous, these Germans on the margins were largely excluded from funds from the Reich and from political power within the minority. The marginalization of the Germans was in part due to their geographic location, which was outside of the formerly Prussian areas. This chapter examines the approximately 60,000 German-speakers in the city of Łódź, one of Central Europe's great industrial metropolises. The polyethnic nature of the city ensured that the Łódź Germans – despite their numerical strength – would remain on the margins of the German minority as a whole. In particular, German activists in Poland internalized and instrumentalized the stereotype of the *lodzermensch,* or person of Łódź, to underscore the national unreliability of these Germans. This regional hierarchy of Germanness was the other side of the nationalist project of turning the minority into a Volksgruppe.

Rogers Brubaker notes that the literature on diasporas often faces a tension between viewing them as examples of interethnic "boundary maintenance" or as "boundary erosion."[1] Indeed, the German activists in Poland constantly struggled to maintain their ethnic boundaries against erosion – especially from within. Thus, there was strong interest in quarantining those

---

1 Rogers Brubaker, "The 'Diaspora' Diaspora," *Ethnic and Racial Studies* 28, no. 1 (2005): 1–19, here 6–7, 11.

elements in the minority itself deemed corrosive to Germanness. Even if not totally excluded, however, these purportedly unreliable Germans served a useful purpose. Whereas the nationality struggle against the Poles may have dominated the self-perception of German activists, the periphery within the minority also served as the internal other for defining the mission and meaning of being German in Poland.

ŁÓDŹ AND RUSSIAN POLAND BEFORE THE FIRST WORLD WAR

Interwar Poland's formerly Russian territories were mainly composed of two historical regions: the Congress Kingdom and Volhynia. More than 400,000 German-speakers lived in these regions. Before 1914, these two territories differed, not only in their legal status, but in their confessional and ethnic composition as well. Although the majority of German-speakers in Congress Kingdom and Volhynia lived in rural areas, a significant number lived in one city: Łódź. A booming textile industry saw the dramatic growth of Łódź in the nineteenth and early twentieth centuries.[2] In 1820, as part of a plan to spur economic growth in the recently created Congress Kingdom of Poland, Łódź was one of seventeen cities slated to become industrial centers.[3] The city became the Russian Empire's third largest industrial center after Moscow and St. Petersburg and the second largest city in partitioned Poland after Warsaw. It was often referred to as the "Manchester of the East" as well as the "Polish Manchester."[4]

Although the Russian administration played an important role, Łódź came to be seen as a city of three nationalities: Jews and Poles as well as Germans. Entrepreneurs and workers from various German states had played a major role in the initial phase of settlement and the growth of the mills and factories.[5] The subsequent immigration of Polish-speakers from the countryside and Jews, however, meant that the German proportion declined rapidly. Although the reduction of complex biographies to national categories can often be misleading, the statistics still allow insight into broader trends. According to one recent Polish study, Germans made up 62.4 percent

---

2 Paweł Samuś, "Lodz. Heimatstadt von Polen, Deutschen und Juden" in *Polen, Deutsche und Juden in Lodz 1820–1939. Eine schwierige Nachbarschaft,* ed. Jürgen Hensel, 13–32 (Osnabrück: Fibre, 1999), here 13.
3 Bianka Pietrow-Ennker, "Ein Klischee lernt das Zwinkern. Der 'Lodzermensch' verkörpert eine Lebensweise, die in Lodz wieder modern wird," *Frankfurter Allgemeine Zeitung* (January 3, 2002): 48.
4 Samuś, "Lodz. Heimatstadt von Polen, Deutschen und Juden," 13.
5 The question of which ethnic group played the dominant role in building Łódź is contested. See Krzysztof Woźniak, "Spóry o genezę Łodzi przemysłowej w pracach historycznych autorów polskich, niemieckich i żydowskich," in *Polacy–Niemcy–Żydzi w Łodzi w XIX-XX w. Sąsiedzi dalecy i bliscy,* ed. Paweł Samuś (Łódź: Ibidem, 1997), 9–26.

of the population in 1862; just three years later, in 1865, this category made up only 44.5 percent. By 1914, Łódź had 500,500 inhabitants. According to one estimate, 50.9 percent were Poles and 32.5 percent were Jews. The some 75,000 German-speakers made up only 15 percent of the population.[6] Despite the declining share of Germans in the city, Łódź nonetheless remained the center of German activity in the Congress Kingdom. Likewise, the city played an important role in the cultural, political, and economic life of Polish Jews: Łódź had become Poland's second-largest Jewish community after Warsaw.[7] As the industrial hub in the Congress Kingdom, Łódź was a flashpoint in the Revolution of 1905–1907 and was central to Polish nationalist aspirations. Given its size and importance, Łódź had become disputed territory for activists from three competing nationalities.[8]

PROMISED LAND AND EVIL CITY: THE CONSTRUCTION OF THE LODZERMENSCH

In the period before the First World War, immigrants and outside observers often associated Łódź with quick and easy economic success but also with cultural pessimism. Already before the First World War, variations of the Yiddish song "Itzek, komm mit nach Lodz" expressed the irony of this "Promised Land."[9] To contemporary observers, Łódź captured the fears of an onrushing capitalist modernity, including increasing individualism and the loss of one's cultural and national roots. The rampant capitalism, the rise and fall of fabulous fortunes, and uncontrolled urban growth also garnered for Łódź the nickname "Antechamber to Hell."[10] The image of Łódź suffered because of the anti-bourgeois and anti-urban attitude of many Polish intellectuals, who idealized the Polish nobility and its agrarian way

---

6 Wiesław Puś, "Die Berufs- und Sozialstruktur der wichtigsten ethnischen Gruppen in Lodz und ihre Entwicklung in den Jahren 1820–1914," in *Polen, Deutsche und Juden in Lodz* (see note 2), 33–43, here 35–37.

7 Samuś, "Lodz. Heimatstadt von Polen, Deutschen und Juden," 13.

8 For more on disputed territories, see Stefan Wolff, *Disputed Territories: The Transnational Dynamics of Ethnic Conflict Settlement* (New York/Oxford: Berghahn, 2003).

9 Austrian soldiers during the First World War adapted the song to "Rosa, wir fahr'n nach Lodz." See Valentin Polcuch, "Wie ein Schmonzeslied zum Schlager wurde," in *Lodz. Die Stadt der Völkerbegegnung im Wandel der Geschichte*, ed. Peter E. Nasarski (Cologne-Rodenkirchen: Liebig, 1978), 78; Valentin Polcuch, "'Theo, wir fahr'n nach Lodz.' Ein Schlager im Wandel der Geschichte," in *Lodz – "Gelobtes Land": Von deutscher Tuchmachersiedlung zur Textilmetropole im Osten. Dokumente und Erinnerungen*, ed. Peter E. Nasarski (Berlin/Bonn: Westkreuz, 1988), 11–12; Andreas Kossert, "'Promised Land'? Urban Myth and the Shaping of Modernity in Manchester and Lodz," in *The Politics of Urban Space, vol. 2 of Imagining the City*, ed. Christian Emden, Catherine Keen, and David Midgley, 169–192 (Oxford/Bern: Peter Lang, 2006), here 180.

10 Richard Breyer, Peter E. Nasarski, and Janusz Piekalkiewicz, *Nachbarn seit tausend Jahren. Deutsche und Polen in Bildern und Dokumenten* (Mainz: Hase & Koehler, 1976), 209.

of life in the era before the partitions. No doubt they were also jealous of the rise of Łódź in competition with the Polish capital Warsaw.[11] Another contemporary Polish writer, Zygmunt Bartkiewicz, coined yet another nickname for Łódź: the "evil city."[12]

By the late 1800s, the city gave birth to the stereotype of the lodzer-mensch.[13] The term, which arose in Yiddish, was also spelled in Polish as *lodzermensz* and often appeared as *Lodzer Mensch* in German. The historian Bianka Pietrow-Ennker sums up the stereotype as the following: "In the urban microcosm of Łódź, the 'lodzermensch' type stood for the businessman of German, Jewish, or Polish heritage. He was characterized by a rational and individual way of life, and his work was dictated by the principles of the market economy. He remained loyal under any given political circumstances in order not to endanger his business dealings."[14] Thus, this economically liberal but politically conservative image of the lodzermensch expressed a form of inter-ethnic accommodation that was commonplace in East Central Europe and elsewhere in the German-Polish borderlands, such as Upper Silesia.[15]

Władysław Reymont, awarded the Noble Prize in literature in 1924, wrote the classic depiction of the lodzermensch in *The Promised Land* (1899). In his story, speculation and greed, fortune and ruin dominated the lives of the three protagonists. These were nominally a German, a Jew, and a Pole, but they were above all ambitious and joined forces to start a textile factory. Reymont's lodzermensch felt equally at home in Polish and German; his characters even spoke a pidgin form that combined elements from both languages. Whereas the lodzermensch was initially associated with the predominantly German-Jewish entrepreneurial class, the concept eventually became metonymic. Even when the lodzermensch was not explicitly mentioned by name, it became commonplace to use coded language that alluded

---

11 Bianka Pietrow-Ennker, "Auf dem Weg zur Bürgergesellschaft. Modernisierungsprozesse in Lodz (1820–1914)," in *Polen, Deutsche und Juden in Lodz* (see note 2), 103–129, here 128–129.

12 Zygmunt Bartkiewicz, *Złe miasto. Obrazy z 1907 roku* (Warsaw: Nakł. Jana Czempińskiego, 1911); Zygmunt Bartkiewicz, *Trzy opowieści* (Warsaw: Dom Książki Polskiej, 1930).

13 Richard Breyer, "Der 'Lodzer Mensch' – Legende und Wirklichkeit," in *Lodz – die Stadt der Völkerbegegnung im Wandel der Geschichte*, 74–75.

14 Pietrow-Ennker, "Ein Klischee lernt das Zwinkern," 48 (translation mine).

15 Two recent works on the "Schlonsaken" and other Upper Silesians include: Kai Struve and Philipp Ther, ed., *Die Grenzen der Nationen. Identitätenwandel in Oberschlesien in der Neuzeit* (Marburg: Herder-Institut, 2002); Manfred Alexander, "Oberschlesien im 20. Jahrhundert – eine mißverstandene Region," *Geschichte und Gesellschaft* 30, no. 3 (2004): 465–489. Also, Tomasz Falęcki compares the German minorities in Upper Silesia and Łódź, but unfortunately he touches on the "lodzermensch" only briefly. See "Niemcy w Łodzi i Niemcy w województwie śląskim w okresie międzywojennym. Wzajemne powiązania oraz podobieństwa i różnice pod względem społeczno-ekonomicznym i świadomościowym," in *Niemcy w Łodzi do 1939 roku*, ed. Marian Wilk, 74–88 (Łódź: Uniwersytet Łódzki, 1996), here 79.

to it. Variations of the lodzermensch, for example, were often ascribed to the city's population at large.[16]

Although the lodzermensch had positive characteristics such as diligence, punctuality, and initiative, the term became increasingly synonymous with dystopian views of Łódź. Many saw this hybridity as a threatening deviation from modern nation-building.[17] Although perceived as a sign of assimilation, the lodzermensch remained inherently foreign at the same time. One Polish observer in 1904 wrote that the German settlers in Łódź had lost their "Germanic patriotism." Instead of becoming Poles, however, they had instead become "patriotic lodzermenschen."[18] The lodzermensch was ethnicized as something essentially German and/or Jewish, a trope that maintained the idea of a pure Polish nation, but the fear that many Poles were also becoming lodzermenschen reflected the cultural pessimism of the intelligentsia. Nor was the lodzermensch a threat for Polish nationalists alone, for other activists could claim their own version of undesired hybridity. Especially the workers seemed to be melting into a homogenous international proletariat.[19] Although the reality behind the lodzermensch is hard to pinpoint, it is important that its discursive foundations existed. German observers often drew the conclusion that the Łódź Germans were somehow not German enough and used the specter of the lodzermensch to explain this situation. Like other stereotypes, elements could be reactivated at a later date and mobilized in different contexts.

In the Russian Empire, German cultural life had been for the most part unpoliticized. The Evangelical Church of the Augsburg Confession remained the center of communal activity for most of the German-speaking immigrants and their descendants. The Church also ran elementary schools (*Volksschulen*) with German instruction throughout Central Poland.[20] During a Russification campaign from 1895 to 1910, the number of evangelical schools in Congress Poland sank from 606 to 584.[21] Łódź tended to fare better than the rural areas, and the city even experienced a growth of German

---

16 Samuś, "Lodz. Heimatstadt von Polen, Deutschen und Juden," 23.
17 On the perceived threat of hybridity, see Tara Zahra, "Imagined Non-Communities: National Indifference as a Category of Analysis," *Slavic Review* 69 (Spring 2010): 93–119, 98.
18 Stefan Gorski, *Łódź Spółczesna. Obrazki i szkice publicystyczne* (Łódź: Księg. Narodowa, 1904), 21–22. Also cited in Samuś, "Lodz. Heimatstadt von Polen, Deutschen und Juden," 23.
19 Breyer, Nasarski, and Piekalkiewicz, *Nachbarn seit tausend Jahren*, 209.
20 Otto Heike, *Das deutsche Schulwesen in Mittelpolen. Ein Kapitel mühsamer Abwehr staatlichen Unrechts* (Dortmund: Ostdeutsche Forschungsstelle im Lande Nordrhein-Westfalen, 1963), 12.
21 Heike, *Das deutsche Schulwesen in Mittelpolen*, 13. Russification entailed changing Church-run schools into public elementary schools with some instruction in Russian. See Ingo Eser, *"Volk, Staat, Gott!" Die deutsche Minderheit in Polen und ihr Schulwesen 1918–1939* (Wiesbaden: Harrassowitz, 2010), 98, 107–109.

schools shortly before the war. By 1914, there were twenty-three public elementary schools and six Church-run (*Kantorat*) schools within the city.[22]

Although it is impossible to gauge the feeling of the majority of the German-speakers, it is likely that the minor successes of Russification policies in Central Poland did not create widespread national resentments or resistance. The overall lack of political freedom, socioeconomic disparities, and rural-urban alignments also hindered national mobilization on the issue. Especially the poor economic conditions in the countryside ensured that schooling in any language would be welcome: in the early interwar period, 25 percent of all German-speakers were illiterate in the Congress Polish territories (compared to 30–35 percent for the general population).[23] The supposed national quietude on the part of the Germans has led to a tendency to project an idealized and peaceful interethnic coexistence on the past. Andreas R. Hofmann has provided a needed corrective by showing that prewar Łódź was not a multicultural idyll disrupted by the First World War, but that the war itself acted as a catalyst for preexisting nationality conflicts.[24]

IMPACT OF WORLD WAR I IN ŁÓDŹ AND CENTRAL POLAND

The outbreak of the First World War saw thousands flee Central Poland in order to evade possible conscription or forced evacuation by the Russian authorities. German troops occupied Łódź in December 1914, which spared the German-speakers there from deportation. More than 100,000 people from the Central Polish countryside, however, were forcibly transported east on account of their supposed Germanness.[25] At the same time, Reich German troops were generally surprised by the number of Germans they encountered in Russian territory.[26] In 1915, the Central Powers divided the occupied Congress Kingdom into two separate zones for civil administration: Germany's Government General Warsaw, which included Łódź, and Austria-Hungary's Military Government Lublin. The German

---

22 Heike, *Das deutsche Schulwesen in Mittelpolen*, 16.
23 Richard Blanke, *Orphans of Versailles: The Germans in Western Poland, 1918–1939* (Lexington: University Press of Kentucky, 1993), 38. In Volhynia, illiteracy rates were even more extreme: 57% of all Germans were illiterate, against 70% for the general population.
24 Andreas R. Hofmann, "Die vergessene Okkupation. Lodz im Ersten Weltkrieg," in *Deutsche-Juden-Polen. Geschichte einer wechselvollen Beziehung im 20. Jahrhundert. Festschrift für Hubert Schneider*, ed. Andrea Löw, Kerstin Robusch, and Stefanie Walter, 59–78 (Frankfurt/Main: Campus, 2004).
25 Otto Heike, *Die deutsche Minderheit in Polen bis 1939. Ihr Leben und Wirken, kulturell, gesellschaftlich, politisch. Eine historisch-dokumentarische Analyse* (Leverkusen: self-published, 1985), 134–135.
26 Richard Breyer, *Das Deutsche Reich und Polen, 1932–1937. Außenpolitik und Volksgruppenfragen* (Würzburg: Holzner, 1955), 47.

Empire's relations to its new subjects, both Polish and German, remained tense. Reich Germans who came to occupied Łódź were forced to rely on traditional elites to govern the city and the region. It was believed that the Polish-speaking population tended to belong to Polish nationalist groupings, whereas the Jewish and the German members of the industrial bourgeoisie continued to support Imperial Russian interests.[27] Disturbed by the lack of national affiliation, the occupiers sneeringly called the local Germans "ruble patriots."[28] Governor General Hans von Beseler himself identified the Germans in Poland with the "Russophilia" of the Łódź industrialists.[29]

On November 15, 1916, Germany and Austria-Hungary announced the creation of an autonomous Polish Kingdom. Yet the plan to resurrect Poland remained largely unconvincing. There was no definition of the borders, and it was likely that Poland was to encompass only the areas belonging to the Russian Empire – including Łódź – but no Prussian or Austrian territory. Moreover, many saw through this attempt to exploit the Polish Question to better conscript Poles for the German war effort. Still, the German administrators tried not to alienate the Polish population and gave the Poles an advisory role in administering Central Poland through the Provisional State Council.[30] The plan to hand Łódź to Poland incensed German activists, who denounced this policy and worked for Germany's direct annexation of the Łódź region. The Deutscher Verein, founded by the businessman Adolf Eichler in March 1916, held demonstrations to voice the desire to "stay here."[31] He was also at odds with the Reich authorities over their choice of the leader of the Evangelical-Augsburg Church, Julius Bursche.[32] In order to limit the interference of these activists and to counter the agitation of various annexationist groups in Germany, Reich administrators restricted the activity, clubs, and press of the German

---

27 Hofmann, "Die vergessene Okkupation," 63.
28 Stefan Pytlas, "Problemy asymilacji i polonizacji społeczności niemieckiej w Łodzi do 1914 r.," in *Niemcy w Łodzi do 1939 roku,* 13–20, here 19; Adolf Eichler, *Das Deutschtum in Kongreßpolen* (Stuttgart: Ausland und Heimat Verlags-Aktiengesellschaft, 1921), 119; also Eduard Kneifel, "Adolf Eichler – Ein Leben im Dienste des Deutschtums," in *Deutschtum im Aufbruch. Vom Volkstumskampf der Deutschen im östlichen Wartheland,* ed. Adolf Kargel and Eduard Kneifel, 11–32 (Leipzig: Hirzel, 1942), here 15.
29 Werner Conze, "'Nationalstaat oder Mitteleuropa?' Die Deutschen des Reiches und die Nationalitätenfragen Ostmitteleuropas im ersten Weltkrieg," in *Deutschland und Europa. Historische Studien zur Völker- und Staatenordnung des Abendlandes, Festschrift für Hans Rothfels,* ed. Werner Conze, 201–230 (Düsseldorf: Droste, 1951), 217.
30 Martin Broszat, *Zweihundert Jahre deutsche Polenpolitik* (Frankfurt/Main: Suhrkamp, 1972), 189–191; Heike, *Das deutsche Schulwesen in Mittelpolen,* 16–19.
31 Breyer, *Das Deutsche Reich und Polen,* 48–49; also in Conze, "'Nationalstaat oder Mitteleuropa," 215–216.
32 Kneifel, "Adolf Eichler – Ein Leben im Dienste des Deutschtums," 21–22.

minority.[33] Still, the Deutscher Verein grew to include 30,000 members and 230 local chapters.[34]

Despite the initial antagonisms with minority leaders, German occupation turned out to be more effective in reviving German cultural institutions in Łódź than in resurrecting a Polish state. The Provisional State Council guaranteed substantial cultural rights to the Germans in Central Poland, who were slated to live as a national minority in the Polish Kingdom. German schools throughout the Government General Warsaw grew at a brisk pace, in part due to the activity of Eichler's Deutscher Verein.[35] By 1918, the number of German elementary schools in Central Poland (including the Austrian zone) exceeded the prewar highpoint of 606 in 1895.[36] Łódź alone had forty German elementary schools. German secondary education also flourished in the city, where the Lodzer Deutsches Gymnasium reached new enrollment highs with 545 pupils in 1915 and 711 pupils in 1918.[37] A second high school, the Luisen-Lyzeum for girls, was established in Łódź, as well as high schools elsewhere in Central Poland.[38]

The marriage of convenience between Reich and Polish leaders quickly soured, however, and the defeat of the Central Powers would reverse the fortunes of Germans in Poland. German occupation had set the stage for future conflict, for the post-Versailles Polish government was intent on dismantling the excessive number of German institutions left in Central Poland. Yet the occupation had also revealed the first signs of mobilization among German activists in Central Poland and laid the groundwork for their future relationship with the Reich. Although members of the Deutscher Verein had used German protection to build more schools, they had shown that they were more than willing to assert their own interests against those of their erstwhile benefactors.

GERMAN POLITICAL LIFE IN ŁÓDŹ UP TO 1933

Because Poznania and Pomerelia did not come under Polish rule until 1920 – and 1922 for eastern Upper Silesia – the first political stirrings of the Polish Germans appeared in Central Poland. This head start gave Germans

33 Conze, "Nationalstaat oder Mitteleuropa," 215–216.
34 Joachim Rogall, *Die Deutschen im Posener Land und in Mittelpolen* (Munich: Langen Müller, 1993), 123.
35 Rogall, *Die Deutschen im Posener Land und in Mittelpolen*, 123.
36 Heike, *Das deutsche Schulwesen in Mittelpolen*, 16–20.
37 Adolf Kargel, "Das Lodzer deutsche Schulwesen im Zeitraffer," in *Das Lodzer Deutsche Gymnasium. Im Spannungsfeld zwischen Schicksal und Erbe, 1906–1981*, ed. Peter E. Nasarski, 11–18 (Berlin/Bonn: Westkreuz, 1981), here 15.
38 Heike, *Das deutsche Schulwesen in Mittelpolen*, 20.

in Łódź the chance to form their own organizations without outside inter-ference by the Germans in Western Poland. Łódź remained the center not just for the 100,000 Germans residing outside the city in Łódź county[39] but also for the entire former Congress Kingdom with its approximately 320,000 Germans.[40] As such, Łódź had the potential to serve as the minor-ity's political bastion, especially given the drawing of the electoral districts that gave urban minorities a better chance at political representation than those in the countryside.[41] Yet for at least the first half of the interwar period, Łódź played only a peripheral role in intra-minority politics, espe-cially as socialist and pro-Polish movements within the minority appeared to threaten the revisionist goals of the Reich and Western Polish German leaders.

Although conservative-nationalist groupings dominated German politi-cal life in Western Poland, these elements were on the defensive in Łódź in the early 1920s. The attempts to build on the nationalist activity of the First World War were initially weak. The Deutscher Verein, for example, disbanded already in 1918.[42] Its leader, Adolf Eichler, and other nationalists from the Deutscher Verein founded a new party, the Deutsche Volkspartei, in December 1918 for the elections in January 1919 to the Constituent Sejm (Sejm Ustawodawczy).[43] Eichler served as Chairman of the Deutsche Volkspartei.[44] Working with Jewish leaders, the Deutsche Volkspartei gath-ered 51,527 votes in Central Poland, and it was able to send two candi-dates to the Constituent Sejm.[45] Having fulfilled its function, however, the Deutsche Volkspartei was disbanded immediately after the elections. Eichler himself fled to East Prussia in the early 1920s because he feared the wrath of Polish authorities. The response of local German leaders to Eichler's flight was mixed,[46] but it was undoubtedly a blow to the fledgling nationalist movement in Łódź.

---

39 Jerzy Tomaszewski, "Jews in Łódź in 1931 According to Statistics," *Polin* 6 (1991): 173–200, here 175.
40 Walter Kuhn [Andreas Mückler, pseud.], *Das Deutschtum Kongreßpolens. Eine statistisch-kritische Studie* (Leipzig/Wien: Franz Deuticke, 1927), 87.
41 Paweł Korzec, "Der Block der Nationalen Minderheiten im Parlamentarismus Polens des Jahres 1922," *Zeitschrift für Ostforschung* 24, no. 2 (1975): 193–220, here 202.
42 Fritz Wertheimer, *Von deutschen Parteien und Parteiführern im Ausland*, 2nd edition (Berlin: Zentral-Verlag, 1930), 108.
43 Korzec, "Der Block der Nationalen Minderheiten im Parlamentarismus Polens des Jahres 1922," 198, 200.
44 Mads Ole Balling, *Von Reval bis Bukarest. Statistisch-Biographisches Handbuch der Parlamentarier der deutschen Minderheiten in Ostmittel- und Südosteuropa 1919–1945*, vol. 1 (Copenhagen: Dokumenta-tion Verlag, 1991), 182.
45 Balling, *Von Reval bis Bukarest*, 182; Rogall, *Die Deutschen im Posener Land und in Mittelpolen*, 132.
46 Kneifel, "Adolf Eichler – Ein Leben im Dienste des Deutschtums," 23.

The search for a successor organization took on new impetus as the 1922 elections neared. On March 24, 1921, German leaders announced the Bund der Deutschen Polens (BDP; also called Bund der Deutschen in Polen).[47] In July 1921, about 3,000 people came to the opening meeting in Łódź. The organizers proclaimed that the Bund der Deutschen Polens would be non-political. They claimed that they would work together with the Poles to rebuild Poland and to stand against communism. Dr. Eduard von Behrens, the director of the publishing company Libertas and editor of the *Lodzer Freie Presse* from 1921 to 1923, served as the chairman of the Bund der Deutschen Polens.[48] Joseph Spickermann, the Sejm deputy who had been part of the Deutsche Volkspartei, was elected to its head committee.[49]

The Bund der Deutschen Polens was the first serious attempt to rebuild a German nationalist party in Łódź and the outlying areas, and its membership increased to about 1,000 by 1923. The Poles, however, saw Behrens' political agitation unfavorably and eyed the Bund der Deutschen Polens with great suspicion.[50] They never authorized the organization.[51] Yet the problems lay just as much with the Germans. The original program of the BDP was to unite all Germans in Poland, but the leaders soon concluded that such an organization would not be likely in the near future.[52] Resistance from other regional parties was a problem.[53] The area of activity was to encompass Congress Poland and Galicia but not Prussian Poland, which had its own organization.[54] The Deutschtumsbund, after all, had just been founded in this period (May 8, 1921), and it served the interests of those Germans in the formerly Prussian areas.

---

47 Przemysław Hauser, "The German Minority in Poland in the Years 1918–1939. Reflections in the State of Research and Interpretation, Proposals for Further Research," *Polish Western Affairs* 32, no. 2 (1991): 13–38, here 22; Mirosław Cygański, *Mniejszość niemiecka w Polsce centralnej w latach 1919–1939* (Łódź: Wydawnictwo Łódzkie, 1962), 22–24.

48 Cygański, *Mniejszość niemiecka w Polsce centralnej*, 22.

49 "Ein neuer Bund der Deutschen in Polen," translation of *Dziennik Gdański*, Nr. 173 v. 28.7 (1921), in "Gesamtüberblick über die poln. Presse," August 2, 1921, in GStA, I HA, Rep. 77, Tit. 856, folder 32, 19; Balling, *Von Reval bis Bukarest*, 202.

50 Cygański, *Mniejszość niemiecka w Polsce centralnej*, 22.

51 Balling, *Von Reval bis Bukarest*, 187, 202.

52 Cygański, *Mniejszość niemiecka w Polsce centralnej*, 22.

53 Cygański, *Mniejszość niemiecka w Polsce centralnej*, 22, Breyer, *Das Deutsche Reich und Polen*, 49; Rogall, *Die Deutschen im Posener Land und in Mittelpolen*, 132. These authors emphasize the regional differences to explain the BDP's failure. In contrast, Richard Blanke sees the Polish government's position as the primary cause for the failure to create a unified minority party. Blanke uses the repression of the League of Germans in Poland as an example. See Blanke, *Orphans of Versailles*, 56.

54 "Ein neuer Bund der Deutschen in Polen," translation of *Dziennik Gdański*, Nr. 173 v. 28.7 (1921), in "Gesamtüberblick über die poln. Presse," August 2, 1921, in GStA, I HA, Rep. 77, Tit. 856, folder 32, 19.

After the Polish government banned the Deutschtumsbund in Western Poland in 1923, the leaders of the Bund der Deutschen Polens dissolved their group as well.[55] Another party called the Bürgerliche Deutsche Partei (confusingly, with the same acronym BDP) was founded on May 8, 1923 – five days before the city council elections – by Alexander Drewing, who had also started the *Neue Lodzer Zeitung*. After the elections, in which it did not do well, the Bürgerliche Deutsche Partei appeared to be without a purpose and sank into inactivity.[56] In part, the name was unattractive for German nationalists in Łódź, where the term "bürgerlich" (bourgeois) usually did not connotate nationalist groupings, as was the case in Western Poland. Rather, the "bourgeois" Germans in Łódź were commonly associated with putatively assimilated or Polonophile patricians. Fritz Wertheimer, the director of the Deutsches Ausland-Institut, claimed that "opportunists" largely made up the party's membership.[57]

On June 1, 1924, the Sejm deputies August Utta and Joseph Spickermann, both from Łódź, founded a new party, the Deutscher Volksverband (DVV).[58] August Utta had belonged to the right wing of the socialist camp before he broke with the party altogether during the communal elections in 1923.[59] The purpose of the party, according to the German Foreign Ministry representative in Łódź, was to provide a völkisch alternative to the local German socialist party and to awaken the "sleeping Germandom" in the countryside, which was allegedly marked by "sluggishness" and "backwardness." Although the DVV strove to mobilize politically all citizens of German descent, it also sought the "unity and peaceful collaboration of all völkisch organizations in the entire territory of the Polish Republic, for the good of the individual, the German minority, and the entire state."[60] The new party attracted the majority of its adherents from the largely inactive Bürgerliche Deutsche Partei. The DVV would become the fulcrum of German nationalist activity in Łódź and Central Poland until 1939. During this time, the Deutscher Volksverband had two major press organs, the daily

---

55 Hauser, "The German Minority in Poland," 23.
56 Zygmunt Stoliński, *Die deutsche Minderheit in Polen* (Warsaw: Instytut Badań Spraw Narodowościowych, 1928), 58.
57 Wertheimer, *Von deutschen Parteien*, 108.
58 Other important Germans involved in the founding were Sejm Deputy Karau from Włocławek and Senator Stüldt from the Voivodeship of Łódź. See Consul in Łódź (Hoffmann-Völkersamb) to German Foreign Ministry, November 26, 1924, in PAAA, Pol IV, Politik 25 Polen, vol. 18, R82198, 213–237. Several copies of the DVV program were included with the report, which inexplicably came five months after the founding of the party.
59 Balling, *Von Reval bis Bukarest*, 186, 209.
60 Grundsätze des Deutschen Volksverbandes in Polen, June 1, 1924, several copies sent as attachments by Consul in Łódź (Hoffmann-Völkersamb) to German Foreign Ministry, November 26, 1924, in PAAA, Pol IV, Politik 25 Polen, vol. 18, R82198, 213–237.

Freie Presse and the weekly paper *Der Volksfreund*, which targeted Germans in the Central Polish countryside. August Utta became the head of the new party. He served as a Sejm deputy from 1922 to 1930, and he was Senator from 1930 until 1935.[61] Under his leadership, the party grew rapidly in the 1920s, albeit primarily in the countryside outside of Łódź. In 1924, the party had 7,000 members; and in 1930, it had 24,000 members organized in 305 chapters.[62] Utta led the party until he stepped down in 1938, and he continued to play a leadership role until his death in 1940.

The creation of an explicitly nationalist German party that differentiated itself from the bourgeois-liberal position of many Germans in the city was an important turning point in polarizing German public opinion in Łódź. It gave voice to those German-speakers who did not want to vote socialist but who also shunned the other German parties that appeared too accommodating to Polish authorities. Like the conservative-nationalist Deutsche Vereinigung (DV) in Western Poland, the DVV leaders continued to cooperate politically with the other national minorities in Poland within the context of the Minorities Bloc. Utta even served as the Minorities Bloc's German representative.

The DVV, however, remained relatively weak in the 1920s. Although the conservative-nationalist German parties dominated the other regions in Poland, the DVV remained largely based in the Central Polish countryside and was unable to win over Germans in Łódź itself. The DVV became the object of attack by those who felt the path taken by the German minority had become too nationalist or chauvinist. In the 1928 Sejm elections, the all-but-defunct Bürgerliche Deutsche Partei claimed in a flyer that the DVV wanted to turn Polish citizens of German nationality into Germans abroad (Auslandsdeutsche). The Bürgerliche Deutsche Partei also criticized the dubious source of the DVV's money and the corruption of its leaders.[63] By the early 1930s, the DVV began to buckle under internal dissent, causing the organization to lose support.[64]

The creation of the Deutscher Volksverband did give the appearance of increased unity among the conservative-nationalist German parties in Poland, but the cooperation between the Deutsche Vereinigung in Western Poland and the Deutscher Volksverband in Central Poland remained limited beyond a few staged campaigns. Not able to dominate its own region, the

61 Jacek Walicki, "Żydzi i Niemcy w samorządzie Łodzi lat 1917–1939," in *Polacy–Niemcy–Żydzi* (see note 5), 359–376, here 360.

62 Petra Blachetta-Madajczyk, *Klassenkampf oder Nation? Deutsche Sozialdemokratie in Polen 1918–1939* (Düsseldorf: Droste, 1997), 61–62.

63 Stoliński, *Die deutsche Minderheit in Polen,* 60.

64 Cygański, *Mniejszość niemiecka w Polsce centralnej,* 42.

DVV could only play the role of junior partner to the Deutsche Vereinigung in Western Poland during the 1920s and early 1930s. A Polish assessment of the DVV's events in the fall of 1932 to be "more than modest" only seemed to confirm the national torpidity of the Łódź Germans.[65] This inactivity left the field open to the German socialists, who dominated minority politics in Łódź for most of the 1920s and to carry on the struggle for Germanness in Łódź.

GERMAN SOCIALIST PARTIES IN A NATIONALIZING STATE

Within interwar Poland's German minority, the socialist parties were the greatest challenge to the near hegemony of the conservative-nationalist organizations. Socialists were less effective in Pomerelia and Poznania, where German communities were overwhelmingly rural and the nationality conflict had been deeply embedded.[66] The socialist movement was, however, a significant political factor among Germans in Łódź, where there had been a long tradition of workers' organization.[67] During the 1920s, the socialists dominated German political life in Łódź, and the city soon became the center of German socialism in Poland.

Although German socialists were not represented in the Constituent Sejm (1919–1922), they were well prepared for the 1922 Sejm elections. The first German socialist party in independent Poland, the Deutsche Arbeitspartei Polens (DAP), was founded in Łódź on January 19, 1922.[68] Because the Polish Socialist Party (PPS) did not want to associate itself officially with the other national minorities in the highly charged nationalist atmosphere of the early 1920s, the German socialists from Łódź limited their cooperation to the other Germans in Poland. For the Sejm elections in November 1922, the Deutsche Arbeitspartei Polens joined with the conservative-nationalists around the Bund der Deutschen Polens to form the Deutsches Zentralwahlkomitee in Lodz (also known as the Deutscher Volksrat für Mittelpolen).[69] In turn, this Central Polish coalition participated with the other regional German committees within the Minorities Bloc for the 1922 Sejm and Senate elections.

65 *Sprawy Narodowościowe* 6, no. 6 (1932): 683; also cited in Breyer, *Das Deutsche Reich*, 249.
66 Otto Heike, *Die deutsche Arbeiterbewegung in Polen, 1835–1945* (Dortmund: Ostdeutsche Forschungsstelle im Lande Nordrhein-Westfalen, 1969), 75.
67 Padraic Kenney, *Rebuilding Poland: Workers and Communists, 1945–1950* (Ithaca: Cornell University Press, 1997).
68 Blachetta-Madajczyk, *Klassenkampf oder Nation*, 45.
69 Blachetta-Madajczyk, *Klassenkampf oder Nation*, 118.

In the 1922 elections, the Minorities Bloc won a total of eighty-seven seats, seventeen of which were allotted to the German participant organizations, making the Germans the third largest fraction in the Minorities Bloc.[70] The cooperation between socialists and conservative-nationalists was fruitful for the Central Polish German activists, with a total of five Sejm mandates and one seat in the Senate for the region. Of the seventeen German seats, four went to the German socialists, and three of these served the Łódź city/region. The only other German socialist seat in the Sejm was Arthur Pankratz from Bydgoszcz in Pomerelia.[71] The urban inflection in German socialism is apparent in the distribution of mandates in the Łódź region (Łódź city and Łódź county). Arthur Kronig received a direct mandate for Łódź city, while Emil Zerbe received a seat through the state list for Łódź county. August Utta, who led the right wing of the DAP, had gained a seat in Łódź county (excluding the city) with the help of Jewish votes in 1922.[72] After Utta's defection to the conservative-nationalist camp, the remaining three socialists in the Sejm continued as part of the German parliamentarian club until the parliament was dissolved on November 28, 1927.

In Central Poland, the German conservative-nationalists had a slow start in its struggle with German socialism. They did not initially have a mandate for Łódź city/region in the 1922 Sejm elections, although Utta's defection from the socialist camp in 1923 gave them an important new spokesman representing Łódź county.[73] In the Central Polish regions outside of Łódź, the conservative-nationalists fared better: Joseph Spickermann and Jakob Karau gained seats in the Sejm for Konin and Wocławek. Of the 111 members of the Polish Senate, 5 belonged to the German parliamentarian club. None of these German senators came from the socialist camp.[74] The one senator from Central Poland was Karl Stüldt, who represented the entire Voivodeship of Łódź.[75]

In the overall political landscape of the German minority, socialism seemed to be an eastern phenomenon. German socialism never took root in Poznania and Pomerelia, where there was little industry. German socialists played a more significant role in the industrial areas of Upper Silesia. In the 1922 Sejm elections, however, the German socialists in eastern Upper

70 Blachetta-Madajczyk, *Klassenkampf oder Nation*, 118–119.
71 Stoliński, *Die deutsche Minderheit in Polen*, 41.
72 Korzec, "Der Block der Nationalen Minderheiten im Parlamentarismus Polens des Jahres 1922," 204.
73 Cygański, *Mniejszość niemiecka w Polsce centralnej*, 24; Heike, *Die deutsche Arbeiterbewegung in Polen*, 81–82; Stoliński, *Die deutsche Minderheit in Polen*, 41; Balling, *Von Reval bis Bukarest*, 186, 209.
74 Blachetta-Madajczyk, *Klassenkampf oder Nation*, 119.
75 Stoliński, *Die deutsche Minderheit in Polen*, 42.

Silesia (annexed to Poland in June of that year) had opted not to join the other German socialists in participating in the Minorities Bloc. Failing to make any list at all, the German socialists in Upper Silesia were not represented in the Sejm elected in 1922, although they had two representatives in the regional parliament, the Silesian Sejm.[76] Despite the industrial infrastructure in Upper Silesia, socialism lagged among both Germans and Poles.[77] Although the Upper Silesian German socialists initially had a larger organization than the DAP in Łódź, they did not do as well, and throughout the 1920s they would lose influence to Łódź.[78] By 1930, the German socialists in Upper Silesia had only 3,200 members.[79]

The formal cooperation between German conservative-nationalists and German socialists in Central Poland ended early. The Deutsches Zentralwahlkomitee in Lodz was disbanded after the 1922 Sejm elections.[80] In the Łódź city council elections in 1923, the Deutsche Arbeitspartei Polens ran separately from the German conservative-nationalist camp, which had coalesced for the time being around the Bürgerliche Deutsche Partei. Despite lingering differences over the extent of minority rights, the German socialists tended to cooperate with the Polish socialists. Working with the PPS but running on their own list, the German socialists made a strong showing in the municipal elections. The DAP received 11,421 votes and five seats on the city council, while the more nationalist-oriented BDP received 5,581 votes and two seats.[81]

This contentious relationship continued with the new conservative-nationalist party, the Deutscher Volksverband. The DVV denounced socialism and there was bitter animosity between the two parties during elections.[82] Yet the German nationalists and socialists did not so much compete as complement one another. In principle, the German socialists tried to cooperate with the conservative-nationalist Germans in cultural and educational issues while refusing political work.[83] In practice, however, all minority cultural activity had political implications, and the DAP collaborated with the DVV on a wide variety of issues, especially when German cultural institutions were threatened. They could coexist because the two parties largely operated in separate spheres. During city council elections, the Łódź German voters tended to side with the socialists. The

---

76 Blachetta-Madajczyk, *Klassenkampf oder Nation*, 118–120.
77 Blanke, *Orphans of Versailles*, 61, 74.
78 Blachetta-Madajczyk, *Klassenkampf oder Nation*, 44, 84–85, 120, 168.
79 Blanke, *Orphans of Versailles*, 74.   80 Balling, *Von Reval bis Bukarest*, 187.
81 Heike, *Die deutsche Arbeiterbewegung in Polen*, 82; Stoliński, *Die deutsche Minderheit in Polen*, 59.
82 Cygański, *Mniejszość niemiecka w Polsce centralnej*, 29.
83 Hauser, "The German Minority in Poland," 23.

conservative-nationalist camp in Congress Poland fared better in the Sejm elections than in the Łódź city council elections because in the nationwide elections they could also count on the German voters in the countryside. Although each tailored their message to an urban or rural electorate, both claimed to serve German interests in Central Poland. Conservative and socialist parties were both essentially nationalist organizations: they faced the same task of mobilizing the German vote, and they both used the theme of cultural defense.[84]

Contrary to the claim made by Petra Blachetta-Madajczyk, the German socialists in Łódź were not any less shy of tackling nationality issues than their cohorts in Upper Silesia.[85] As a minority party in a nationalizing state, German socialists ranked national issues as high as – often even higher than – socialist goals, and a distinctly nationalist bent was apparent in DAP politics. After all, German socialists still relied on a voter base that identified itself first and foremost as German. Just like the conservative-nationalists, German socialists likewise feared that the Germans in Central Poland were somehow not national enough. Before the Sejm elections in November 1922, the newspaper of the Deutsche Arbeitspartei Polens had expressed its dissatisfaction with the political development of the Germans:

The vast majority of the Germans in Congress Poland is politically indifferent and unorganized. They are not this way because they are incapable of political thought and political organization, but because those who call themselves the leaders of Germandom have totally misinterpreted their role and taken the wrong path. We must change this path if we do not want to lead our Volkstum toward total degeneration.[86]

Although the German socialist author used "political" to mean socialist, it also implies national here. By warning of degeneration, the author argued that socialism was the right path to greater national consciousness among the Germans. It is apparent that the German socialists loathed the qualities associated with the lodzermensch just as much as the German nationalists.

For better or for worse, the Łódź German socialists were unable to abandon an agenda oriented toward German cultural concerns. Although historians such as Przemysław Hauser, Mirosław Cygański, and Otto Heike blame the growing nationalism among German groups for the fall of the German socialists, it is also likely that the socialists were hurt by the fact that their program remained *too* nationalist. Despite its cooperation with the

84 Breyer, *Das Deutsche Reich und Polen*, 249; Hauser, "The German Minority in Poland," 17.
85 Blachetta-Madajczyk, *Klassenkampf oder Nation*, 45.
86 *Die Arbeit*, March 22, 1922, untitled excerpt reprinted in Heike, *Die deutsche Arbeiterbewegung in Polen*, 81.

Polish socialists, the efforts to mobilize the German minority often made the DAP's commitment to socialism appear thin. The fact that the socialists concentrated on the same cultural themes decreased the differences between them and the conservative-nationalists; as a consequence, the DAP was in danger of losing its distinct position in Łódź politics. The difference between right and left, never great to begin with in minority politics, continued to shrink.

Despite the national outlook of the German socialists, however, others doubted the DAP's loyalty to the national cause. Although the German socialists were in most ways just as interested as the conservative-nationalists in maintaining a strong Germandom in Poland, the German Foreign Ministry and other authorities continued to see them as less capable in the nationality struggle. It was claimed that whereas Polish socialists were nationalist first and socialist second, the reverse was true for the German socialists.[87] The DAP's leadership, for example, did not send petitions to the League of Nations, a tactic through which the DAP hoped to show its loyalty to the Polish government.[88] No matter how tenaciously the DAP's members fought for German schools, they could only appear as a weaker alternative in protecting German cultural institutions. One writer in the conservative-nationalist camp noted that the two German socialist deputies from Łódź in the Polish Sejm could only be considered partial representatives of Germandom.[89] The German socialists fell between all the stools: they were too nationalist for the Poles and not nationalist enough for German conservative-nationalists and even the socialists in the Reich and Western Poland.

SOCIALISM AND REGIONALISM

The question of supraregional unification dogged the German socialists in Poland throughout the 1920s. There were early attempts to unify the various groupings, but their leaders recognized that the differing needs of the regional organizations remained the biggest problem.[90] In 1925, the various German socialist parties in Łódź, Bydgoszcz, Bielsko, and Katowice united to form the Deutsche Sozialistische Arbeitspartei Polens, which was based in Łódź. The DSAP joined the Socialist Workers' International the

---

87 Blachetta-Madajczyk, *Klassenkampf oder Nation*, 113–127, especially 121.
88 Blanke, *Orphans of Versailles*, 57.
89 Friedrich Heidelck, "Die Stellung des Deutschtums in Polen. Kritische Untersuchungen zu Zygmunt Stoliński. *Die deutsche Minderheit in Polen*," in *Deutsche Blätter in Polen* 6, no. 2 (February 1929): 49–104, here 77–78.
90 Blachetta-Madajczyk, *Klassenkampf oder Nation*, 79.

following year.[91] Like the German nationalists, the German socialists tried to work within the Polish system. While the nationalists cooperated with the other minorities in the Minorities Bloc, however, the socialists continued to ally themselves with parties of the ethnic majority, and primarily with the Polish Socialist Party. In the next Łódź city council elections on October 9, 1927, the German socialists, now organized as the DSAP, did even better than they had in the last local elections in 1923. The DSAP obtained 16,643 votes (seven seats in the city council, two more than in 1923), while the German conservative-nationalists grouped around the Deutscher Volksverband received 7,365 votes (three seats, only one more than in 1923).[92] Of the overall increase of 7,000 "German" votes since the last election in 1923, the socialists accounted for 5,000 of these.[93] The German socialists became the second largest party in Łódź, after the PPS.[94]

The Sejm and Senate elections of 1928, however, revealed once more the regionalist threat to the German socialists in Poland. There had been an attempt to work with other minority socialist organizations to form a single electoral bloc, but strong disagreements between the Jewish parties Bund and Poalej Syjon destroyed this possibility.[95] In the end, the DSAP campaigned with the PPS, although anti-Semitic tendencies in the latter made it difficult to cooperate with the Bund.[96] The DSAP leadership's decision not to participate in the Minorities Bloc was widely criticized not just by German nationalists but also within the German socialist camp.[97] The German socialist party in Western Poland, called the Deutsche Sozialdemokratische Partei Polens, followed an agenda more in tune with the German revisionist nationalism particular to that region.[98] Under the leadership Arthur Pankratz, the Western Polish German socialists tended to cooperate more with the local nationalist Deutschtumsbund than with Polish socialists or German socialists elsewhere in the country. Citing "different circumstances in Poznania-Pomerelia," Pankratz's socialists broke with the rest of the DSAP and ran on a list with the other German conservative-nationalist organizations in the Minorities Bloc.[99] The political schisms within the

---

91 Hauser, "The German Minority in Poland," 25.
92 Cygański, *Mniejszość niemiecka w Polsce centralnej*, 29; Blachetta-Madajczyk, *Klassenkampf oder Nation*, 84.
93 Heike, *Die deutsche Arbeiterbewegung in Polen*, 82–83.
94 Blachetta-Madajczyk, *Klassenkampf oder Nation*, 84.
95 Otto Heike, *Die deutsche Arbeiterbewegung in Polen*, 85.
96 Blachetta-Madajczyk, *Klassenkampf oder Nation*, 165.
97 "Für und wider den Minderheitenblock." January 14, 1928, *Bielitz-Bialer Deutsche Zeitung*, quoting the *Kattowitzer Zeitung* from January 12, 1928.
98 Blanke, *Orphans of Versailles*, 74.
99 Blachetta-Madajczyk, *Klassenkampf oder Nation*, 51; Harald von Riekhoff, *German-Polish Relations, 1918–1933* (Baltimore: The Johns Hopkins University Press, 1971), 210.

Table 3.1. *1928 Sejm Elections: Results in Łódź*

PPS (with DSAP)	74,100 votes	(3 seats)
Communists	49,200 votes	(2 seats)
BBWR	44,000 votes	(1 seat)
Minorities Bloc (with DVV)	31,900 votes	(1 seat)
Bund	12,500 votes	
Deutscher Bürgerblock	6,300 votes	
Others	39,200 votes[100]	

socialist camp coincided with regional cleavages, and the German socialists in Western Poland found more in common with fellow residual Reich citizens than with other socialists, German or otherwise. As with German minority activity more generally, German socialism in Poland could be regionally differentiated between its Reich-oriented, secessionist western and Poland-oriented, unification eastern variants.

Overall, German organizations overall fared even better in the 1928 Sejm and Senate elections than in 1922, with a total of twenty-one mandates compared to the previous seventeen. The socialists, however, did not improve their position, doing worse than the conservative-nationalists. Significantly, Łódź remained the stronghold of German socialism, in large part due to the general dominance of socialism there, as the results for the Sejm elections in the city show (see Table 3.1).

Given the mixed constituencies of these parties, it is not possible to determine how many socialist votes were actually "German." Nor do the statistics allow for a precise counting of how many Germans answered the call of the DVV to vote for the Minorities Bloc. Notably, the moderate Deutscher Bürgerblock received a high percentage of the overall estimated number of Germans in Łódź. All the same, the intra-German divisions between the socialist city and the nationalist small town/countryside offered a repeat of the elections of 1923: of the five German Sejm delegates elected from Central Poland in 1928, the socialist Emil Zerbe won the only German seat from Łódź city. Arthur Kronig, the other DSAP delegate, did not win a district but came in on the state list again. Of the German nationalists, August Utta won his seat from the Łódź region (excluding the city), Jakob Karau came from Włocławek, and Julian Will – the only change in the Sejm lineup from Central Poland – represented Konin. The only senator from Central Poland representing a German party was Joseph Spickermann, who

100 Blachetta-Madajczyk, *Klassenkampf oder Nation*, 167–168.

belonged to the DVV and replaced Karl Stüldt. Spickermann was elected from a district encompassing the entire Voivodeship of Łódź.[101]

Although the DSAP was able to hold on to its seats, the divisions and weaknesses in the DSAP were evident. While Arthur Kronig and Emil Zerbe from Łódź sat with the PPS fraction in the Sejm, Arthur Pankratz from Bydgoszcz sat with the conservative-nationalists in the German parliamentarian club.[102] Significantly, the Upper Silesian German socialists failed once again to get a Sejm seat despite their large organization, nor did they do well in the communal elections at the end of 1929.[103] The Silesian weakness within the German socialist movement in Poland resulted in the decision by the DSAP in Katowice in 1929 to recognize Łódź as the official seat of the party, thus ending four years of uncertain rivalry.[104] Still, regional tensions continued to express themselves in various ways. German socialists in Central Poland, for example, were often seen as more energetic than elsewhere.[105] In general, the German socialists in Łódź had an easier time working with their Polish cohorts, whereas the bad feelings induced by the plebiscite and violence of the early 1920s haunted German-Polish cooperation in Upper Silesia.[106]

The Reich's preferential treatment for the formerly Prussian parts of Poland was apparent in the case of the German socialists as well, especially in the subsidies to socialist newspapers. Upper Silesian German socialists maintained their own paper, the *Volksstimme*, which later became the *Volkswille*. The Bydgoszcz paper was called the *Bromberger Volkszeitung*, and the DSAP newspaper in Łódź was called the *Lodzer Volkszeitung*. The German state provided subsidies for all German socialist papers in the 1920s, although the Upper Silesian paper received considerably more (about RM 5,000 per month) than the paper belonging to the more successful organization in Łódź (about RM 2,000 per month). Between May 1928 and April 1930, the Łódź newspaper received no subsidies at all; and until January 1933, it received small subsidies on an irregular basis. The Upper Silesian *Volkswille* received a reduced monthly amount of RM 3,300, and the *Bromberger Volkszeitung* in Pomerelia received RM 900 per month in this period. That the Bydgoszcz German socialists received anything at all is probably due to their town's strategic placement within the Corridor. The German socialist newspaper in Bielsko in formerly Austrian Silesia received just a one-time

101 Stoliński, *Die deutsche Minderheit in Polen,* 40.
102 Heike, *Die deutsche Arbeiterbewegung in Polen,* 85; Hauser, "The German Minority in Poland," 28.
103 Blachetta-Madajczyk, *Klassenkampf oder Nation,* 84.
104 Heike, *Die deutsche Arbeiterbewegung in Polen,* 85.
105 Blachetta-Madajczyk, *Klassenkampf oder Nation,* 85–86.
106 Blachetta-Madajczyk, *Klassenkampf oder Nation,* 157, 163.

payment of RM 2,000 in August 1929.[107] The Germans' political successes in the late 1920s were short-lived, for the Polish government began to crack down on minority political organizations at the end of the 1920s. In November 1930, all German parties throughout Poland won a total of only five seats in the Sejm and three seats in the Senate.[108] The pressure by the Poles and their own internal divisions made the Deutscher Volksverband and the German socialists susceptible to another German organization that sought accommodation with the Polish state on a radically loyalist basis.

DEUTSCHER KULTUR- UND WIRTSCHAFTSBUND

What seemed even more menacing than the socialists to the German national activists was the rise of a pro-Polish organization in the early 1930s, the Deutscher Kultur- und Wirtschaftsbund (German Cultural and Economic Association, DKuWB).[109] Johannes Danielewski founded the DKuWB in Łódź in 1929. The idea for the organization originally came from the Upper Silesian Voivode Michał Grażyński, but Łódź soon became the party's stronghold.[110] The DKuWB advanced itself as the only German organization that was truly loyal to the Polish state. The banner of the association's newspaper, *Der Volksbote,* proclaimed the newspaper to be a "weekly paper for politics, culture, economics, and understanding." Danielewski's program of cooperating with the Polish government led the Polish Advertising Agency's catalog of periodicals to list the political orientation of *Der Volksbote* as "sanacja" (the Polish government bloc).[111] One 1932 article in the *Der Volksbote* claimed that German-Polish reconciliation could only be achieved if the minority cut off all political contacts with Germany. It asserted that the other German parties, including the DVV and the DSAP, were in the pay of the revisionist Weimar government and warned that any association with those parties would make the German minority appear disloyal, and a Polish backlash against Germans would inevitably result.[112] The paper accused German cultural organizations, such as the German boy scouts (*Pfadfinder*), of anti-Polish attitudes and militarism.[113] The DKuWB also voiced suspicions of corruption in connection with subsidies to the

---

107 Blachetta-Madajczyk, *Klassenkampf oder Nation*, 130–133.
108 Hauser, "The German Minority in Poland," 30.
109 Hauser, "The German Minority in Poland," 31.
110 Blachetta-Madajczyk, *Klassenkampf oder Nation*, 69.
111 Franciszek Krajna, *Katalog Prasowy PARa. Rocznik IX 1934–35* (Poznań: Polska Agencja Reklamy, 1934–1935).
112 "Urteilsmotive in Gymnasiumprozeß," *Deutscher Volksbote*, January 31, 1932, in AP Łódź.
113 "Jugend und Pazifismus," *Deutscher Volksbote*, January 17, 1932, in AP Łódź.

minority, especially about minority functionaries in Western Poland and Upper Silesia.[114] In a letter to Ewald Ammende, the leader of the European Nationalities Congress,[115] the DKuWB claimed that the paid "Prussian agents" and the Reich-supported minority press only wanted to use the Germans in Congress Poland as "electoral chattel" (*Stimmvieh*), but that these supposed German leaders would not support the Germans in their economic and cultural needs.[116] Such statements suggested that helping the local DSAP or DVV would serve the interests of the Germans in Western Poland more than the Germans in Central Poland.

There has been little research on the DKuWB, and historians have tended to take a negative view of the organization. Richard Blanke, for example, notes that the organization, funded by the Polish government, was corrupt and "openly collaborationist."[117] Likewise, Petra Blachetta-Madajczyk sees the DKuWB as an example of the Polish government's "undemocratic measures" against the minority, with the goal of being divisive and assimilationist. Besides assessing the organization as ultimately unsuccessful, she also repeats the oft-claimed view that the loosely affiliated *Neue Lodzer Zeitung* was "nationally indifferent."[118] Indeed, German nationalists of the time considered the *Neue Lodzer Zeitung*, a liberal German daily newspaper, to be too friendly to Poland and an organ of the "bourgeois" elements in Łódź.[119] Yet the *Neue Lodzer Zeitung* often carried articles that were similar in tone to nationalist newspapers when standing up for German cultural institutions, and the newspaper commonly reprinted nationalist articles from Western Polish German newspapers.[120] The stigma remained even though German nationalists often used the paper's printing presses. During the Second World War, one German minority leader, the pastor Eduard Kneifel,

---

114 "Die deutsche Minderheit am Scheideweg," *Deutscher Volksbote. Wochenschrift für Politik, Kultur, Wirtschaft und Verständigung – Organ des deutschen Kultur- und Wirtschaftsbundes in Polen*, September 20, 1931, sent as attachment by Polish Interior Ministry (M. Sochański) to Polish Foreign Ministry, Wydział Zachodni, September 22, 1931, in AAN, MSZ, folder 2234, 22–25, here 24.

115 For an excellent account of the European Nationalities Congress, see Sabine Bamberger-Stemmann, *Der Europäische Nationalitätenkongreß 1925 bis 1938. Nationale Minderheiten zwischen Lobbyistentum und Großmachtinteressen* (Marburg: Verlag Herder-Institut, 2000).

116 Deutscher Kultur- und Wirtschaftsbund (Bundesvorstand) to Ammende, September 6, 1931, copy sent by Gebauer to Polish Interior Ministry, undated but received September 21, 1931, in AAN, MSW, 1003, 18–24, here 19–20.

117 Blanke, *Orphans of Versailles*, 93.

118 Blachetta-Madajczyk, *Klassenkampf oder Nation*, 68–69.

119 German Passport Agency in Łódź (Drubba) to German Foreign Ministry, February 6, 1922, in PAAA, Pol IV, Politik 25 Polen, vol. 9, R82189, 22–23; Heidelck, "Die Stellung des Deutschtums in Polen," 82.

120 Maria Dehmer, "Die deutsche Minderheit in Lodz nach dem Ersten Weltkrieg bis zum Ende der Ära Pilsudski (1920–1931). Die Schulpolitik anhand ihrer Darstellung in der *Neuen Lodzer Zeitung*" (M.A. thesis, University of Konstanz, 1999), 4–5, 21, 25, 28.

also referred to the newspaper as the organ of the lodzermenschen,[121] and Theodor Bierschenk considered it "Polonophile."[122] The DKuWB seemed to concentrate those nationally suspect elements that were despised by the German Consul in Łódź and the nationalist German press.

It would be more accurate, however, to say that the organization's membership reflected the complexities of different pressures on the German minority. Professionals, especially civil servants, may have joined the organization to advance their careers. The growing tensions between Weimar Germany and Poland probably encouraged many a wary German-speaker to join up with the government-backed German party as insurance against possible reprisals. Still, coercion had many faces, and support by the Polish government does not exclude the possibility that the organization enjoyed genuine support from a wide spectrum of German minority members. In important ways, the DKuWB was a continuation of the Bürgerliche Deutsche Partei of the mid-1920s. As a pacifist organization with a German profile seeking reconciliation and compromise, it may have found fertile ground among the Łódź Germans. Notably, the DKuWB also functioned as a protest party against the allegedly chauvinistic nationalism that ran in both the DVV and the DSAP. The Germans in the DKuWB could thus do something against what they perceived to be a hijacking of local minority politics by the Germans in Western Poland and a growing dependency on the Reich government.

The DKuWB grew quickly in the early 1930s, causing anxiety among the other German parties.[123] It also attempted to gain a foothold in Volhynia, a development that must have been worrisome to the German nationalists who had just discovered this supposedly young Germandom, as described previously. In turn, the Deutscher Volksverband and the German socialists were united in their bitter criticism of the DKuWB, denouncing it as a puppet of the Polish government. Their contempt led many to call it simply the "Danielewski-Bund" or the "Kultur- und Wirtschaftsbund," consciously questioning or omitting the adjective "Deutscher."[124] As expected, the greatest conflict between the DKuWB and the traditional German parties arose over the issue of German education. The DKuWB's accusations of subversive activity in the Lodzer Deutsches Gymnasium caused the high school's administrators to take legal action against Danielewski and other

---

121 Kneifel, "Adolf Eichler – Ein Leben im Dienste des Deutschtums," 15–16.
122 Theodor Bierschenk, *Die deutsche Volksgruppe in Polen, 1934–1939* (Würzburg: Holzner, 1954), 52.
123 Hauser, "The German Minority in Poland," 31.
124 "Die Jungdeutsche Partei erkennt Versailler Vertrag an," *Volkszeitung*, December 2, 1934, in PAAA, Pol IV, Politik 25 Polen, vol. 34, R82214, 58.

DKuWB members; not surprisingly, a court trial the next year acquitted the defendants of slander.[125]

In September 1931, the DKuWB also tried to organize German teachers in the Verband deutscher Lehrer in Polen, which competed with the older organization, the Deutscher Lehrerverein. Initially, forty-two German teachers joined, and this development spurred the DSAP and the DVV to campaign against the supposed threat within the minority to German schools and the German community. For German nationalist and socialist activists, the DKuWB-backed association seemed to be a manifestation of increasing Polonization. One article from the socialist newspaper *Volkszeitung* on September 23, 1931, reveals the typical tactic of shaming the 42 German teachers for their decision to join the Verband deutscher Lehrer in Polen while simultaneously showing some understanding for their dilemma:

Whoever is impressed by the number of 42 should consider that the teachers were forced to come together, for besides a few hard-bitten careerists, no one went there voluntarily. The fear of being fired drove the teachers together, just as fear drives together the sheep to the slaughter.... Necessity will break iron.... The Verband deutscher Lehrer thus exists. Forty-two people have found their way to Danielewski, and these people are ready to commit moral suicide. Teachers are in the process of digging a grave for teachers! Gravediggers! This word will stick to these people. Forever.... And it is an ugly word. It carries the stench of corpses. It is not honorable to be a hangman.[126]

This passage plays not only upon how German teachers and their organizations were helpless vis-à-vis the Polish government ("like sheep to the slaughter") but also how concerns about their jobs had made these Germans willing to commit "moral suicide" and to become the "gravedigger" for Germanness in Łódź. These purported turncoats would always have the "stench of corpses" about them. Here, the socialists pleaded that only an intensified national consciousness, wrought by active political participation, could successfully defend German rights and culture. Although the influence of the DKuWB remained minimal, the heated rhetoric signaled a shift in Łódź German politics. A more hostile atmosphere now replaced the previously tense but practical coexistence of the DSAP and DVV. The allegedly assimilationist DKuWB uncovered the confusion and insecurity of these mainstream German parties, which became increasingly

---

125 Heike, *Das deutsche Schulwesen in Mittelpolen*, 87–88.
126 "Der Sänger seiner eigenen Schande," *Volkszeitung*, September 21, 1931, reprinted in Heike, *Das deutsche Schulwesen in Mittelpolen*, 106–108. Significantly, Otto Heike referred to this DKuWB-affiliated organization as "morally very questionable."

worried by the apparent ease with which Germans could lose their national consciousness.

Yet the attacks on the DKuWB also wrought collateral damage in the project of building a Volksgemeinschaft in Poland. In their attempts to undermine the DKuWB, the established parties in Western Poland played upon regional antagonisms. Indeed, one could see an attempt to localize and quarantine the danger. In the eyes of many Germans, the DKuWB was the political manifestation of the national apathy that accompanied the stereotype of the lodzermensch. A short circular by the Deutsche Vereinigung to farmers in Western Poland played upon such fears and resentments. The juxtaposition of "our local Germandom" against the "Lodzer party" (used three times) was unmistakable: The "Lodzer gentlemen" and "elements from Łódź" were foreign not only in a geographical sense but also in a national one. The writer's references to the DKuWB as German-speaking makes clear that the group was not properly German, but a crypto-Polish organization in actuality.[127] By operating on stereotypes associated with the lodzermensch, the German author from Western Poland ethnically and territorially externalized the national threat to Łódź.

DEFINING THE MARGINS: THE REVIVAL OF THE LODZERMENSCH

Łódź Germans represented the largest concentration of German-speakers in Poland.[128] Moreover, Łódź set the tone for German political activity in the rest of Central Poland. As the German population in Central Poland grew, so should have Łódź's role in the political life of the German minority. Despite the fact that German socialists were just as adamant about protecting Germandom as the German conservative-nationalists, the two camps together in Central Poland had difficulty in converting their political achievements into a leadership role within the minority as a whole. Throughout the 1920s and early 1930s, Łódź remained a periphery in German minority activity. It was not only the geographic position of these Germans in the central and eastern parts of Poland that made them less important to the Reich's revisionist plans; reinforcing this second-class status was the discursive position these Germans occupied on the totem pole of Germanness. This hierarchy

---

127 Hauptgeschäftsstelle der Deutschen Vereinigung (Wiese), "Deutsche Bauern und Volksgenossen!" Bromberg/Bydgoszcz, dated October 1933, sent as attachment by Major Szaliński, Sztab Główny, Oddział II to Suchenek-Suchecki, head of the Nationalities Department in the Polish Interior Ministry, memorandum "Kontrakcja Niemców b. zaboru pruskiego przeciw łódzkiemu towarzystwu 'Kultur und Wirtschaftsbund,'" January 8, 1934, in AAN, MSW, folder 1003, 4–6.

128 Bielsko (Bielitz), on the other hand, had the highest percentage of Germans of any city in Poland. See Blanke, *Orphans of Versailles*, 3.

within the minority drew upon preexisting conceptions that saw a west-east gradient in the German settlements in Central and Eastern Europe.[129]

The previous chapter showed how the Volhynian Germans were "orientalized" and in a sense colonized by the Germans in Western Poland and Bielsko. Łódź was likewise marginalized in this discourse because the local Germans were perceived to be somehow less German than the Germans in Western Poland. The process of ascribing regional similarities and differences was also an expression of power relations within the German minority in Poland. Western Polish Germans strove to educate the German-speakers in Poland's eastern regions about how to become better Germans. Although Łódź Germans themselves were not necessarily the primary focus of such efforts, they were collectively part of those non-Prussian Germans in need of guidance, be it moral, political, or financial, from their brethren in Western Poland.

In part, the west-east phantom borders within the minority were reinforced by the general lack of contact with one another, which then distorted the experience and meaning of the rare encounters that occurred. Gotthold Rhode attended the Schiller Gymnasium in Poznań between 1924 and 1934. Later a professor in West Germany, he suggested in an essay written in 1986 how exotic the Germans in Central Poland had been to the Poznań Germans. There were no school excursions or hiking trips from Poznań to Łódź. Sport competitions took place with other German schools in Poznania and Pomerelia, but not with those in Łódź.[130] As Rhode recalls, the chance meeting between Poznań and Łódź youth would take place in Berlin, when they encountered one another at the train station on their way to holiday camps for children. On such occasions, the Poznań German teenagers would note how the Łódź German girls were more promiscuous in dress and makeup; the Poseners, on the other hand, dressed "faithfully German." The Łódź German youth also appeared to be "more generous" in purchasing bananas, chocolate, and souvenirs. Their Poznań counterparts, according to Rhode, were raised to be frugal even when they came from well-to-do families and would only buy "useful" things.[131] Rhode tried to make light of the differences, stressing how the two regions were just variant expressions of Germanness in Poland. What others may have seen as financial profligacy, as Rhode seemed to suggest, he ultimately deemed

---

129 Breyer, *Das Deutsche Reich*, 232.
130 Gotthold Rhode, "Lodzer Deutsche – Posener Deutsche. Keine wissenschaftliche Untersuchung, sondern eine Plauderei," in *Suche die Meinung. Karl Dedecius, dem Übersetzer und Mittler zum 65. Geburtstag*, ed. Elvira Grözinger and Andreas Lawaty, 237–256 (Wiesbaden: Harrassowitz, 1986), here 244–245.
131 Rhode, "Lodzer Deutsche – Posener Deutsche," 245–246.

as generosity. Yet Rhode's descriptions of this interaction reveal not just the lack of contact between the Germans, but also the Poseners' preconceived notions of the eastern Germans, easternness, and the relations of power within the minority. Rhode's aside about how the "mostly well-to-do and cultivated" Jewish schoolchildren at the German Gymnasium in Poznań disdainfully treated their "Ostjuden" classmates from Congress Poland could also stand in for the Posener–Lodzer relationship.[132] Living together did not necessarily erode stereotypes between Germans but reinforced them.

Such hierarchical understandings of Germanness corresponded to the belief that the nation-state embodied and fostered the highest form of national consciousness. As former citizens of the Reich, the Germans in Western Poland felt themselves to be more advanced economically, culturally, and nationally than the Germans in the formerly Russian and Austrian regions. Excluded from any experience of life in the German nation-state, the diaspora Germans in Central and Eastern Poland were often considered culturally inferior and less supportive of the German (i.e., the Reich's) cause. Their passive acceptance, even enthusiasm, for the new Polish state did not (yet) square with the revisionist aims of the German leaders in Western Poland and in Germany, and the more völkisch-minded nationalists were alarmed by the apparent ease with which these Germans seemed to suppress their national consciousness. The widespread fear that the Germans in Central and Eastern Poland were somehow not national enough was reflected in their stigmatization.

Differing relationships to the Polish and German states seemed to dovetail with such understandings. In her analysis of the German language press in Poland, Beata Lakeberg has noted that the Łódź Germans often used the term "Polish-speaking Germans" or "Polish Germans," whereas the Germans in Western Poland tended to use "German minority" to describe their situation. Lakeberg suggests that Germans in Łódź seemed to be more accepting of the Polish state than those Germans in Western Poland.[133] Yet there is the danger of equating this stance of the Łódź Germans as being intrinsically less nationalistic (because not revisionist), nationally indifferent, or even pro-Polish.[134] Even a German nationalism not centered on the

---

132 Rhode, "Lodzer Deutsche – Posener Deutsche," 244.

133 Beata Lakeberg, "Identitätsfragen in der deutschen Minderheitenpresse während der ersten Jahre der Zweiten Polnischen Republik," in *Grenzdiskurse. Zeitungen deutschsprachiger Minderheiten und ihr Feuilleton in Mitteleuropa bis 1939*, ed. Sibylle Schönborn, 81–93 (Essen: Klartext, 2009), 83–86; Beata Lakeberg, *Die deutsche Minderheitenpresse in Polen 1918–1939 und ihr Polen- und Judenbild* (Frankfurt/Main: Peter Lang, 2010), 136–140, 148–149.

134 Tara Zahra suggests this connection between national indifference and the lodzermensch: "Imagined Non-Communities," 103–104.

Reich was still nationalism. German activists in Łódź felt that they were doing their part for the German cause, even if it was not popular for fellow nationalists elsewhere. Accepting programmatic statements of a somehow lesser German nationalism in Central Poland also contributes to a romanticized, idyllic vision of prewar Łódź, which in turn serves as evidence of proto-multiculturalism and cultivates a "good German" myth.

The important point here is to understand how these perceptions of national hierarchy were deployed to construct a pecking order of regions. Left on the discursive and political margins and relatively underfunded by the Reich, the Germans in the eastern regions of Poland formed what could be termed the minority's underclass. As is common in such views, a sense of differentiation often evolves to naturalize this lower status. Indeed, intra-ethnic categories within the German minority drew on elements of racism, such as hierarchy and the immutability of certain characteristics, without being explicitly racial. As Eric Weitz has argued about Soviet nationality policy, racialized categories can exist without the concept of race itself.[135] Even for Germans seemingly contaminated by life in the East, their national defects did not easily go away even after long exposure to their western cousins. The German consulate in Toruń reported complaints about those Germans "of Russian citizenship" who had been resettled in Prussian Poland by the Settlement Commission in the Imperial period. The "local and established" Germans believed that the immigrants were politically less reliable because they tended to vote with the Poles; moreover, there were rumors that one should treat them with caution in business relations.[136] The differentiation was also racial in the sense that this inferiority was genetic and passed on from generation to generation. Not biological determinants per se, but the poor conditions in the countryside as well as the urban milieu in Łódź reproduced this problem by acting as incubators for this underclass. Moreover, the fears of cross-cultural contamination and racial mixing with Poles and Jews led many German nationalists to see Łódź as a nest of "renegade Germandom." As Gotthold Rhode notes, the Germans in Łódź used many more Slavic words, and even their grammatical construction of German seemed to have been influenced by the Polish double negative.[137] For some, this was a sign not just of linguistic and cultural decline but also national and even racial contamination.

---

135 Eric Weitz, "Racial Politics Without the Concept of Race: Reevaluating Soviet Ethnic and National Purges," *Slavic Review* 61, no. 1 (Spring 2002): 1–29, here 3–8.

136 Consulate in Toruń (Mulert) to German Foreign Ministry, "Polnische Strömungen unter den Rückwanderern aus Kongresspolen," April 24, 1924, in PAAA, Pol IV, Politik 25 Polen, vol. 17, R82197, 187.

137 Rhode, "Lodzer Deutsche – Posener Deutsche," 246.

Although observers may have seen an inadequately German elite as part of the problem, they also perceived the lack of national consciousness as a general affliction among the Łódź Germans. Rightist ideologues especially found it difficult to fit the urban and socialist-leaning Lodzers into their conceptions of what Germandom outside of the Reich should be. As we have seen, conservative-nationalist groupings dominated German political life in Western Poland, but they were considerably weaker than the socialists in Łódź. Especially the growth of the pro-Polish DKuWB in the city reinforced the purported dangers of Łódź for the rest of the German minority.[138] The organization appeared to be the political embodiment of the lodzermensch, and its mere existence confirmed fears of the increasing Polonization of the Germans and the decreasing potency of the German national cause in Łódź. Only against this background is it possible to understand why a small group such as the apparently pro-Polish Deutscher Kultur und Wirtschaftsbund created so much anxiety among German activists in Poland and officials in the Reich.

REICH AUTHORITIES AND THE MARGINALIZATION OF ŁÓDŹ

In order to explain this apparent anomaly of the anational German, Reich officials, minority leaders, and Ostforscher regurgitated and applied the trope of the lodzermensch throughout the 1920s. Especially Reich authorities invoked stereotypes associated with the lodzermensch when it served a particular cause. Paul Drubba, head of the Reich's passport agency in Łódź, did not hold the local Germans in high regard.[139] As we have already seen in the previous chapter, he advocated a unified minority position, but with the formerly Prussian Germans taking the lead. He complained that the wealthy Germans in Łódź were largely politically passive and indifferent, as well as only interested in making money. Drubba argued that the local Germans must be made aware that they were not alone, and that there were Germans in other parts of Poland who were fighting for Germandom. Their example, Drubba claimed, would strengthen the local Germans' backbone and help them become "conscious Germans" once more. He said it was good that the local Germans were slowly beginning to acknowledge their

---

138 Prussian Minister for Science, Art, and Public Education, July 1, 1931, in Staatsarchiv Münster, StAM VII no. 35, microfiche 5952. My thanks to Brian McCook for bringing this document to my attention.

139 Drubba helped set up the passport agency in September 1920. He served there until September 1922, becoming consul in July 1922. Maria Keipert and Peter Grupp (Auswärtiges Amt, Historischer Dienst), *Biographisches Handbuch des deutschen Auswärtigen Dienstes 1871–1945*, vol. 1: A–F (Paderborn: Ferdinand Schöningh, 2000), 464–465.

Germanness as well as their own faults. Still, Drubba noted that the German nationalists there could not succeed on their own. Although he recognized that the local German Sejm deputies, Friese and Spickermann, had possessed "a certain courage" to run as German candidates in Poland, Drubba dismissed them as "decent average people." There had to be "new blood" brought to the local Germandom, with leaders who were at least on a par with their opponents.[140] Although Drubba did not specify where this new talent should come from, he advocated several months later (in November 1921) the "immediate personal influence" of German leaders from Western Poland.[141] In another memo later that month, Drubba argued that "the rotten construction" of the Łódź Germans had to be propped up and improved in order to prevent its collapse. Only later could one lay a new foundation and build a superstructure that would make the Germans in Poland into a "unified organism."[142] In short, there had to be a transformation within the Łódź German community before it could be incorporated into the larger minority-building project, for which the Western Polish regions were supposed to serve as a model and template.

Yet at the same time, Drubba understood that the attempt to construct a unified German minority would require acknowledging and preserving the dignity of the Germans in the non-Prussian regions. The German Foreign Ministry had been upset by Łódź German leader Eduard von Behrens for his role in proposing a loyalty telegram at the first Congress of the Germans in Poland in 1921.[143] As we have already seen, the resulting tensions between German delegates from Łódź and Western Poland had almost wrecked this important meeting for German unity. In October 1921, a month after the congress, Drubba stated that he himself had heard rumors that Behrens was "a drunkard and politically unreliable." Still, Drubba defended Behrens by stating the following principle for the whole German population of Łódź: "In my reports I have always stressed the fact that the local Germans cannot be judged by Reich German standards, but that that is no reason to doubt their reliability in völkisch terms, at least not in those circles that openly declare themselves for Germandom."[144] In another report one

---

140 German Passport Agency in Łódź (Drubba) to German Foreign Ministry, April 27, 1921, in PAAA, Pol IV, Politik 25 Polen, vol. 4, R82184, 105–106.

141 German Passport Agency in Łódź (Drubba) to German Foreign Ministry, November 12, 1921, in PAAA, Pol IV, Politik 25 Polen, vol. 8, R82188, 17.

142 German Passport Agency in Łódź (Drubba) to German Foreign Ministry, November 20, 1921, in PAAA, Pol IV, Politik 25 Polen, vol. 8, R82188, 48–50.

143 Draft of letter from German Foreign Ministry to German Passport Agency in Łódź, October 31, 1921, in PAAA, Pol IV, Politik 25 Polen, vol. 7, R82187, 151.

144 German Passport Agency in Łódź (Drubba) to German Foreign Ministry, October 20, 1921, in PAAA, Pol IV, Politik 25 Polen, vol. 7, R82187, 149–150.

month later, Drubba explained that Behrens had grown up and studied in the Russian Empire, thus accounting for why he had so little comprehension of Germany, Reich German thinking, and Reich German policies. Behrens' alleged lack of "correct understanding" was responsible for his apparent deviant behavior, for he had no idea of how far he could push an issue. At the same time, Drubba called Behrens an "undoubtedly German leader" and considered him to be völkisch reliable, despite his strong political orientation toward Russia. Behrens had told Drubba that he (Behrens) had to "play the Polish patriot" occasionally in order to create a "political alibi" for his sharp attacks against the Polish government. Indeed, the Polish government had just initiated legal proceedings against Behrens for an article he had written in the *Freie Presse*. According to Drubba, Behrens had also backtracked from the controversial loyalty statement that he had demanded at the beginning of the Congress of the Germans in Poland. Behrens explained that he had merely wanted a telegram informing the president and premier that the congress was to take place. Drubba pointed out that all the German leaders in Łódź had felt the same way as Behrens on this issue. In any case, Behrens was not just the best but the "only horse in the stable." Drubba repeated the mantra of optimism that there was growing solidarity of Germans in Central Poland with the formerly Prussian areas, and that Behrens would never do such a thing again. In Drubba's view, the task at hand was to build a Germandom in Łódź on a purely völkisch basis, and an understanding for Reich policies would grow by itself.[145]

Drubba's conflation of state and völkisch interests was typical for many Reich German observers. Although Drubba claimed that the local Germans should not be judged according to Reich German standards, he constantly did so himself and reduced German needs to Reich German policy. Not just his position as consul, but also his background facilitated the need to see the East as backward and as needing help. Drubba, who had studied Turkish languages at the Seminar für orientalische Sprachen in Berlin and served in the German consulate in Beirut before the First World War,[146] was well suited to "orientalize" the Germans in the East. Drubba's statements expressed the tension in the view of these Germans in Poland. On the one hand, he believed that Germans in the former Congress Kingdom lacked real leaders and needed guidance from Germans in Western Poland,[147] who

---

145 German Passport Agency in Łódź (Drubba) to German Foreign Ministry, November 20, 1921, in PAAA, Pol IV, Politik 25 Polen, vol. 8, R82188, 48–50.
146 Keipert and Grupp, *Biographisches Handbuch*, vol. 1: A–F, 464–465.
147 German Passport Agency in Łódź (Drubba) to German Foreign Ministry, November 12, 1921, in PAAA, Pol IV, Politik 25 Polen, vol. 8, R82188, 17.

in his opinion were probably justified in feeling "intellectually superior" vis-à-vis the local Germans.[148] Hence, the reins of power within the minority were to remain in the hands of the formerly Prussian Germans in Western Poland. On the other hand, Drubba argued, this superiority should not be made too obvious. The Germans in Central Poland should be given the feeling that they were needed and respected, especially after the Germans in Western Poland had bruised their dignity by sending a complaint to the League of Nations without consulting them first.[149] This embittering experience of the Łódź Germans would have serious consequences for the unity of the minority. All the same, Drubba believed that the German leaders in Western Poland should not give up on the Germans in the East; otherwise the process would lead to even greater mistrust.[150] Yet Drubba's push for greater cooperation boiled down to a tactical maneuver to save the peace between east and west and to rein in the Central Polish Germans. This task was all the more urgent in light of the political necessities. The German embassy in Warsaw was concerned that the "unpolitical posture" of the Łódź Germans could hurt the German cause.[151] It was clear that Reich German officials considered the Łódź Germans to be a threat to their vision of a German minority in Poland.

In 1922, the passport agency in Łódź became a consulate, and Hermann Hoffmann-Fölkersamb replaced Drubba. Originally from the Alsace region, Hoffmann-Fölkersamb, like Drubba, had studied Turkish languages at the Seminar für orientalische Sprachen in Berlin. He even received his degree (Diplom) in Turkish the day after Drubba, on July 19, 1896. As a university student, Hoffmann-Fölkersamb had led high school pupils from Berlin-Steglitz on excursions that would become the Wandervogel movement. After joining the diplomatic corps, he served in various posts during the war in Damascus, Haifa, and Aleppo.[152] Like his predecessor, Hoffmann-Fölkersamb lamented in 1925 the apparent lack of national consciousness of the Łódź Germans – both socialists and non-socialists – while half-admiring the national tenaciousness of the Poles in Łódź: "The German

148 German Passport Agency in Łódź (Drubba) to German Foreign Ministry, December 7, 1921, in PAAA, Pol IV, Politik 25 Polen, vol. 8, R82188, 189–193.
149 German Passport Agency in Łódź (Drubba) to German Foreign Ministry, December 7, 1921, in PAAA, Pol IV, Politik 25 Polen, vol. 8, R82188, 189–193.
150 German Passport Agency in Łódź (Drubba) to German Foreign Ministry, November 12, 1921, in PAAA, Pol IV, Politik 25 Polen, vol. 8, R82188, 17.
151 German Embassy in Warsaw (Schoen) to German Foreign Ministry, telegram dated September 12, 1921, in PAAA, Pol IV, Politik 25 Polen, vol. 7, R82187, 33.
152 Maria Keipert and Peter Grupp (Auswärtiges Amt, Historischer Dienst), ed., *Biographisches Hand-buch des deutschen Auswärtigen Dienstes 1871–1945*, vol. 2: G–K (Paderborn: Ferdinand Schöningh, 2005), 339–341.

is simply . . . in the first place a socialist or a bourgeois, and in second place or even lower a German. The Pole is a Pole in the first place." He also complained that Russian rule had left the Germans "ethnically socio-politically divided."[153] Yet Hoffmann-Fölkersamb also did little to promote a more German nationalist cause, in part because he felt (in contradiction to his other statements) that the local Germans were doing well on their own, and in part because he did not want to spoil his good relations with Polish officials.[154] Hoffmann-Fölkersamb stated that he had been wary of reporting problems to the Foreign Ministry because he knew that Reich finances were in a dire situation. Again, he noted that the Łódź Germans were "too accustomed" to self-help when it came to providing for their cultural needs – a sentence that seemed to have drawn a puzzled reaction from the desk officer at the German Foreign Ministry.[155] Hoffmann-Fölkersamb's claims of a self-sufficient German community, it seems, did not square with his previous and oft-repeated statements about the lack of an active Germandom.[156]

Erich von Luckwald replaced Hoffmann-Fölkersamb in 1926 and served as consular head in Łódź until 1932.[157] Luckwald was more aggressive in getting support from the Reich for the Germans in Central Poland. Luckwald and the German ambassador in Warsaw did have a vested interest in supporting Utta and the Germans in Central Poland. They wanted the German voice in their respective jurisdictions (Łódź in particular, Poland as a whole) to increase: the more German votes and political influence, the better the results would reflect on them. By advocating the needs of "their" Germans and showing their progress, Foreign Ministry officials could show that they were doing a good job. Consul Luckwald especially asserted that the Germans in "Congress Poland" (like many of his contemporaries, he omitted the modifier "former") deserved as much attention as those in the once Prussian regions. He described their national-minded activity and expressed his hope that they would get more help from Germany in the

153 Blachetta-Madajczyk, *Klassenkampf oder Nation*, 121.
154 Consulate in Łódź (Hoffmann-Fölkersamb) to German Foreign Ministry (Zechlin), November 15, 1923, in PAAA, Pol IV, Politik 25 Polen, vol. 16, R82196, 52–53.
155 Consulate in Łódź (Hoffmann-Fölkersamb) to German Foreign Ministry, March 6, 1925, copy for Abteilung IV, in PAAA, Pol IV, Politik 25 Polen, vol. 19, R82199, 120–122.
156 The consul did apply for Reich funds to obtain a projector and legal aid for August Utta, although it cannot be determined here whether these were approved. Consulate in Łódź (Hoffmann-Fölkersamb) to German Foreign Ministry, January 9, 1925, in PAAA, Pol IV, Politik 25 Polen, vol. 19, R82199, 41–44.
157 Maria Keipert and Peter Grupp (Auswärtiges Amt, Historischer Dienst), ed., *Biographisches Handbuch des deutschen Auswärtigen Dienstes 1871–1945*, vol. 3: L-R (Paderborn: Ferdinand Schöningh, 2008), 129–131.

future.[158] Luckwald had previously noted the inequity in Reich funds for the Germans in his consular district, where the amounts for the 250,000 "tribal brothers" in Central Poland were miniscule in comparison to the formerly Prussian regions.[159]

Luckwald thus tried to find the right mix of adversity, optimism, and justice in order to argue for support for his Germans in Central Poland and to increase his own influence in German minority affairs. Luckwald strongly sympathized with the German nationalist circles in Łódź and encouraged more support for the "conscious Germans" there. In 1928, he wrote that the local Germans were "in bloom,"[160] but he also did not deny how low the starting point was for these Germans:

> The heading ["Lodzer Germandom"] encompasses a term that has not been honorable up to now. The "Lodzer German" has held and still holds today the sound of hard cash, the value of one's assets, in the highest regard. The goal of material wealth is to be achieved at all cost; and because the changing political situation has not always made it "advantageous," but rather dangerous to show one's allegiance to the German homeland, one has avoided any positive völkisch views. The wealthier circles of Łódź industrialists like to use the term "cosmopolitanism" to cover up their meager interest in the homeland and to shake off any expectations of giving active help.[161]

Luckwald's own language thus revealed how little he thought of the local Germans. Although he relegated the "mushy masses of cowardly, provincial philistines" to the recent past, there is the sense that he privately believed that the same characteristics still applied to the Germans at large in the city. He stated in the same document, for example, that the "golden Russian age" remained unforgotten in the hearts of the Germans in (former) Congress Poland.[162] Other reports by Luckwald stressed the need for a "strong hand" to guide these Germans.[163] Luckwald thus continued a line of thinking that saw the Germans in Łódź as somehow contaminated; the few active

---

158 Consulate in Łódź (Luckwald) to German Foreign Ministry, December 1, 1931, copy to Krahmer-Möllenberg, in BA Berlin, R8043, folder 942, 425–427.

159 Consulate in Łódź (Luckwald) to German Foreign Ministry, "Lodzer Deutschtum," August 20, 1928, copy for Abteilung IV, in PAAA, Pol IV, Politik 25 Polen, vol. 25, R82205, 35-37, here 35; also found in BA Berlin, R8043, folder 941, 424–429.

160 Consulate in Łódź (Luckwald) to German Foreign Ministry, March 12, 1928, copy for Abteilung IV, in PAAA, Pol IV, Politik 25 Polen, vol. 24, R82204, 187–188.

161 Consulate in Łódź (Luckwald) to German Foreign Ministry, report "Lodzer Deutschtum," March 14, 1928, in PAAA, Pol IV, Politik 25 Polen, vol. 24, R82204, 191–194; also found as copy for Krahmer-Möllenberg, in BA Berlin, R8043, folder 940, 14–16, here 14.

162 Consulate in Łódź (Luckwald) to German Foreign Ministry, report "Lodzer Deutschtum," March 14, 1928, in PAAA, Pol IV, Politik 25 Polen, vol. 24, R82204, 191–194; also found as copy for Krahmer-Möllenberg, in BA Berlin, R8043, folder 940, 14–16, here 14.

163 Consulate in Łódź (Luckwald) to German Foreign Ministry, August 20, 1928, copy for Abteilung IV, in PAAA, Pol IV, Politik 25 Polen, vol. 24, R82204, 35.

German nationalists there appeared to be the exception that proved the rule. Surely the national situation of the Germans in Central Poland could be described as improving or worsening, depending on the motives of the actor involved. One Polish commentator feared that the Germans in Łódź were becoming more German in the Prussian sense.[164] But the idea of the stridently non-national lodzermensch remained the yardstick in assessing the Germans in Central Poland.

Despite the concern of some officials, the Reich did relatively little to help the Germans in Congress Poland. The German state remained stingy when it came to the Germans in the formerly Russian and Austrian regions although the German leaders there were often quite active and paid a heavy price for their political engagement. In 1927, the Minorities Bloc began publishing *Natio*, a pamphlet concerning minority issues in Poland. The leader of the Central Polish DVV, August Utta, served as the Minorities Bloc's German representative, and Polish officials responded by closing the newspaper and moving Utta's assignment as a schoolteacher from Łódź to a remote location near Kielce.[165] Because the new location was twenty-two hours away from Łódź, Wilhelm Wallroth, a ministerial director in the Foreign Ministry, asked to fund Utta so he could resign from his post as schoolteacher and devote his time entirely to the DVV. Wallroth noted that Utta had four children and that his wife was seriously ill. Wallroth recognized Utta's merits, stating that he was slowly bringing the "sluggish" German upper class in Łódź back to national consciousness.[166] The German consul in Łódź, Erich von Luckwald, also intervened on Utta's behalf. Although the Foreign Ministry offered help to Utta, a German who did not live in the formerly Prussian areas, the small amount Utta received underlines how little concrete support the Foreign Ministry was willing to provide to persons and organizations in these areas. Utta's benefactors at the German consulate in Łódź asked for RM 3,000 per annum for five years, but he was granted the full sum for only the first year (1928), and only after considerable teeth pulling. Utta apparently also received an additional RM 1,500 in 1928 to take care of emergency needs. In 1929, he received RM 2,000, and in 1930 only RM 1,500.[167] Starting in 1931, he received no more money at

---

164 Zygmunt Stoliński, *Liczba i rozmieszczenie Niemców w Polsce* (Warsaw: Wydawnictwo Instytutu Badań Spraw Narodowościowych, 1927), here 3.
165 Blanke, *Orphans of Versailles*, 92.
166 "Aufzeichung des Ministerialdirektors Wallroth," January 5, 1928, in *ADAP*, ser. B, vol. 8, document no. 6, pp. 12–14, here 13.
167 "Aufzeichung des Ministerialdirektors Wallroth," January 5, 1928, in *ADAP*, ser. B, vol. 8, document no. 6, pp. 12–14, here 14n5.

all because he had become a Polish senator and thus was deemed to have an adequate salary.[168]

In general, Reich officials considered the importance of the Central Polish Germans in terms of how they could best serve Reich and Western Polish German interests. Despite the concern of some Reich officials for Utta, significant aid from Germany was not forthcoming for even nationalist German political organizations in Central Poland. Given Wallroth's arguments about how important Utta was for rallying the Germans in Central Poland in the upcoming elections – and hence his importance for the entire minority in Poland – the Foreign Ministry's aid to Utta was miserly when compared to the large sums flowing into Poznania, Pomerelia, and Upper Silesia. After all, the Foreign Ministry had transferred RM 3,000,000 to the Deutschtumsbund in September 1922 to pay for its services.[169] The Foreign Ministry apparently did not think that Central Poland was worthy of the same kind of investment, and Central Polish minority leaders and institutions could only hope for leftovers at best. The local German's purported political passivity, strongly associated with prevailing stereotypes of the lodzermensch, seemed to underline the nationalists' weakness in Central Poland and justified their inequitable treatment.

OSTFORSCHUNG AND THE LODZERMENSCH

Even the Ostforscher, who generally held all things German in great esteem, contributed to this pattern of racialization. Indeed, they were among the most vehement critics of the lodzermensch condition. Most Ostforscher were at home in rightist milieus, and they tended to see the conservative, patriarchal, and agrarian structures of the various German minorities as an idealized community that could be juxtaposed against developments in the much-despised Weimar Republic.[170] Yet it was precisely this outlook that led them to despise the urban Germans in Łódź all the more because they did not fit easily into these views. Hence, Ostforscher observers of the Germans in Poland largely repeated the trope of the denationalized Germandom in Łódź, thereby underlining the cultural contamination of the local Germans and their danger to Germany's revisionist goals. Such references functioned as a kind of coded racism that referred back to the

---

168 Schwarz memo, February 3, 1936, in PAAA, Pol IV-Geheimakten, Politik 25 Polen, vol. 9, R30868k.
169 Blanke, *Orphans of Versailles*, 73–74.
170 Rudolf Jaworski, "Der auslandsdeutsche Gedanke in der Weimarer Republik," *Annali dell'Istituto storico italo-germanico in Trento* 4 (1978): 369–386, here 379–380.

archetype of the lodzermensch. Moreover, anti–Semitic language – in part due to the ethnic makeup of the city, in which the Jews made up a large minority of the population – informed the image of the Łódź Germans that included intellectual sterility, business orientation, and cosmopolitanism. By insinuating their cultural proximity to the Jewish population, this brand of anti–Semitism could be used to peripheralize and discipline the German minority in Łódź.

Significantly, members of the German minority were involved in much of the *Ostforschung*, or the German study of the East, as it related to Poland. Indeed, research on the Germans in Poland was to a great extent "German research in Poland."[171] Therefore, the program and the results of Ostforschung in Poland could never be separated from power relations among different minority groupings, especially regional ones. Exacerbating the dominance of Germans in Western Poland (both thematically and as researchers) in Ostforschung were the organizational and funding structures within the minority: the Historische Gesellschaft in Poznań managed the projects and research funds that the Reich sent to Poland.[172] Hence, Ostforschung on and in Poland was heavily biased toward the Germans in Western Poland.

In an article in *Deutsche Blätter in Polen*, Dr. Johann Reiners, a German economist from Western Poland, bemoaned the stunted intellectual level of all national groups in Łódź. He compared Łódź with America in order to describe the shallowness of the city's inhabitants, who were purportedly only interested in business and avoided activities of deeper intellectual and cultural value. According to Reiners, the Łódź German could speak two or three languages, but due to business concerns, he remained nationally cautious: he considered himself a Lodzer first and German second, and he certainly did not want to be identified as a Prussian–German. Reiners did not deny that there were signs that the "sleeping ethnic group" was indeed waking up, but it was to be a slow selection process, a separation of the "chaff from the wheat."[173] The overall tone of his article was pessimistic and was dominated by his criticism of the signs of cultural hybridity and

---

171 Wolfgang Kessler, "Die 'Ostforschung' und die Deutschen in Polen," *Nordost-Archiv* 9, no. 2 (2000): 379–411, here 396. Kessler bases his assessment in part on the following work: Alfred Lattermann, "Deutsche Forschung im ehemaligen Polen 1919–1939," in *Deutsche Ostforschung. Ergebnisse und Aufgaben seit dem ersten Weltkrieg*, ed. Hermann Aubin, Otto Brunner, Wolfgang Kohte, and Johannes Papritz, vol. 2 (Leipzig: Hirzel, 1943), 461–487.

172 Kessler, "Die 'Ostforschung' und die Deutschen in Polen," 396.

173 Johann Reiners, "Von der Struktur des Deutschtums in Polen," in "Ständischer Aufbau" special issue, *Deutsche Blätter in Polen* 2, no. 1 (January 1925): 18–34, here 27. Dr. Reiners' dissertation to the University of Breslau in 1923 was titled "Die landwirtschaftliche Produktivgenossenschaft in Theorie und Praxis, hinsichtlich ihrer Bedeutung für die innere Kolonisation."

national contamination. In 1931, another writer complained in *Deutsche Blätter in Polen* that the most serious problem of the Łódź Germans was "the indifference of the acquisitive people in the industrial city of Łódź to intellectual and völkisch questions."[174]

While German activists bemoaned the lack of national feeling in Łódź, this discussion remained a largely internal German debate. Polish commentators also noted that regional as well as class cleavages determined the political life of the Germans in Poland, and they also made references to the lodzermensch.[175] Yet German authorities were quick to close ranks and defend the honor of the Łódź Germans when outsiders – especially Poles – questioned their Germanness. In 1929, the DV functionary and high school teacher Friedrich Heidelck reviewed a book on the German minority written by Zygmunt Stoliński. In his review, Heidelck criticized the Łódź-based Bürgerliche Deutsche Partei, which Stoliński's book had praised for its apparent loyalty to Poland. Heidelck complained that the "bourgeois" groups in the Bürgerliche Deutsche Partei had little to do with Germandom. These "Assimilanten" had cooperated with the Poles in the 1928 Sejm elections, and Heidelck was especially incensed by the temerity of renegade elements in the Bürgerliche Deutsche Partei who had leveled charges of treason against those Germans working within the Minorities Bloc. Heidelck's defense of the general wholesomeness of Łódź's Germandom was a natural reaction to a perceived Polish attempt to divide and conquer the Germans. At the same time, however, Heidelck himself was not free from playing on common prejudices. Heidelck complained that one could understand these attacks only if one was familiar with the "atmosphere in Łódź" – where the "purely materialist attitude" of the bourgeois party supporters dominated.[176] The coded qualities of the lodzermensch thus persisted even in attempts to downplay its existence.

Even Central Polish German nationalists had largely incorporated these eastern and hybrid discourses, and they did not hesitate to apply the archetype of the hated lodzermensch when they found it expedient to do so. Many Germans from Łódź played an active role in nationalist minority politics and in Ostforschung, but they were the rare exceptions who proved the rule of stigmatization. Often they seemed to be much harsher in their judgment than their Western Polish colleagues. Adolf Eichler, considered one of the fathers of Central Polish German nationalism, noted that

---

174 D. Borse, "Der Deutsche Schul- und Bildungsverein zu Lodz," Deutsche Blätter in Polen 8, nos. 8/9 (August/September 1931): 470–471, here 470.

175 Stoliński, *Die deutsche Minderheit in Polen*, 40.

176 Heidelck, "Die Stellung des Deutschtums in Polen," 49–104.

the Łódź Germans still had to "excrete" the "creeping poison" of their "renegade disposition."[177] In an issue of *Deutsche Blätter in Polen* from 1925, one commentator, apparently from Central Poland, complained about the "cultural immaturity," the "political ignorance," and the lack of a "conscious Volksgemeinschaft" among the German inhabitants in Łódź.[178] The already named Eduard von Behrens, a leading figure in the city, likewise complained of the textile workers' preference for "internationalism" in "völkisch uncertain" Łódź.[179] There is considerable irony in his statements, which suggest an internalization and circumvention of dominant stereotypes about the Łódź Germans. As we have seen, Reich authorities had long considered Behrens himself to be nationally unreliable and obsequious to the Polish state.

Rural–urban antagonisms played a role in informing the (self-)criticism of the Germans in Łódź. The rural Germans fared somewhat better in many assessments: countless essays, stories, and anecdotes recounted the alleged cultural and economic superiority of the Central Polish Germans over their Slavic neighbors.[180] Because Łódź was the undisputed center for the Germans in the former Congress Kingdom,[181] however, the lodzermensch could also strike beyond municipal borders. Just as the concept had been metonymically conveyed from the industrial elites to the whole of Łódź's (German) population, its characteristics were readily transferable from the city to the entirety of Central Poland. Walther Burchard, a German from Poznań who received a doctorate for a dissertation submitted in Marburg in 1922, noted that the general ignorance about Central Poland caused people to apply the somewhat infamous and not always flattering qualities of the Łódź Germans to the rural Central Polish colonists.[182] In 1931, Albert Breyer, a school teacher from Central Poland (but not Łódź) who wrote often on the German minority in Poland, complained of the low evolutionary development of the German settlements and stated that the Central

---

177 Adolf Eichler, "Die nationale Selbstbehauptung der Lodzer Deutschen," in "Vom Deutschtum in Kongreßpolen I," special issue, *Deutsche Blätter in Polen* 1, no. 5 (November 1924): 193–198, here 197.

178 T.R., "Innere Zerrissenheit," in "Vom Deutschtum in Kongreßpolen II," special issue, *Deutsche Blätter in Polen* 2, no. 3 (March 1925): 109–113, here 112.

179 Eduard von Behrens, "Das Deutschtum in Kongreßpolen," in "Vom Deutschtum in Kongreßpolen I," special issue, *Deutsche Blätter in Polen* 1, no. 5 (November 1924): 199–203, here 203.

180 En Plattdütscher [pseud.], "Die Weichselkolonisten," in "Vom Deutschtum in Kongreßpolen I," special issue, *Deutsche Blätter in Polen* 1, no. 5 (November 1924): 203–205; Walther Th. Burchard, "Weichselkolonisten," *Deutsche Blätter in Polen* 2, no. 6 (June 1925): 278–295, here 279, 287.

181 German Passport Agency in Łódź (Drubba) to German Foreign Ministry, February 6, 1922, in PAAA, Pol IV, Politik 25 Polen, vol. 9, R82189, 22–23; Heidelck, "Die Stellung des Deutschtums in Polen," 82.

182 Burchard, "Weichselkolonisten," 294.

Polish Germans there were driven by primitive instincts and thought only in pragmatic terms. He concluded that one could have only low expectations for the cultural-intellectual production of these Germans.[183] The emphasis on the local Germans' purported lack of national vigor perhaps served as a justification for why the German nationalists in Central Poland were unable to win more people for their cause.

Generally, the assumption of many völkisch and nationalist thinkers that the peasantry "represented culture in its most intuitive and innocent form"[184] could also be turned around to promote greater political intervention. Eduard von Behrens complained of the low cultural development of the German colonists, whose alleged frugality – otherwise a virtue – hindered them from buying any books or newspapers. Their deep religiosity was also a problem because they did not read anything beyond the Bible and hymnbooks. As an expression of his frustration and of his own acceptance of a west-east gradient, Behrens was pleased that "real German gentlemen" from the Prussian and Austrian regions were taking an increased interest in the "forgotten" German colonists. For Behrens, these Central Polish Germans could "look up proudly" to the knowledge and capabilities of the visitors, who would help them in their struggle for their nationality.[185]

Several articles by Germans in Western Poland brought out clearly the tensions between their pronounced unity with the Germans in Central Poland and their tacit claim to dominate them. Words of support often revealed a patronizing attitude, especially toward the Łódź Germans. Hermann Rauschning, who was editor of *Deutsche Blätter in Polen* before moving to Danzig, called for greater unity through mutual understanding in his introduction to a special issue devoted to the Germans in Central Poland. Rauschning's essay seemed designed to enlighten Western Polish Germans about their exotic eastern cousins and to ask for understanding of their sometimes strange ways: one should realize that their long exposure to foreign elements may have taken forms that appear "alienating and not straightforward" to the Germans in Western Poland, who as "newcomers" were still new to their situation as Germans abroad.[186] Rauschning even praised the Łódź Germans for their "powers of resistance and tenacious perseverance"

183 Albert Breyer, "Neuerscheinungen im Deutschen Schrifttum Mittelpolens (1925–1930)," *Deutsche Blätter in Polen* 8, no. 4 (April 1931): 227–230, here 227.
184 Roger Chickering, *We Men Who Feel Most German: A Cultural Study of the Pan-German League, 1886–1914* (Boston: Allen & Unwin, 1984), 89.
185 Behrens, "Das Deutschtum in Kongreßpolen," 200; Eser, *Volk, Staat, Gott*, 231.
186 Hermann Rauschning, "Zur Einführung," in "Vom Deutschtum in Kongreßpolen I," special issue, *Deutsche Blätter in Polen* 1, no. 5 (November 1924): 190–193, here 191–192.

that the Germans in Western Poland did not yet possess.[187] According to the historian Richard Breyer (born in Central Poland and the son of the afore-mentioned school teacher and minority activist Albert Breyer), Rauschning was one of the few Germans in Western Poland who saw the value of all Germans in Poland and the necessity of working together.[188] Despite Rauschning claims that some "fruitful" aspects could be gleaned from the Central Polish experience, however, his programmatic appeal to the Western Polish Germans to drop their haughty attitude toward the Łódź Germans only underlined the persistence of such views. His admiration for the endurance of the Germans in Łódź accompanied his own apparent doubts about whether all German-speakers in the city could be considered Germans.

In a later issue of *Deutsche Blätter in Polen*, a contributor named Walther Burchard wrote a rambling exegesis relying heavily on circular argumentation about the organic foundations of the German minority in Poland. Following the ideas of Othmar Spann,[189] Burchard proposed that the Germans in Poland could only be united on a corporatist basis that would spring from an "intellectual-spiritual origin." He contrasted an organic unity against mere material organization and suggested that the Germans in Poland had grown too far apart. A community of common goals was either lacking or only artificially created as a negative reaction to Polish repression. Yet Burchard back-pedaled later in his essay, stating that there was enough commonality for establishing a corporatist community.[190] In another essay a few months later on German settlers along the Vistula River, Burchard admitted that the differences in the way of life and thinking between "us" (the Germans in Western Poland) and those Germans further east often aroused "strong feelings of displeasure." Still, he found that the settlers served as a good example of Germans who had remained German while fulfilling their duties as Polish citizens. He concluded the essay by proclaiming how much the Vistula colonists were waiting to be "newly fertilized" by "real German spirit," and "we" (again, presumably the Germans in Western Poland) should not let them wait in vain.[191]

Another article that appeared in *Deutsche Blätter in Polen* by Erich Monens similarly expressed these relations of power within the minority. Besides the

---

187 Rauschning, "Zur Einführung," 192.
188 Breyer, *Das Deutsche Reich und Polen*, 57n41.
189 On Othmar Spann, see Kurt Sontheimer, *Antidemokratisches Denken in der Weimarer Republik. Die politischen Ideen des deutschen Nationalismus zwischen 1918 und 1933* (Munich: Nymphenburger Verlagshandlung, 1962), 249–252.
190 Walther Th. Burchard, "Vom kommenden ständischen Aufbau der deutschen Minderheit in Polen," *Deutsche Blätter in Polen* 2, no. 2 (Februar 1925): 66–72, here 67.
191 Burchard, "Weichselkolonisten," 279, 295.

usual verbiage about the Germans as bearers of culture, he insisted that "we Germans in Western Poland must get rid of our really unwarranted pride vis-à-vis the Germans in Congress Poland and try to become closer to them." Germans in Western Poland could thus learn "German loyalty and steadfastness" from the Germans who had withstood more than three centuries of living in a foreign environment. Monens also warned of the influence of glossy cultural magazines with a "Reich German viewpoint," which would inevitably lead to the uprooting of the German man. Despite his apparent respect for the Germans in Central Poland, however, Monens also appealed to the Germans in Western Poland, who according to Monens had a stronger sense of nationality, to strengthen their contacts with the Germans in Central Poland and to "fertilize" them. It was also their duty to encourage the Germans in Central Poland to send their children to German-language schools. Finally, drawing on prevailing images and clichés, Monens said that the Germans in Central Poland had to be educated so that they would not be too timid and too stingy when it came to standing up for their nationality.[192]

It is telling that Rauschning, Burchard, and Monens came from the Western Polish territories and were based in Poznań. Their visions of a German Volksgemeinschaft in Poland envisioned a corporatist community that was also hierarchical. The condescending (and gendered) language they used made it unmistakable that the Germans in Western Poland would assume first place in this hierarchy. In their view, there was very much a need to discipline and educate those on the minority's margins. True, the Western Polish Germans often stated that there was something to be learned from the toughness of the Germans in Central Poland, but such a position was far from seeing the Łódź Germans as equals, much less as a viable model for the Western Polish Germans. Rather, such statements merely confirmed the primacy of the Western Polish regions and legitimated their further management of the East. Self-criticism was overshadowed by the self-aggrandizing, larger mission to raise their eastern cohorts.

Throughout the 1920s and 1930s, references to the lodzermensch played a disciplining function in this project of building a German Volksgruppe in Poland. German activists used the anti-model as a warning of insufficient national affinity and of cosmopolitanism in order to keep cultural issues at the forefront. The Germans of Łódź, as the embodiment of cultural contamination, became the negative Other of what a good German

---

192 Erich Monens, "Wir Deutschen in Polen. Ein Querschnitt durch die rechtlichen und moralischen Grundlagen unseres Volkskörpers, seine Nöte und Kämpfe," *Deutsche Blätter in Polen* 3, no. 1 (January 1926): 23–42, here 39.

should be. Being a member of a national minority inevitably led to compromises with the host state and society. Even German conservative-nationalists routinely cooperated with the Jews and other minorities, as the rather fruitful elections with the Minorities Bloc in the 1920s show. Confining ethnic betrayal to the imagined renegade Łódź Germans allowed these nationalist Germans, even those in Łódź, to differentiate their own cooperation with Polish society and government from purportedly traitorous activity. In other words, dealing with the Poles was acceptable as long as it did not go so far as the lodzermensch. Rather than bridging social, cultural, and racial boundaries, the lodzermensch idea served very much to maintain them.

For the Ostforscher and German activists, Germanness was a privilege that had to be protected; and the rootless, accommodating Łódź German, lacking national self-respect, seemed to question the nature of this privilege and the durability of the German Volk. As a transgressor who had failed in the implicit duty to uphold his nationality, the Łódź German also appeared to lack principles or morals. Although it was not doubted that many of the inhabitants in Łódź were somehow German, their dedication to Germandom remained under scrutiny. Łódź Germanness was considered both endangered and a danger. This in-between condition was proof of the need for redoubling efforts to mobilize Germandom in Poland and to disassimilate the Germans from the other nationalities. Thus, the Łódź Germans served as a warning for cultural danger that simultaneously reified the existence of pure national essences: as a crossbreed, he was perceived as inferior to Germans and Poles. Chad Bryant's insightful work on the Sudetenland is valuable here, for the Łódź German also represented what Nazi scholars would refer to as "amphibians" – those persons who were purportedly able to switch their public nationality or who could not be nationally identified with ease.[193] As Bryant notes, "[a]mphibians threatened the myth that the nation was eternal, unified, and homogenous; they threatened to bring the project of making nations to a halt."[194] As not-quite-Germans, the Łódź Germans as lodzermenschen likewise posed a danger to unitary Germanness and thus challenged the concept of Volksgemeinschaft.

Similarities can be found in other west-east hybrid discourses.[195] The internalization of eastern differences was apparent in the debates between

193 Chad Bryant, "Either German or Czech: Fixing Nationality in Bohemia and Moravia, 1939–1946," *Slavic Review* 61, no. 4 (Winter 2002): 683–706, here 684–685; Chad Bryant, *Prague in Black: Nazi Rule and Czech Nationalism* (Cambridge: Harvard University Press, 2007).
194 Bryant, "Either German or Czech," here 701.
195 Maria Todorova, "The Balkans: From Discovery to Invention," *Slavic Review* 53, no. 2 (1994): 453–482, here 455.

Westernizers and Slavophiles/nationalists in Russia, which served as one of the constitutive "Easts" for Western Europe. As Iver B. Neumann has argued, Russian intellectuals could construct themselves as European by making the Turks into the barbarous Other.[196] Similarly, as Maria Todorova argues, Balkanism allowed (Western) European intellectuals to project their frustrations onto an Other that was still somehow undeniably part of the self. This alterity "served as a repository of negative characteristics against which a positive and self-congratulatory image of the 'European' and the 'the west' has been constructed." For Reich Germans and Germans in Western Poland, such dynamics were at work when they confronted "wavering forms" in Central and Eastern Poland.[197] Especially the Germans in Łódź were not just on the margins of the Volksgemeinschaft, but like the Balkan Other in (Western) European identity formation, they represented the "dark side within."[198]

Because this purportedly unhealthy Łódź Germandom could be regionally isolated from the rest of the national body, this periphery fulfilled another important function. As a part of a racialized discourse, the externalization and construction of a negative milieu in the East supported a politics of domination and subordination within the minority by keeping the regional hierarchy in place. Despite the constant invocation of Volksgemeinschaft and the calls for greater unity, regional distinctions persisted and indeed widened throughout the 1920s: Germans continued to be treated differently and to see themselves as different according to where they lived. These phantom borders did not simply linger over time but were politicized and dynamically reconstructed throughout the interwar period. Although they remained unseen, they continued to haunt German activists despite the National Socialist promise of national community.

---

196 Iver B. Neumann, *Uses of the Other: "The East" in European Identity Formation* (Minneapolis: University of Minnesota Press, 1999), 160–182.

197 On "wavering figures," see Todorova, "The Balkans: From Discovery to Invention," 476.

198 Todorova, "The Balkans: From Discovery to Invention," 482.

4

Negotiating Volksgemeinschaft

National Socialism and Regionalization (1933–1937)

Support within the minority for Hitler had been present before 1933, and it grew especially during the increasing economic hardships and the high tide of Nazi electoral successes in 1932. As in Germany, minority elites in Poland saw in Hitler a chance to unify the German people.[1] Although Polish authorities were concerned about close ties between National Socialism and the German minority before 1933, Hitler's appointment as chancellor troubled minority leaders themselves at the beginning. Affected were not only the German socialists in Poland but also members of the conservative-nationalist camp. Their reserved stance was a result of tactical as well as ideological considerations. The private enthusiasm of some minority leaders may have been tempered in part by apprehensions of possible reprisals by the Polish government. National Socialism was also an unknown political factor that could threaten the power base of the traditional minority leadership. Some were concerned about the movement's anti-Semitic slogans,[2] an issue that was especially important where Jews were members of German organizations.[3] Many established minority leaders

---

1 According to the Polish officials, the following newspapers "carefully" gave their support for Hitler in 1932: *Deutsche Rundschau, Pommereller Tageblatt*, and *Culmer Zeitung*. See Office of the Voivode in Toruń to Polish Interior Ministry, situation report on the German minority (June 1932), sent July 1932, document 61, 323, in Rudolf Jaworski et al., eds., *Deutsche und Polen zwischen den Kriegen. Minderheitenstatus und "Volkstumskampf" im Grenzgebiet. Amtliche Berichterstattung aus beiden Ländern, 1920–1939* (Munich: Saur, 1997).

2 Mirosław Cygański, *Mniejszość niemiecka w Polsce centralnej w latach 1919–1939* (Łódź: Wydawnictwo Łódzkie, 1962), 51; Przemysław Hauser, "The German Minority in Poland in the Years 1918–1939. Reflections in the State of Research and Interpretation, Proposals for Further Research," *Polish Western Affairs* 32, no. 2 (1991): 13–38, here 33.

3 During a meeting of the Volksbund in 1933, a priest named Pszczyński defended those Jews who had proven their cultural political ties to Germandom. See Karol Gostyński, "Przewrót Hitlerowski w Niemczech i Niemcy w Polsce (Dokończenie)," *Sprawy Narodowościowe* 10, no. 3 (1936): 220–221.

worried about National Socialism as a pagan or otherwise un-Christian ideology.[4]

It was not long, however, before conservative-nationalist German leaders across Poland openly declared their adherence to the Third Reich. By the end of 1933, virtually all of the important minority organizations had undergone a more or less voluntary *Gleichschaltung*, a falling into line with the National Socialist government in Germany.[5] Others, like the Catholic German leader Eduard Pant, the pro-Polish Deutscher Kultur- und Wirtschaftsbund, or the German socialists, opposed National Socialism on principle, but they were too small in number to make a notable difference. Their example proved increasingly rare by the mid-1930s.

The growing Nazification of German political life in Poland is often attributed to Polish repression. This chapter offers a different perspective by looking into how Polish authorities did much to foster – both intentionally and unintentionally – support for National Socialism in Poland. Despite the apparent ideological conformity, Polish German activists adapted National Socialist precepts to their particular conditions, which deepened regional cleavages within the minority. By examining the conflict between "Old Germans" and "Young Germans" in Poland, this chapter explores how German parties articulated ideological claims that played upon regional protest within the minority. It also shows how many German activists found positive answers within Nazism to their troubles. Especially with its focus on the qualities of race and its clear separation from the state, National Socialism helped Germans in Poland resolve a fundamental question of their existence as a national minority: How could one simultaneously be a good German and a loyal Polish citizen?

IMPACT OF *GLEICHSCHALTUNG* AND THE UNITY QUESTION

It would seem that this period of heightened national feeling and apparently broad support for National Socialism should have been most favorable for minority leaders to carry out at last the long-proclaimed goal of achieving organizational unity. Already in the fall of 1932, German leaders in Poland had come up with yet another (stillborn) plan to create a supraregional

---

4 Ingo Eser, "*Volk, Staat, Gott!*" *Die deutsche Minderheit in Polen und ihr Schulwesen 1918–1939* (Wiesbaden: Harrassowitz, 2010), 199, 201.
5 Richard Breyer, *Das Deutsche Reich und Polen, 1932–1937. Außenpolitik und Volksgruppenfragen* (Würzburg: Holzner, 1955), 244.

organization.[6] Despite the enthusiastic proclamation of minority leaders, however, the Nazi rise in Germany had minimal effect on unification attempts in Poland. Indeed, the increased pressure on the minority briefly revived regional tensions even between Poznania und Pomerelia. The loose structure of the Deutsche Vereinigung in the 1920s had generally helped to defuse conflict among several very ambitious personalities in Western Poland. The new uncertainty after 1933 and the perceived need to centralize leadership, however, led to a renewed jockeying for power.

A major change was the replacement of the two main DV leaders, Chairman Eugen Naumann and Director Kurt Graebe. The two were long-standing rivals who represented the Poznanian and Pomerelian camps, respectively, within the DV.[7] Naumann's fatal mistake was the publication of a New Year's article in January 1933, in which he outlined his ideas for reorganizing German life in Poland. Drawing upon völkisch thinking that clearly delineated the state from ethnic concerns, Naumann proposed a deal whereby the German minority would agree not to assert its political rights in exchange for a guarantee of cultural autonomy. On February 12, 1933, twenty German leaders of the largely ceremonial Zentralausschuss had gathered in Łódź to discuss Naumann's article and how to make him leave his post as chairman of the Zentralausschuss. They decided to replace him with Erwin Hasbach from Hermanowo-Freda[8] (near Starogard) in Pomerelia, in part because of his prior parliamentary experience and his command of Polish. Although Hasbach had long opposed Naumann, the other members of the Zentralausschuss had to convince the compunctious Hasbach that Naumann's dismissal was neither a matter of personal rivalry between them nor an opportunistic stab in the back.[9] Naumann was also forced to resign his post as deputy in the Sejm in December 1933, which was passed on to Berndt von Saenger from Obornik county in Poznania.[10] Naumann's

---

6 Office of the Voivode in Toruń to Polish Interior Ministry, situation report on the German minority (February 1933), sent March 1933, in Jaworski et al., *Deutsche und Polen zwischen den Kriegen*, document 62, 337.

7 Richard Blanke, *Orphans of Versailles: The Germans in Western Poland, 1918–1939* (Lexington: University Press of Kentucky, 1993), 89; various correspondence from Consulate General in Poznań (Lütgens) to German Foreign Ministry, December 23, 1929, January 21, 1930, and June 5, 1930, in PAAA, Pol IV-Geheimakten, Politik 25 Polen, vol. 6, R30865.

8 Małgorzata Smogorzewska, *Posłowie i senatorowie Rzeczypospolitej Polskiej 1919–1939: Słownik biograficzny*, vol. 2: E–J (Warsaw: Wydawnictwo Sejmowe, 2000), here 208–210. Hasbach was born near Białystok, but he acquired the estate in Pomerelia in 1922.

9 Protokoll der Sitzung des deutschen Zentralausschusses in Lodz vom 12.2.1933, BA Berlin, R8043, folder 942, 114–119, here 115–116.

10 Dariusz Matelski, *Mniejszość niemiecka w Wielkopolsce w latach 1919–1939* (Poznań: Wydawnictwo Naukowe UAM, 1997), 93n136.

position as chairman of the DV fell to Erich von Witzleben from Lisykowa in Wrzysk (Wirsitz) county in Pomerelia.[11]

Richard Blanke argues that Eugen Naumann was replaced as the chairman of the DV because he was not convincing enough in his support for National Socialism.[12] The Zentralausschuss proceedings in early February 1933 suggest, however, that there had already been discontent in both the DV and the Zentralausschuss with Naumann's overall leadership. The article in question, after all, had appeared before Hitler came to power. Indeed, Naumann had apparently turned to National Socialist ideas early on, but that probably did him more harm than good, for the plan he proposed in his New Year's article may have sounded *too* National Socialist for his colleagues at the time. At the Zentralausschuss meeting in February, even Eduard Pant, the Catholic Party leader and later the minority's most notable opponent of National Socialism, welcomed Naumann's replacement. Concerned with these long-standing leadership issues, the Zentralausschuss members devoted relatively little attention to recent events in Germany, or if so it was not recorded. When they did discuss their position on National Socialism at the end of the meeting, they agreed on the need to halt the growth of "National Socialist cells" among the Germans in Poland.[13] The speeches of the various Zentralausschuss members at the ninth DVV congress in Łódź also made little or no mention of the events in the Reich.[14] Thus, whether Naumann was too little or too much engaged with National Socialism was probably irrelevant – he would have been replaced in any case.

Although the removal of Naumann was in many ways a victory for the Pomerelian faction within the DV, Kurt Graebe, the vice-chairman and director of the DV, did not enjoy his success for very long. He too was soon criticized within the DV (and later by the Young Germans) for being an unsuitable leader in light of the new events in the Reich. The leader of the Volksbund (formerly Verein) für das Deutschtum im Ausland, Hans Steinacher, called Graebe a "frustrated Reich German."[15] In other words, it

11 Matelski, *Mniejszość niemiecka w Wielkopolsce*, 93n136.
12 Blanke, *Orphans of Versailles*, 166.
13 Protokoll der Sitzung des deutschen Zentralausschusses in Lodz vom 12.2.1933, BA Berlin, R8043, folder 942, 114–119.
14 "Die 9. Tagung des Deutschen Volksverbandes," *Freie Presse*, February 12, 1933, newspaper clipping in BA Berlin, R8043, folder 942, 103–104. Also interesting to note was that the German leaders from Western Poland repeated how bad their situation was, while the DVV leader, August Utta, emphasized how well the DVV was doing.
15 Blanke, *Orphans of Versailles*, 166.

appeared that Graebe was devoted more to cultivating his own connections with the Reich than to the needs of a diverse German minority. Graebe eventually resigned his various posts, although he served out his term as Sejm deputy until 1935. After losing his Polish citizenship, Graebe left Poland in 1937 for Berlin, but he remained suspect in Germany, in part due to his ties to Free Masonry.[16] He only gained German citizenship again after joining the army during the Second World War. Eugen Naumann, who stayed in Poland, was killed during the roundup of Germans by Polish authorities in September 1939.[17]

The impulses for a Gleichschaltung of the Germans in Poland came not from the Reich but from within the minority. Most German minority leaders readily adapted to the new roles expected of them, and they carried out a self-cleansing that coincided with long-standing political factionalism. In the end, however, relatively few leaders were ousted.[18] The Zentralausschuss itself was refounded as the Deutscher Zentralverein on July 5, 1933. Erich von Witzleben, who was already chairman of the DV, became the Zentralverein's chairman, and Hasbach became vice-chairman.[19] For the time being, the Deutsche Vereinigung and the other conservative-nationalist parties elsewhere in Poland remained basically unchanged; they were still rather cliquish clubs of a few thousand members. Despite the new course in Germany, the DV leadership initially refused to reach out to become a broad, mass movement. In short, the conservative German organizations could claim to be National Socialist without really having to prove it. Nor did it appear that the German leaders in Western Polish regions would give up their claim to lead the Germans in all parts of Poland. Witzleben, it appears, took his position as leader of the DV and of the Zentralverein seriously: in January 1934, he pronounced himself the "Führer of Germandom in Poland."[20] Yet at precisely the same time, a serious challenge to his leadership and to Western Polish dominance was rising from the regional periphery of Austrian Silesia. Not National Socialism from Germany, but National Socialism from within Poland would be the dominant factor in shaking up German minority politics.

16 For an overview of Graebe's life, see Mads Ole Balling, *Von Reval bis Bukarest. Statistisch-Biographisches Handbuch der Parlamentarier der deutschen Minderheiten in Ostmittel- und Südosteuropa 1919–1945*, vol. 1 (Copenhagen: Dokumentation Verlag, 1991), 224–225.

17 Blanke, *Orphans of Versailles*, 222.

18 Blanke, *Orphans of Versailles*, 166.

19 Mads Ole Balling, *Von Reval bis Bukarest*, 217, 225.

20 Office of the Voivode in Poznań to Polish Interior Ministry, situation report on the German minority (January 1934), February 9, 1934, in Jaworski et al., *Deutsche und Polen zwischen den Kriegen*, document 224, 640. See also Blanke, *Orphans of Versailles*, 173.

FOREIGN POLITICAL RAPPROCHEMENT

Besides financial concerns and political posturing within the minority, the growing acceptance of National Socialism among minority leaders can only be fully understood in light of the diplomatic context of Poland's relations with Germany. From 1930 to 1933, German-Polish tensions increased, a situation largely driven by Reich Chancellor Heinrich Brüning's attempt to steal the political thunder from the National Socialists.[21] Hitler's "seizure of power" in 1933 was at first deeply worrisome: Polish newspapers, for example, reported the disturbing signs of Nazification in the minority press.[22] Still, the reception of events in Germany was differentiated and heterogeneous. Especially Polish nationalists had a love-hate relationship with National Socialism.[23] The National Democrats, who represented the far right in Polish politics and were usually antagonistic toward the Germans, remained wary but admired the nationalist dynamism of the Nazis.[24] Some Poles sought parallels in the nationalist thought of the Nazis, especially in their anti-Semitism. The nationalist weekly journal *Myśl Narodowa* even praised the book burnings in May 1933 as a cleansing of European culture and came up with its own list of censured authors – most of whom were Jewish.[25]

Many across the Polish political spectrum, including those on the right, saw Hitler's policies as a break with the revisionist policies of the Weimar Republic.[26] In the nationalist quarterly *Strażnica Zachodnia*, which was published by the Związek Obrony Kresów Zachodnich (ZOKZ, Union for the Defense of the Western Borderlands),[27] the foreign correspondent Kazimierz Smogorzewski wrote a cautiously optimistic article titled "A Historical Change in Polish-German Relations?" Poles, he wrote, should not overreact to Nazism.[28] Whereas the Weimar Republic tried to use revisionism

21 Harald von Riekhoff, *German-Polish Relations, 1918–1933* (Baltimore: Johns Hopkins Press, 1971), 357; Martin Broszat, *Zweihundert Jahre deutsche Polenpolitik* (Frankfurt/Main: Suhrkamp, 1972), 233.

22 "Die deutsche Minderheit in Polen unter dem Kommando Berlins," from an article translated from Polish: *Dzień Pomorski*, September 3, 1933, in GStA, I HA, Rep. 77, Tit. 856, folder 752.

23 Albert S. Kotowski, *Hitlers Bewegung im Urteil der polnischen Nationaldemokratie* (Harrassowitz: Wiesbaden, 2000), 129, 185.

24 Wojciech Wrzesiński, *Sąsiad, czy wróg? Ze studiów nad kształtowaniem obrazu Niemca w Polsce w latach 1795–1939* (Wrocław: Wydawnictwo Uniwersytetu Wrocławskiego, 1992), 614–616.

25 Kotowski, *Hitlers Bewegung im Urteil der polnischen Nationaldemokratie*, 39–40. He cites *Myśl Narodowa* from May 14, 1933.

26 Kotowski, *Hitlers Bewegung im Urteil der polnischen Nationaldemokratie*, 190; Wrzesiński, *Sąsiad, czy wróg*, 609–613.

27 In 1934, the Związek Obrony Kresów Zachodnich became the Polski Związek Zachodni, and the *Strażnica Zachodnia* became *Front Zachodni*.

28 Kazimierz Smogorzewski, "Czy dziejowy zwrot w stosunkach polsko-niemieckich?" *Strażnica Zachodnia* 12, no. 4 (October–November 1933): 447–477, here 450.

in foreign policy to unite a contentious and splintered society, Hitler's strong leadership made this stance superfluous.[29] Smogorzewski stated, perhaps naively, that the German minority in Poland was too small to pose an irredentist danger and that the lessening of tensions was already bearing fruit.[30] In his eyes, Germans and Poles were not doomed to be enemies.[31] It is important to note the fluidity of stereotypes on both sides during this period. As John Connelly has argued, German perceptions of the Poles were likewise not uniformly negative in the interwar period and changed according to specific situations.[32]

Despite continuing anxieties regarding Germany, the Polish government soon found that cooperation with Hitler was both possible and desirable.[33] Nazi Germany offered new political opportunities that the previous Weimar governments had not. Poland's authoritarian leader, Józef Piłsudski, and others identified Hitler with Catholic Austria and Bavaria and hence saw a break with Protestant Prussia and its previous aggressive policies to Germanize the Eastern Marches.[34] Austrian policies in Galicia before the First World War, in contrast, had given Poles considerable local political authority and were generally deemed to have been the most mild of the partitioning powers. Moreover, Piłsudski found Nazism's anti-communist stance appealing.[35] Improved relations served above all the revisionist aims of the Polish government, which sought to rid itself of the humiliating limitations on its sovereignty imposed by the Minorities Protection Treaty.

On January 26, 1934, the German government concluded a non-aggression pact with Poland.[36] Hitler was interested in a revision of Versailles but not in a mere restoration of the 1914 borders.[37] Hitler's far-reaching strategic aims for a "New Order" were subordinate to the immediate goal of remilitarization, which required cooperation with the Polish state to secure Germany's eastern flank during this process. The policy of rapprochement

29 Smogorzewski, "Czy dziejowy zwrot w stosunkach polsko-niemieckich?" 456.
30 Smogorzewski, "Czy dziejowy zwrot w stosunkach polsko-niemieckich?" 465, 467.
31 Smogorzewski, "Czy dziejowy zwrot w stosunkach polsko-niemieckich?" 477.
32 John Connelly, "Nazis and Slavs: From Racial Theory to Racist Practice," *Central European History* 32, no. 1 (1999): 1–33; John Connelly, "Why the Poles Collaborated So Little – And Why That Is No Reason for Nationalist Hubris," *Slavic Review* 64, no. 4 (Winter 2005): 771–781.
33 Wrzesiński, *Sąsiad, czy wróg,* 609–613.
34 Kotowski, *Hitlers Bewegung im Urteil der polnischen Nationaldemokratie,* 190. Interestingly, Piłsudski did not make the same positive association with Chancellor Franz von Papen of the Center Party. See Riekhoff, *German-Polish Relations,* 365; Eser, *Volk, Staat, Gott,* 202.
35 Broszat, *Zweihundert Jahre deutsche Polenpolitik,* 235; Breyer, *Das Deutsche Reich und Polen,* 68; Blanke, *Orphans of Versailles,* 184–185.
36 Blanke, *Orphans of Versailles,* 184–185.
37 Gerhard L. Weinberg, *Germany, Hitler, and World War II: Essays in Modern German and World History* (Cambridge/New York: Cambridge University Press, 1995), 35.

was at least, in Hitler's view, an attempt to assert German control over Poland – if not yet through war.[38] The policy was nonetheless a stark change in policy for the Reich. The German ambassador in Bern, Ernst von Weizsäcker, noted that no German statesman could have made such a move toward rapprochement with Poland during the Weimar Republic, when politics and policy making were often subjugated to nationalist and anti-Polish passions.[39] Both governments soon reaped the rewards of the treaty, which was to last for ten years. The Nazi regime stood by as Poland virtually dismantled the Minorities Protection Treaty in September 1934, and Poland reciprocated by quietly accepting Hitler's declaration of German rearmament in March 1935.[40]

In any case, even this cautious enthusiasm for the Nazis soon subsided as fears of Germany and the Germans reasserted themselves. Many expected Hitler to resume a revisionist policy vis-à-vis Western Poland at a later date. Polish nationalists also called for more control over the German organizations in Poland, including infiltrating them with Poles with German-sounding last names. Such calls for harsher treatment, however, were in line with domestic political posturing. As part of the political opposition in Warsaw, the National Democrats hoped to use any information gleaned this way to accuse the government of being too soft on the minority and of neglecting Poland's security needs.[41] Still, Polish-German relations in the mid-1930s were better than they had been during the Weimar Republic, and they remained outwardly cordial even if mutual suspicions remained. To a large degree, Polish authorities tolerated the pro-Nazi position of the German minority and, as will be explained later, even encouraged it.

NATIONAL SOCIALISM AND THE GERMAN MINORITY'S RELATIONSHIP TO POLAND

The sense of uncertainty within the German minority following the Polish government's crackdown on opposition parties in the early 1930s gave way to a sense of relief with the German-Polish treaty. Polish authorities reported that the news of the non-aggression pact brought out spontaneous singing of the Polish national anthem and praise for Piłsudski and the

---

38 Karina Pryt, *Befohlene Freundschaft. Die deutsch-polnischen Kulturbeziehungen 1934–1939* (Osnabrück: Fibre, 2010), 466–467.
39 Ian Kershaw, *Der NS-Staat. Geschichtsinterpretationen und Kontroversen im Überblick* (Reinbek bei Hamburg: Rowohlt Taschenbuch, 1994), 224.
40 Blanke, *Orphans of Versailles*, 186, 187.
41 Kotowski, *Hitlers Bewegung im Urteil der polnischen Nationaldemokratie*, 40–41, 112–113, 128–129, 168–169.

Polish president.[42] The first few months following the treaty, the "era of good feeling," seemed to confirm this optimism. Hans-Jürgen Seraphim, an agricultural economist who specialized in Eastern Europe,[43] remarked in a lecture in Rostock in 1934 that the German-Polish treaty allowed the Volhynian Germans more freedom, including the ability to form dairy cooperatives.[44] A copy of a speech that circulated around Western Poland, presumably around 1936, claimed the rapprochement between Hitler and Piłsudski had made it possible for the German minority to pursue völkisch activities.[45] Official reconciliation and high words from statesmen did not mean, however, that popular nationalism and pressure on the minority had died down, and the treaty may have actually worsened the situation for the minority. Despite promises by the Polish government to fight discrimination, for example, the situation for German-language schools continued to deteriorate.[46] In the interest of maintaining good relations, however, the press in Nazi Germany became more restrained in its reporting of abuses against the German minority in Poland. This self-censorship would last until 1939.[47]

Many German leaders in Poland expressed deep disappointment after the high expectations in the honeymoon period following the 1934 treaty.[48] Viktor Kauder, editor of *Deutsche Monatshefte in Polen* (the successor publication to *Deutsche Blätter in Polen*), optimistically wrote in the July 1934 issue that the treaty had finally broken the stalemate between Germany and Poland. He criticized those naysayers who thought Germany had given up on the minority in Poland. He not only thought the lessened tensions

---

42 Office of the Voivode in Poznań to Polish Interior Ministry, situation report on the German minority (January 1934), February 9, 1934, in Jaworski et al., *Deutsche und Polen zwischen den Kriegen*, document 224, 640. Piłsudski's popularity is documented in an article by Heidi Hein, "Der Piłsudski-Kult in der Woiwodschaft Schlesien. Ein Mittel zur politischen Integration?" in *Dzieje Śląska w XX w. w świetle badań młodych historyków z Polski, Czech i Niemiec*, ed. Krzysztof Ruchniewicz, 102–113 (Wrocław: Instytut Historyczny Uniwersytetu Wrocławskiego, 1998).

43 Hans-Jürgen Seraphim was the older brother of Peter-Heinz Seraphim, an Ostforscher who also specialized in Jewish matters. See Alan E. Steinweis, *Studying the Jew: Scholarly Antisemitism in Nazi Germany* (Cambridge: Harvard University Press, 2006), 143–151; Claudia Koonz, *The Nazi Conscience* (Cambridge: Belknap Press of Harvard University Press, 2003), 199.

44 Reich and Prussian Minister of the Interior, memorandum on lecture by H. J. Seraphim at the Volksdeutscher Klub in Rostock (November 7, 1934), November 8, 1934, in BA Berlin, R8043, folder 946, 334–336.

45 Copy of speech "Völkischer Sozialismus," in BA Koblenz, R57-Neu, folder 1094 (Nr. 1), undated (presumably around early 1936), 2.

46 Blanke, *Orphans of Versailles*, 192–193.

47 Martin Burkert, *Die Ostwissenschaften im Dritten Reich, Teil I: Zwischen Verbot und Duldung. Die schwierige Gratwanderung der Ostwissenschaften zwischen 1933 und 1939* (Wiesbaden: Harrassowitz, 2000), 636, 638; Blanke, *Orphans of Versailles*, 202–203, 205; Breyer, *Das Deutsche Reich und Polen*, 316.

48 Blanke, *Orphans of Versailles*, 195, 202.

would allow the Germans to recover economically, but following a kind of constructivist logic, he indicated that good formal relations would eventually awaken real trust between Poles and Germans.[49] Just fourteen months later, however, Kauder lamented in the same journal that many of these new freedoms had been insignificant or shallow, and the deterioration of the economic basis had gone on unhindered despite the treaty. Indeed, he seemed to suggest that it was the treaty itself that had brought the minority to its desperate situation by giving the Polish government a free hand to do as it pleased.[50] One should note, however, that his words appeared in a German journal published in Poland.

Hans Kohnert, the new leader of the DV in 1935, also announced in a speech to the DV representatives in September 1936 that the period of greater freedom had come to an end. He claimed that the problem lay not in the leadership but in the lower echelons of administration and among the Polish "fellow citizens": indeed, Kohnert appealed to the government to enforce the rights that it had guaranteed.[51] Other anecdotal evidence shows that there was a marked improvement immediately after the treaty and then a rapid deterioration. Walburg Lehfeldt, a manorial estate owner in Western Poland, notes in her memoirs that there were many little advantages at first.[52] In a wartime essay looking back at the so-called nationality struggle of the interwar period, the German minority leader in Central Poland, Ludwig Wolff, also stated that the pact had brought initial relief for the Germans.[53] Hence, the focus has been on the fleeting nature of these good feelings.

Yet one should not underestimate the psychological effect of the treaty and its effect in binding Germans to the Polish state. Despite continuing repression in many cases, the new political rapprochement following the pact in 1934 made it safer than ever − politically and physically − to be a German in Poland. As the historian Przemysław Hauser has noted, "The policy of apparent rapprochement, skillfully pursued by Germany, made it impossible for the Polish authorities to take a tough line towards the elements supporting National Socialism."[54] Indeed, the Polish-German

---

49 Viktor Kauder, "Blick in die Zeit," *Deutsche Monatshefte in Polen* 1 (11), no 1 (July 1934): 1–4.
50 Viktor Kauder, "Mutterland und Auslanddeutschtum," *Deutsche Monatshefte in Polen* 2 (12), no. 3 (September 1935): 79–84, here 83; Blanke, *Orphans of Versailles*, 195.
51 Hans Kohnert, *Dr. Kohnert spricht. Zwei Reden an die Delegierten der Deutschen Vereinigung* (Bydgoszcz: Deutsche Vereinigung, 1936), 14–15.
52 Walburg Lehfeldt, *Gut Lehfelde. Eine deutsche Geschichte, 1932–1950 (Wie konnte das geschehen?)* (Wiesbaden: Limes, 1986), 70–71.
53 Ludwig Wolff, "Der Volkstumskampf des Deutschtums im Osten des Warthelandes," in *Der Osten des Warthelandes. Herausgegeben anläßlich der Heimatschau in Litzmannstadt*, ed. Müller, Hubert, 176–195 (Stuttgart: Stähle & Friedel, 1941), here 192.
54 Hauser, "The German Minority in Poland," 34.

political constellation did much to encourage National Socialism within the minority. For those Germans who were politically active, adherence to a pro-National Socialist organization seemed to minimize the risk of state repression. It even appeared that the Polish government preferred to deal with National Socialist-oriented minority leaders.[55] There was little support for German groups that opposed Hitler, in part because they also opposed the increasingly authoritarian streak in Polish politics.[56] Instead, Polish authorities cracked down on anti-Nazi organizations, including the German socialists, and others who questioned Poland's new friend.[57] Arthur Trunkhardt, a German pacifist in Upper Silesia, was brought to court for insulting Hitler. His initial sentence of ten months in prison was thrown out only because the charges had passed the statutes of limitations.[58] Given this kind of treatment, it is not surprising that all openly anti-Nazi German organizations had been reduced to insignificance by 1934.[59]

Ironically, the increasing Nazification of German activists in Poland also meant that the German minority became more tightly bound to the Polish state. As an apparent foreign policy success of Nazi Germany, the improved relations served to legitimate the Polish state in the eyes of minority leaders as well.[60] German minority leaders, of course, often found it beneficial to underline the improved German-Polish relations in public in order to give the sense that they were in line with the Reich's position. At least one Polish correspondent recognized the lessening of tensions in Upper Silesia and appreciated the new atmosphere in which German coolheadedness was gaining the upper hand.[61] If German nationalists still did not love Poland, they could at least learn to live with it. The treaty seemed to provide a breakthrough, and they sought to translate this optimism and progress into political gain. At the same time, the treaty made room for forces within the minority to challenge the established leadership. As will be seen later in this chapter, different National Socialist organizations competed with one another by asserting their loyalty to Poland.

---

55 Otto Heike, *Die deutsche Arbeiterbewegung in Polen, 1835–1945* (Dortmund: Ostdeutsche Forschungsstelle im Lande Nordrhein-Westfalen, 1969), 102; Eser, *Volk, Staat, Gott,* 202–203.

56 Eser, *Volk, Staat, Gott,* 202–203.

57 Otto Heike, *Die deutsche Minderheit in Polen bis 1939. Ihr Leben und Wirken, kulturell, gesellschaftlich, politisch. Eine historisch-dokumentarische Analyse* (Leverkusen: self-published, 1985), 435.

58 Eser, *Volk, Staat, Gott,* 202–203n585.

59 Hauser, "The German Minority in Poland," 34.

60 Office of the Voivode in Toruń to Polish Interior Ministry, situation report on the German minority (February 1934), sent March 1934, in Jaworski et al., *Deutsche und Polen zwischen den Kriegen,* document 63, 358.

61 Lektorat Polen, "Tagesbericht über die polnische Presse," November 15, 1934, in GStA, I HA, Rep. 77, Tit. 856, folder 752, 102.

The treaty provided new rhetorical opportunities for the Germans in making cultural, if not political, claims on the Polish state. Kohnert's admonishment of Polish officials to enforce existing rules suggests that minority leaders directed their discontent not at the Polish state per se or at its highest leaders. Instead, they blamed the largely anonymous low-ranking bureaucrats or the agitation of the National Democrats, who were particularly strong in Western Poland.[62] The appeal to higher authorities to crack down on those elements threatening the good relations between the Reich and Poland showed their willingness to participate in the political system. Another form of participation was the personality cult around Marshal Józef Piłsudski that had taken root in Poland. As Heidi Hein has demonstrated, the rituals surrounding the cult served as a means of integrating the Germans in the Polish state.[63] German minority leaders also hoped that their public approval of Piłsudski would prove their loyalty to the Polish state, which would then enable them to pursue other claims.

The depth of the Piłsudski cult within the minority had its limits, for the espousal of Polish nationalism did not go well with minority demands. Still, German leaders in Poland and in the Reich expressed great respect for Piłsudski. The German press in the Reich continued to show Piłsudski as a leader of the National Socialist type.[64] When Piłsudski died in May 1935, Germans participated in funeral services and wrote eulogies in the minority press. The German general consulate reported that the *Kurier Poznański* saw the grief of the Germans in the Reich and in Poland as sincere.[65]

In April 1935, shortly before Piłsudski's death, the Polish government introduced a new constitution that strengthened the executive branch and diminished the power of the Sejm and Senate. It also reduced the number of seats from 444 to 208 in the Sejm and from 111 to 96 in the Senate – 32 of which could be named by the president.[66] This situation made it even more

---

62 Kohnert, *Dr. Kohnert spricht*, 15.
63 See various works by Heidi Hein: "Der Piłsudski-Kult in der Woiwodschaft Schlesien. Ein Mittel zur politischen Integration?" (see note 42); Heidi Hein, "Die Piłsudski-Feiern in der *Kattowitzer Zeitung* und dem *Oberschlesischen Kurier*. Ein Beitrag zum Piłsudski-Bild und zur Rezeption des Piłsudski-Kultes der deutschen Minderheit in der Wojewodschaft Schlesien (1926–1939)," in *Die Geschichte Polens und Deutschlands im 19. und 20. Jahrhundert. Ausgewählte Beiträge*, ed. Markus Krzoska and Peter Tokarski, 124–141 (Osnabrück: Fibre, 1998).
64 Heidi Hein, *Der Piłsudski-Kult und seine Bedeutung für den polnischen Staat 1926–1939* (Marburg: Herder-Institut, 2002), 357–359. See also Martina Pietsch, *Zwischen Verachtung und Verehrung. Marschall Józef Piłsudski im Spiegel der deutschen Presse 1926–1935* (Cologne/Weimar/Vienna: Böhlau, 1995).
65 Consulate General in Poznań to German Foreign Ministry (Copy for Warsaw), May 15, 1935, in PAAA, PI 2e, Botschaft Warschau, Tod des Marschalls Pilsudski, 1935–6.
66 Balling, *Von Reval bis Bukarest*, 177–179.

difficult for minority parties to gain representation. Still, the conservative-nationalist Germans supported the government's election bloc in the 1935 elections, even though the bloc's list had no German candidates.[67] This development completely wiped out the already low number of Sejm mandates that the Germans had won in the 1930 elections. As a concession, the Polish president Ignacy Mościcki appointed two Germans to serve in the Senate, Rudolf Wiesner and Erwin Hasbach, who represented different camps but were both in favor of National Socialism.[68] German socialists, of course, were not considered. In 1938, President Mościcki once again chose two Germans, Max Wambeck and again Erwin Hasbach, to serve in the Senate. These were not minor concessions given the increasingly undemocratic and nationalistic atmosphere of the late 1930s in Poland.

NATIONAL SOCIALISM AND THE GERMAN MINORITY'S RELATIONSHIP TO GERMANY

The relationship of German activists in Poland to National Socialism is difficult to assess, even in very localized studies. The historian Mieczysław Wojciechowski concedes his frustration concerning the lack of sources about the Toruń Germans' political activity during the Nazi period.[69] Many scholars have focused on social and political conformity to explain the success of National Socialism among the Germans in Poland. Przemysław Hauser, for example, notes how one German newspaper headline proclaimed, "If you are German, then you must also be National Socialist." In his assessment, minority members lacked civil courage and feared being cast outside of the Volksgemeinschaft.[70] Other scholars have preferred to see the minority's devotion to National Socialism as a natural result of repressive Polish policies, which forced the minority to look to a strong Germany to alleviate its misery. The focus on Polish repression, however, can obscure the challenges that National Socialism posed for the minority, especially in Western Poland. Likewise, a concentration on German revanchism in explaining the minority's support for the Third Reich would conceal the other reasons for the Polish Germans' enthusiastic reception of National

---

67 Heike, *Die deutsche Arbeiterbewegung in Polen*, 109.

68 The two senators appointed were Erwin Hasbach from the Deutsche Vereinigung in Western Poland and Rudolf Wiesner from the Jungdeutsche Partei.

69 Mieczysław Wojciechowski, "Mniejszość niemiecka w Toruniu w latach 1920–1939," in *Mniejszości narodowe i wyznaniowe w Toruniu w XIX i XX wieku*, ed. Mieczysław Wojciechowski, 59–80 (Toruń: Uniwersytet Mikołaja Kopernika, 1993), 69.

70 Przemysław Hauser, "Die deutsche Minderheit in den Wojewodschaften Posen und Pommerellen 1919–1939," in *Deutsche und Polen zwischen den Kriegen* (see note 1), 273–282, here 277.

Socialism. Finally, focusing on the issue of irredentism would privilege the Germans in the Western Polish areas and suggest a misleading continuity between Weimar revisionism and Nazi Germany's wartime annexations.

Devotion to the mother country and attraction to National Socialist ideas were certainly major factors in many Germans' acceptance of National Socialism, but there were also powerful pragmatic reasons for German leaders to support National Socialism and to incorporate its ideological trappings. With the suppression of other political parties in Germany, there was no other available framework of political cooperation for those German nationalists who wanted to maintain ties with what they considered to be their mother country.[71] German conservative-nationalist leaders had to support the Reich government and its German minority agenda or risk appearing un-German or even anti-German. In Western Poland especially, where the minority had grown dependent on subsidies from the Reich, loyalty to the new regime was necessary for the continued existence of many organizations and individuals. A powerful motive, too, was the desire to appropriate the dynamism associated with National Socialism, which had become an important factor of legitimacy in German minority politics.

Yet the alignment with the Third Reich had its costs for minority leaders who expected too much. In Western Poland in particular, many Germans had never come to terms with Polish rule, a fact noted in the Reich press.[72] Hitler's rise to power increased expectations that the time for a revision had come. Polish reports in the mid-1930s indicated that many Germans in the so-called Corridor (i.e., Pomerelia) believed that a stronger Germany could at last begin the process of a peaceful, negotiated settlement of the border question. The voivodeship administration in Poznań noted a "lively satisfaction" among local Germans already in February 1933.[73] As events would show, however, these hopes were disappointed rather than fulfilled in the next few years. After the 1934 Polish-German treaty, shrill support for a border revision was no longer seen as an asset but as a foreign political liability. The new priorities shifted attention away from questions of border revision and hence away from the borderland Germans in Western Poland. Hitler proved more than willing to sacrifice the well-being of the minority

---

71 Hauser, "The German Minority in Poland," 33.
72 See "Mit dem Hakenkreuz in Polen. Polnischer Terror gegenüber den Deutschen – Alle hoffen auf Hitler," *Völkischer Beobachter*, June 9, 1932, in GStA, I HA Rep. 77, Tit. 856, folder 325, unpaginated.
73 Office of the Voivode in Poznań to Polish Interior Ministry, situation report on the German minority (January 1933), February 14, 1933, in Jaworski et al., *Deutsche und Polen zwischen den Kriegen*, document 221, 622; see also Office of the Voivode in Toruń to Polish Interior Ministry, situation report on the German minority (February 1934), sent March 1934, ibid., document 63, 349.

for foreign political aims.[74] For the Germans in Western Poland, the chances for a border revision became more remote than ever until 1939.[75] At the same time, the established minority leadership was being challenged by new groups on the periphery.

THE YOUNG GERMAN CHALLENGE

It was precisely the period of National Socialism that saw the German minority and its parties drift further than ever from the long-proclaimed goal of creating a national community. Despite enthusiastic shows of National Socialist affiliation and unity, the German minority quickly became embroiled in infighting and intrigue, destroying the political equilibrium between the western center and the eastern periphery. As previous chapters have shown, political life within the minority grew increasingly regionalized in the 1920s. After 1933, Reich authorities and certain German leaders renewed attempts to unify the minority under the banner of Volksgemeinschaft, yet these efforts only aired and worsened unresolved regional tensions and resentments. Especially loud in its claim to represent true National Socialism was the Jungdeutsche Partei für Polen (JDP), a party based in Bielsko. The attempt of these Young Germans to expand to other regions in Poland, although a failure, was the first major challenge to the system built around the dominance of the Germans in Western Poland.

AUSTRIAN SILESIA AND THE RISE OF THE JUNGDEUTSCHE PARTEI

Nestled in Poland's mountainous southern frontier with Czechoslovakia, Bielsko was once an important textile center in the Austrian lands. Located in the former Duchy of Teschen (Cieszyn), the city was cut off from the rest of Silesia after Frederick the Great's victories over Maria Theresa in the mid-eighteenth century. Increasingly, Bielsko came under the sway of the Bohemian lands. After the first partition of Poland in 1772, the bordering western Galician town of Biała – separated by a small river – also grew rapidly, and in many aspects the two towns had become one community by the end of the nineteenth century.

As we have previously seen, the formerly Austrian regions played a role between center and periphery within the minority after 1918. The Germans in Bielsko had not been the Staatsvolk in Austria the same way the Germans

---

74 Ronald M. Smelser, *The Sudeten Problem, 1933–1938: Volkstumspolitik and the Formulation of Nazi Foreign Policy* (Middleton: Wesleyan University Press, 1975), 18–20.

75 Blanke, *Orphans of Versailles*, 205–206.

in Western Poland had been in prewar Prussia, but neither had they been partially oppressed minorities like the Germans in Russian Poland or even in Austrian Galicia. The majority German-speaking population in Bielsko (estimated to be 30,000 strong[76]) assured that German parties would dominate municipal politics. As in many ethnically and religiously mixed areas, reactions to cohabitation varied greatly in Teschen Silesia. Significantly, the Austrian cultural matrix produced many völkisch scholars who researched German settlements in Poland and elsewhere. Viktor Kauder, a Volkstumsforscher and editor of *Deutsche Monatshefte in Polen*, was born in Łódź in 1899 but went to school in Bielsko (then Bielitz). Walter Kuhn and Alfred Karasek, both of whom took part in the Volhynia Expedition of 1926, were key members of the influential Bielitzer Kreis. That their works remained respectable in the post-1945 period is in part due to the fact that they focused less on the highly politicized and revisionist goals of the interwar period than on broader völkisch and ethnographic concepts. Yet Bielsko was also the hometown of Eduard Pant, the leader of the German Catholic Party in Poland who was also a key opponent of National Socialism within the minority. Teschen Silesia was especially fertile in producing German activists who could simultaneously play the roles of insider and outsider.

In 1921, members of the nationalist club Deutschbund founded the Deutscher Nationalsozialistischer Verein für Polen, the forerunner to the Jungdeutsche Partei. Rudolf Wiesner (1890–1973), an engineer from Bielsko, took over the party's leadership in 1923. Despite many affinities with National Socialism in Germany, however, the party's origins had little to do with the Hitler's party in Germany, but with conditions specific to Austrian Silesia.[77] Bielsko's geographical proximity to Bohemia had already acculturated the Germans there to the idea of nationality struggle between Czechs and Germans before the First World War. The founding members of Deutscher Nationalsozialistischer Verein für Polen had advocated creating an independent Sudetenland that would include Teschen Silesia, and after Poland took over the region, they maintained strong ties to German nationalists in Czechoslovakia.[78]

By 1928, however, the party had largely restricted its activities to Teschen Silesia, and even there its influence was limited.[79] Polish authorities became increasingly wary of Wiesner's organization, and they conducted several

---

76 Blanke, *Orphans of Versailles*, 3.
77 Breyer, *Das Deutsche Reich und Polen*, 240; Hans-Adolf Jacobsen, *Nationalsozialistische Außenpolitik, 1933–1938* (Frankfurt/Main: Metzner, 1968), 584–585; Eser, *Volk, Staat, Gott*, 193–194.
78 Zygmunt Stoliński, *Die deutsche Minderheit in Polen* (Warsaw: Instytut Badań Spraw Narodowościowych, 1928), 55.
79 Stoliński, *Die deutsche Minderheit in Polen*, 55.

house searches to look for organizational connections with Nationalist Socialists in Germany and Czechoslovakia. In order to become less conspicuous, the party leadership changed the organization's name in 1928 to Jungdeutsche Partei für Polen.[80] Polish authorities remained suspicious, however, and they continued to regard the JDP as a Polish branch of the Deutsche Nationalsozialistische Arbeiterpartei, the precursor to Konrad Henlein's Sudetendeutsche Partei in Czechoslovakia.[81] As the "for Poland" in the party's name suggests, however, the JDP was never meant to be strictly regional, and it would represent the first serious effort to unite all Polish Germans into one party. Several reasons account for why the JDP broke out of Teschen Silesia and pursued a Poland-wide expansion. As previous chapters have shown, various factors (e.g., demographics, the electoral system, territorial revisionist tendencies) led to a hardening of German parties along regional lines. The Austrian Silesian Germans were not only geographically isolated from Germans in Poznania and Central Poland, but also confessionally from Germans elsewhere in Upper Silesia. The Germans in Bielsko were divided fairly evenly between Catholics and Protestants (the leader of the JDP, Wiesner, came from an evangelical family), whereas the Germans in formerly Prussian Upper Silesia were by and large Catholic. To complicate this confessional divide, the two Silesian territories enjoyed different legal statuses under Polish rule. The Geneva Accord of 1922 for Upper Silesia, signed by Poland and Germany, called for the international regulation of German and Polish Upper Silesia for fifteen years. In the voivodeship of Silesia, however, the treaty held only for the formerly Prussian part, thus excluding the Germans in Bielsko from this protection.[82]

The Germans in formerly Austrian Silesia, then, were in a semi-peripheral position within the German political landscape in Poland, a position reinforced by the general lack of attention from Germany. Moreover, the German political and cultural scene in Teschen Silesia in the 1920s was dominated by parties from Prussian Upper Silesia, for example, the Deutsche Katholische Volkspartei (German Catholic People's Party), the Deutsche Partei, and the Volksbund. In Bielsko communal politics, the JDP remained a junior partner to the Deutsche Partei until 1933. The Volksbund,

---

80 Jacobsen, *Nationalsozialistische Außenpolitik*, 584–585. Blachetta-Madajczyk claims the name was changed in 1931: *Klassenkampf oder Nation? Deutsche Sozialdemokratie in Polen 1918–1939* (Düsseldorf: Droste, 1997), 59.

81 Martin Broszat, "JDP und DV in Posen-Pommerellen," *Gutachten des Instituts für Zeitgeschichte* 1 (1958): 404–407, here 404.

82 Pia Nordblom, *Für Glaube und Volkstum. Die katholische Wochenzeitung "Der Deutsche in Polen" (1919–1939) in der Auseinandersetzung mit dem Nationalsozialismus* (Paderborn: Ferdinand Schöningh, 2000), 60.

the largest minority organization in the voivodeship of Silesia and led by Otto Ulitz, largely limited its distribution of subsidies to the formerly Prussian areas there.[83] The JDP received little, if any, of the subsidies flowing in from the Reich. Hans Steinacher, the leader of the Volksbund für das Deutschtum im Ausland, one of the largest organizations devoted to helping Germans abroad, described how excluded JDP leaders felt like "pariahs" in view of the privileges enjoyed by the "aristocrats" in formerly Prussian territories.[84]

Conditions in Austrian Silesia, however, encouraged ambitious leaders to break out of the region. Whereas other German parties in Poland could content themselves with organizing the Germans in their respective regions, the German population base in Austrian Silesia was relatively small. A local party would not have been able to reach an adequate economy of scale to become a major player in the minority. In order to be influential within the German minority as a whole, Wiesner had to think big and escape the confines of Bielsko. At the same time, the very outsider status of the Young Germans made their party less dependent on the goodwill of Reich authorities and minority leaders elsewhere. The JDP had much to gain and nothing to lose.

BREAKOUT FROM THE PERIPHERY: THE JDP INCURSION INTO WESTERN POLAND

The general crisis of the Polish political system and the shakeup of the German parties after 1930 opened new opportunities for the JDP. In 1931, the JDP set up its first local group in Katowice, in formerly Prussian Upper Silesia.[85] Like the pacifist-loyalist Deutscher Kultur- und Wirtschaftsbund, the JDP tried to capitalize on the growing discontent within the minority. The economic depression of the early 1930s hit industrial Upper Silesia especially hard, and the increasingly authoritarian politics of the Piłsudski regime was unpopular with Germans and Poles alike. The advent of the Nazis in Germany in 1933 was decisive in giving the JDP new momentum. Wiesner took advantage of his party's strong formal affinities to National Socialism and claimed, with some justification, that the JDP was the oldest

83 Nordblom, *Für Glaube und Volkstum*, 60. Nordblom notes that Germans in Teschen Silesia and Upper Silesia had trouble getting along due to the differences in their legal status as well as psychological and financial support.

84 Hans-Adolf Jacobsen, ed., *Hans Steinacher. Bundesleiter des VDA 1933–1937. Erinnerungen und Doku-mente* (Boppard am Rhein: Boldt, 1970), 528–529; Jacobsen, *Nationalsozialistische Außenpolitik*, 585n48.

85 Jacobsen, *Nationalsozialistische Außenpolitik*, 585.

National Socialist organization in Poland. The JDP grew quickly in the voivodeship of Silesia, giving him a much-needed power base. With this increased leverage and territorial springboard, Wiesner could then take on the old guard in the minority's center of power: Poznania and Pomerelia.

The JDP announced in late 1933 its intention to establish party chapters in Western Poland.[86] In February 1934, the first local chapter (Ortsgruppe) was established in Poznań, followed in April by the first chapter in Bydgoszcz.[87] The JDP in Poznania and Pomerelia grew rapidly, and entire local chapters of the DV soon defected to the JDP. With 13,000 members by the end of 1934, it had reached almost the same size as the DV in less than a year. The JDP's vehement attacks against the established German parties quickly escalated, and brawls at meetings became routine.[88] In 1934, local JDP members in Grudziądz (Graudenz) disrupted a rally held by the Jungblock, a youth group affiliated with the DV. In the melee that followed, Erich Makus from the JDP was killed. Like Horst Wessel for the Nazi Party in Germany, Makus was celebrated as a martyr for the JDP cause.[89] Established German leaders in Poland now saw the JDP as a greater threat to unity than the German socialists or pacifists. For some, they were even more dangerous than the Poles.

The initial success of the JDP in Western Poland can be attributed to a convergence of class, generational, and regionalist claims. Contemporaries tended to see the conflict through the prism of National Socialist experience, interpreting it as a young-old or left-right struggle.[90] Indeed, JDP leaders cultivated this idea of class conflict. They claimed that only the more radical socialist concepts of the JDP could carry out the minority's rejuvenation by ridding it of reactionary elements. The Jungdeutsche members liked to allude to the NSDAP's victory in Germany over the conservative DNVP.[91] Well into the late 1930s, the JDP organ *Der Aufbruch* continued

---

86 Office of the Voivode in Toruń to Polish Interior Ministry, situation report on the German minority (February 1934), sent March 1934, in Jaworski et al., *Deutsche und Polen zwischen den Kriegen*, document 63, 349.

87 Broszat, "'Jungdeutsche Partei' und 'Deutsche Vereinigung' in Posen-Pommerellen," 405.

88 "Deutsche gegen Deutsche in Polen," *Ostsee-Beobachter* (Memel), June 9, 1935, in GStA, I HA, Rep. 77, Tit. 856, folder 753, 44.

89 "Die deutsche Uneinigkeit. Die politischen Auseinandersetzungen unter den deutschen in Polen und Pommerellen," *Glaube und Heimat*, May 27, 1934, in PAAA, Pol IV, Politik 12D Polen, vol. 3, R 82088, 173. Theodor Bierschenk claims that Makus was the only German to be killed during the infighting between Young Germans and Old Germans, although the common perception was that many more had died. See Theodor Bierschenk, *Die deutsche Volksgruppe in Polen, 1934–1939* (Würzburg: Holzner, 1954), 384n22.

90 Edward Wynot, "The Polish Germans, 1919–1939: National Minority in a Multinational State," *The Polish Review* 17, no. 1 (Winter 1972): 23–64, here 63.

91 Blanke, *Orphans of Versailles*, 172.

to carry the subheading "For Volkstum and Socialism." JDP leaders constantly chastised Old German minority leaders for their alleged bourgeois backgrounds and neglect of poorer Germans.[92] One Polish commentator noted that the JDP invoked the prewar antagonisms between small farmers and Junker in order to drum up support for the JDP-backed German Farmer Association (Deutscher Bauernbund). The JDP played on class resentments by accusing the "old bigwigs" of possessing luxury limousines and palaces.[93] The JDP often took its claim of being more National Socialist to extremes. For example, the JDP continued to use the Nazi calendar system until at least 1937, even though it had never caught on in the Reich.[94] For their part, the Old Germans likened the radicalism of the JDP to that of Ernst Röhm, the leader of the *Sturmabteilung* (SA), or the Nazi leftist Gregor Strasser; both were executed in the Night of the Long Knives in 1934. Comparisons of the Young German movement to Bolshevism were also common.

Yet for all the verbal posturing, the JDP was not really more left than its rivals. Polish reports claiming the existence of a left–right conflict often merely recited what the Germans themselves had claimed, and many Poles saw no substantial ideological difference. The JDP and DV's platforms praising National Socialism were virtually identical, as the Austrian ambassador to Poland in the 1930s noted.[95] The JDP often accused the "reactionary" DV and its allies of harboring Jews in their ranks.[96] The Volksbund in Upper Silesia indeed had Jewish members in the organization until 1936, when Julius Streicher's rabidly anti-Semitic weekly newspaper in Germany, *Der Stürmer*, discovered this apparent scandal.[97] Yet both the JDP and its established rivals used anti-Semitic slogans early on, and the younger generation of leaders in the DV was just as adamant about a "purification" of the

---

92 State Police station in Wałdowo to county administrator (Starosta) in Sępólno Krajeńskie, "Zebranie 'DV' (3.XII 1934 r.)," December 5, 1934, in Jaworski et al., *Deutsche und Polen zwischen den Kriegen*, document 97, 425; "Politik ist Planung der Zukunft," *Deutsche Nachrichten*, June 9, 1935, in GStA, I HA, Rep. 77, Tit. 856, folder 753, 45.

93 "Verstärkte Aktivität der Deutschen in Posen und Pommerellen," report on article by Józef Winiewicz, title translated as "Organisiertes Chaos," *Gazeta Polska* from October 10, 1935, in "Gesamtüberblick über die poln. Presse," October 19, 1935, in GStA, I HA, Rep. 77, Tit. 856, folder 753, 129.

94 Blanke, *Orphans of Versailles*, 171.

95 Anthony Tihamer Komjathy and Rebecca Stockwell, *German Minorities and the Third Reich: Ethnic Germans of East Central Europe Between the Wars* (New York: Holmes & Meier, 1980), 78; see also Blanke, *Orphans of Versailles*, 179.

96 "Reaktionärer Kampf gegen die jungdeutsche Bewegung in Posen," *Völkischer Beobachter* (Berlin Edition), June 3–4, 1934, in GStA, I HA, Rep. 77, Tit. 856, folder 752, 59.

97 Blanke, *Orphans of Versailles*, 166.

German community of all Jewish influences.[98] Finally, the JDP may have had a high percentage of younger Germans in its ranks, but in the end, most of the politicized German youth went with the DV.[99] Thus, the radicalism of the JDP had little to do with traditional political categories. The intra-minority conflict in Western Poland essentially involved marginalized groups against the established German leaders in the DV, and this protest cannot be ideologically or even generationally pinned down. Yet as the JDP sought to reshuffle power within the minority and to reinvent the Volksgemeinschaft, the outsider party became the catch-all platform for the discontented.

The initial successes of the JDP in Western Poland can thus be attributed to the tremendous dissatisfaction after a decade and a half of what was essentially the same leadership, and a showdown over the future course of the German minority was long in coming. In the early 1930s, for example, the leadership of the DV remained mostly in the hands of the generation born in the 1870s and 1880s. These aging activists had been able to quell opposition because they also controlled access to the Reich funds. Having already established a stable relationship with the DV, Reich officials were also wary of taking chances with new leaders. The discontent only increased after Piłsudski's general political crackdown of 1930. By 1933, many German activists in Western Poland believed that the DV leadership had grown out of touch with changes in the Reich.[100] Because the DV had effectively suppressed all organizations not within its control, there was no outlet for this discontent.

Many excluded Germans, especially junior DV functionaries, thus welcomed the JDP incursion in Western Poland. That the JDP was a "foreign" party was important for an insurrection in Western Poland. With its base in Bielsko, the JDP was largely immune to the politics and intervention of the DV and Reich authorities. As a challenger from the outside, the JDP was able to speak to many disenfranchised Germans both in and outside of the DV. The relationship between Bielsko and the rebellious elements in Western Poland was, at least in the beginning, a two-way street. The JDP offered the disaffected locals the organizational and ideological resources to change minority politics in Western Poland. The party's mobilization rallies were not only exciting in themselves, but the timing of the JDP's

98 See Hans Kohnert and Gero von Gersdorff, eds., *Wille zur Einheit. Reden und Aufsätze. Eine Schrift der Deutschen Vereinigung* (Bydgoszcz: Deutsche Vereinigung, 1937).

99 Breyer, *Das Deutsche Reich und Polen*, 250–252.

100 Office of the Voivode in Toruń to Polish Interior Ministry, situation report on the German minority (February 1934), sent March 1934, in Jaworski et al., *Deutsche und Polen zwischen den Kriegen*, document 63, 349.

expansion gave it a strong association with the momentous changes in the Reich. In return, the local Germans gave the JDP leadership in Bielsko an opportunity to expand and become a major player within the minority. The regional challenge of the JDP in Bielsko hence coincided with the generational challenge of the local JDP leaders in Poland. As the first truly Poland-wide German minority party, the JDP appeared to be a tangible manifestation of the vaunted Volksgemeinschaft.

REICH RESPONSES TO THE JDP

Organizations responsible for ethnic Germans abroad viewed the events in Western Poland with great concern, yet their reactions were mixed. The support in the Reich for the competing factions tended to fall along the lines of party and state: the more established institutions such as the Volksbund für das Deutschtum im Ausland and the Foreign Ministry supported the Deutsche Vereinigung, while Nazi Party organizations such as the Auslands-Organisation der NSDAP and the Hitler Youth supported the JDP.[101] Later, the Volksdeutsche Mittelstelle, technically a part of the Nazi Party and linked to the Schutzstaffel (SS), was sympathetic to the JDP as an organization, if not to its leader. Just as German minority leaders tried to place their conflict in the context of National Socialism in Germany, authorities in the Reich projected their notions of the power struggle between party and state on events in Poland.

German officials who represented both the Reich government and the Nazi party in Poland often found themselves in an especially difficult position. Hans Steinacher recalled the attempt by the German consul in Toruń to mediate between the different German organizations in Western Poland:

Consul Bernardt of the German Reich in Toruń, simultaneously a representative of the AO [Auslands-Organisation der NSDAP], received a delegation of "Young Germans" from his administrative district. They asked him for a decision regarding the conflict between the "Deutsche Vereinigung" and the "Young Germans." The Consul gave the following classic answer: As a representative of the Foreign Ministry, he was supposed to say that the "Deutsche Vereinigung" was the organization officially recognized in the Reich. As a National Socialist, however, he would recommend that they support the "Jungdeutsche Partei."[102]

Rather than working to unify the Germans in Poland, governmental and party organizations created confusion within the minority and among themselves. Thus, the constellation of competing authorities in Germany

---

101 Blanke, *Orphans of Versailles*, 175.   102 Cited in Jacobsen, *Hans Steinacher*, 531.

contributed to the persistence of the conflict between the DV and JDP in Western Poland. This infighting was more than just embarrassing episodes that flagrantly exposed the fiction of German unity. It also clearly dampened any Reich German hopes to use the minority for foreign policy aims.[103] As early as 1934, the *Völkischer Beobachter* severely criticized the JDP for its divisive actions.[104] Yet the lack of clear authority and of a neutral organization for mediation allowed for a great degree of independence and agency, and each party exploited this situation in order to further its own particularistic interests. Each was "working towards the Führer," or at least toward the Volksgemeinschaft.[105] With incoherent signals coming from the Reich, the Polish response to the conflict would be decisive.

THE JDP AND THE POLISH STATE

There is good reason to believe that many Polish officials, despite private reservations, did not see National Socialism, especially as manifested in the JDP, as necessarily detrimental to Polish interests. As we have seen earlier, Polish nationalists could see Hitler's policy of rapprochement as a basis for further reconciliation and as an opportunity for Poland to improve its foreign – and domestic – position. Instead of regarding the JDP as an element fostering disloyal sentiment within the minority, some Polish officials initially treated the Young Germans as the element to bind the minority to Poland. Indeed, just as Hitler's Austrian heritage seemed to many Poles to reduce the danger of a revanchist Prussia-Germany, the Austrian heritage of the JDP gave Wiesner's party an edge over the other German organizations. Given that Bielsko had not belonged to the prewar Reich, the JDP disavowals of German territorial revisionism sounded more sincere and were perceived as such for the time being.[106] Unlike German organizations in Western Poland, the JDP was not heavily enmeshed in the subsidies network from the Reich.

The issue of loyalty to the Polish state was particularly important, for Polish goodwill was a valuable political resource in this intra-minority conflict. Both the DV and the JDP curried favor with Polish authorities in the period after the non-aggression pact with the hope that they could expand their activities and block their rivals. The JDP repeatedly affirmed its loyalty

---

103 Jacobsen, *Nationalsozialistische Außenpolitik,* 593.
104 Blanke, *Orphans of Versailles,* 180.
105 On this concept, see Ian Kershaw, "Working Towards the Führer," in *Stalinism and Nazism: Dictatorships in Comparison,* eds. Ian Kershaw and Moshe Lewin, 88–106 (Cambridge/New York: Cambridge University Press, 1997).
106 Jacobsen, *Nationalsozialistische Außenpolitik,* 585.

to Poland and its financial independence from Germany, claiming to work only for the good of the Germans in Poland.[107] Wiesner's insistence on the lack of Reich aid can be seen as an attempt to turn a weakness into a political virtue, and the JDP was not afraid to accuse the other German leaders of irredentism. The Polish press often recognized the JDP's efforts, and the German embassy was somewhat disturbed that the *Gazeta Polska* reported that the JDP was more loyal than its German opponents.[108] Indeed, Wiesner's loud assertions of loyalty to the Polish state brought back the old fear of turncoats and traitors within the German minority. Old German minority leaders and Reich authorities suspected that Polish authorities were supporting the JDP, and they accused JDP functionaries of being crypto-Poles or of having belonged to Polish nationalist organizations. Otto Ulitz of the Volksbund in Upper Silesia claimed that Georg Drzymalla, the chief treasurer of the JDP, had been part of the Polish nationalist Sokół organization and had thus been thrown out of the Volksbund.[109] Even the German socialist *Volkszeitung* in Łódź, probably in an attempt to polish its own national credentials, compared the JDP to the much maligned pro-Polish Deutscher Kultur- und Wirtschaftsbund.[110] The Gestapo also reported Polish support for the JDP. In April 1935, some 550 people gathered near Ostrowo in Poznania for a DV meeting. When a JDP functionary appeared and asked the German farmers to join the JDP instead, he received little support. Indeed, the only people who applauded were Polish criminal police officers in attendance. One of the Polish officers later spoke at the meeting and asked the attendees not to join the DV, whose intention according to him was to "Germanize the Poles."[111] The Polish support for the JDP in this case, whatever the motives, was unmistakable.

Cynicism clearly played a role for those Poles who saw the JDP as an effective bulwark against the influence of the German conservative-nationalists. In a report to county-level administrators, the voivodeship office in Poznań ordered local authorities in March 1934 not to interfere with the JDP so

107 Bierschenk, *Die deutsche Volksgruppe in Polen*, 34; Blanke, *Orphans of Versailles*, 189.
108 German Embassy in Warsaw to German Foreign Ministry, "Tagung der Jungdeutschen Partei in Posen," December 5, 1934, with translation of article from *Gazeta Polska* from December 1, 1934, in PAAA, Pol IV, Politik 25 Polen, vol. 34, R82214, 51–55.
109 Nationalities Department of the Polish Interior Ministry, *Sprawozdanie z życia mniejszości narodowych za II kwartał 1936 r.* (Warsaw, 1936), in AAN, MSZ, folder 2348, 3–163 (1–161), here 72 (70).
110 "Die Jungdeutsche Partei erkennt Versailler Vertrag an," *Volkszeitung*, December 2, 1934, in PAAA, Pol IV, Politik 25 Polen, vol. 34, R82214, 58.
111 Gestapo to German Foreign Ministry and Deputy Führer and Reich Minister Rudolf Hess (Munich), "Deutsche Vereinigung in Polen," April 6, 1935, in PAAA, Pol IV, Politik 25 Polen, vol. 34, R82214, 403; Blanke, *Orphans of Versailles*, 179–180.

that it could break the German "front."[112] This divide-and-conquer tactic seemed to pay off, and the conflict did increase the vulnerability of German minority organizations. Not only did the rising memberships allow the Polish police to infiltrate both organizations with considerable thoroughness, but rival German activists willingly denounced their opponents to Polish authorities.[113] Thus, Polish police reports that recorded the DV–JDP conflict have been tremendously useful in reconstructing events and meetings. Hans Steinacher, the head of the VDA, recalled that the Polish police minister had openly boasted that he no longer needed to spend money to pay German informants because he could gather confidential information by perusing the party newspapers.[114] This instrumental attitude toward the JDP also meant that the Poles were willing to turn against the party as soon as the costs outweighed the benefits. The costs were indeed high from the start, since authorities recognized early on that they were playing with fire: the intra-minority conflict tended to politicize an ever greater number of Germans.[115] Despite the bitter competition and the eager statements of loyalty, the Polish press noted that the German factions were all fighting in the name of Germandom and that organized activity was growing.[116] By tolerating or even encouraging the JDP, Polish officials helped to intensify the Nazification of the German minority in Poland.

Such unintended consequences highlight the need to reevaluate how the Polish government contributed to the JDP's growth. Germany's invasion of Poland in 1939 has meant that, until recently, Polish historiography has tended to brand the Germans in Poland as a fifth column, thus ignoring the Polish government's own role in aiding and abetting Nazified elements in Poland. Likewise, postwar German apologists for the DV have tended to paint the JDP as the only National Socialists in Poland. Decades after the war, many expellees still view the JDP as *the* troublemakers who were responsible for minority disunity and Nazi activity against the Polish state.[117] Whereas

---

112 Office of the Voivode in Poznań to county administrators (do starostów), "Zachowanie się wobec 'JDP,'" March 30, 1934, in Jaworski et al., *Deutsche und Polen zwischen den Kriegen*, document 225, 654.

113 Blanke, *Orphans of Versailles*, 179, 189.

114 Jacobsen, *Hans Steinacher*, 530; Blanke, *Orphans of Versailles*, 179.

115 Voivode in Poznań to Political Department of the Polish Interior Ministry, memorandum "JDP-działalność niezgodna ze statutem," July 15, 1936, in AAN, MSW, folder 1005, 1–4, here 1–2.

116 "Verstärkte Aktivität der Deutschen in Posen und Pommerellen," report on article by Józef Winiewicz, title translated as "Organisiertes Chaos," *Gazeta Polska* from October 10, 1935, in "Gesamtüberblick über die poln. Presse," October 19, 1935, in GStA, I HA, Rep. 77, Tit. 856, folder 753, 129.

117 This view of the JDP as somehow more Nazi and more troublesome than the DV can be found in the memoirs of a German landowner, Walburg Lehfeldt: *Gut Lehfelde*, 70–71. See also Georg W. Strobel, "Das multinationale Lodz, die Textilmetropole Polens, als Produkt von Migration und

this postwar viewpoint is problematic because it conveniently externalizes Nazi activity away from the members of the DV, it also misrepresents the Polish state's relationship with the JDP as fundamentally antagonistic. It also oversimplifies the relationship between National Socialism, the Geman minority, and Poland. As Ingo Eser posits, "It is questionable if a turn to National Socialism can be interpreted automatically as a conscious act of disloyalty towards the Polish state."[118] Although the Nazi-oriented Germans were not nationally indifferent, it remains difficult to categorize their political choices. But such was everyday practice in the ethnically mixed regions of East Central Europe, despite – or even because of – the increasing nationalist atmosphere of the interwar period.[119]

NATIONAL SOCIALISM: A TRANSNATIONAL APPROACH

Völkisch thinkers had attempted to differentiate nationhood from statehood well before 1933, but the improved relations between Germany and Poland that existed for most of the mid-1930s made the accommodation between Volk and state appear feasible. By decoupling formal citizenship from national belonging, völkisch thought allowed Germans in Poland to find a connection to the Reich while also seeing their own role in Poland. Indeed, the clear distinction of Volk from state was an important resource in propagating allegiance to both. German activists in Poland had often found that religion could serve as a model for this distinction between state and nationality. As Ingo Eser points out, German-nationalist Protestant pastors in Poland often referred to Martin Luther's division of secular and religious authority into "two kingdoms" when preaching the necessity of subordination to the state while upholding German culture. Eser provides a lucid example from a newspaper for Polish German schoolteachers that praised a religion teacher who had been fired in 1933: "He rendered unto his Volkstum the things that are the Volk's, and he rendered unto the Polish state the things that are the state's."[120] For many Germans in Poland, National

Kapitalwanderung," in *Wanderungen und Kulturaustausch im östlichen Mitteleuropa. Forschungen zum ausgehenden Mittelalter und zur jüngeren Neuzeit*, ed. Hans-Werner Rautenberg, 163–223 (Munich: Oldenbourg, 2006), 210; Valdis O. Lumans, *Himmler's Auxiliaries: The Volksdeutsche Mittelstelle and the German National Minorities of Europe, 1933–1945* (Chapel Hill: University of North Carolina Press, 1993), 96, 98.

118 Eser, *Volk, Staat, Gott*, 204.
119 On "national indifference," see Tara Zahra, "Imagined Non-Communities: National Indifference as a Category of Analysis," *Slavic Review* 69, no. 1 (Spring 2010): 93–119, 103.
120 Eser, *Volk, Staat, Gott*, 594, see also 209, 242. Eser points out that the example refers to the New Testament's Gospel of Matthew 22:21.

Socialism was not seen as a program of political activity but as simply a "way of life."[121]

German political leaders in Poland made similar statements that distinguished state from ethnic authority. Rudolf Wiesner's speech to the Polish Senate on December 14, 1936, illustrates this attempt to square Volkstum with citizenship:

1. We recognize the principle that the Polish people are the people of the state and the host nation. They alone have the right to organize the state and to build it according to their needs.
2. Only German principles and our Weltanschauung can guide our völkisch life.
3. As honest and decent citizens, we want to participate in the building of the state and to devote all our energy to it.
4. We declare that we are loyal citizens of the state and also loyal members of our Volk. That is not a contradiction, and it is necessary.
5. Our work is founded upon the laws governing the state. We are not influenced by factors outside of the state, and we want to shape our lives only according to the possibilities given by this state.

   As Germans abroad, we feel that we are brothers of the entire German Volk. We give to the state what belongs to the state, and we want to support it in all aspects wherever possible for us. But our most holy good, our German ethnicity [Volkstum], cannot be surrendered.[122]

Wiesner attempted to alleviate the cognitive dissonance of being a good German and being a good Polish citizen. In this way, ties to both countries were strengthened, and the conflict between mother country and host state could be resolved. The rhetoric and the ritualization of loyalty in turn created their own expectations and attachments. Most members probably did not have any reason to doubt that these statements from their German leaders were sincere. It is not unlikely that such proclamations of loyalty to Poland in turn conditioned the Germans to practice what they preached. Whether National Socialist or not, the rise of völkisch precepts provided an increasingly deterritorialized view of national belonging, allowing Germans in Poland to consider themselves to be as real in their Germanness as Reich Germans. National Socialist tenets, too, fostered such transnational identities across political boundaries.[123]

In practice, however, the demands of the mother country could contradict those of the host state, and these tensions could never fully be

---

121 Eser, *Volk, Staat, Gott*, 243.
122 Theodor Bierschenk, "In Memoriam Rudolf Wiesner," in *Heimat Wolhynien*, ed. Alfred Cammann, 42–43 (Marburg/Lahn: N.G. Elwert, 1988).
123 On defining this concept, see Patricia Clavin, "Defining Transnationalism," *Contemporary European History* 14, no. 4 (2005): 421–439.

resolved.[124] Nazi Germany's völkisch practice followed goals that were different from the völkisch ideology that many of Hitler's proponents preached. Far from seeing the equality of the Germans abroad with the Germans in the Reich, Nazi leaders would readily sacrifice the needs of the ethnic Germans abroad to the interests the of core state.[125] The separation of state and Volk was clearly discernible in Nazism's racialized and racist approach to German citizenship. As Dieter Gosewinkel has noted, the National Socialists actually broke the traditional practice of citizenship in which people not of German ethnicity, however defined, could still gain German citizenship and pass it on to their descendants. Their citizenship, once acquired, could only be revoked with great difficulty. In the Nazi period, however, citizenship was fragmented into different hierarchical categories, and a biologicized concept of race rather than subjective-cultural or legal-political understandings had become the important criterion in considering who would be a proper German citizen.[126] Because völkisch thought in Nazi Germany was increasingly coopted for a racist and expansionist agenda, it lost any transnational affinities in practice. The prerogative of a racial state that claimed that ethno-national borders should be congruent with political ones legitimated at first the "Heim ins Reich" programs to repatriate ethnic Germans to the Reich, and later the war for territorial expansion and racial cleansing.

DEALING WITH DIVERSITY: REGIONALISM AND THE USES OF VOLKSGEMEINSCHAFT

Despite the Young Germans attempt to revamp minority politics, it ultimately failed to become dominant in any region outside its home base in Austrian Silesia. Although certain regional factors favored JDP inroads into Western Poland, other regional factors would later work against the JDP challenge. As the generational pressure subsided as younger functionaries took control of the DV, regionalism began to reassert itself. It was precisely over the issue of regional diversity and organizational unity that the rival organizations feuded most bitterly. A close study of these competing visions thus reveals the salience of individual and particular interests behind the façade of Volksgemeinschaft.[127]

124 Eser, *Volk, Staat, Gott*, 247.   125 Smelser, *The Sudeten Problem*, 17–20.

126 Dieter Gosewinkel, *Einbürgern und Ausschließen. Die Nationalisierung der Staatsangehörigkeit vom Deutschen Bund bis zur Bundesrepublik Deutschland* (Göttingen: Vandenhoeck & Ruprecht, 1991), 383, 387, 393, 399, 403, 425–426.

127 The instrumental functions of Volksgemeinschaft are explored in John F. Connelly, "The Uses of Volksgemeinschaft: Letters to the NSDAP Kreisleitung Eisenach, 1939–1940," *The Journal of Modern History* 68 (December 1996): 899–930.

Although the inflated rhetoric of national community often presented the same slogans, the competing German parties presented fundamentally different ideas when it came to the regional question. The DV's sphere of influence remained limited to Poznania and Pomerelia, in part out of deference to its allies elsewhere and in part to concentrate its resources in Western Poland. DV leaders thus advocated a loose confederation of regional organizations. The JDP, however, had a free hand to operate throughout Poland. In the JDP's interpretation, the National Socialist movement was an organizational matter, and the JDP approach to Volksgemeinschaft was to equate it with a single centralized party, which could then achieve a "welding together" of all the regions.[128] Only this kind of unity could allow the Germans to assert their minority's rights vis-à-vis the Polish state and to fight the established system within the minority.

In JDP eyes, a "revolutionary völkisch renewal" could only be achieved in an explicitly political organization.[129] Although the JDP recognized certain differences as legitimate, region was not to be an issue of division in a true Volksgemeinschaft. Indeed, the JDP saw existing regional differences as a confirmation of the need to create a unified organization. As a consequence, the JDP ostentatiously and self-servingly bemoaned "cantonization" and "swissification" within the minority,[130] as well as "regional separatism."[131] The JDP's call for a centralized party seemed to converge with National Socialist precepts of Volksgemeinschaft, into which all class, generational, and regional conflicts would be subsumed. Over and over, the JDP repeated its motto "It shall be all of Germandom."[132]

The expanding JDP not only had to convince the local Germans that a supraregional party was in their interest, but that the established parties in Western Poland and elsewhere stood in the way of the unification of all Germans in Poland.[133] It was especially relentless in its criticism of the DV,

---

128 "'Alles für unser Volk.' Gewaltige Kundgebung der Jungdeutschen Partei auf dem Unterparteitag in Posen am 18. November 1934," *Deutsche Nachrichten*, November 27, 1934, in GStA, I HA, Rep. 77, Tit. 856, folder 752, 111; "Ja, warum aber . . . ?" *Deutsche Nachrichten in Polen,* March 10, 1935, in GStA, I HA, Rep. 77, Tit. 856, folder 752, 196.

129 "Zur Einheit," *Deutsche Nachrichten in Polen,* November 21, 1934, in GStA, I HA, Rep. 77, Tit. 856, folder 752, 113.

130 Peter-Jacob Esch, "Falsche Rivalität," *Danziger Tageblatt,* November 25, 1934, in GStA, I HA, Rep. 77, Tit. 856, folder 752, 122. Rudolf Wiesner and Walter Günzel also used the word "Verschweizerung" in their speeches. See Jungdeutsche Partei für Polen, *Reden und Berichte vom Parteitag 1934.* Second Edition (Bielsko: Jungdeutsche Partei für Polen, 1934), in BA Koblenz, R57-Neu, folder 1093 (Nr. 21).

131 "Und die Wirklichkeit?" *Deutsche Nachrichten in Polen,* June 20, 1935, in GStA, I HA, Rep. 77, Tit. 856, folder 753, 53.

132 Flyer titled "Das ganze Deutschtum soll es sein!" in *Deutsche Nachrichten in Polen,* May 3, 1935, in GStA, I HA, Rep. 77, Tit. 856, folder 753, 17.

133 "Aus Mittelpolen: Sompolno jungdeutsch. Ortsgruppe des Volksverbandes geht geschlossen zur JDP über," *Deutsche Nachrichten in Polen,* October 20, 1935, in GStA, I HA, Rep. 77, Tit. 856, folder 753, 131.

which it alleged had a strong interest in keeping the minority regionally divided. Indeed, the JDP accused the DV of actively cultivating regional differences in order to avoid the work of unification. According to the JDP, the old "cliques" had thus followed a politics of interest that contradicted the very tenets of Volksgemeinschaft: the DV's resistance to völkisch renewal had brought the minority to the brink of destruction.[134] These accusations of "regional mania" in turn fed latent suspicions of self-profit and corruption among DV leaders.[135] Countless JDP speakers and journalists staged the JDP as the only true brotherhood of Germans across Poland, while the DV, limited to Poznania and Pomerelia, was said to be comprised of incorrigible and arrogant regionalists.[136]

The JDP's self-representation as the true party of egalitarian unity served to win over not just Germans in Poland, but also authorities in the Reich. The rhetoric of Volksgemeinschaft and harmony across regional and class lines reflected the new ideological priorities emanating from Germany. The JDP challenge to Western Poland received tailwind from Reich authorities who were increasingly frustrated with the established German leaders there. As we have seen, the German Foreign Ministry stressed the need for the Germans in Western Poland finally to come to terms with being "Germans abroad" and to rid themselves of their "acute irredentist mentality."[137] Around the same time, Krahmer-Möllenberg from the Deutsche-Stiftung expressed an analogous desire for the Germans in Western Poland to learn how to survive abroad.[138] This language suggested that the Germans in Western Poland were not better than the other Polish Germans after all. The diminishing importance of residual Reich citizenship and the growing importance of völkisch belonging in Nazi rhetoric put the eastern diaspora Germans and the Germans in the Western Polish provinces on increasingly equal footing.

In the end, however, the JDP became its own greatest enemy. Because the JDP leadership sustained its self-perception as a party from the disadvantaged periphery, the JDP itself recklessly played the regional card in its attacks on its enemies. While the JDP's goal was to overcome regional

---

134 Flyer titled "Das ganze Deutschtum soll es sein!" in *Deutsche Nachrichten in Polen*, May 3, 1935, in GStA, I HA, Rep. 77, Tit. 856, folder 753, 17.

135 "Deutsche Ostern in Polen," *Deutsche Nachrichten in Polen*, in GStA, I HA, Rep. 77, Tit. 856, folder 753, 11.

136 Peter-Jacob Esch, "Falsche Rivalität," *Danziger Tageblatt* Nr. 57, November 25, 1934, in GStA, I HA, Rep. 77, Tit. 856, folder 752, 122.

137 Fritz von Twardowski, "Aufzeichnung betreffend die deutsche Volksgruppe in den an Polen abgetretenen Gebieten," November 30, 1936, in PAAA, Inland II geheim, vol. 2 (221), microfiche nos. 2322–2323, 222–229. Cf. Blanke, *Orphans of Versailles*, 205.

138 Blanke, *Orphans of Versailles*, 205.

antagonisms, the very discussion of such problems reinforced old regional resentments and invoked, reformulated, and crystallized new ones. Moreover, it fostered regionalism in its own ranks. Local JDP chapters soon chafed under "Bielitzer centralism."[139] Trying to head off a rebellion in Poznania and Pomerelia in the summer of 1934, Wiesner made concessions for greater autonomy of the JDP in Western Poland. Yet the conflict with the DV and within the JDP only made Wiesner more intent on tightening his control through administrative reorganization and the purging of local chapter leaders. Local JDP members felt betrayed.[140] That these tensions had come to the fore at the height of JDP successes illustrates the salience of regional antagonisms. Not surprisingly, these internal power struggles only intensified as the JDP declined. The bad blood between the Western Polish JDP and the JDP leadership in Bielsko continued until the outbreak of the Second World War.

Caught between his previously pro-Polish course and the growing rebellion among his lieutenants, Wiesner opted for a harder line against the Polish government by late 1936. Polish observers saw the Reich's manipulation of the minority behind this growing anti-Polishness.[141] Yet the growing anti-Polish stance and militancy of the JDP troubled German officials as well. As one Polish report noted, the German consul in Katowice, Wilhelm Nödelcke, had gone so far as to send a complaint to the Foreign Ministry on October 15, 1936, about the JDP's anti-Polish behavior.[142] Not surprisingly, the Poles began to see less value in tolerating the JDP in Western Poland. In the fall of 1936, Wiesner had promised the social-political affairs officer at the Poznanian Voivodeship to suppress anti-Polish sentiments in his party. Disappointed by Wiesner's failure to keep his promises, the voivodeship administration concluded that the JDP was playing a dirty game against the Polish government.[143] The situation became a vicious circle: lacking the beneficence of Polish officials, the JDP functionaries felt compelled to use

---

139 Breyer, *Das Deutsche Reich und Polen*, 247.

140 "Die Vorgänge in der JDP im Sept./Okt. 1934," in BA Koblenz, R57-Neu, folder 1093 (Nr. 21); For Steinacher's account of different German minority leaders, see "Zur Lage der deutschen Volksgruppen in Europa und Übersee," reprinted as Appendix B in Jacobsen, *Hans Steinacher*, 527; Jacobsen, *Nationalsozialistische Außenpolitik*, 588; Blanke, *Orphans of Versailles*, 173–174.

141 Office of the Voivode in Poznań to Polish Interior Ministry, situation report on the German minority (May 1937), June 13, 1937, in Jaworski et al., *Deutsche und Polen zwischen den Kriegen*, document 229, 657–658.

142 Karol Grünberg, *Nazi-Front Schlesien. Niemieckie organizacje polityczne w województwie śląskim w latach 1933–1939* (Katowice: Wydawnictwo Śląsk, 1963), 66n1.

143 Office of the Voivode in Poznań to county adminstrators (do starostów), "Krytykowanie władz polskich ze strony 'JDP,'" December 3, 1936, in Jaworski et al., *Deutsche und Polen zwischen den Kriegen*, document 227, 655–656.

more anti-Polish statements to garner support. In early 1937, the voivode for Poznań suggested that it was time to "shake up" the JDP.[144]

Germany's expansionist path heightened concerns about the role of the ethnic Germans in Hitler's plans. The advantage of the JDP's Austrian heritage waned in 1938 with the incorporation of Austria and the Sudeten German crisis in Czechoslovakia, for it was now apparent that Germany would attempt to annex territory outside of its 1914 borders. Yet the increasing radicalization in the minority in general and the JDP in particular was not just due to high politics; it was also a result of the logic of hypernationalism. The constant talk of national unity, and the inevitable disappointment that followed, led to the search for familiar enemies. Although enough opponents could be found within the German minority at first, it was inevitable that the focus would eventually swing back to the Polish state. Moreover, the initially pro-Polish attitude of the party became harder to sustain as the party expanded into Western Poland. In many cases, the JDP was forced to adapt to the prevailing revisionist attitudes of the German population there. The JDP leaders in Bielsko had failed to see how the incorporation of so many Germans in Western Poland would tear their organization apart.

A large part of the JDP's failure in Western Poland derived from the fact that it was a party from the political periphery, taking on the minority's political center. Regional conditions and resentments had determined the JDP challenge in Western Poland, and despite its claim to represent all Germans, the JDP never really could rid itself of its roots in Austrian Silesia. Moreover, the JDP also had considerable difficulty in maintaining control over its local members, many of whom had previously been in the DV: accustomed to being privileged within the hierarchy of regions, JDP members in Western Poland were less apt to follow commands emanating from Bielsko. On multiple fronts, the outsiders could not dislodge or replace the insiders in Western Poland.

UNITY IN DIVERSITY? THE DV'S REGIONAL RESPONSE

Facing a growing defection of Germans to the JDP in the mid-1930s, Deutsche Vereinigung leaders had sought to reform their organization. Perhaps the most immediate, if not serious, problem for the established minority leaders was the lack of a comparable structure able to compete with the JDP. Although the JDP had been overly centralized in its organization, the

---

144 Polish Interior Ministry, "Jungdeutsche Partei," memorandum dated March 20, 1937, in AAN, MSW, folder 1005, 68–69, here 69.

Deutsche Vereinigung was too loosely organized. Prior to 1934, the DV was formally a network of the German delegates to the Polish parliament. Thus the DV leadership sought an organizational makeover that would make it more like a party. On September 8, 1934, the Polish government approved the refounding of the DV.[145] The new name was the Deutsche Vereinigung in Westpolen (DVW), but most continued to call the organization simply Deutsche Vereinigung and to use the same (abbreviated) acronym DV. Pressure to imitate the JDP led to the establishment of a single leader within the DV. After some initial missteps, Dr. Hans Kohnert from Bydgoszcz took over the DV on June 24, 1935.[146] Kohnert (1905–1972) was a relatively young man within the DV and enjoyed the respect of many JDP members, and his choice was intended to draw support away from the JDP. Under Kohnert, the DV implemented new organizations explicitly geared toward younger members and strove for closer cooperation between Old German youth groups from other areas.

Based in Western Poland and hounded by suspicions of revisionism, the DV was at a disadvantage vis-à-vis the JDP when it came to showing loyalty to Poland. DV leaders felt especially compelled to deal with the issue of irredentism, which the JDP often accused the DV leadership of harboring. Kohnert, for example, tried to show that a younger, less revisionist leadership was now in place:

We all know that we are Polish citizens and as such we are to fulfill obediently our duties to the state. It has been said that especially we Germans in the formerly Prussian territories have been following irredentist thoughts. We have always denied these claims and do so today as well. After 15 years of Polish rule, we have accustomed and adapted ourselves to the new construction of the state, and we will loyally fulfill our civic duties. Especially the young generation, which today has taken an important step in responsibly participating in the representation of German interests through the election of the new executive, desires an understanding coexistence with the Polish neighbors, with whom they have maintained good relations since serving together in the Polish army.[147]

Thus Kohnert had to walk the fine line of denying that the Western Polish Germans had ever supported irredentist tendencies in the past, but at the same time claiming that the DV had undergone a major transformation in its outlook. His public statements stressed the need to have the trust of Polish authorities.[148]

145 Matelski, *Mniejszość niemiecka w Wielkopolsce*, 95.
146 Bierschenk, *Die deutsche Volksgruppe in Polen*, 39.
147 Kohnert, *Dr. Kohnert spricht*, 5.
148 *Sprawy Narodowościowe* 10, nos. 4–5 (1936): 499–500.

Despite its new statutes, the DV and its affiliated organizations remained less convincing than the all-in-one solution of the JDP. In order to compete with the JDP, therefore, the Old Germans pursued two parallel, and somewhat contradictory, unification projects. One project was to coordinate the various regional parties within a confederation, the Rat der Deutschen in Polen (RDP), founded in October 1934. Erwin Hasbach, who replaced Eugen Naumann as the head of the Zentralausschuss/Zentralverein in early 1933, served as the leader of the RDP until 1939. Hasbach had been a Sejm deputy from 1919 to 1922 and senator from 1922 to 1930, and he would serve again as senator from 1935 to 1939. Despite the appearance of greater cohesiveness of the German minority, the RDP was really a loose umbrella organization of the various regional German organizations with the primary purpose of working against the JDP.[149] Although the council drew its twelve regular members from throughout Poland, the organization reproduced the dominance of the formerly Prussian territories, which could be seen in their disproportionate weight in the council: Poznań/Pomerelia had four seats, and Upper Silesia had three. The formerly Austrian regions of Teschen Silesia (Bielsko) and Little Poland (Galicia) were each allotted only one seat. The formerly Russian territories of Central Poland and Volhynia had two slots and one slot, respectively.[150] According to this breakdown, the formerly Prussian territories maintained a slim majority of seats, which meant that the other regions could not outvote them. Although Poznanian-Pomerelian Germans did not necessarily get along with each other or with the Upper Silesian Germans, the Prussian advantage was clear because the regional cleavages on the non-Prussian side were even greater. Having more clout to begin with, the DV members in the RDP could ensure that only acquiescent members would be picked from the non-Prussian regions, especially Volhynia and Galicia. Finally, the council could call in specialists, and parliamentarians and senators were allowed, ex officio, to sit in on meetings with full voting privileges.[151] The last measure in particular favored the

149 Breyer, *Das Deutsche Reich und Polen*, 252.
150 Walter Kuhn, "Das Deutschtum in Polen und sein Schicksal in Kriegs- und Nachkriegszeit," in *Osteuropa Handbuch: Polen*, ed. Werner Markert, 138–164 (Cologne/Graz: Böhlau, 1959), here 149.
151 *Sprawy Narodowościowe* 9, nos. 1–2 (1935): 81. The report listed the DVV members of the RDP to be J. Krause and T. Blin. Alfred Kleindienst represented Volhynia, and Bolek represented Galicia. The other members were not yet known. In 1937, a Polish police report listed thirteen members, including the female secretary whose home served as the RDP office, to be: Erwin Hasbach (leader, Hermanowo), August Utta (first member of the board of directors, Łódź), Otto Ulitz (second member of the board of directors, Katowice), Helena Pahl-Binkowska (secretary, Warsaw), Ludwig Bolek (Lwów), Alfred Kleindienst (Łask), Leo Brauer (Łódź), Dr. Hans Kohnert (Bydgoszcz), Gero von Gersdorff (Bydgoszcz) Heinrich Hauss (Długa Goślina, Poznania), Robert Piesch

western areas and Upper Silesia, which in 1934 still accounted for four of the five Sejm deputies and two of the three German senators in Poland.

Not surprisingly, the RDP enjoyed very little support even among the Old Germans.[152] For those who wanted a true political unification of the Germans in Poland, its loose federal structure was a poor substitute. Far from solving the unity question, in many ways the council furthered the construction of regions by institutionalizing them within the RDP. Hence, the organizational structure of the RDP was out of touch with demographic and political developments in Poland; it can even be seen as a last ditch attempt to maintain the dominance of the formerly Prussian regions. For Germans in the non-Prussian regions who resented Western Polish domination, the Rat der Deutschen in Polen must have looked like old wines in new bottles. JDP leaders saw through this pseudo-unification attempt and ridiculed the arrangement as "national communities unto themselves and regional reclusiveness" (Volksgemeinschaften unter sich und Teilgebietseigenbrötelei).[153] The JDP claimed that the RDP encouraged separatism and was merely a "liberal means," that is, an inorganic and artificial process, for bridging the differences between the regions.[154] Yet the RDP's loose federal structure was also its greatest strength: the RDP did not demand true unification and thus accepted the continuing existence of regional organizations. Left alone within the RDP, regional German leaders did not feel threatened by one another and could continue to cooperate.

The other project was to change the DV statutes that had limited its activities only to Poznania-Pomerelia, thereby allowing it to operate like the JDP. Yet the plan for turning the DV into a Poland-wide organization met with considerable skepticism. Ongoing regional antagonism within one's own party was a sensitive subject that German functionaries did not like to talk about publicly or discuss in their correspondence with Reich

(Bielsko), Paul Golletz (Katowice), Jan Rosumek (Siemianowice – Upper Silesia). See Voivodeship Office of the State Police in Toruń (Investigation Department) to State Police Headquarters (Investigation Department) in Warsaw, memorandum "Rat der Deutschen in Polen – struktura organizacyjna," September 7, 1937, copy for Main Office of the Silesian Voivodeship Police (Investigation Department) in Katowice, September 22, 1937, in AP Katowice, Policja Województwa Śląskiego, folder 197, 112–113. See also Gostyński, "Przewrót Hitlerowski w Niemczech i Niemcy w Polsce (Dokończenie)," 219–220. Gostyński discusses the distribution of power within the RDP.

152 Gostyński, "Przewrót Hitlerowski w Niemczech i Niemcy w Polsce (Dokończenie)," 220.

153 Breyer, *Das Deutsche Reich und Polen*, 251. Dr. R. Fritsch, perhaps anxious to justify the VDA's support for the conservative-nationalist parties, attributed the JDP's absence in the council to the JDP leadership's own stubborness; the Rat der Deutschen in Polen, Fritsch claimed, had made an effort to include the JDP. See VDA Lecture by R. Fritsch, in Jacobsen, *Hans Steinacher*, 542.

154 *Wir schmieden die Zukunft. Der Kampf der "Jungdeutschen Partei" in Posen-Pommerellen* (Geschäftsstelle Bromberg der JDP: Bydgoszcz, 1935), 30–32, in PAAA, Pol IV, Politik 25 Polen, vol. 36, R82216, 64; "Erwachen des völkischen Lebens in Mittelpolen," *Deutsche Nachrichten in Polen*, March 16, 1935, in GStA, I HA, Rep 77, folder 752, 197.

officials. Hence, Polish sources are invaluable in filling in the blanks for such taboo topics. In January 1936, 900 DV delegates from across Poznania and Pomerelia attended a meeting in Bydgoszcz to discuss the plans to expand into Silesia, the Łódź voivodeship, Volhynia, and Galicia. The vote to change the statutes was unanimous. Yet a Polish report of the DV meeting, claiming to draw upon "unofficial" sources and looking "behind the scenes," shows that the unanimous vote for unity was a mere façade. Although the "famous German solidarity and discipline" had prevented them from speaking openly about their reservations, certain circles in the DV were clearly unhappy with the proposed plan for expansion. Above all, these DV members harbored doubts about the Germans in Upper Silesia. Some feared that a merging of the DV with other German organizations would allow Upper Silesian Germans to dominate the top positions and to "outvote" the Germans from Poznania-Pomerelia. Indeed, the Polish report indicated that Kohnert himself was unsure of his own proposal, and that certain functionaries regarded his support for the fusion as bowing to pressure from the Upper Silesian Germans. Some believed Kohnert's acquiescence would mean the end of his political career.[155] Another report by Polish authorities on the JDP in Łódź from the same time revealed that Germans in Poznań and Pomerelia often expressed their dislike toward German Silesians by derisively calling them "Galician Germans."[156]

The DV's apparent focus on the Upper Silesians as a threat can be accounted for by their similar status as a former Reich region and thus a serious organizational and financial rival. The fears of DV members were exaggerated, however, as the worried reaction of the Upper Silesian Germans to the DV expansion plans reveals. While the DV expected the Upper Silesians to greet the planned unification enthusiastically,[157] their leader, Otto Ulitz, worked feverishly in early 1936 to extend the activities of the Volksbund in order to maintain his influence *against* a possible DV incursion into Upper Silesia.[158] Likewise, German activists in the Central Polish regions also expressed their wariness of DV expansion plans through backchannels to the meeting in Bydgoszcz. Still, the suggestive power of Volksgemeinschaft

155 Voivode in Poznań to Political Department of the Polish Interior Ministry, memorandum "Deutsche Vereinigung – zjazd delegatów w Bydgoszczy," February 1, 1936, in AP Bydgoszcz, Urząd Wojewódzki Pomorski, folder 2788, 25–30.
156 Social-Political Department of the Voivodeship of Łódź, monthly report, no. 12 for December 1-31, 1935, dated January 9, 1936, in AP Łódź, Urząd Wojewódzki Łódzki, folder 2507 L.
157 Voivode in Poznań to Political Department of the Polish Interior Ministry, memorandum "Deutsche Vereinigung – zjazd delegatów w Bydgoszczy," February 1, 1936, in AP Bydgoszcz, Urząd Wojewódzki Pomorski, folder 2788, 25–30.
158 Nationalities Department of the Polish Interior Ministry, *Sprawozdanie z życia mniejszości narodowych za II kwartał 1936 r.* (Warsaw, 1936), in AAN, MSZ, folder 2348, 3-163 (1–161), 72 (70).

meant that Kurt Lück gave a lecture at the meeting on how Poznanian and Pomerelian settlers had colonized Central Poland and Volhynia in the past – and hence the current plan to incorporate the Germans there in a unified organization would awaken their feelings of affinity.[159] Yet the mutual suspicions harbored by these supposedly allied regional organizations were exacerbated, and not ameliorated, by the rhetoric of Volksgemeinschaft. On the one hand, the repetitive call for unity became a force in itself, creating pressure to unify and to consolidate the various parties. On the other hand, the weight of public solidarity prevented people from openly voicing their opinions and forced regional resistance into the back room.

Fortunately for those Germans who felt threatened by the DV plans to "go national," the DV never received approval from the Polish state to expand beyond Poznania and Pomerelia. The plans were dropped and never revived in this form again. Minority leaders saw this development as yet another example of Polish repression of the German minority, suggesting that the Poles were responsible for the failure of the minority to unify. Yet there must be a fairer assessment of the *causes* for the inability of the DV to encompass all parts of Poland. Just as the Polish government's role in the rise of the JDP has been underestimated, the impact of the Polish government on the inability of the DV to expand has been grossly exaggerated. Probably most Polish authorities objected to the expansion, and the Polish government had the last say in the matter, but German inhibitions surely made the process impossible right from the start. Whereas the Germans in the other regions feared being swallowed up by the traditional center, the German leaders in Poznania-Pomerelia were likewise wary of being dominated from outside.

More importantly, it is necessary to reevaluate the *impact* of the failure of the expansion of the DV. Rather than a setback, it was a political windfall for the Old German leaders. As many have argued, the infighting between the German groups caused more people to become engaged in political activity.[160] Yet the greatest advantage for minority leaders was yet another opportunity to blame the Polish government for their failures. The focus on repression represented a cynical use of adversity, for it allowed the Germans to avoid talking about the real reasons for the lack of progress – that is, personal and regional fears and rivalries. Even though many German minority functionaries did not want the unification themselves, the Polish

---

159 Voivode in Poznań to Political Department of the Polish Interior Ministry, memorandum "Deutsche Vereinigung – zjazd delegatów w Bydgoszczy," February 1, 1936, in AP Bydgoszcz, Urząd Wojewódzki Pomorski, folder 2788, 25–30.
160 Bierschenk, *Die deutsche Volksgruppe in Polen*, 46–48.

government's reluctance to approve the plan became yet another page in the litany of repression that served the minority leaders' mobilization of the Germans in Poland. At the same time, minority leaders could use repression as an excuse to avoid the hard work and sacrifice that organizational unity would have entailed.

Having to deal with the existence of several regional groupings for the foreseeable future, the conservative-nationalist DV leaders had to take a very different approach to unity and unification than the JDP. The DV now championed the loosely organized Rat der Deutschen in Polen, which did not represent a serious attempt at organizational unification. Yet the rhetoric of national community proved to be remarkably flexible, and DV leaders quickly adjusted their concept of Volksgemeinschaft to fit the limitations they faced. They especially pushed for a vision of national community that included regional heterogeneity and maintained the status quo. Disingenuously ignoring their own role in the schism, DV leaders argued that minority unity had existed before the arrival of the JDP on the political scene.[161] Above all, the DV tried to counter the party-organizational interpretation that the JDP proffered. DV functionaries argued that to unify all Germans in Poland in a single party would only endanger the Volksgemeinschaft by bringing on Polish repression:

We cannot take many of the external forms of National Socialism. We live under the laws of our state, and we naturally respect these. Moreover, we cannot forget one thing: unlike its mother nation, the small Volksgruppe abroad cannot strive for the highest goal: rather, the Volksgruppe must struggle to keep its national land [Volksboden], its farmland, its culture – otherwise it will lose everything. For many of us, this fact will appear bitter – and perhaps even like self-denial. But it is a clear necessity, we must limit ourselves to maintaining our Volkstum. It has already been said that this renewal will be demanding for all of us, and so we will have to carry out the great idea according to its spirit.[162]

According to DV logic, the necessity of protecting German nationality and conforming to Polish laws justified the bitter "self-denial" of political forms. Although the DV did not back away completely from the creation of a unified organization for all Germans in Poland, DV leaders opposed the creation of parties, which Hans Kohnert called the "source of all evil."[163] A similar speech by the DV youth leader Gero von Gersdorff in 1936 warned against aping overly grandiose political forms that would be unsuitable for

---

161 Gero von Gersdorff, "Lebensfragen unserer Volksgruppe. Die Front unseres Kampfes. Oktober 1936," in Kohnert and Gersdorff, *Wille zur Einheit*, 61.

162 Copy of speech: "Völkischer Sozialismus," in BA Koblenz, R57-Neu, folder 1094 (Nr. 1), undated (presumably around early 1936), 2.

163 Kohnert, *Dr. Kohnert spricht*, 7, also 20 ("Gegen Parteigeist – für die Einheit!").

a minority in Poland: "The organization of a 60 million strong people cannot be schematically applied to a minority that consists of 1.2 million people. Although it is easy for a person in the Reich to fall into a philistine somnolence, abroad he will be kept awake by the constant conflict with the foreign environment. A skyscraper has its place in New York, but not in Schmiegel!"[164] Thus, the DV version of a German Volksgemeinschaft in Poland largely encompassed an "inner renewal."[165] Old Germans elsewhere in Poland likewise stressed the importance of the "intellectual bearing" and not formal arrangements in determining the value of a German minority organization.[166] At a meeting in Łódź, Fritz Zeller from Upper Silesia supported the idea of cultivating a unified spirit, which he claimed would inevitably lead to organizational unity.[167] The focus on a mental construction of the German Volksgruppe thereby provided an argument for postponing political unification to the indeterminate future.

Yet this quasi-spiritual definition of unity, be it across regional or social barriers, could lead to grotesque forms of definitional hairsplitting, as the DV functionary Gero von Gersdorff attempted to show in a speech in June 1936: "The Deutsche Vereinigung recognizes that this struggle is not about a visible seizure of power, but rather that our only power exists in the establishment of an internally hardened community. That is why we do not want a unification [Einigung], but unity [Einung]."[168] The DV leadership was of course aware of the problems that such vague definitions of Volksgemeinschaft could raise. In a later speech, for example, Gero von Gersdorff dismissed criticism that the DV represented a "nebulous cultural Germandom." He reassessed the importance of cultural work, which he claimed was

---

164 Gero von Gersdorff, "Verwaltung und Bewegung," June 4, 1936, reprinted in Kohnert and Gersdorff, *Wille zur Einheit*, 44. See also "Hohn und Tragik," *Kattowitzer Zeitung*, June 2, 1935, in GStA, I HA, Rep. 77, Tit. 856, Nr. 753; Copy of speech: "Völkischer Sozialismus," in BA Koblenz, R57-Neu, folder 1094 (Nr. 1), undated (presumably around early 1936), 2. Schmiegel (Śmigiel in Polish) is a small town in Poznania.

165 An die Ortsgruppen, February 8, 1935, 1 – attachment to cover letter: Adelt, Stellungnahme der Hauptgeschäftsstelle der Deutschen Vereinigung in Bromberg, February 12, 1935), in BA Koblenz, R57 Neu, folder 1094 (Nr. 1).

166 "Hohn und Tragik," *Kattowitzer Zeitung*, June 2, 1935, in GStA, I HA, Rep. 77, Tit. 856, folder 753.

167 "Deutsche Jugend will leben! Über 1000 Vertreter der jungen Generation aus allen Gauen Polens bekunden ihre Einheit," *Freie Presse*, November 2, 1937 (newspaper clipping sent by Consul Berchem to German Foreign Ministry on November 3, 1937, then forwarded by German Foreign Ministry to Reich Interior Ministry, Volksdeutsche Mittelstelle, and Deutsche Stiftung on November 16, 1937), in BA Berlin, R8043, folder 943, 67–71, here 70 backside.

168 Gero von Gersdorff, "Verwaltung und Bewegung," June 4, 1936, reprinted in Kohnert and Gersdorff, *Wille zur Einheit*, 48. Gersdorff used the term "Einung" in at least one other speech: "Unser Leben heißt: Volk," ibid., 68: "Aber dies [sic] Leid macht uns hart. Hart in der Entschlossenheit, diesen Kampf bis zur Einung des Deutschtums in Polen zu Ende zu führen."

not political according to "reactionary definitions," but rather "authentically political" [urpolitisch] in the sense of maintaining and expanding Germandom.[169] In this interpretation, the DV embodied National Socialism as a movement rather than a party, and the unity it sought was not necessarily incompatible with regional pluralism.

The apparent stubbornness of the DV in defending regional organizational forms only nurtured suspicions of the DV's particularism and appeared to confirm its disdain for the Germans in other regions. These accusations, once voiced, could not be easily explained away, and they continued to dog the DV leadership. Despite their own resentments and real prejudices vis-à-vis other Germans in Poland, the confrontation with these charges of arrogance did not resonate well within the ranks or elsewhere, and the DV leadership was forced to explain to the Germans of Western Poland why there was discontent on the minority's periphery. The following excerpt from a program sent by DV headquarters to the local chapters in 1935 makes it clear that there was the need to address the accusations of regional snobbery on the part of the Germans in Western Poland:

[W]e do not think at all that we are better than our German brothers in Central, Southern, and Eastern Poland. That has been proven practically for years by the help rendered (especially in Volhynia and Congress Poland)! Admittedly, we have not imposed ourselves because the differences between the individual groups of our Germandom in Poland that have grown out of varying historical developments usually make meddling in the particulars appear unwanted.[170]

The passage reveals the desire to show sensitivity to the peripheral Germans while simultaneously asserting Western Polish German privilege over them. The reference to the DV's financial generosity in the past suggests solidarity, but it also reinforces the stereotypes of the needy, and hence less capable, Germans in the eastern parts of Poland. The desire not to interfere in the internal affairs of the other regional parties because of their different development was portrayed as a concession to the needs and feelings of the other regions, although the real reasons might have well been a lack of interest, aversion, failure of will, or unwillingness to provide funds. The program reiterated the futility of a "schematic unitary organization" and the need for a "certain elasticity" in the diversity of regional organizations.[171] In short, the DV tried to convince the Germans that by defending its

---

169 Gero von Gersdorff, "Lebensfragen unserer Volksgruppe. Die Front unseres Kampfes. Oktober 1936," in Kohnert and Gersdorff, *Wille zur Einheit*, 53.
170 "An die Ortsgruppen," February 8, 1935, 2, in BA Koblenz, R57 Neu, folder 1094 (Nr.1).
171 "An die Ortsgruppen," February 8, 1935, 2, in BA Koblenz, R57 Neu, folder 1094 (Nr.1).

own interests first and by keeping separate regional parties, it was indeed defending all.

By 1937, the JDP was a spent force in Western Poland. Polish authorities noted the growing dissatisfaction and the loss of discipline within its ranks,[172] and the JDP could not halt the hemorrhaging of its membership. The JDP news organ in Western Poland, *Deutsche Nachrichten*, lost 200 subscribers in a matter of a few weeks in the spring of 1937.[173] By then, the JDP could only count 12,000 members in Pomerelia and Poznania. The DV, in contrast, had benefited greatly from the minority infighting, counting some 60,000 members in 1937.[174] The conflict between the JDP and the DV in Western Poland was at its core a turf war, in which the JDP's incursion triggered a vigorous reaction by the threatened organizations. Prior to 1934, there had been little conflict between the two organizations because they had both stayed regional. Thereafter, both organizations deployed a common National Socialist rhetoric to wage their battles. Using a mixture of its own local patriotism and a loose interpretation of Volksgemeinschaft, the DV successfully defended what many saw as its own territory.

Yet the DV triumph over the JDP was a pyrrhic victory. The conflict with the JDP deepened the regional cleavages, not just between the DV and the JDP, but within the JDP and between the DV and its regional allies. In particular, the high expectations aroused by the rhetoric of Volksgemeinschaft and the ensuing disappointment fostered regional mistrust. The chances for unifying the minority in one organization became more difficult, not easier, with the passage of time. By advocating and embodying the new appreciation for the eastern, non-Prussian regions, the JDP had changed the balance of power in Polish German politics. Established German activists in Western Poland were triumphant in their struggle with the JDP, but their authority within the minority was vulnerable to a yet greater challenge coming from the East.

172 Office of the Voivode in Poznań to Polish Interior Ministry, situation report on the German minority (May 1937), June 13, 1937, in Jaworski et al., *Deutsche und Polen zwischen den Kriegen*, document 229, 659.

173 Office of the Voivode in Poznań to Polish Interior Ministry, situation report on the German minority (May 1937), June 13, 1937, in Jaworski et al., *Deutsche und Polen zwischen den Kriegen*, document 229, 666.

174 Blanke, *Orphans of Versailles*, 182.

5

Revenge of the Periphery

German Empowerment in Central Poland (1933–1939)

Two weeks after Hitler became chancellor in 1933, Kurt Graebe, the director of the Deutsche Vereinigung in Western Poland, came to Łódź to attend the annual meeting of the local German party, the Deutscher Volksverband. In a brief report to the Deutsche Stiftung in Berlin, Graebe stated that he was surprised by the sizable attendance, and the rally made a "very good impression." The mood of the Germans had appeared "transformed" and "much more German." This change could be seen in the Łódź Germans' more positive attitude toward the Reich. According to Graebe, this development was a reaction to the repressive Polish policies of years past. Notably, Graebe did not mention the recent events in Germany.[1] Graebe's observations reveal that his own perception of the Germans in Łódź had changed as well. The recent upheaval in the Reich had reformulated the question among proponents and opponents of National Socialism alike: What makes a good German outside of Germany?

The previous chapters explained the deepening regional cleavages within the German minority. The JDP-DV struggle in Western Poland played a key part of in this regionalization process. Yet this process was concomitant with another development: the eastern empowerment of the minority. Throughout the interwar period, the center of gravity – demographic, ideological, and political – was slowly shifting from the formerly Prussian areas to Central Poland. The undermining of established regional hierarchies would have important consequences for unifying the German minority in Poland. Especially the growing fetish for völkisch ideas would allow the so-called diaspora Germans in the East to renegotiate their role within the minority and to turn the tables on the Germans in Western Poland.

1 Graebe to Krahmer-Moellenberg, February 14, 1933, in BA Berlin, R8043, folder 942, 109.

Categories such as Volk, Volksdeutsche (ethnic Germans), and Volksgemeinschaft became increasingly important in this reshuffling, precisely
because they were unclear and opened up competing interpretations of
Germanness. Moreover, for those on the margins seeking entry into the
club, this lack of clarity and uncertainty could exacerbate tensions with
other ethnic groups. In multiethnic Łódź, this radicalization would lead to
the breakdown of German-Jewish-Polish relations.

THE SILENT REVOLUTION: DEMOGRAPHY AND THE GERMAN MINORITY

The dramatic population change in the western parts of Poland resulted
in demographic patterns that reflected and reaffirmed the new eastern self-
assertiveness. More than a decade of heavy subsidies to the German minority
in Western Poland had failed to stem the demographic slide there. Rather
than holding on to land and businesses, the Germans continued to flee
Poland for Germany. According to Theodor Oberländer, the leader of the
Bund Deutscher Osten and an Ostforscher specialist in agriculture (and
in the 1950s, minister for expellees in the Federal Republic of Germany),
economic and cultural life in Western Poland was deteriorating rapidly, a
problem he attributed in part to the region's separation from Germany.[2]

These demographic developments within the German minority also
encouraged the new appraisal of the Germans in the eastern regions of
Poland. Throughout the interwar period, the number of Germans in the
non-Prussian regions continued to grow, a development that helped to
ensure that the dominance of the German leaders in Western Poland would
steadily diminish. An overview of the minority's demographic development
in the various Polish regions shows that a silent revolution was taking place
within the minority; see Table 5.1.

While the German population declined in the formerly Prussian territories during the interwar period, the number of Germans in formerly
Austrian and Russian lands actually increased both absolutely and propor-
tionally to the entire minority. Taking into account the 40,000 Germans in
Teschen Silesia, Table 5.2 shows that by 1939 the majority of Polish Germans lived in the regions that had never belonged to the German Empire.[3]

---

2 Theodor Oberländer, "Die wirtschaftliche Notlage der früher preußischen Provinzen Posen und
  Westpreußen," *Jomsburg. Völker und Staaten im Osten und Norden Europas* 1 (1937): 143–154, especially
  153–154.
3 Richard Blanke, *Orphans of Versailles: The Germans in Western Poland, 1918–1939* (Lexington: University Press of Kentucky, 1993), 3.

Table 5.1. *Distribution of German Populations in Interwar Poland*[4] *(P = formerly Prussian, A = formerly Austrian, R = formerly Russian)*

	1921				1931			
	Polish Census		"German" Estimate by Joseph Czech		Polish Census		"German" Estimate by Joseph Czech	
	Number	%	Number	%	Number	%	Number	%
Pomerelia (P)	175,771	16.1	561,000	41.6	105,400	14.2	335,000	29.4
Poznania (P)	327,846	30.0			193,080	26.1		
Eastern Upper Silesia (P)	322,759*	29.6	333,000	24.7			310,000	27.2
Teschen Silesia (A)	29,681*	2.7	40,000	3.0	99,645	13.5	40,000	3.5
Galicia (A)	39,810	3.6	65,000	4.8	40,676	5.5	70,000	6.2
Congress Poland (R)	166,280	15.2	300,000	22.3	245,600	33.1	330,000	28.9
Volhynia (R)	24,960	2.3	48,000	3.6	46,883	6.3	55,000	4.8
Northeast Territories (R)	5,264	0.5	–	–	9,811	1.3	–	–
Total	1,092,371	100.0	1,347,000	100.0	741,095	100.0	1,140,000	100.0

* estimated with expected growth, based on 1910 census.
Source: Matelski, *Niemcy w Polsce w XX wieku*, 44.

The consequences of these demographic trends were manifold. Although Western Poland had made up the dominating majority at the beginning of the interwar period, the growing parity of the populations in Western Poland, the semi-autonomous voivodeship of Silesia (both formerly Prussian and Austrian parts), and Central Poland had made it impossible for any one organization to represent the majority of the Germans in Poland. This population dispersal helped to ensure that regional German parties would dominate the political life of the German minority. Yet the long-term trend benefited the Germans in the non-Prussian regions. One estimate put the German population in Bielsko in formerly Austrian Teschen Silesia at more than 60 percent German in 1921, making it the only German-majority city in Poland.[5] The changes were even more dramatic in Central Poland. More than 60,000 Germans lived in formerly Russian Łódź, thus representing

4 Dariusz Matelski, *Niemcy w Polsce w XX wieku* (Warsaw/Poznań: Wydawnictwo Naukowe PWN, 1999), 44.
5 Otto Heike, *Das Deutschtum in Polen, 1918–1939* (Bonn: self-published, 1955), 33; Blanke, *Orphans of Versailles*, 3.

Table 5.2. *German Population in Poland in 1939*[6]

Poznania and Pomerelia (Prussian)	312,000
East Upper Silesia (Prussian)*	180,000
Teschen Silesia (Austrian)*	40,000
Other regions (Russian, Austrian)	490,000
Total:	1,022,000

* my own adjustments for separating Teschen Silesia from Upper Silesia.

Source: Pia Nordblom, *Für Glaube und Volkstum*, 40.

the largest concentration of Germans in Poland. By 1939, the Germans in formerly Prussian lands – the traditional core of German activity in Poland – had become a minority within the minority, ensuring that the dominance of the German leaders in Western Poland would steadily diminish. The East, and especially Łódź, was becoming the minority's "biological center."[7]

The steady demographic easternization complemented and affirmed the racialized völkisch ideologies espoused in the Third Reich. Many observers believed Germany was facing a demographic crisis in the interwar period.[8] Not surprisingly, the high birth rates and ethnic steadfastness of the more rural ethnic Germans in the East were highly esteemed.[9] Hans-Jürgen Seraphim reported that in 1932 the Germans in Volhynia had 36 babies per 1,000 people, almost twice as many as Germans in Poznań (17 per 1,000).[10] These demographic and ideological developments, especially the egalitarian emphasis of völkisch thought, brought a certain downclassing for the Germans in Western Poland. Increasingly placed on the same footing with the ethnic Germans in Central and Eastern Poland, these former citizens saw their special relationship with the Reich diminish.

6 Pia Nordblom, *Für Glaube und Volkstum. Die katholische Wochenzeitung "Der Deutsche in Polen" (1919–1939) in der Auseinandersetzung mit dem Nationalsozialismus* (Paderborn: Ferdinand Schöningh, 2000), 40.

7 Richard Breyer, *Das Deutsche Reich und Polen, 1932–1937. Außenpolitik und Volksgruppenfragen* (Würzburg: Holzner, 1955), 45.

8 Christiane Reinecke, "Krisenkalkulationen. Demographische Krisenszenarien und statistische Expertise in der Weimarer Republik," in *Die "Krise" der Weimarer Republik. Zur Kritik eines Deutungsmusters*, ed. Moritz Föllmer and Rüdiger Graf, 209–240 (Frankfurt/Main: Campus, 2005), 232–236.

9 For an analysis of the image of the "tough" German in Central and Eastern Poland, see Wilhelm Fielitz, *Das Stereotyp des wolhyniendeutschen Umsiedlers. Popularisierungen zwischen Sprachinselforschung und nationalsozialistischer Propaganda* (Marburg: N.G. Elwert, 2000), 94.

10 Reich and Prussian Minister of the Interior, memorandum on lecture by H.J. Seraphim at the Volksdeutscher Klub in Rostock (November 7, 1934), November 8, 1934, in BA Berlin, R8043, folder 946, 334–336.

ETHNIC GERMAN ADVOCACY IN TRANSITION

As we have previously seen, the Gleichschaltung of the organizations that worked with German minorities proceeded rather smoothly. Because the Reich sought to improve its image abroad in the early years, it initially left its Volkstumspolitik largely to existing organizations and to semi-clandestine official channels.[11] Although the Foreign Ministry played a small role in Volkstum affairs in general,[12] the affiliated Deutsche Stiftung under Krahmer-Möllenberg maintained considerable control over the German organizations in Western Poland. The Verein für das Deutschtum im Ausland renamed itself as the less elitist-sounding Volksbund für das Deutschtum im Ausland (VDA; People's Union for Germandom Abroad) and received a new leader, Hans Steinacher. Many other smaller organizations were conglomerated within the Bund Deutscher Osten (Union for the German East), which was led by Alfred Rosenberg (and later Theodor Oberländer). Still, the scene became increasingly splintered again with the rise of other party organizations, especially the Auslands-Organisation der NSDAP and even the Hitler Youth, and later the Volksdeutsche Mittelstelle (VoMi; Ethnic German Liaison Office). The fractured landscape gradually undermined the influence of the VDA and the Deutsche Stiftung and fostered deepening divisions in the minority.

As Martin Broszat has noted, völkisch terminology could bridge enormous differences in various camps.[13] There were older Volkstum theorists, notably Max Hildebert Boehm, who had advocated Reich expansion and a national reordering of Europe.[14] Other anti-democratic and völkisch advocates did not initially welcome the National Socialists, or they were too nonconformist for the new regime to accept them readily. Among these were Edgar Jung, Wilhelm Stapel, Oswald Spengler, and Othmar Spann.[15] Recent work by the sociologist Stefan Breuer has also detailed the complicated strands in German right-wing and nationalist thinking.[16] But even if

11 Ronald M. Smelser, *The Sudeten Problem, 1933–1938: Volkstumspolitik and the Formulation of Nazi Foreign Policy* (Middleton: Wesleyan University Press, 1975), 20.
12 Smelser, *The Sudeten Problem*, 15.
13 Martin Broszat, "Die völkische Ideologie und der Nationalsozialismus," *Deutsche Rundschau* 84, no. 1 (1958): 56–57.
14 Ingo Haar, *Historiker im Nationalsozialismus. Deutsche Geschichtswissenschaft und der "Volkstumskampf" im Osten* (Göttingen: Vandenhoeck & Ruprecht, 2000), 35; see also Max Hildebert Boehm, *Grenzdeutsch – Großdeutsch. Vortrag anläßlich der Hauptausschußtagung des V.D.A. im November 1924* (Dresden: Verein für das Deutschtum im Ausland, 1925), 5.
15 Kurt Sontheimer, *Antidemokratisches Denken in der Weimarer Republik. Die politischen Ideen des deutschen Nationalismus zwischen 1918 und 1933* (Munich: Nymphenburger Verlagshandlung, 1962), 370.
16 Stefan Breuer, *Ordnungen der Ungleichheit – die deutsche Rechte im Widerstreit ihrer Ideen 1871–1945* (Darmstadt: Wissenschaftliche Buchgesellschaft, 2001); Stefan Breuer, *Die Völkischen in Deutschland. Kaiserreich und Weimarer Republik* (Darmstadt: Wissenschaftliche Buchgesellschaft, 2008).

their goals may have been similar, it is important to note the distinctions. Hence, the categories of "traditionalist" and "radical" as used by Ronald Smelser and Tammo Luther, although unable to capture all the nuances, are useful here.[17]

For most traditionalist Volkstum experts, the Volk was not necessarily racially defined, and many völkisch advocates did not match what many radical Nazi racial theorists would later formulate.[18] Hans Steinacher was perhaps typical of the traditionalist school. He felt a völkisch orientation in politics would help settle national minority conflicts and bring about peaceful relations. In a position paper from 1935, Steinacher contrasted etatist with what he called *volklich*[19] thought. He claimed that state-centered thinking treated territories with conationals abroad (*Volksboden*) as land to recover; or it ignored them completely for political reasons. Either way, there would not be a lasting solution. Volklich thought in his opinion, however, sought a compromise between states and nationalities, thus providing real peace.[20] It is likely that Steinacher and many German minority leaders truly believed that the Nazi revolution allowed a way out for national minorities who faced the difficult dilemma of assimilation or exit. A cross-border völkisch community could ensure the survival of Germanness in both liberal democratic and authoritarian nation-states.

In essence, established völkisch activists like Steinacher postulated the following: (1) Germans outside of the core-state were still essentially German in regard to their Volkstum (culture/ethnicity/nationality); and (2) Germans in the core state and Germans abroad were equal. This flattening could be seen in the use of the term volksdeutsch. Rudolf Hess, as nominal head of the Volksdeutscher Rat (Ethnic German Council), a new organization meant to coordinate work among ethnic Germans, proclaimed in 1934 that the classification Auslandsdeutsche was to be reserved for German citizens abroad.[21] Volksdeutsch was to be used for all Germans, however defined, without Reich citizenship. As Dieter Gosewinkel notes, the term

---

17 Smelser, *The Sudeten Problem*, 14–41 and Appendix B, 258; Tammo Luther, *Volkstumspolitik des deutschen Reiches 1933–1938. Die Auslanddeutschen im Spannungsfeld zwischen Traditionalisten und Nationalsozialisten* (Stuttgart: Franz Steiner, 2004).
18 Smelser, *The Sudeten Problem*, 14–20.
19 Steinacher insisted on using "volklich" rather than "völkisch" because he felt the latter had pejorative undertones, and he compared the difference to the words *kindlich* (child-like) and *kindisch* (childish). See Hans-Adolf Jacobsen, ed., *Hans Steinacher. Bundesleiter des VDA 1933–1937. Erinnerungen und Dokumente* (Boppard am Rhein: Boldt, 1970), xxix. See also Günter Hartung, "Völkische Ideologie," in *Handbuch zur "Völkischen Bewegung" 1871–1918*, ed. Uwe Puschner, Walter Schmitz, and Justus H. Ulbricht, 22–41 (Munich: Saur, 1996): 23–24.
20 Rudolf Luther, *Blau oder Braun? Der Volksbund für das Deutschtum im Ausland (VDA) im NS-Staat 1933–1937* (Neumünster: Wachholtz, 1999), 69.
21 Luther, *Blau oder Braun*, 81.

Volk in the interwar period increasingly lost its legal-political meaning and was often reduced to ethno-nationality (Volkstum).[22] The purported ethno-racial characteristics of the Germans living in other countries allowed them to belong fully to the German nation and be the equal of the Reich Germans. Hitler was, after all, also an ethnic German from Austria. This sentiment was reflected in countless speeches and semi-official publications in Germany. An example of this attempt at popular reeducation can be found in a pamphlet from 1935. Its title proclaimed: "You Must Become Ethnic German!" The author enthusiastically invoked the long experience of the self-help of Germans abroad as a model for Germans in Germany as well.[23] For the former Reich Germans in Western Poland, in particular, these tenets would appear to relieve them of their status as second-class Germans.[24] Yet this development also meant that their residual citizenship, that is, their special place among Germans living outside of the Reich, would increasingly lose its significance as the easternization in politics and scholarship continued.

THE EASTERNIZATION OF OSTFORSCHUNG

The historian Martin Burkert has argued that the new prohibitions and the racial emphasis during National Socialism actually destroyed traditional Ostforschung.[25] It appears, however, that Ostforschung as a discipline moved relatively smoothly into the roles demanded by party and state.[26] Even if not a perfect fit, pre-1933 Ostforschung was not dissolved, but rather redeployed. As Ian Kershaw has noted about German society as a whole, the majority of these scholars had no problem with "working towards the Führer."[27] Indeed, there was a biographical continuity of many key

22 Dieter Gosewinkel, *Einbürgern und Ausschließen. Die Nationalisierung der Staatsangehörigkeit vom Deutschen Bund bis zur Bundesrepublik Deutschland* (Göttingen: Vandenhoeck & Ruprecht, 1991), 367.

23 Horand Horsa Schacht, *Du mußt volksdeutsch sein!* (Dortmund: Crüwell, 1935), 13. See also Franz von Papen, *Volksdeutscher Durchbruch. Aufrufe und Bekenntnisse zur gesamtdeutschen Verbundenheit* (Berlin: VDA, 1934).

24 Blanke, *Orphans of Versailles*, 163.

25 Burkert, *Die Ostwissenschaften im Dritten Reich*.

26 Michael Burleigh, *Germany Turns Eastwards: A Study of Ostforschung in the Third Reich* (Cambridge/New York: Cambridge University Press, 1988), 33, 39; Eduard Mühle, "Institutionelle Grundlegung und wissenschaftliche Programmatik der westdeutschen Beschäftigung mit 'deutscher Geschichte' im östlichen Mitteleuropa (1945–1959)," in *Doświadczenia przeszłości. Niemcy w Europie Środkowo-Wschodniej w historiografii po 1945 roku = Erfahrungen der Vergangenheit. Deutsche in Ostmitteleuropa in der Historiographie nach 1945*, ed. Jerzy Kłoczowski, Witold Matwiejczyk, and Eduard Mühle, 25–66 (Marburg: Herder-Institut; Lublin: Instytut Europy Środkowo-Wschodniej, 2000), 26.

27 For further analysis of Kershaw's concept, see Ian Kershaw, "Working Towards the Führer," in *Stalinism and Nazism: Dictatorships in Comparison*, eds. Ian Kershaw and Moshe Lewin, 88–106 (Cambridge/New York: Cambridge University Press, 1997).

figures, and the reorganization of the various research programs had begun well before the Nazi period.[28] Albert Brackmann, the general director of the Prussian State Archives since 1929, initiated the centralization of Ostforschung. In 1931, he created the Publikationsfonds, which became the Publikationsstelle Dahlem (PUSTE) in March 1933. When the Bund Deutscher Osten moved to create its own research institute in cooperation with the Volksbund für das Deutschtum im Ausland, Brackmann preempted this move by creating the Nordost-Deutsche Forschungsgemeinschaft.[29] The name was changed in 1936 to the Nord- und Ostdeutsche Forschungsgemeinschaft (NOFG) to respond to the research agenda of the Baltic Institute (Instytut Bałtycki), which focused on northern Europe. The NOFG was part of the Publikationsstelle, and both were funded by the Reich Ministry of the Interior. Brackmann was general director of the PUSTE until 1936, when Johannes Papritz took over, but he remained chairman of the steering committee of the NOFG until 1945. In 1938, the PUSTE was moved organizationally from the Prussian State Archives and placed directly under the auspices of the Reich Ministry of the Interior. After 1943, the SS-Reichssicherheitshauptamt exerted increasing control.[30]

It proved initially more difficult for the Nazi regime to effect the Gleichschaltung of the Deutsches Ausland-Institut (DAI; German Foreign Institute) in Stuttgart. Its general secretary, Fritz Wertheimer, was of Jewish ancestry but had converted to Protestantism. Even though many conservative völkisch activists wrote in support of Wertheimer (including Kurt Graebe from the Deutsche Vereinigung in Western Poland), he was relieved of his post in 1933.[31] After some other changes, the members of the Deutsches Ausland-Institut in Stuttgart continued to operate as usual, building contacts with minorities abroad, collecting information on them, and writing various articles. At the DAI, a notable new employee was Wilhelm Gradmann, who started out in the library but would later become a junior officer in the SS and a part of the Volksdeutsche Mittelstelle.[32] As the next chapter will show, he would play a major role in the resettlement of

28 Burleigh, *Germany Turns Eastwards*, 32–39.
29 Jörg Hackmann, "Deutsche Ostforschung und Geschichtswissenschaft," in *Deutsche Ostforschung und Polnische Westforschung im Spannungsfeld von Wissenschaft und Politik. Disziplinen im Vergleich*, ed. Jan M. Piskorski, Jörg Hackmann, and Rudolf Jaworski, 25–45 (Osnabrück: Fibre, 2002), 34–35.
30 Hackmann, "Deutsche Ostforschung und Geschichtswissenschaft," 35.
31 Blanke, *Orphans of Versailles*, 165.
32 SS-Anwärter Wilhelm Gradmann, R.u.S.-Fragebogen, in BA Berlin, former BDC, SS-O und RS: Gradmann, Wilhelm (Dr.), 07.05.1909, Film B5-264-91, 786–788.

Germans in occupied Poland. He was part of Germany's "uncompromising generation" that would plan and implement the New Order.[33]

By showing that Germans abroad were full-fledged national brothers of the Reich Germans, Ostforschung contributed to the easternization of the Germans in Poland. The close relationship between Ostforscher, the minority leadership, and the Reich resulted in a research agenda tied not just to foreign political questions between states but also to politics within the minority. Weimar's official revisionist agenda had encouraged Ostforschung to focus on the lands and Germans within the borders of 1914. After the signing of the friendship treaty with Poland, however, political expediency meant avoiding politically charged taboo subjects such as the so-called border Germandom in Western Poland. Moreover, the rise of biologicist and racist tenets awoke new interest in the German settlements further to the East. Ironically, Ostforschung, which had received much of its initial impetus from the loss of the Prussian territories after the First World War, increasingly turned east and away from these areas.

OVERTURNING THE HIERARCHY OF GERMANNESS

One could now discern a reversed hierarchization taking place within the minority, with the Germans in Western Poland becoming the new discursive underclass. It was increasingly apparent that the Germans in Western Poland, rather than being the natural leaders of the minority, now faced serious problems themselves: they were overly dependent on handouts from Germany, plagued by corruption, and tied to the Weimar system.[34] There were increasing calls in Reich circles for these borderland Germans to learn from diaspora Germans, and especially to copy the self-help activities of these Germans. Especially the German Foreign Ministry saw the need for the Germans in Western Poland to finally come to terms with being "Germans abroad" and to rid themselves of their "acute irredentist mentality."[35] Although similar statements had been common before 1933, the Nazi regime imbued such calls with greater legitimacy and urgency. The circulation of such ideas concurred with an increasing appreciation of

33 Michael Wildt, *Generation des Unbedingten. Das Führungskorps des Reichssicherheitshauptamtes* (Hamburg: Hamburger Edition, HIS Verlag, 2002).

34 Albert S. Kotowski, "Die deutsche Minderheit in Polen 1919–1939/45. Forschungsstand und -desiderata," *Nordost-Archiv* 9, no. 2 (2000): 483–506, here 492–493; Blanke, *Orphans of Versailles*, 150, 165–166, 175–177.

35 Fritz von Twardowski, "Aufzeichnung betreffend die deutsche Volksgruppe in den an Polen abgetretenen Gebieten," November 30, 1936, in PAAA, Inland II geheim, vol. 2 (221), microfiche nos. 2322–2323, 222–229; cf. Blanke, *Orphans of Versailles*, 205.

the Germans in Poland's central and eastern territories. As will be shown, what had once been on the margins became increasingly central in the project to build a Volksgruppe in Poland.

Wilhelm Fielitz's work on the stereotype of the Volhynian Germans indicates that the positive portrayal of the Volhynian Germans arose during the Second World War.[36] Yet this reassessment was already well underway in the mid-1930s among the Ostforscher. They imbued the eastern Volksdeutsche with positive characteristics that had been derived from their long experience with nationality conflict. In such imaginations, the diasporic language islands were pockets of racially pure Germandom, whose national instincts at most needed only to be awakened. They were widely admired for not just holding on to German Volksboden but for even flourishing on it – and importantly with little or no financial assistance from Germany. This change was of course not uniform, nor did it progress in a linear pattern. In 1934, Franz Anton Doubek, who was born in Graz and taught at the University in Vilnius from October 1927 to March 1934,[37] still spoke of borderland Germans as being nationally stable, whereas the language island Germans were weak.[38] More and more, however, minority advocates saw in Poland's central and eastern territories the very model of how an embattled Germandom could and should fend off foreign influences. In contrast, their soft and worldly Reich German cousins – including those incorporated into Western Poland after World War I – had been long pampered by the state and had never had to fight to assert their Germanness. The self-sufficiency and higher birthrates of the Eastern Polish Germans – and especially of the Volhynian Germans in formerly Russian Poland – appeared to prove their purported racial value and went well with völkisch conceptions of a rough and hardy Germandom.[39]

Many of the Polish German Ostforscher imbibed these ideas and contributed to the fetishization of the Germans in Eastern Poland. The Bielitzers Walter Kuhn and Alfred Karasek and the Posener Kurt Lück are notable examples. At the same time, they found that their funding sources in the Reich were increasingly subject to Gleichschaltung. This stark change was apparent in the writings of Viktor Kauder, who in 1931 had still written of the need for "cultural assistance" from Western Poland to encourage

---

36 Fielitz, *Das Stereotyp des wolhyniendeutschen Umsiedlers*, 300.
37 Burleigh, *Germany Turns Eastwards*, 86–87. According to Burleigh, Doubek and his wife were living on a very modest 250 Złoty (approximately RM 125) per month.
38 Wolfgang Kessler, "Die 'Ostforschung' und die Deutschen in Polen," *Nordost-Archiv* 9, no. 2 (2000): 379–411, here 396; Haar, *Historiker im Nationalsozialismus*, 219–220.
39 Fielitz, *Das Stereotyp des wolhyniendeutschen Umsiedlers*, 94.

self-help among the Germans in Volhynia.[40] In 1934, Kauder became editor of *Deutsche Monatshefte in Polen*, which in many aspects became the successor to *Deutsche Blätter in Polen*.[41] In the first issue, Kauder called for the Western Polish Germans to become more "auslanddeutsch" and hence more self-reliant. A few months later, Kauder wrote "Basic Principles of Ethnic German Policy in Poland," in which he repeated the call for a radical intellectual reorientation of the Germans in Western Poland. Kauder recounted many of the older complaints concerning the Germans in the Prussian East, including their purported blind dependence on the state. Notably, this blemish continued to stain the Germans in Western Poland, albeit now reconfigured in a pan-minority context – residual Reichness, after all, had its disadvantages as well. According to Kauder, Germans in Western Poland should not just understand their eastern cousins but also learn self-initiative and self-sufficiency.[42] With the help of the usual suspects (Alfred Karasek, Walter Kuhn, and Kurt Lück), Kauder also published a volume on the Germans in Eastern Poland in 1939, and here the picture was much more optimistic than the 1931 publication by Alfred Karasek and Kurt Lück.[43] Captions to the many photos portrayed the "Volksgemeinschaft in Volhynia" and the hardiness of the German men who had endured a physical form of nationality struggle since their youth. It is significant, however, that the identities of the Volhynian German settlers were still reduced to mostly nameless pictures that were supposed to exemplify this "tough race" as a whole.[44]

EXORCISING THE LODZERMENSCH IN CENTRAL POLAND AFTER 1933

The increased interest in issues concerning the Germans in Central Poland could be seen in the journal *Deutsche Monatshefte in Polen*, in which a good quarter of all articles in the late 1930s were devoted to Central Polish issues and subjects. In 1934, Walter Kuhn, a German in Poland from Austrian Silesia who was a prodigious writer on the German minority in Poland,

40 Viktor Kauder, "Vorwort," in *Die deutschen Siedlungen in Wolhynien. Geschichte, Volkskunde, Lebensfragen*, ed. Alfred Karasek and Kurt Lück (Leipzig: Hirzel, 1931), v.

41 *Deutsche Blätter in Polen* ceased in 1931. *Deutsche Monatshefte in Polen* was a continuation of *Schaffen und Schauen*, which was published in Katowice and edited by Viktor Kauder, but the style and thematic emphasis made the link to *Deutsche Blätter in Polen* clear. Poznań as the site of publication was also important for establishing this continuity.

42 Viktor Kauder, "Grundlagen volksdeutscher Politik in Polen," *Deutsche Monatshefte in Polen* 1 (11), no. 3 (September 1934): 75–78, here 76–77.

43 Alfred Karasek and Kurt Lück, eds., *Die deutschen Siedlungen in Wolhynien. Geschichte, Volkskunde, Lebensfragen* (Leipzig: Hirzel, 1931).

44 Viktor Kauder, *Das Deutschtum in Ostpolen*, vol. 5 of *Das Deutschtum in Polen. Ein Bildband*, ed. Viktor Kauder (Leipzig: Hirzel, 1939), 78, 96.

applauded the "healthy" aspects of the German farmers in Central Poland but lamented the lack of a "really German" leadership for the Germans in Łódź. Still, he ended on the optimistic note that things were changing.[45] Likewise, in a 1938 article in *Jomsburg*, Albert Breyer from Central Poland revised his earlier assessment of a weak intellectual life of the Germans in Łódź, now claiming its sturdiness and unity.[46]

Especially the increasingly racialized brand of Ostforschung propagated by the SS was reflected in the strong interest in the Germans of Central Poland. Dr. Hans Joachim Beyer, the leader of the Arbeitsstelle für auslandsdeutsche Forschung and later an influential racial expert in the SS, found these Germans useful for demonstrating his "volk-biological" theses on ethnic and racial assimilation. For "Heydrich's professor," even populations that had been denationalized could and should be regained for Germandom, but the process would not succeed without first removing all Jewish influence.[47] In an article that was published around the time of the German invasion of Poland, Beyer insisted that the early German settlers in Central Poland had already been deeply anti-Semitic. It was precisely their aversion to the Jews, he claimed, that drove many Łódź Germans who were facing Jewish economic competition into the arms of Polish nationalists. Beyer also described how pastors of Jewish descent had steadily undermined the German leadership of the Evangelical Church of the Augsburg Confession in the nineteenth century, turning it into a potential instrument of Polonization. Despite these allegedly Polonizing Jewish pastors and the "materialistic indifferentism" of the Łódź Germans, Beyer also acknowledged the beginnings of an ethnic German renewal after 1905. Returning to the current situation in interwar Poland, he believed that the deeply rooted "community of fate" among Germans in Poland would triumph over all "appearances of foreign infiltration."[48] For the racial theorists of the SS, the Łódź Germans were increasingly becoming the living proof of the triumph of Germandom. This biological history of the Germans in Poland was of course a dehistoricized depiction: change over time gave way to a stable and static German essence that was not just separate from the Jews but in every way antagonistic to them. By drawing a sharp line between

45 Walter Kuhn, "Das Deutschtum in Kongreßpolen und Ungarn. Ein sprachinselkundlicher Vergleich," *Deutsche Monatshefte in Polen* 1 (11), no. 1 (July 1934): 5–14.
46 Albert Breyer, "Das Deutschtum in Mittelpolen. Bemerkungen zu der anliegenden Karte," *Jomsburg. Völker und Staaten im Osten und Norden Europas* 2 (1938), 74–77.
47 Karl Heinz Roth, "Heydrichs Professor. Historiographie des 'Volkstums' und der Massenvernichtungen: Der Fall Hans Joachim Beyer," in *Geschichtsschreibung als Legitimationswissenschaft 1918–1945*, ed. Peter Schöttler, 262–342 (Frankfurt/Main: Suhrkamp Taschenbuch, 1999), here 273.
48 Hans Joachim Beyer, "Mittelpolen in der neueren deutschen Volksgeschichte," *Vergangenheit und Gegenwart* 29, nos. 9/10 (1939): 510–524, here 514, 518–524.

Germans and Jews, the Germans in Łódź – whose purported cosmopolitan leanings had caused such concern in the past – could now be fully included in the Volksgemeinschaft. The weaknesses of the Łódź Germans were now reinterpreted as virtues, and this shift in the politics of symbols allowed the Germans in Central Poland to begin playing a real political role.

What happened to the despicable lodzermensch? German nationalists still talked about the problem of renegade Germandom, but its application to the Germans in Łódź as a whole diminished noticeably. Rather, lack of national feeling was now attributed mainly to the dwindling members of the pro-Polish DKuWB or seen as a past affliction from which the Germans in Łódź had since recovered. Eugen Oskar Kossmann, for example, noted that a new intellectual spirit was overtaking that of the "purely economically determined structure of the 'Lodzer Mensch.'"[49] Others preferred to reinterpret the lodzermensch altogether. In 1936, Kurt Lück published an essay claiming that the literary and historically grounded lodzermensch was proof that the Germans had played the role of the "industrial pioneers" in the Łódź region. For Lück, the generally negative image of the Łódź Germans – and by association the lodzermensch – in Polish literature was unwarranted. Lück criticized Władysław Reymont's *The Promised Land* and other Polish literary works for ignoring the productive side of the lodzermensch and for failing to grasp the circumstances in which the Łódź Germans had acted the way they did. He supported his case with one Polish economic historian's demographic research, which Lück credited with "saving the honor of the 'Lodzer Mensch.'"[50] In other words, the lodzermensch had become a very German phenomenon for Lück. Clearly, Central Polish Germans remained a versatile screen for projecting manifold ideological precepts.

GERMANS VERSUS JEWS? "BLACK PALM SUNDAY" OF 1933 IN ŁÓDŹ

As we have seen previously, Polish animosity against Germans initially increased with Hitler's appointment as chancellor, for most Poles were familiar with the chauvinist and irredentist rhetoric of the Nazis. These tensions, however, diminished over the course of the year, culminating in the Polish-German treaty in January 1934. German relations with Jews in Łódź, however, took a different turn. The growing nationalist atmosphere

---

49 Eugen Oskar Kossmann, "Deutsche auf Lodzer Boden," *Deutsche Monatshefte in Polen* 2, no. 1–2 (July/August 1935): 58–76, here 76.
50 Kurt Lück, "Deutsches Wesen im Spiegel der polnischen Literatur und Volksüberlieferung," *Deutsche Monatshefte in Polen* 2 (12), no. 8 (February 1936): 307–318, here 311–316.

in Poland and Germany created opportunities for confrontation and conflict among all three major ethnic groups. The attitude of many Germans in Łódź toward the Nazi rise to power in Germany was initially a mixture of curiosity and apprehension. Jews outnumbered the Germans about four to one in the city, and a souring of relations could have been devastating for the local German population, both politically and economically. In early 1933, boycotts in Germany against Jewish stores led to small-scale Jewish demonstrations in Łódź against products from Germany. Although these boycotts did not specifically target Germans in Poland, many German minority-owned stores dealt with goods originating from Germany. The general perception was that the boycotts were aimed at the Germans in Łódź as a whole.

On Palm Sunday in April 1933, a demonstration organized by the Polish nationalist Związek Obrony Kresów Zachodnich (Union for the Defense of the Western Borderlands) took a violent turn. Demonstrators damaged the Lodzer Deutsches Gymnasium and the Deutsche Genossenschaftsbank, while others ransacked two German bookstores and the offices and printing presses of Libertas, which published the German nationalist newspapers *Freie Presse* and *Der Volksfreund*.[51] The incident was one of the most significant outbreaks of anti-German violence in interwar Poland, although it remains unclear how the rioting began. Despite the destruction of property, there were no personal injuries during the violence. Moreover, the participants were not senseless in their choice of targets: in Łódź, the attacks were directed against the high school and the presses, those sites that were perceived as centers that propagated German nationalism.

The nationalist German press in Łódź and elsewhere immediately concluded that the crowd had been mostly Jewish and had been whipped up by a Jewish party, Organizacja Syjonistyczna (Zionist Organization). It did not matter that Dr. Jerzy Rozenblat, the leader of the local chapter of Organizacja Syjonistyczna, had issued an "appeal from Jews to German public opinion in Łódź," in which he condemned the violence and denied the allegations that Jewish organizations were behind the outbreak. Although DVV leader August Utta met with Rozenblat, Utta did not back down from his assertion about the role of Organizacja Syjonistyczna. Indeed, rumors

51 Blanke, *Orphans of Versailles*, 183; Breyer, *Das Deutsche Reich und Polen*, 250; Beate Kosmala, "Lodzer Juden und Deutsche im Jahr 1933. Die Rezeption der nationalsozialistischen Machtübernahme in Deutschland und ihre Wirkung auf das Verhältnis von jüdischer und deutscher Minderheit," in *Polen, Deutsche und Juden in Lodz 1820–1939. Eine schwierige Nachbarschaft*, ed. Jürgen Hensel, 237–245 (Osnabrück: Fibre, 1999), here 241.

continued to circulate that Jews were planning additional anti-German demonstrations in other cities.[52]

Among German nationalists, the incident became known as "Black Palm Sunday": the DVV and later the JDP regularly commemorated the incident and referred to it in their speeches in their effort to rally the Germans. The incident was important for future German and Jewish relations in the city, less because it exacerbated existing tensions, and more because it allowed the German activists to stage a confrontation with the Jewish population. Although they had previously worked closely with Jewish parties, Łódź German nationalists instrumentalized the incident to break with their former allies. They quickly terminated other contacts with Jewish groups in Łódź.[53] The marked anti-Semitic turn could be seen in other DVV-related organizations, including the Deutscher Schul- und Bildungsverein (German Club for School and Education).[54] In the era of good relations between Germany and Poland, such an incident helped the mobilization strategy of German activists in Łódź. The violence weakened the idea of interethnic cooperation, which hurt the DVV's rivals, the German socialists and German pacifists (DKuWB). Both of these groups insisted on working with the other nationalities in the city. The DSAP, for example, cooperated with the PPS and the Bund to issue a proclamation that decried the excesses against Jews as well as Germans.[55] Many on the other side could not avoid the nationalist temptation, however, and in many ways the DVV leaders succeeded in provoking Jewish groups. In response to German accusations, the Jewish leaders in Łódź called for more economic boycotts in September and October of 1933 as well as in subsequent years.[56] For some Jewish leaders, the anti-German protests likewise served to integrate the heavily splintered Jewish parties.[57] Thus, Germans and Jews played into the hands of their respective nationalist camps. The community of shared interests between Polish Germans and Polish Jews in the 1920s had unraveled into a community of conflict.

In his analysis of the anti-Semitic pogroms in Lwów in 1918, William Hagen explains how Polish participants had projected their own violent behavior on the Jews, thus justifying the pogrom.[58] There are obvious

---

52 Janusz Wróbel, "Between Co-Existence and Hostility: A Contribution to the Problem of National Antagonisms in Łódź," *Polin* 6 (1991): 201–206, here 204.
53 Kosmala, "Lodzer Juden und Deutsche im Jahr 1933," 204.
54 Wróbel, "Between Co-Existence and Hostility," 204–205.
55 Wróbel, "Between Co-Existence and Hostility," 205.
56 Kosmala, "Lodzer Juden und Deutsche im Jahr 1933," 244.
57 Kosmala, "Lodzer Juden und Deutsche im Jahr 1933," 238.
58 William W. Hagen, "The Moral Economy of Ethnic Violence: The Pogrom in Lwów, November 1918," *Geschichte und Gesellschaft* 31, no. 2 (2005): 203–226. See also David Engel, "Lwów, 1918: The

differences in the Łódź case, of course. According to the categories proposed by Donald L. Horowitz, the Black Palm Sunday would not even
qualify as a "deadly ethnic riot" but rather as a "violent protest."[59] In the
moral economy of German minority activists, however, the "exclusionary
violence" was interpreted as an anti-German pogrom.[60] The Black Palm
Sunday remained a recurrent theme because it could serve various needs,
including justifying the violence of ethnic Germans against their Polish and
Jewish neighbors during the Second World War.

Hence, the events of Black Palm Sunday were significant less in themselves than in how ethnic entrepreneurs used them to mobilize the Germans
in Poland and construct a narrative of national awakening. As the historian
Beate Kosmala has noted, the Black Palm Sunday became a "mythologi-
cal event," a useful tool for disassimilating Germans from their Jewish and
Polish surroundings and for building a common sense of identity.[61] In the
narrative of national becoming, the Black Palm Sunday was the point of
demarcation, or trauma, that initiated the awakening of the Germandom
in Łódź.[62] By ostensibly proving Jewish maliciousness, the DVV leaders
could freely bring their program in line with National Socialist tenets and
propaganda. The alleged Jewish victimization of the Germans attracted the
attention of the new Nazi regime, as praise, advice, and funds began to flow
from the Reich to Łódź.[63] The Black Palm Sunday allowed German leaders
in Łódź to wash themselves of past political cooperation with the Jews and
rinse away the sticky association with the lodzermensch.

German historians in the postwar period have perpetuated many myths
about the Black Palm Sunday. Notably, Richard Breyer attributed the violence to a "Polish-Jewish crowd."[64] More generally, the Black Palm Sunday
is portrayed as a regrettable but ultimately positive event for the development
of the German minority into a proper Volksgruppe. Theodor Bierschenk, a

Transmutation of a Symbol and its Legacy in the Holocaust," in *Contested Memories: Poles and Jews during the Holocaust and its Aftermath*, ed. Joshua D. Zimmerman, 32–44 (New Brunswick/London: Rutgers University Press, 2003). In general, there is a need to understand here what Helmut Walser Smith calls "process" in his analysis of anti-Semitic violence in Konitz in 1900: *The Butcher's Tale: Murder and Anti-Semitism in a German Town* (New York/London: Norton, 2002), 21–23.

59 Donald L. Horowitz, *The Deadly Ethnic Riot* (Berkeley/Los Angeles: University of California Press, 2001), 19–20.

60 Various case studies that broaden the perspective on pogroms can be found in Christhard Hoffmann, Werner Bergmann, and Helmut Walser Smith, eds., *Exclusionary Violence: Antisemitic Riots in Modern German History* (Ann Arbor: The University of Michigan Press, 2002).

61 Beate Kosmala, *Juden und Deutsche im polnischen Haus. Tomaszów Mazowiecki 1914–1939* (Berlin: Metropol, 2001), 290–292.

62 Social-Political Department of the Voivodeship of Łódź, monthly report no. 1 for 1–31 January 1935, dated January [sic] 9, 1935, in AP Łódź, Urząd Wojewódzki Łódzki, folder 2507 L.

63 Wróbel, "Between Co-Existence and Hostility," 201–206.

64 Breyer, *Das Deutsche Reich und Polen*, 250.

former JDP functionary from Central Poland, creates a narrative that relies on the negative characteristics associated with the lodzermensch:

In Central Poland around 1930, the stagnating Germandom, especially in part in Łódź, had believed that it could most easily "earn" the toleration of a life of its own by behaving passively. The events on Palm Sunday 1933 shook up this Germandom.... This Black Sunday caused the Łódź Germans either to wake up from their lethargy, to give up the inner reserve they had lately practiced, or to reexamine their previous political behavior.[65]

Bierschenk's use of pejorative language for interethnic accommodation ("lethargy") reveals his assumption that the nationalization was right and necessary, even if the process was guided by Nazi tenets and with the hindsight of what happened in the war years. It became common to say that minority leaders in Poland had been naive and never really knew what National Socialism was about, thus excusing them for what would happen in the war. In the case of Łódź, such apologists failed to see that the Nazification of German political life had already destroyed the fabric of a polyethnic city before German troops arrived in 1939. Rather than answering why the Łódź Germans were nationalized, the Black Palm Sunday incident requires us to ask why so many German activists in Łódź embraced Nazism. A host of many other reasons – conviction, opportunism, and fear – made Germans in Łódź sympathize with pro-National Socialist groupings. The lack of viable political alternatives to prove their Germanness only exacerbated the situation.

JDP VERSUS DVV IN CENTRAL POLAND

The JDP recognized early on that the struggle for Central Poland would become critical for the future course of the party. Central Poland was after all a major prize in itself: the Ostforscher Walter Kuhn, writing under the alias Andreas Mückler, had estimated the number of Germans in the former Congress Kingdom in 1927 to be 320,000.[66] Moreover, taking control of the region would have provided a base to expand into the German settlements in neighboring Volhynia. In 1936, JDP leaders even considered plans to move their headquarters to Łódź.[67] In late 1938, Wiesner sought

---

65 Theodor Bierschenk, *Die deutsche Volksgruppe in Polen, 1934–1939* (Würzburg: Holzner, 1954), 40–41.
66 Walter Kuhn [Andreas Mückler, pseud.], *Das Deutschtum Kongreßpolens. Eine statistisch-kritische Studie* (Leipzig/Wien: Franz Deuticke, 1927), 87.
67 Social-Political Department of the Voivodeship of Łódź, monthly report no. 12 for December 1–31, 1935, dated January 9, 1936, in AP Łódź, Urząd Wojewódzki Łódzki, folder 2507 L.

to recruit and train leaders from the eastern and northeastern provinces of Poland.[68] For the upstart party from Bielsko, the move toward the East became more important as its influence in Western Poland waned.

The Young Germans established a local chapter in Łódź in early 1934, but problems prevented a more definite expansion until 1935. Young German leaders were aware that their party, as a newcomer to Central Poland, would have difficulties finding resonance in Łódź and the region.[69] Much of the initial difficulties for the JDP, however, had to do with the continuing leadership disputes in Western Poland, where Wiesner expended much of his time and energy. Learning from his bitter experience with the rebellion in Western Poland, Wiesner made every attempt to ensure that the party chapters in Central Poland would remain loyal to him. Downplaying these problems, the JDP press described this inactivity as a necessary resting period to build a "core troop" that would carry the battle into the countryside.[70] In fact, the JDP spent much of the early period attacking the German socialists. Already on the decline, the "Marxists" provided a convenient enemy for the JDP, both in newspaper attacks and in the "hall battles," or brawls at political meetings.[71] The nationalist DVV was still largely based in the countryside and had not yet been established among the German workers in Łódź. Despite the JDP's own socialist pretensions, however, the disillusioned DSAP rank and file tended to join the DVV or abstained from politics altogether.

As the previous chapter has shown, the JDP stylized itself not just as the champion of the underprivileged. The JDP tried to use the egalitarian rhetoric of Volksgemeinschaft to win over the disaffected Germans in Western Poland, where generational and class issues had divided the haves from the have-nots. In Central Poland, however, the already peripheral role of the Germans there added another dimension. The Young Germans, having their origins in formerly Austrian Bielsko, enjoyed the advantage of having an apparently non-privileged background, and they relentlessly played on the resentments of the other have-not regions. JDP activists tried to convince the Germans in Central Poland that only their party would take them seriously and remediate their underrepresented role within the minority.

68 Polish Interior Ministry (Nationalities Department), Weekly Report, October 20, 1938, in AAN, MSZ, folder 2352, 283.
69 "Deutsche Volksgemeinschaft in Mittelpolen. Deutscher Gemeinschaftsabend der J. D. P. O. G. Pabjanice," *Deutsche Nachrichten in Polen*, March 29, 1935, in GStA, I HA, Rep. 77, Tit. 856, folder 752.
70 "Vormarsch der J.D.P. in Lodz," *Deutsche Nachrichten in Polen*, January 9, 1935, in GStA, I HA, Rep. 77, Tit. 856, folder 752, 152.
71 "Vormarsch in Lodz: Gegen den Marxismus – für den deutschen Arbeiter," *Deutsche Nachrichten in Polen*, January 24, 1935, in GStA, I HA, Rep. 77, Tit. 856, folder 752, 164.

JDP speakers, for example, accused the DV in Western Poland of thinking of themselves as the better Germans, especially vis-à-vis the Germans in Central Poland.[72] According to JDP newspapers, the Old German leadership had long written off the Central Polish Germans as a hopeless cause.[73]

JDP functionaries from Central Poland who felt that their party finally gave them a voice in minority politics helped to spread this missionary zeal elsewhere. Speaking at the JDP party congress in Chorzów in Upper Silesia in 1934, Walter Günzel stated: "Without a doubt the Young German Party alone deserves credit if the recent efforts to unify all the areas of German settlement have become apparent." He added, "Today there are only Germans. Not Poseners, not Upper Silesians, not Lodzers!" Günzel bemoaned the fact that there were still those in the JDP who still thought in terms of regional differences, but he hoped that the influence of the JDP would eliminate such nonsensical views with time. Near the end of his speech, Günzel revealed his deep-seated desire for the recognition of his home region: "Tell your fellow Germans that the flags will also wave in Congress Poland, that there are Germans living, working and striving there – not the so-called 'also-Germans' [auch-Deutsche], but Germans like you in Poznania and Pomerelia or Upper Silesia and Bielsko or Galicia and Volhynia."[74] But even JDP members from Central Poland were not free of self-stereotyping, and they played the lodzermensch card when it suited their needs. In another speech in Łódź, Walter Günzel noted that the Germans in the former Congress Kingdom did not enjoy a good reputation in the Reich and in the other Polish territories, but their growing support for the JDP had proved their German spirit and character.[75]

The JDP bitterly criticized the apparent accommodation that had been reached by the Deutsche Vereinigung in Western Poland and the Deutscher Volksverband in Central Poland. The JDP especially ridiculed their umbrella organization, the Rat der Deutschen in Polen, for its inability to bridge the differences between the various regions. Yet the Bielsko-based JDP made even less progress in Central Poland, a fellow peripheral region, than in Western Poland. For all its other failings, the JDP leadership was correct

---

72 "Erwachen des völkischen Lebens in Mittelpolen," *Deutsche Nachrichten in Polen*, March 16, 1935, in GStA, I HA, Rep. 77, folder 752, 197. At the 1935 rally in Lodz, a JDP leader from Western Poland referred to himself as a "Posen-Pommereller."

73 "Frühjahrsoffensive in Lodz," *Deutsche Nachrichten in Polen*, May 22, 1935, in GStA, I HA, Rep. 77, Tit. 856, folder 753, 32.

74 Jungdeutsche Partei für Polen, "Rede von Pg. Dr. Günzel, Lodz," *Reden und Berichte vom Parteitag 1934* (Bielsko: Jungdeutsche Partei für Polen, 1934), 23–30, here 23, 30, in BA Koblenz, R57-Neu, folder 1093 (Nr. 21).

75 Social-Political Department of the Voivodeship of Łódź, monthly report no. 1 for January 1–31, dated January (sic) 9, 1935, in AP Łódź, Urząd Wojewódzki Łódzki, folder 2507 L.

in assessing the stubborn persistence of regional parties and their pursuit of their own interests. As the JDP had discovered in Western Poland, the Germans in Central Poland likewise harbored a strong sense of particularism – itself a reaction to the JDP incursion.

THE HOMEFIELD ADVANTAGE

The Deutscher Volksverband responded swiftly to the challenge from the JDP. A flurry of newspaper articles pronounced the JDP's threat to National Socialist German unity and renewal. By doing so, they legitimated the right of the established conservative-nationalist organizations to dominate their own home ground.[76] As in Western Poland, the conflict was an ideological battle, but not one between different ideologies. Rather, each side portrayed itself as the true representative of National Socialist ideas, while trying to discredit the other's commitment to their common credo, as the following newspaper article shows:

> It is not enough to call oneself a National Socialist, one must also be one. It is impossible to stand at the head of a renewal movement and to want to renew others without having been taken up by this movement and without having taken it in. If we take a look at Bielitz, where you [Wiesner] have allegedly already done fifteen years of national work, then we have to ask in vain what the accomplishments and successes are.[77]

Der Volksfreund, the weekly paper of the DVV, castigated the JDP as a "so-called renewal movement" and pointed out that the "JDP-Terror" displayed a very un-National Socialist "lack of discipline."[78] The newspaper also carried out ad hominem attacks on Rudolf Wiesner and other JDP leaders, calling into question their integrity and leadership ability.[79]

The rough JDP tactics, especially as the party lost ground to the DVV, did not help the Young German cause. In his memoirs, Eugen Oskar Kossmann recalled how at one rally a JDP speaker slapped an elderly DVV speaker – it was probably Joseph Spickermann, who had served as Sejm deputy and as senator.[80] In the January 1936 incident already recounted in the Introduction, JDP members crashed a DVV public meeting and harassed

76 "Die Lage des Deutschtums in Westpolen," *Der Volksfreund*, May 31, 1936, 2–3, in AP Łódź.
77 "Ein Brief. Pastor Harlfinger an Senator Wiesner," *Der Volksfreund*, January 5, 1936, 2–4, here 4, in AP Łódź.
78 "Organisierter Überfall jungdeutscher Sprengtrupps auf deutsche Versammlungen," *Der Volksfreund*, January 12, 1936, 3–5, here 3, in AP Łódź.
79 "Herr Wiesner bittet ums Wort," *Der Volksfreund*, January 26, 1936, 3–4, in AP Łódź.
80 Eugen Oskar Kossmann, *Es begann in Polen. Erinnerungen eines Diplomaten und Ostforschers* (Lüneburg: Nordostdeutsches Kulturwerk, 1989), 131.

the speakers. Playing on class tensions, the JDP shouted down one speaker, Leo Brauer, telling him to leave the stage because he was the son of a factory owner. When the JDP members rushed the stage and tore apart the DVV banner, a general melee ensued. Only the DVV's calling of the Polish police to intervene restored temporary order before more fighting broke out. The meeting was ended, but the exiting JDP members ridiculed August Utta, who had not been present, by calling him a "swine." The Polish report noted that many "non-organized" Germans at the meeting had been outraged by the JDP's behavior.[81]

Yet a large share of the JDP's failure was due to its inability to break down, overcome, or transcend the regional particularism of the Central Polish Germans. In many ways, the JDP actually triggered a strengthening of regional alignments. The decline of the other parties with strong local roots, the DSAP and the DKuWB, only reinforced the view of the DVV as a homegrown party. The following assertion by the DVV youth leader Ludwig Wolff reveals his stylization of the party's role as simultaneously regional and totalizing: "As the organization of the Germans in Central Poland, the Deutscher Volksverband is for all these people not one organization among others, but rather the organization, and our success lies in our ability to make this happen."[82] The German Foreign Ministry also recognized the DVV as *the* party for the Germans in Central Poland, and the local consulate supported the DVV over the JDP. During the city council elections at the end of September 1936, the German consulate in Łódź asked for RM 3,000 to help the DVV campaign.[83]

As in the DV's struggle with the JDP in Western Poland, the Deutscher Volksverband conflated the support of National Socialism and German unity with the party's own particularist tendencies. Before 1933, conservative-nationalist parties had been quite satisfied with their regional arrangement in Poland. The JDP challenged the existing order by taking seriously the commonly espoused call for organizational unity. The DVV-friendly *Volksfreund*, in turn, cynically used the rhetoric of unity to cut into the JDP:

---

81 Voivodeship of Łódź (Vice-Voivode A. Potocki) to Nationalities Department of the Interior Ministry in Warsaw, January 8, 1936, copy as attachment sent by Skarbek, Interior Ministry to Polish Foreign Ministry (Wydział Ustrojów Międzynarodowych), January 14, 1936, in AAN, MSZ, folder 2238, 1–3. See the Introduction for more on this incident.

82 "Deutsche Jugend will leben! Über 1000 Vertreter der jungen Generation aus allen Gauen Polens bekunden ihre Einheit," *Freie Presse*, November 2, 1937 (newspaper clipping sent by Consul Berchem to German Foreign Ministry on November 3, 1937, then forwarded by German Foreign Ministry to Reich Interior Ministry, Volksdeutsche Mittelstelle, and Deutsche Stiftung on November 16, 1937), in BA Berlin, R8043, folder 943, 67–71, here 69 back side.

83 Consulate in Łódź (Kurschat) to German Foreign Ministry, July 30, 1936, in PAAA, Pol V, Politik 25 Polen, vol. 1, R104198, 89–90.

This campaign by the Jungdeutsche Partei against German unity in Poland has also encouraged the Marxists anew. They also have held a party congress in Łódź and have called for a continuation of the class struggle among us Germans. The so-called Kultur- und Wirtschaftsbund is trying to collect the remnants of its few members and to continue the scam [Bauernfang] through demagogic promises.[84]

By making a causal connection between the rise of the JDP and the revival of the socialists and the pro-Polish loyalists in the German camp, the author was able to demean the JDP as a real threat to Germandom in Poland. Such statements in *Der Volksfreund* reveal less the DVV leadership's desire for an idealized German unity in Poland, however, than its determination to maintain its recently won hegemony in Central Poland. After all, the phantom threats of the DSAP and the DKuWB pertained mainly to Central Poland.

Perhaps most critical for the DVV success was its ability to draw upon a well of popular mistrust among local Germans toward other German groups in Poland. *Der Volksfreund* printed an acrimonious letter from an Upper Silesian German pastor who claimed that the JDP was merely a Bielitzer club, thus ridiculing JDP pretensions to lead the entire German minority.[85] As in Western Poland, the regional foreignness of the JDP easily communicated a kind of ethno-national foreignness. The accusations that various JDP leaders had belonged to Polish organizations in their youth thus fed fears of their crypto-Polishness:

Suddenly there appeared new men in our midst, men who during our greatest need had sat in cozy club salons drinking beer and playing cards and performed their "national work" in "undercover"; some even tried to pursue a career in Polish-national organizations, failed students who had tried their luck elsewhere in Poland and have now attempted to establish the "Jungdeutsche Partei" amongst us.[86]

Having long experienced marginalization themselves, the German activists in Central Poland, especially those from Łódź, knew very well how to make others appear as outsiders and "less German." At the same time, this foreignness changed in different contexts. The DVV, which claimed to represent the large number of rural Germans in Central Poland, also used perceived antagonisms toward Łódź in its struggle against the JDP.

84 "Ein Volk, ein Wille, eine Front. Zur 12. Tagung des Deutschen Volksverbandes in Polen," *Der Volksfreund*, February 2, 1936, 1–2, in AP Łódź.
85 "Ein Brief. Pastor Harlfinger an Senator Wiesner," *Der Volksfreund*, January 5, 1936, 2–4, here 3, in AP Łódź.
86 "Ein Volk, ein Wille, eine Front. Zur 12. Tagung des Deutschen Volksverbandes in Polen," *Der Volksfreund*, February 2, 1936, 1–2, in AP Łódź.

Der Volksfreund referred to JDP activists as "25 fellows from Lodz" and "intruders" at a meeting of farmers in rural Central Poland.[87]

The school issue, which had previously united German socialists and conservatives against the Polish government, now became a source of conflict between the DVV and the JDP. An example of this political instrumentalization of the school issue took place in 1936, when Wiesner, who was then serving as a Polish senator, made a proposal to introduce Polish language instruction beginning with the first grade at public elementary schools with German instruction. *Der Volksfreund* reported that Germans throughout Poland were outraged over Wiesner's proposal. August Utta sarcastically suggested that the German minority would be better off under the Poles than under Senator Wiesner: "He is more Polish than the Polish Ministry of Education. He is going the same direction that the pseudo-German Kultur- und Wirtschaftsbund has gone: in word solidly German, in deed more Polish than the Polish ministries themselves."[88] By questioning Wiesner's Germanness and comparing the JDP to the much-maligned Deutscher Kultur- und Wirtschaftsbund, Utta underlined Wiesner's threat to Germandom in terms that local Germans could understand. In a reversal of regional hierarchies, Utta was able to project the specter of the stridently anti-national lodzermensch on the outsider JDP.

At the same time, the DVV effectively copied the JDP's language of renewal. *Der Volksfreund*, edited by August Utta, appropriated slogans that the JDP had used to attack the Old Germans. *Der Volksfreund* announced the upcoming DVV annual meeting in 1936 with the proclamation: "It shall be all of Germandom."[89] At the congress, the banner hanging above the stage announced: "You are nothing – Your Volk is everything!" The speakers discussed the need to heal class differences and displayed supraregional unity with guests from across Poland. Senator Erwin Hasbach, a Poznanian German and the leader of the Rat der Deutschen in Polen, gave a speech attacking Wiesner and in which he asked "who is the better National Socialist."[90]

87 "Die Landbevölkerung steht treu zum Deutschen Volksverband. Ortsgruppenversammlung in Adamow – Jungdeutsche Eindringlinge werden aus dem Versammlungslokal entfernt," *Der Volksfreund*, January 19, 1936, 10, in AP Łódź.

88 "Der Bärendienst Senator Wiesners," *Der Volksfreund*, April 26, 1936, 1–2, here 1; "Ein harter Schlag gegen die deutsche Schule," *Der Volksfreund*, April 12, 1936, 3–4, in AP Łódź.

89 "Das ganze Deutschtum soll es sein! Zur Jahrestagung des DVV am 15. Februar 1936," *Der Volksfreund*, February 9, 1936, 1, in AP Łódź.

90 "Gewaltige Kundgebung für die Volksdeutsche Front. Die 12. Jahrestagung des Deutschen Volksverbandes," *Der Volksfreund*, February 23, 1936, 1, in AP Łódź; "Gewaltige Kundgebung für die Volksdeutsche Front. Die 12. Jahrestagung des Deutschen Volksverbandes (Schluss)," *Der Volksfreund*, March 1, 1936, 2, in AP Łódź; also "Die Tagung des Deutschen Volksverbandes. Im Zeichen der

Like the DV in Western Poland, the DVV's attacks on the JDP walked a fine line when it praised cultural-spiritual unity while rejecting a unified political organization for all Germans in Poland.[91] DVV leaders did not take this stance merely out of consideration for their Western Polish partners. The Central Polish DVV was still relatively small in relation to the Deutsche Vereinigung, and it would have been vulnerable in any organizational merger with its allies. While preaching the supraregional unity of a Volksgemeinschaft, both the DVV and the JDP actually instrumentalized particularist feelings: a positive regionalism on the one hand, peripheral have-not resentment against the privileged have regions on the other.

The failure of the JDP was even more disastrous in Central Poland than in Western Poland, where Wiesner's party had at least managed to remain a political factor. The JDP never had more than 800 members in Central Poland, and according to VDA sources, the JDP organ for Central Poland, the *Völkischer Anzeiger*, had a circulation of only 400–500 copies.[92] An early setback occurred already in 1935, when the JDP leader for Łódź county, Walter Günzel, was sent to Poznań to be head of press and propaganda and to take an editorial position at *Deutsche Nachrichten*. His replacement was Theodor Bierschenk, later a postwar historian of the minority. According to Polish reports, Bierschenk was energetic and had organizational talent, but he lacked Günzel's speaking abilities.[93]

The overwhelming triumph of DVV over the JDP incursion in Central Poland can be largely attributed to the preference of Germans in Central Poland for their homegrown party. Despite its ultimate failure, however, the JDP left a fateful legacy in Central Poland. Its rhetoric of recognizing the underprivileged within the minority empowered German nationalists in Central Poland, who increasingly looked to themselves for leadership. Moreover, there was one point where the JDP seemed to score against the DVV; the Young Germans relentlessly assaulted August Utta's integrity and his leadership of the DVV.[94] The criticism apparently struck a chord within the DVV, allowing a new star to rise within the party. Ludwig Wolff

jungen Mannschaft. Eindrucksvoller Verlauf des gestrigen Aufmarsches der volksdeutschen Front im Sängerhaus," *Freie Presse*, February 16, 1936, 1–4.

91 Voivodeship of Łódź (Vice-Voivode A. Potocki) to Nationalities Department of the Interior Ministry in Warsaw, January 8, 1936, copy as attachment sent by Skarbek, Interior Ministry to Polish Foreign Ministry (Wydział Ustrojów Międzynarodowych), January 14, 1936, in AAN, MSZ, folder 2238, 1–3.

92 VDA lecture by Reinhard Fritsch (November 1937), reprinted in Jacobsen, *Hans Steinacher*, 538–539.

93 Social-Political Department of the Voivodeship of Łódź, monthly report no. 9 for September 1–30, 1935, dated October 9, 1935, in AP Łódź, Urząd Wojewódzki Łódzki, folder 2507 L.

94 Social-Political Department of the Voivodeship of Łódź, monthly report no. 6 for May 1–31, 1935, dated June 8, 1935, in AP Łódź, Urząd Wojewódzki Łódzki, folder 2507 L.

was as energetic as he was ruthless, and as leader of the DVV youth wing he was able to take the wind out of the JDP's sails. With their appetite for power whetted, the attitude of the German leaders in Central Poland toward a possible political unification also changed as they grew numerically and politically. Whereas the Germans in Western Poland increasingly appeared tired and impotent, Łódź became the center of an "awakening Germandom."[95] The hour of the German nationalists in Łódź had struck.

THE POLITICAL EASTERNIZATION OF THE GERMAN MINORITY

The steady subversion of the negative image of the Łódź German informed and reflected the overturning of the regional hierarchy within the German minority in Poland. Especially the internecine conflict between the Deutsche Vereinigung and the JDP undermined the dominance of the Germans of Western Poland. German activists there had traditionally flexed their muscle within the minority through their large number of Sejm and Senate seats, but the Polish constitutional reform in April 1935 made it virtually impossible for any Sejm representatives from the German minority to be elected, thus contributing to a flattening of political hierarchies within the minority.

There were those in Western Poland, of course, who readily recognized that the Volksgruppe was now supposed to rely on itself (and not on aid from Germany), and that the Germans in the formerly Prussian regions should look east and not west for inspiration.[96] Still, many Western Polish German leaders were reluctant to acknowledge the sea change within the minority in the 1930s. A 1935 speech in Łódź by Erich Spitzer, the Gauleiter of the Young German Party in Pomerelia, exemplified this ambivalence:

Despite a long period of foreign rule during which you have suffered some losses, we recognize that you have still kept the core of your Germandom intact. You have thus had experience as Auslandsdeutsche, which we do not yet have in the western regions. On the other hand, we have been quicker to discern the goal and the road to renewal because we have had greater opportunity to draw strength from the mother country.[97]

The idea of learning from the East about coping with minorityness was not new, but Spitzer's statement reveals that this reversal of fortune for the

---

95 Breyer, *Das Deutsche Reich und Polen*, 250.
96 "Unsere Revolution von 1918," *Deutsche Nachrichten in Polen*, August 18, 1935, in GStA, I HA, Rep. 77, Tit. 856, folder 753, 93.
97 "Erwachen des völkischen Lebens in Mittelpolen," *Deutsche Nachrichten in Polen*, March 16, 1935, in GStA, I HA, Rep. 77, Tit. 856, folder 752, 197.

Western Polish Germans was not easy. His narrative of völkisch progress dwelled on many of the allegedly bad qualities of the Łódź Germans, although these sins were now seen as part of the past. His attempt to reassert what his own region had to offer underlines how difficult it was for the Germans in Western Poland to understand their diminishing influence as the schoolmaster for their eastern cousins. With the value of their Staatsvolk heritage depreciating rapidly, the Germans in Western Poland were increasingly forced to concede that they were not better than the Łódź Germans after all. The time was passing when Western Polish Germans in the DV or JDP could give an occasional patronizing compliment to the Łódź Germans without undermining their own self-worth.

THE LIMITS OF REICH CONTROL

The apparently reduced possibility of a border revision in the short term due to the German-Polish Non-Aggression Pact focused attention on the long-term survival of the German minority in Poland. The overall amount of subsidies from the Reich to the German minority actually decreased during the 1930s.[98] Despite the overall reduction in funds, the distribution of money to the minority had by no means become fairer. The ceded territories remained important to various Reich institutions. The Deutsche Stiftung, for example, wrote to the Reich Economics Ministry in 1936, demanding RM 314,400 per month to cover its expenses. It complained that the ceded territories still required a considerable amount of money, but the general reduction in funds had stalled its operations.[99] In a 1936 summary by the Foreign Ministry, the cover organization, Ossa, had distributed RM 3,000,000 to cooperatives and banks in Poznania-Pomerelia and a further RM 600,000 to Upper Silesia, but it had given only RM 50,000 to Congress Poland, Galicia, and Volhynia combined. Ethnic German advocacy should be supported, but on the cheap. There was still the belief that that one could "get relatively good results with little money" in Central Poland.[100] These eastern regions also received money through the Deutscher Schulverein, but the discrepancy with Western Poland was still marked.[101] At least in the

---

98 Blanke, *Orphans of Versailles*, 161–162, 203–204.
99 Krahmer-Möllenberg to Reich Economics Ministry, June 10, 1936, in PAAA, Inland II geheim, vol. 1 (220), microfiche 2319, 207–215.
100 L.R. Schwager to IV Polen (Lieres, Consul Dr. Schwarz), February 22, 1936, with attachment of draft memorandum "Finanzierung der Ossa-Aufgaben nach Ablauf des Dreijahresplans" to Reich Finance Ministry, in PAAA, Pol IV-Geheimakten, Politik 25 Polen, vol. 9, R30868k.
101 Volhynia was allotted RM 55,000, Central Poland was to receive RM 45,000, Catholic elementary schools in Galicia were to receive RM 21,000, and the high school (Gymnasium) in

first few years after 1933, the old channels that privileged the old Prussian territories remained in place.

With an increasing interest in Germany for Germandom abroad, however, the differences in subsidies became an issue among minority members and outsiders alike. In 1934, one observer from Königsberg who had traveled through Volhynia claimed that Poznania-Pomerelia was a "giant dam" for Reich funds flowing into Poland.[102] This accusation by an apparent amateur to such issues angered the Deutsche Stiftung's Krahmer-Möllenberg, who wrote the following to the German consulate in Poznań:

> Time and again, Reich Germans who have not been overly burdened with professional knowledge have traveled to a region of German settlement. Based on a 14-day visit, they believe that they can make profound evaluations regarding the problems facing Germandom. Unfortunately, the belief in the credibility of such reports is also widespread here in the Reich. As a consequence, such elaborations often make things extremely difficult.[103]

This ethnic German advocacy from below appeared to have touched a nerve, and as Krahmer-Möllenberg's statement suggests, there was widespread willingness to believe such stories. The new ideological wind provided additional urgency for organizations in the Reich to address minority issues before other, newer forces would speak for them.

The established German authorities in Western Poland and the Reich, however, still felt in the early Nazi period that they could continue to harness the Germans in Central Poland for their own purposes. Many hoped that the meager funds that made their way into Central Poland would be sufficient to hold the Germans there in line. In 1934, the representative of the Deutscher Schulverein in Bydgoszcz, Otto Schönbeck, was wary of handing more than RM 15,000 from the VDA to August Utta. Schönbeck believed that the money should be conditional on the Germans in Łódź building a "responsible committee." In a word play, he complained that Congress Poland wanted to be "emancipated" (*mündig*), but that it still lacked a real mouthpiece (*Mund*). Scribbled next to the sentence, presumably by the Deutsche Stiftung's Krahmer-Möllenberg, was "Utta is all mouth."[104] Utta had become quite unpopular among both Reich authorities and German

Lwów/Lemberg was to receive RM 20,000. See Deutsche Stiftung to Deutscher Schulverein, May 26, 1937, in BA Berlin, R8043, folder 943, 124.

102 Theo Walther, Bericht über die Lage des Deutschtums in Wolhynien, September 15, 1934 (copy), in BA Berlin, R8043, folder 946, 313.

103 Krahmer-Möllenberg to Consulate General in Poznań (Tucher), September 18, 1935, in BA Berlin, R8043, folder 946, 199.

104 Schönbeck to Krahmer-Möllenberg, June 6, 1934, in BA Berlin, R8043, folder 943 [found on Film 62662], 389.

activists elsewhere in Poland, and they now hoped for a leadership change within the DVV. Krahmer-Möllenberg had long complained about Utta's "lack of ability."[105]

Just what Schönbeck implied with creating responsible Germans in Łódź could be inferred in a letter by Krahmer-Möllenberg to Schönbeck a year later. The Deutsche Stiftung gave its confidant Dr. Schweikert RM 15,000 with the intention of supporting a "decisively German direction" at the German Gymnasium in Łódź.[106] Krahmer-Möllenberg agreed fully with Schönbeck's pressure tactics to couple financial aid with German obligations. Drawing on the negative stereotypes of the local Germans, both writers repeated the assertion that money was the only effective means of influencing the school in Łódź. Passing on the money as a no-interest loan, Krahmer-Möllenberg said, would make the Lodzers "docile."[107] The correspondence between the Deutsche Stiftung in Berlin and the Deutscher Schulverein in Bydgoszcz reveals an unease with the growing influence of the Germans in Central Poland, but the letters also show the persistence of familiar patterns in answering these new challenges: money should be used to condition change. There was a clear effort to make the minority conform to the goals of the Third Reich. Established authorities like Krahmer-Möllenberg may not have been loud about their National Socialist credentials, but they were no less ideological in their actions.

Although the Deutsche Stiftung mediated and even supported different factions within the minority, Krahmer-Möllenberg could rarely get the best-case scenarios he wanted. Despite the desire to control the Germans in Central Poland and repeated attempts to foster a leadership change in the DVV, for example, Utta managed to cling to power. In early 1938, Schönbeck stated how unfortunate it was that Utta was still the leading man in what Schönbeck still called Congress Poland. While complaining that nobody, including Wolff, had the courage to tell Utta to quit, Schönbeck also said he did not want to be the one to "saw him off" and be drawn in the "line of fire."[108] The difficulties were in part self-made. Even though Central Poland received far fewer subsidies than the western regions, or perhaps because of this fact, money was still an untested tool. Because there

---

105 Krahmer-Möllenbeg to Schönbeck, March 24, 1934, in BA Berlin, R8043, folder 943 [found on Film 62662], 461; Krahmer-Möllenberg to Consul Molly, March 24, 1934, in BA Berlin, R8043, folder 943 [found on Film 62662], 462.

106 Dr. Schweikert to Schönbeck, March 12, 1935, in BA Berlin, R8043, folder 943 [found on Film 62662], 295; Schönbeck to Schweikert, March 1, 1935, ibid., 294; Schönbeck to Deutsche Stiftung, May 1, 1935, in ibid., 293.

107 Krahmer-Möllenberg to Schönbeck, May 15, 1935, in BA Berlin, R8043, folder 943 [found on Film 62662], 292.

108 Schönbeck to Deutsche Stiftung, February 8, 1938, in BA Berlin, R8043, folder 943, 27–29.

was little transparency in the disbursement of subsidies, uncertainty and jealousy marked the relations between the Reich and German leaders in Łódź. This situation fostered the reluctance of Reich agencies in becoming too exposed in intra-minority politics, especially in Central Poland. Rather than being in the driver's seat in its relationship with minority activists, the Deutsche Stiftung functioned as a fire brigade that reacted to various queries, rumors, and denunciations coming in from often dubious German characters in Central Poland.[109] Krahmer-Möllenberg himself was aware of the enormous influence that Germans from Poland could exert if they simply spent enough time in Berlin.[110] Indeed, the Deutsche Stiftung tended to jump on the bandwagon after events were already going a certain way. As the next sections will show, even the more ambitious SS would prove unable to bring minority leaders under its control.

Although the growing assertiveness of Central Polish German activists caused concern, the growing easternization of the minority could not be denied. With much of the leadership now going into Wolff's hands, the Deutscher Volksverband in Central Poland enjoyed a new burst of activity and growth in the later 1930s as it organized rallies and membership drives throughout Central Poland and in neighboring Volhynia. Claiming more than 25,000 members in 1937, the Łódź-based Deutscher Volksverband had become a major player in minority politics. This dynamic display of nationalism impressed Polish and German officials alike.[111] Ludwig Wolff, the DVV's rising star, also began to play a larger role in pan-minority politics. At the Youth Congress of the Germans in Poland in 1937, the *Freie Presse* stated that the Germans in Central Poland should be proud that the DVV had taken on the task of creating the German minority's intellectual front of unity. Wolff spoke of the need for inner unity, and he emphasized that the fate of Germandom abroad encompassed more than just Reich German fate. To be a German abroad was to involve growing beyond the individual and becoming a conscious "national comrade."[112]

---

109 "Voranschlag 1936, Kongresspolen. Abrechnung über das Etatsjahr 1.4.35–31.3.36," in BA Berlin, R8043, folder 943, 219–220; Schönbeck to Deutsche Stiftung (Ewert), October 26, 1937, with attachment "Kongresspolen. Abrechnung über das Etatsjahr 1.4.1936 bis 31.3.1937," ibid., 82–83; Deutscher Schulverein to Deutsche Stiftung, November 2, 1937, ibid., 87.

110 Krahmer-Möllenberg to Schönbeck, January 19, 1938, in BA Berlin, R8043, folder 943, 48.

111 VDA lecture by Reinhard Fritsch (November 1937), reprinted in Jacobsen, *Hans Steinacher*, 537–538; Polish Interior Ministry (Nationalities Department), Weekly Report, August 11, 1938, in AAN, MSZ, folder 2352, 129–130; Werner Lorenz to German minority leaders in Poland, May 18, 1938, with attachment: "Vorschlag für die Neubildung der deutschen Volksgruppe in Polen (I. Projekt)," in PAAA, Inland II geheim, vol. 8 (227), microfiche 2347, 156–160, here 159.

112 "Deutsche Jugend will leben! Über 1000 Vertreter der jungen Generation aus allen Gauen Polens bekunden ihre Einheit," *Freie Presse*, November 2, 1937 (newspaper clipping sent by Consul

After years of waiting, Wolff officially replaced August Utta as the leader of the DVV at the fourteenth annual party meeting in May 1938. Wolff was the only candidate and was elected unanimously. Utta did not even come to the conference, allegedly due to health problems. He papered over tensions in a letter that was read to the DVV delegates before they elected the new leader. Utta offered his continued cooperation and expressed his desire that all German leaders would finally sit down one day and form the long-desired organization to represent the entire minority. Although addressed to Wolff, there was no mention of him, and certainly no praise or thanks. It is significant that this letter was also published in the German press in Western Poland.[113]

This leadership change had little to do with the will of Reich authorities but much to do with Wolff's own ambition. Indeed, the rising star of the DVV caused unease among Reich authorities even before his formal takeover. Schönbeck from the Deutscher Schulverein suspected Wolff and his colleagues of working behind his back.[114] Krahmer-Möllenberg from the Deutsche Stiftung also had doubts about Wolff, but the Western Polish German leader Kohnert assuaged them, saying that Wolff merely had personal problems concerning his engagement to a Reich German woman. The engagement had been called off because the woman's parents did not want their child to go to, as Kohnert continued to call it, Congress Poland. Kohnert himself emphasized his good working relationship with Wolff.[115] He had previously cooperated with Wolff in processing applications for money from the Reich.[116] If Kohnert thought he could trust Wolff, however, he would soon be proved wrong. Utta's exit from the political stage and Wolff's rise to power only replaced one Central Polish headache with another – and it was not just to be a problem for the Deutsche Stiftung, but also for the new growing authority in ethnic German affairs – the Volksdeutsche Mittelstelle.

Berchem to German Foreign Ministry on November 3, 1937, then forwarded by German Foreign Ministry to Reich Interior Ministry, Volksdeutsche Mittelstelle, and Deutsche Stiftung on November 16, 1937), in BA Berlin, R8043, folder 943, 67–71, here 70 back side.

113 "August Utta an Ludwig Wolff," *Deutsche Rundschau*, May 18, 1938, in PAAA, Pol V, Politik 25 Polen, vol. 3, R104200, 199–205.

114 Schönbeck to Deutsche Stiftung, January 11, 1938, with attachment Schönbeck to Wolff, in BA Berlin, R8043, folder 943, 49–51.

115 Kohnert to Krahmer-Möllenberg, February 13, 1937, in BA Berlin, R8043, folder 943, 150–152.

116 Schönbeck to Deutsche Stiftung, January 11, 1938 with attachment Schönbeck to Wolff, in BA Berlin, R8043, folder 943, 49–51.

The Volksdeutsche Mittelstelle (VoMi), a Nazi Party bureau that was strongly linked to the SS, led the drive to coordinate German minority groups abroad. Its head, Werner Lorenz, and his lieutenant, Hermann Behrends, had tried to unify the various regional German groups in Poland as early as 1937.[117] The project was put on ice until the next year, when the VoMi had settled its disputes with the VDA by forcing Hans Steinacher to retire. The political amalgamation of Sudeten Germans under Konrad Henlein had always been tenuous, but the outward appearance of a unified German minority in Czechoslovakia created a demonstration effect and increased pressure to do the same in Poland.[118]

It is likely that the VoMi gave the impetus for German leaders to reconcile in early 1938. According to the monthly report of the Poznanian Voivodeship Office, the Old Germans in the Rat der Deutschen in Polen were to meet with JDP leaders in Poznań on March 4–5, 1938.[119] Yet the very attempt to find a location to meet almost wrecked the talks. The Rat der Deutschen representatives were afraid that JDP leaders, including Senator Wiesner, would claim a victory if the meeting took place at the JDP's office in Poznań, so the Rat der Deutschen insisted on the hotel where many of its own members were staying. Both sides refused to budge, and there arose a comical situation in which no real meeting between the two groups took place at all. Rather, the Rat der Deutschen and JDP delegates only met amongst themselves, and then they exchanged letters and discussed issues within a "committee for understanding." At the end of the conference, both sides claimed to have overcome their outstanding differences. The reality was, however, that negotiations had reached a dead end before they had even started. It is significant that the Polish report remarked that opinion within the loosely organized Rat der Deutschen in Polen was divided, and that the tensions there were apparent. The report described how the Western Polish DV leaders remained obstinate, while the leaders from other areas – probably he meant the Germans of Central Poland – were "liberal" in their approach to the JDP.[120] If there was hope for a possible

---

117 Valdis O. Lumans, *Himmler's Auxiliaries: The Volksdeutsche Mittelstelle and the German National Minorities of Europe, 1933–1945* (Chapel Hill: University of North Carolina Press, 1993), 96.

118 Office of the Voivode in Poznań, report on national minorities from May 1, 1938 to May 31, 1938, dated June 18, 1938, in AP Poznań, Urząd Wojewódzki Poznański, folder 5709, 2.

119 Office of the Voivode in Poznań, report on national minorities from March 1, 1938 to March 31, 1938, dated April 15, 1938, in AP Poznań, Urząd Wojewódzki Poznański, folder 5708, 66.

120 Office of the Voivode in Poznań, report on national minorities from March 1, 1938 to March 31, 1938, dated April 15, 1938, in AP Poznań, Urząd Wojewódzki Poznański, folder 5708, 71.

organizational unification of the Germans in Poland, the initiative would probably not come from Western Poland.

Events thereafter showed the rift once again between German activists in Western and Central Poland. In late April 1938, the VoMi voiced its concern over the Rat der Deutschen in Polen's lack of progress toward consolidating the minority in Poland. Old German leaders, it seems, bent under this pressure. Meeting in Warsaw on April 20–21 and in Poznań on April 25–26, the representatives in the Rat der Deutschen in Polen announced their intention to create a comprehensive organization for all Germans in Poland. The direction the Rat der Deutschen in Polen was taking, however, appeared to unsettle Ludwig Wolff from the DVV in Central Poland. When the JDP renegade leader Wilhelm Schneider contacted Wolff about possibly cooperating together, Wolff abruptly broke ranks with his Old German allies in the RDP. According to a Polish police report, Wolff and Schneider agreed to create a new youth movement that would eliminate senior German leaders and functionaries. Although their primary hope was to win over the bulk of the JDP, Wolff and Schneider expressed their desire to get various splinter organizations, such as the Deutscher Arbeitskreis and the Volksblock, a youth organization affiliated with the Volksbund in Upper Silesia, on board.[121] On May 1, 1938, they published a joint declaration in the *Freie Presse* calling for a merger of German organizations that would be based on equal partnership and that would not create any winners or losers.[122] Clearly, Wolff had felt that he would be a loser in the merger planned by the RDP.

Wolff's announcement of his cooperation with Schneider shocked the Old Germans in the Rat der Deutschen in Polen, which called a special meeting for May 5 in Warsaw to discuss Wolff's defection.[123] True, other Old Germans had considered working with Wilhelm Schneider before to weaken the JDP,[124] but Wolff's defection right after the Rat der Deutschen in Polen's momentous announcement about unifying the minority must have greatly annoyed the established leaders. That this disturbance came from the often ill-regarded but increasingly important Łódź periphery added

---

121 Report sent by Police Headquarters in Katowice to Silesian Voivodeship Administration (Social-Political Department) in Katowice, May 6, 1938, in AP Katowice, Dyrekcja Policji – Katowice, folder 312, 5.

122 Police Headquarters in Katowice to Silesian Voivodeship Administration (Social-Political Department) in Katowice, May 6, 1938, in AP Katowice, Dyrekcja Policji – Katowice, folder 312, 6–8.

123 Police Headquarters in Katowice to Silesian Voivodeship Administration (Social-Political Department) in Katowice, May 6, 1938, in AP Katowice, Dyrekcja Policji – Katowice, folder 312, 5.

124 Office of the Voivode in Poznań, report on national minorities from March 1, 1938 to March 31, 1938, dated April 15, 1938, in AP Poznań, Urząd Wojewódzki Poznański, folder 5708, 71–75.

another layer of anxiety for the German leaders in Western Poland. All the same, the Old Germans ignored or downplayed the seriousness of the incident. On the same day, Senator Erwin Hasbach went to see Polish Prime Minister Felicjan Sławoj Składkowski to discuss the formation of a united organization for the Germans in Poland, but he failed to get approval for the plan.[125] Polish newspapers were also critical of the political fusion of the Germans in Poland.[126] Still, speakers at meetings of the Deutsche Vereinigung portrayed this meeting as a positive, and the chances for an eventual approval were described as good. Articles in the *Deutsche Rundschau* carried titles such as "The Volk Wants Unity" and "On the Way to Unity for the German Volksgruppe in Poland."[127]

Why would Wolff risk a confrontation with the Rat der Deutschen in Polen? It appears that both Wolff and Schneider were eager to work together to strengthen their positions in any future reorganization of the minority. Wolff was particularly interested in proving his ability to unify the Germans in Poland, and the fact that Schneider's JDP separatists in Central Poland had joined his DVV appeared to underline his leadership skills. To demonstrate his desire for peace within the minority, Wolff also promised to stop attacking the mainstream JDP, which was already weakened.[128] It is significant that Wolff tried to present himself as an authentic supraregional leader, for the VoMi leadership in Berlin was also thinking along the same lines when it finally ordered the Germans to unify.[129]

On May 20, 1938, VoMi chief Werner Lorenz presented his first draft for the new organization of the Germans in Poland. In this draft, Lorenz emphasized that conditions in Poland made a unification of the minority both politically and legal-administratively feasible. He underlined that the reorganization would create "an effective unity of the Germandom that would lead to fulfilling the obligations belonging to a Volksgruppe."[130] The plan was to unify the German minority through two components, a cultural union and a political party. The leader of the cultural union was to be Heinrich Weiss (JDP), but with two powerful Old Germans as his deputy and managing director: Otto Ulitz (Volksbund in Upper Silesia) and

125 Bierschenk, *Die deutsche Volksgruppe in Polen*, 46.
126 Erwin Hasbach, "Unser guter Wille," *Deutsche Rundschau*, May 21, 1938, in PAAA, Pol V, Politik 25 Polen, vol. 3, R104200, 217.
127 "Das Volk will die Einheit" and "Dr. Kohnert: Auf dem Wege zur Einheit der Deutschen Volksgruppe in Polen. Rede auf der öffentlichen Kundgebung in Bromberg am 16. Mai 1938," *Deutsche Rundschau*, May 18, 1938, in PAAA, Pol V, Politik 25 Polen, vol. 3, R104200, 205.
128 Bierschenk, *Die deutsche Volksgruppe in Polen*, 43.
129 Lumans, *Himmler's Auxiliaries*, 97.
130 Werner Lorenz to German minority leaders in Poland, May 18, 1938, with attachment: "Vorschlag für die Neubildung der deutschen Volksgruppe in Polen (I. Projekt)," in PAAA, Inland II geheim, vol. 8 (227), microfiche 2347, 156–160, here 156.

Hans Kohnert (DV in Western Poland). Ludwig Wolff was to be the party leader, and Ernst Fenner, the JDP Gauleiter in Pomerelia, was to be deputy party leader.[131] Formally, the cultural union leader was to be the highest authority for minority affairs. The VoMi plan tried to reach a compromise within the leadership by balancing JDP functionaries with those from the Old German camp.[132]

By creating two key leadership positions, the union leader and the party leader, the dual-track approach could also balance regional ambitions. Ludwig Wolff was the only German from outside Western Poland to be represented in the planned leadership, but it is significant that the VoMi plan also recognized the importance of the eastern margins of the minority by naming him to lead the political wing. In the initial draft, Lorenz based his decision on the grounds that Wolff had turned the DVV into an "authoritative organization."[133] Given the turmoil resulting from Wolff's designation as party leader, it was likely that this position would be the most important in the reorganization of the minority. The appointment of Heinrich Weiss, a pharmacist from Jarocin in Western Poland, to the position of cultural union leader did not provoke any comparable resistance. Indeed, Weiss himself did not appear too keen on fulfilling this assignment, and he declined with the excuse that illness prevented him from devoting the necessary energy to master the organizational task.[134] Wolff alone would be the highest leader.

The proposal left the Old Germans in Western Poland out of the key positions of party leader and union leader, and generally the DV's Hans Kohnert must have felt let down. In a letter to the Foreign Ministry describing his consultation with the VoMi leader Lorenz in Berlin on May 12, 1938, Kohnert argued that the creation of separate cultural and political wings would allow personal animosities to flare up and cause incessant battling between the two groups.[135] The VoMi plan had deviated from Kohnert's proposals by not having one clear leader for the minority. The VoMi did realize the danger of this bifurcation, and the initial draft stated that the

---

131 Volksdeutsche Mittelstelle to German Foreign Ministry, Kult. A (Fritz von Twardowski), May 28, 1938, with attachment: "Vorschlag für die Neubildung der deutschen Volksgruppe in Polen (endgültige Fassung)," undated, in PAAA, Inland II geheim, vol. 8 (227), microfiche 2347, 191–194. A second copy can be found as "Vorschlag für die Neubildung der deutschen Volksgruppe in Polen (endgültiger Vorschlag)," undated, ibid., microfiche 2346, 140–142.

132 Edith Warmbier of the JDP was to serve as the head of the women's section in the cultural union.

133 "Vorschlag für die Neubildung der deutschen Volksgruppe in Polen (I. Projekt)," in PAAA, Inland II geheim, vol. 8 (227), microfiche 2347, 156–160, 158–159.

134 Consul General in Poznań (Walther) to German Foreign Ministry, "Neuordnung der deutschen Volksgruppe in Polen," May 31, 1938, in PAAA, Inland II geheim, vol. 9 (228), microfiche 2348, 1–2.

135 Hans Kohnert, May 12, 1938, copy of letter in PAAA, Inland II geheim, vol. 8 (227), microfiche 2346, 137–138.

leadership of the party and the cultural organizations would later be fused in a personal union.[136] Kohnert also insisted that the unification of the minority "can only spring from the free will and the personal initiative of the Volksgruppe." Although suggestions from the Reich would be welcome, Kohnert thought that orders coming from abroad were dangerous because they could not be kept secret from Polish authorities.[137] Kohnert probably wanted to keep decision making reserved for the DV, but he couched his concerns in the possibility of Polish repression. The VoMi must have likewise been frustrated, however, with the inability of the German leaders in Poland to unify on their own, and Lorenz was determined to pick the form of the proposed unification as well as its leaders.

The reaction of the German Foreign Ministry to the plan of its increasingly powerful rival was also cool. One official asked if it was the appropriate time for a unification project directed from Berlin and if it was wise to include a political party in the project. Both, he said, could lead to difficulties within the minority and between Germany and Poland. He thought that the consolidation of cultural, political, and economic organizations was especially dangerous because it would be putting all the minority's eggs into one basket, and he proposed to leave out at least the economic organizations.[138] Another official in the Foreign Ministry likewise worried about the political fallout if the Poles were to find out that Berlin was behind the unification plans.[139]

Regional alignments continued to pose a special problem within the Foreign Ministry. In August 1938, Martin Schliep of the Foreign Ministry prepared a document to Lorenz to warn about the hardline centralization approach that the VoMi was taking. The draft's attachment pointed out the regional differences of the Germans. Above all, it spelled out the difficulties that the Germans in the formerly Prussian areas faced and the "moral obligations" of the Reich to these areas. The memorandum noted how Reich policies had too often tended to sacrifice the interests of these Germans. In reference to VoMi plans to tie the minority more closely to the Reich, the document suggested that established contacts within the minority should not be sidelined – a possible jab at the upstart Ludwig Wolff. In the thoughts

---

136 "Vorschlag für die Neubildung der deutschen Volksgruppe in Polen (I. Projekt)," in PAAA, Inland II geheim, vol. 8 (227), microfiche 2347, 156–160, here 159.
137 Hans Kohnert, May 12, 1938, copy of letter in PAAA, Inland II geheim, vol. 8 (227), microfiche 2346, 137–138.
138 Memorandum (author unknown), May 20, 1938, in PAAA, Inland II geheim, vol. 8 (227), microfiche 2346, 135–136, here 135 (backside).
139 Schliep (Pol. Abt. V), May 24, 1938, in PAAA, Inland II geheim, vol. 8 (227), microfiche 2346, 139.

expounded in draft, it seems that the Foreign Ministry still clung to a position that favored the Reich's residual citizens. The Foreign Ministry was hence increasingly out of touch with new actors such as the VoMi, which tended to recognize the shift of power to the East within the minority. Significantly, the Foreign Ministry apparently never sent the document to the VoMi.[140]

For different reasons, the most stridently National Socialist organization in Poland, the Young German Party, also did not like the VoMi plan. At first glance, the plan appeared to concede to earlier JDP proposals of creating a double organizational track. Rather than making the JDP the elite political wing, however, the various VoMi proposals wavered between a major shakeup of the JDP and its dissolution altogether. The initial draft suggested that the new minority party would be a Poland-wide expansion of Wolff's Central Polish DVV, which already possessed the necessary statutes as a party.[141] Despite the word party in the JDP's name, the VoMi in Berlin noted that the JDP was not officially registered as such in Poland. The final version of the proposal now seemed to favor the JDP, which was already active throughout Poland and had a proven record of "German accomplishment." Yet Rudolf Wiesner was not only denied any leadership role in the proposed overhaul of minority organizations, but the VoMi contemplated taking the JDP away from him completely and transforming it into an enlarged DVV in everything but name – the new JDP would have to accept Ludwig Wolff as its head. Moreover, the VoMi stipulated that the JDP would have to change its statutes and become a party based on the Ministerial Decree from December 17, 1920, just like the DVV.[142] Not surprisingly, Wiesner was "visibly shocked" when he heard the proposal for the Bund der Deutschen in Polen.[143]

Whereas Wiesner would not have voluntarily given up the leading role in his own party, Young German functionaries in Western Poland likely did not want an Old German outsider from Central Poland to be their new leader, as their objections to Ludwig Wolff reveal. Heinrich Weiss, the proposed cultural union leader, complained that Wolff's association with

---

140 "Vortragender Legationsrat Schliep an Obergruppenführer Lorenz," dated August 1938 (unsent draft), in *ADAP*, ser. D, vol. 5, document no. 51, pp. 59–63.
141 "Vorschlag für die Neubildung der deutschen Volksgruppe in Polen (I. Projekt)," in PAAA, Inland II geheim, vol. 8 (227), microfiche 2347, 156–160, 158–159.
142 Volksdeutsche Mittelstelle to German Foreign Ministry, Kult. A (Fritz von Twardowski), May 28, 1938, with attachment: "Vorschlag für die Neubildung der deutschen Volksgruppe in Polen (endgültige Fassung)," undated, in PAAA, Inland II geheim, vol. 8 (227), microfiche 2347, 191–194.
143 Consul General in Katowice (Wilhelm Nöldeke) to German Foreign Ministry, "Neuordnung der deutschen Volksgruppe in Polen," June 3, 1938, in PAAA, Inland II geheim, vol. 9 (228), microfiche 2348, 26.

former JDP deputy leader Wilhelm Schneider made him untrustworthy and that Wolff was unknown among most Germans in Poznania-Pomerelia. He argued that it would be very difficult to convince the JDP members to accept him.[144] At another meeting, Weiss and Ernst Fenner, Wolff's deputy in the VoMi unity proposal, declared their solidarity with Wiesner.[145] A rejection of Wolff, and hence of the VoMi's plans, could not have been any clearer. In August 1938, Wiesner sent a "tendentious" report to the VoMi to denounce his enemies,[146] but it was apparent that Wiesner had fallen out of favor. Notably, he was not invited for a personal audience with Hitler during a visit he made in the summer to Berlin.[147]

However, this weakness of the JDP did not translate into a victory for the Old Germans. As the events immediately preceding the VoMi unification proposal have shown, Wolff also continued to play a double game with his purported allies. Events soon confirmed the distrust of the German leaders in Western Poland: Wolff, who was very likely stung by the vigorous resistance to his candidature by the JDP and others, probably wanted to emphasize his own indispensability by now working against the Old Germans. According to Polish police reports, Wolff continued to meet with Wilhelm Schneider throughout the summer of 1938. As the former JDP deputy leader, Schneider could still attract support among the many disgruntled Young Germans, allowing Wolff to play a strategic middle position in the ongoing struggle between the Old German RDP and the JDP. Around August 1938, an Old German delegation including Gero von Gersdorff, the DV youth leader, traveled to Łódź to shepherd Wolff back into the fold, but their hopes for a "conversion" were in vain. Wolff refused any meaningful cooperation with the RDP and informed Schneider right away of the delegation's visit.[148] The Old Germans still needed the Central

144 Consul General in Poznań (Walther) to German Foreign Ministry, "Neuordnung der deutschen Volksgruppe in Polen," May 31, 1938, in PAAA, Inland II geheim, vol. 9 (228), microfiche 2348, 1–2.

145 Telegram from Consul General in Katowice (Wilhelm Nöldeke) to German Foreign Ministry, June 4, 1938, in PAAA, Inland II geheim, vol. 9 (228), microfiche 2348, here 28; Consul General in Katowice (Wilhelm Nöldeke) to German Foreign Ministry, "Neuordnung der deutschen Volksgruppe in Polen," June 21, 1938, in ibid., 49.

146 Police Headquarters in Katowice to Silesian Voivodeship Administration (Social-Political Department) in Katowice, August 30, 1938, in AP Katowice, Dyrekcja Policji – Katowice, folder 310, 35; Municipal and County Police Command of the Silesian Voivodeship (Investigation Department) to State Police Headquarters (Investigation Department) in Warsaw, September 7, 1938, in AP Katowice, Policja Województwa Śląskiego, folder 197, 134.

147 Police Headquarters in Katowice to Silesian Voivodeship Administration (Social-Political Department) in Katowice, August 30, 1938, in AP Katowice, Dyrekcja Policji – Katowice, folder 312, 12.

148 Municipal and County Police Command of the Silesian Voivodeship (Investigation Department) to Police Headquarters in Katowice, July 27, 1938, in AP Katowice, Dyrekcja Policji – Katowice, folder 312, 10–11; Police Headquarters in Katowice to Silesian Voivodeship Administration (Social-Political Department) in Katowice, August 30, 1938, in ibid., 12.

Polish DVV to present a united front, so they downplayed this rift, but the tensions could not be concealed. At a meeting of the Rat der Deutschen in Polen in Warsaw on August 19, Wolff sent a substitute (whose identity was unknown to Polish authorities) in his stead. The meeting was all the more important because the new leadership for the Rat der Deutschen in Polen was to be chosen. Through his substitute, Wolff forced the participants to appoint August Utta, who was also present at the meeting, to become deputy leader of the RDP – a position Utta had already more or less held.[149] This maneuvering allowed Wolff to feign continued cooperation with the RDP while relegating his former rival Utta to a symbolic post.[150]

The Polish Interior Ministry's Nationalities Department noted in the summer of 1938 that the DVV's vigorous activity was strengthening its claim to be the strongest and territorially largest German organization in Poland.[151] In September 1938, Wolff undertook a renewed effort to recon- cile his DVV with the JDP in order to take advantage of Wiesner's crumbling stature. A Polish report claimed that the purpose of this effort was to par- alyze the Old Germans in the Rat der Deutschen, who were still working on creating the VoMi-inspired Bund der Deutschen in Polen. The Polish source doubted that Wolff's plan would be successful because Wiesner had already found out about it and introduced countermeasures.[152] Only in November 1938 could the Volksdeutsche Mittelstelle force Wolff to stop his open conspiring against his Old German cohorts. Yet Wolff continued his furtive contacts with the JDP renegade Schneider.[153]

The triangular tug-of-war between the established German leaders in Western Poland, the JDP, and the Wolff/Schneider factions made it impos- sible for any party to be the clear winner. Neither the JDP nor the Old Germans could speak with one voice, but Reich authorities were also unable to act decisively. The VoMi's drive to unify the German minority, which had encountered opposition from different quarters at the start, was quickly

149 Police Headquarters in Katowice to Silesian Voivodeship Administration (Social-Political Depart- ment) in Katowice, August 30, 1938, in AP Katowice, Dyrekcja Policji – Katowice, folder 310, 35; Municipal and County Police Command of the Silesian Voivodeship (Investigation Department) to State Police Headquarters (Investigation Department) in Warsaw, September 7, 1938, in AP Katowice, Policja Województwa Śląskiego, folder 197, 134.
150 The new officers of the RDP were: Erwin Hasbach from Hermanowo (chair), August Utta from Łódź (deputy chair), Hans Kohnert from Bydgoszcz (member of the board), and Otto Ulitz from Katowice (member of the board).
151 Polish Interior Ministry (Nationalities Department), Weekly Report, August 11, 1938, in AAN, MSZ, folder 2352, 129–130.
152 Police Headquarters in Katowice to Silesian Voivodeship Administration (Social-Political Depart- ment) in Katowice, August 30, 1938, in AP Katowice, Dyrekcja Policji – Katowice, folder 312, 12.
153 Police Headquarters in Katowice to Silesian Voivodeship Administration (Social-Political Depart- ment), November 10, 1938, in AP Katowice, Dyrekcja Policji – Katowice, folder 312, 15.

losing momentum. As early as the summer of 1938, the VoMi proposed creating a Committee of Six in order to allow the negotiations for the Bund der Deutschen in Polen to continue.[154] Like the VoMi's previous proposal for the BDP leadership, it was composed of three Young Germans and three RDP representatives, and Heinrich Weiss from the Western Polish group of the JDP served as its head. The VoMi recognized it as the highest organization for the Germans in Poland.[155] Intended as a stopgap measure to further the VoMi's unification plans, it represented in fact a ceasefire between the JDP and Old Germans.

Even the early Sejm elections in November 1938 did not change the situation. The JDP cooperated with the Old Germans in these elections, in part because they knew they would not win any seats on their own. Rather, they encouraged the minority to vote for the ruling party, the Camp of National Unity (Obóz Zjednoczenia Narodowego), which won a large majority because of the electoral boycott by the opposition. German candidates did not gain any seats in the Sejm, but as in 1935, two Germans were appointed to the Senate. President Ignacy Mościcki reappointed Erwin Hasbach as senator, but he rejected Rudolf Wiesner for another JDP member, Max Wambeck. Many saw this move as a major setback for the JDP, and Polish and German observers alike thought that Wiesner's weakened position would foster the minority's consolidation.[156] Yet Wiesner was not about to give up his last remaining bastion of power, the JDP leadership, and a merger between the Old and Young Germans became ever more unlikely. According to a report by Krahmer-Möllenberg in December 1938, Max Wambeck's appointment as senator only seemed to split the political scene further, for it reinvigorated the scheming of the ever-lurking Wilhelm Schneider, who was friendly toward Wambeck. With an eye on how these developments affected Central Poland, the Deutsche Stiftung's Krahmer-Möllenberg noted that Schneider's activity in turn only fueled his ally Ludwig Wolff's obstinacy. Krahmer-Möllenberg complained that Ludwig Wolff's position had become "in many aspects unclear."[157]

154 The members included three JDP members: Weiss (Jarocin), Fenner (Bydgoszcz), Gorgon (Lwów); and three Old Germans: Ulitz (Katowice), Kohnert (Bydgoszcz), and Wolff (Łódź). Hasbach and Wiesner, both Polish senators and the leaders of the RDP and JPD, respectively, were excluded. Police Headquarters in Katowice to Silesian Voivodeship Administration (Social-Political Department), September 25, 1938, in AP Katowice, Dyrekcja Policji – Katowice, folder 310, 36.

155 Dr. Luig, "Verhältnis zu den deutschen Volksgruppen," July 7, 1939, in BA Koblenz, R57, folder 1050 (4 pages, p. 2).

156 Polish Interior Ministry (Nationalities Department), Weekly Report no. 50, December 16, 1938, in AAN, MSZ, folder 2352, 462–463.

157 Krahmer-Möllenberg circular, December 9, 1938, in PAAA, Pol V, Politik 25 Polen, vol. 4, R104201, 199.

German authorities had hoped that the minority's support for the Polish government party during the election campaigns would finally lead to official approval for the Bund der Deutschen in Polen.[158] Yet this scenario only became more unlikely after the Munich Agreement and the annexation of the Sudetenland. It was no secret to the Poles that the VoMi in Berlin had been behind the plan to build the Bund der Deutschen in Polen.[159] According to Krahmer-Möllenberg, a newly reappointed Senator Hasbach discussed the plans for the BDP at the Polish Interior Ministry on November 30, 1938. At the meeting, the ministerial director dissimulated by saying that the plan was currently inopportune for the Polish government, but he said that Hasbach should introduce it to Warsaw's Commissarial City President. The report attributed the lukewarm reception to heightened political tensions between Germany and Poland, especially in regard to the territorial autonomy of Carpathian Ruthenia. Krahmer-Möllenberg, who had always been wary of the VoMi plan, stated that Polish resistance to the Bund der Deutschen in Polen could have been foreseen from the very beginning. Still, he believed that the reasons for the recent lack of progress toward unification lay elsewhere. A Polish approval could have given the Germans the needed impulse to unify, he wistfully remarked.[160] The internecine conflict within the minority had reached such an absurd state that Krahmer-Möllenberg had to condemn the Poles' impending rejection of the BDP, not as a suppression of the German minority's innate drive for unity, but as a missed opportunity to encourage the fractious Germans to come together!

The various machinations over the Bund der Deutschen in Polen resulted in confusion all around: within the minority, among their caretakers in the Reich, and among Polish authorities. A Polish report from January 1939 stated that Kohnert was to be the leader of a new unified party; discussions also circulated that the Polish government feared that he would "play a role similar to Henlein,"[161] a reference to the recent events that had begun the dismemberment of Czechoslovakia. Although the historian Marian Wojciechowski asserts that the report's reference to Kohnert was based on

---

158 Krahmer-Möllenberg circular, December 8, 1938, in PAAA, Pol V, Politik 25 Polen, vol. 4, R104201, 197.

159 Police Headquarters in Katowice to Silesian Voivodeship Administration (Social-Political Department), September 25, 1938, in AP Katowice, Dyrekcja Policji – Katowice, folder 310, 36.

160 Krahmer-Möllenberg to German Foreign Ministry, Reich Interior Minister, and Volksdeutsche Mittelstelle, with attached report (unsigned, undated copy), December 8, 1938, in PAAA, Pol V, Politik 25 Polen, vol. 4, R104201, 197–198.

161 Main Office of the Police of the Silesian Voivodeship (Investigation Department) in Katowice, report "Partie niemieckie – połączenie," January 25, 1939, in AP Katowice, Policja Województwa Śląskiego, folder 197, 204.

rumor – suggesting that Wolff was still the proposed leader for the planned party[162] – it cannot be so easily brushed aside as a mistake.[163] There was more than enough reason for the VoMi to distance itself from Wolff and to rework its plans for the Bund der Deutschen in Polen or to drop it altogether.

In any case, Polish approval for the Bund der Deutschen in Polen was not forthcoming. In late December 1938, the German Desk at the Nationalities Department of the Interior Ministry in Warsaw proposed to deny approval to the Bund der Deutschen in Polen.[164] Yet the issue remained on the table for the Polish government in early 1939.[165] German leaders continued to be in the dark, or at least feigned not knowing. Erwin Hasbach gave a speech in the Senate on March 9, 1939, about the necessity of creating a Bund der Deutschen in Polen. Although negotiations within the Committee of Six would still go on until the spring of 1939, it appears that the VoMi had long ceased to be enthusiastic about its own proposal. It is probable that rapidly deteriorating relations with Poland may have led to new possibilities of solving the minority question once and for all.

Historians have portrayed the efforts to build the Bund der Deutschen in Polen as further proof that the German minority was on the way to unity. Theodor Bierschenk, for example, argued that infighting had decreased starting in 1938, and he used the BDP as an example of greater cooperation between the Old Germans and the JDP.[166] The failure of the VoMi's planned unification of the German minority is largely attributed to the Polish government's opposition as well as to objections of the German Foreign

162 Marian Wojciechowski, "Die deutsche Minderheit in Polen (1920–1939)," in *Deutsche und Polen zwischen den Kriegen. Minderheitenstatus und "Volkstumskampf" im Grenzgebiet. Amtliche Berichterstattung aus beiden Ländern, 1920–1939,* ed. Rudolf Jaworski et al., 1–26 (Munich: Sauer, 1997), here 19n37.

163 The following replies to the January 25 report reiterated the name Dr. Hans Kohnert of the Deutsche Vereinigung, although these replies also show that there had been no contact between Kohnert and the Upper Silesian German nationalists: District Office of the Silesian Voivodeship Police in Rybnik to the Main Office of the Silesian Voivodeship Police (Investigation Department) in Katowice, "Partie niemieckie – połączenie," February 20, 1939, in AP Katowice, Policja Województwa Śląskiego, folder 197, 214; District Office of the Silesian Voivodeship Police in Frysztat to the Main Office of the Silesian Voivodeship Police (Investigation Department) in Katowice, report "Partie niemieckie – połączenie," June 13, 1939, ibid., 222.

164 Nationalities Department at the Polish Interior Ministry (referat niemiecki), memorandum "Restrykcje wobec Jungdeutsche Partei i org. 'starych' za wykluczenie sen. Wambecka," December 29, 1938, in AAN, MSW, folder 1005, 110–111.

165 A Polish report from March 1939 noted that the application was waiting for approval: Voivodeship Office of the State Police (Investigation Department) in Łódź to State Police (Investigation Department) in Katowice, "Partie niemieckie – połączenie," March 24, 1939, in AP Katowice, Policja Województwa Śląskiego, folder 197, 218–219.

166 Bierschenk, *Die deutsche Volksgruppe in Polen,* 45–46.

Ministry and the JDP's Rudolf Wiesner.[167] Yet the plan for the Bund der Deutschen in Polen was inherently flawed. At best, the plan did not take into account the international context and assumed that Poland would still accept the creation of the Bund der Deutschen in Polen after the Sudeten German crisis. At worst, the plan fully underestimated the regional cleavages within the minority and itself further politicized and deepened these divisions. The VoMi may have correctly discerned the growing influence of the East by choosing Wolff to be the minority's single political leader, but it also worked along ideological lines that supposed that a natural unity would come about once a leader had been chosen. The VoMi failed to see how regional interests crosscut simplistic generational and class divisions among German activists in Poland. By applying pressure on these German fault lines, the VoMi fractured the political picture even further. Various third actors, such as Ludwig Wolff and Wilhelm Schneider, believed that they could parlay the rush to unity into political advantage for themselves.

Although the Bund der Deutschen in Polen never came about and Wolff never became the political leader for all the Germans in Poland, these events show just how influential Central Poland had become within the minority. The events in 1938–1939 reveal that the Deutscher Volksverband in Central Poland was not just the little sister of the Deutsche Vereinigung in Western Poland. As the leader of the DVV, Ludwig Wolff had his own agenda and did not belong to any political camp but his own. He remained confident of his own role and that of the Germans in Central Poland. To this end, Wolff played minority leaders against one another and against the various Reich officials.

Other developments further supported Wolff's claims to power. In the communal elections in Łódź on December 18, 1938, the DVV and the JDP entered the elections with a German Unity List. It received 23,150 votes, which resulted in five seats in the city council.[168] The extent of unity in this unity list was very clear: the DVV took all five seats that the list won. Although the election result did not produce the greatest number of total votes cast for German parties – the elections in 1927 had a slightly better turnout for the German nationalist and socialist parties combined – it was the most German votes ever cast for one list (and in effect, for one party) in Łódź.[169] The results were even more impressive in the countryside, where

---

167 Wojciechowski, "Die deutsche Minderheit in Polen (1920–1939)," 18.
168 Ludwig Wolff, "Der Volkstumskampf des Deutschtums im Osten des Warthelandes," in *Der Osten des Warthelandes. Herausgegeben anläßlich der Heimatschau in Litzmannstadt*, ed. Hubert Müller, 176–195 (Stuttgart: Stähle & Friedel, 1941), here 192.
169 Bierschenk, *Die deutsche Volksgruppe in Polen*, 43.

the DVV won 404 of 606 seats up for election in forty-nine rural localities in Łódź county. There were eighty-six seats more (a 27 percent increase) than what had been won in 1936.[170] The elections were a clear triumph for the DVV and a boost to Wolff's already swelling ego. In February 1939, Wolff boldly asserted that the greater Łódź area with its 180,000 Germans had become the "metropolis" not only for the German minority in Poland but for all German minorities in the world. He expected that all German minority organizations in Poland would soon be based in the city.[171] Wolff had become the voice of a newly empowered periphery, but he also symbolized the growing contradiction within the minority over race and space. On the one hand, Wolff's growing stature reflected the influence of deterritorialized, völkisch notions of national belonging. On the other hand, his DVV and the JDP revealed the resurgence of regional alignments.

DIVISION AND RADICALIZATION

The paralysis in leadership complicated the situation of the Germans in Poland and only added to the hopelessness of the situation in late 1938 and 1939. Reports indicated that Germans in Poland often believed Hitler's assertions that Germany no longer had any territorial demands after the Munich Agreement and the annexation of the Sudetenland.[172] Disappointed, many Western Polish Germans began to leave Poland, leading to yet another exodus. It is notable that despite their claims of having become Germans abroad at last, these formerly Prussian Germans had never fully given up their hope of returning to Germany or their belief that Germany should help them. Krahmer-Möllenberg stated that the mood within the minority was similar to the pessimism in 1919–1920, before the official handover of Poznania and Pomerelia, and the idea of holding out in Poland found less and less support.[173] The Germans left in such numbers that in

---

170 Bierschenk, *Die deutsche Volksgruppe in Polen*, 303.
171 Daily reports of the Nationalities Department of the Polish Interior Ministry, undated but part of report from February 11, 1939, in AAN, MSW, folder 971, 51–52.
172 Consulate General in Toruń (Küchler) to German Foreign Ministry, October 4, 1938, in PAAA, Pol V, Politik 25 Polen, vol. 4, R104201, 5; Krahmer Möllenberg report to SS-Oberführer Dr. Behrends, Legationsrat Bergmann, October 5, 1928, with report by Kohnert, October 2, 1938, in PAAA, Pol V, Politik 25 Polen, vol. 4, R104201, 8–13; Consulate General in Toruń to German Foreign Ministry (Küchler), October 5, 1938, in PAAA, Pol V, Politik 25 Polen, vol. 4, R104201, 24–28; Consulate General in Poznań (Walther) to German Foreign Ministry, October 11, 1938, in PAAA, Pol V, Politik 25 Polen, vol. 4, R104201, 34–38. See also Blanke, *Orphans of Versailles*, 203.
173 Krahmer-Möllenberg to Foreign Ministry (Kult A, copy for Pol V), Reich Interior Minister, and Volksdeutsche Mittelstelle, November 4, 1938, in PAAA, Pol V, Politik 25 Polen, vol. 4, R104201, 93–94.

December 1938 the editors of *Deutsche Rundschau* reprinted an article from a German newspaper in the Bukovina that denounced the flight of Germans there as "ethnic desertion." Although the editors made no explicit connection to the situation of the Germans in Poland, the parallels were unmistakable.[174]

Nazi politics and foreign expansion also left the Germans vulnerable to Polish hostility. The rising tensions were in part due to the increasingly nationalist atmosphere in Poland, which the authoritarian government in Warsaw stoked. Nazi propaganda concerning the unity of the German people only convinced Polish nationalists that the Germans in Poland were in league with Reich policy. As discussed previously, many Poles feared that the Reich would use the Germans in Poland as a fifth column as it had with the Sudeten Germans.[175] In Toruń, Polish nationalist clubs such as Sokół staged a boycott of German stores in December 1938 – one month after the anti-Jewish violence in Germany commonly called Kristallnacht (Crystal Night, or Night of the Broken Glass).[176] In February 1939, German stores in Toruń were attacked over four days. The police did little to prevent the vandals from hurling stones through windows. The local German consulate also reported having seen a sign stating: "Germans, Jews, and Dogs: No Entrance."[177] During this time, heightened national tensions easily led to mixtures of anti-Semitic and anti-German sentiments. The German consular official in Cieszyn (Teschen) reported that in early 1939 the local district office had placed a poster with the command: "Chase the Jews and Germans from the country." After several German–owned businesses were attacked, the official submitted photos including one with a Star of David painted over a storefront.[178]

Minority leaders found that they had steadily less room to maneuver in 1939 as the Polish government cracked down on minority organizations and as the VoMi sought to keep the minority from acting on its own lest they create an international incident that would force Hitler's hand.[179] After the dismemberment of rump Czechoslovakia in March 1939, Hitler steered Germany toward war against Poland, a development that became

174 "Völkische Fahnenflucht?" *Deutsche Rundschau*, December 24, 1938, copy sent as attachment by Consulate General in Toruń (Küchler) to German Foreign Ministry, January 2, 1939, in PAAA, Pol V, Politik 25 Polen, vol. 5, R104202, 5–7.

175 Albert S. Kotowski, *Hitlers Bewegung im Urteil der polnischen Nationaldemokratie* (Harrassowitz: Wiesbaden, 2000), 172.

176 Hugo Rasmus, *Pommerellen-Westpreußen 1919–1939* (Munich: Herbig, 1989), 310.

177 Blanke, *Orphans of Versailles*, 219, 302n75.

178 Consulate in Cieszyn (Damerau) to German Foreign Ministry, "Ausschreitungen und Provokationen im Olsagebiet," May 8, 1939, in PAAA, PIII 9i.

179 Lumans, *Himmler's Auxiliaries*, 97–99.

explicit in April after he terminated the non-aggression pact. Germany became louder in its calls for the return of Danzig and the Corridor, and the threat of war was met with a wave of anti-German sentiment in Poland. The tensions erupted periodically in renewed attacks against Germans in Poland. The most severe violence occurred in Tomaszów Mazowiecki (near Łódź) in May 1939, when gangs attacked several dozen Germans and their property.[180] There were no deaths, but according to the report of the German consul in Łódź, at least ten Germans were severely injured in what the consul called a "German pogrom."[181] Now Germans began to leave Central Poland for the Reich in droves, which caused anxiety among DVV leaders.[182] They feared that there might no longer be a minority left to lead. There was a brief respite after the spring of 1939 when attacks subsided. The German consul in Łódź probably overestimated the Polish government's control over such matters when he attributed the lack of further disturbances to the propaganda goals of the Polish government. Yet the situation was still deemed critical. The consul complained that hundreds of German businesses were closing, without remarking that Germany itself was fostering the increasingly acrimonious atmosphere of 1939.[183] New acts of violence began to appear in the hypercharged atmosphere of late August.[184] By then, intensified pressure from the Polish government had all but disbanded the German minority's political parties.

Extensive documentation of the plight of the Germans from throughout Poland was frequent in the period right before the war. The various German consulates in Poland spared no effort in cataloging every act that could be construed as an attempt to exterminate Germandom in Poland, which were later compiled as Germany's so-called White Book to justify the war against Poland.[185] Various subheadings in this chapter included

---

180 Kosmala, *Juden und Deutsche im polnischen Haus*, 362–368.
181 Reprinted as document nos. 370 and 371 in Auswärtiges Amt (Deutsches Reich), *Dokumente zur Vorgeschichte des Krieges* (Berlin: Carl Heymanns, 1939), 247, 248.
182 Kosmala, *Juden und Deutsche im polnischen Haus*, 368.
183 Consulate in Łódź (Berchem) to German Foreign Ministry, reprinted as document no. 381 in Auswärtiges Amt, *Dokumente zur Vorgeschichte des Krieges*, 251–252.
184 Otto Heike, *Die deutsche Arbeiterbewegung in Polen, 1835–1945* (Dortmund: Ostdeutsche Forschungsstelle im Lande Nordrhein-Westfalen, 1969), 116; Breyer, *Das Deutsche Reich und Polen*, 221. The fact that only windows were broken and a sign destroyed in a city near Łódź during such a tense period may also point to more restraint than some German authors have been willing to admit.
185 Auswärtiges Amt, *Dokumente zur Vorgeschichte des Krieges*. This "Second White Book" provides a longer-range view than the first "White Book," which focused more exclusively on the problem of Danzig in August 1939. See Auswärtiges Amt, *Urkunden zur letzten Phase der deutsch-polnischen Krise* (Berlin: Reichsdruckerei, 1939). For another retroactive justification for the attack on Poland, see Karl C. von Loesch, "Polnische Ausrottungspolitik," in *Der befreite Osten*, ed. Max Hildebert Boehm and Karl C. von Loesch (Berlin: Hofmeyer, 1943), 50–86.

"Poland's War against Germandom in Poland and against Danzig, 1919–1933," "No Improvement in the Situation of the German Volksgruppe with the German-Polish Politics of Reconciliation (November 1933 to August 1934)," and "Increasing Intensity of Polish Action against the German Volksgruppe (October 1938 to March 1939)."[186] Concern for the welfare of the ethnic Germans, whose interests had often been ignored or sacrificed by the Nazi regime before 1939, now took the forefront in justifications for the war against Poland.[187]

The VoMi, to the bitter end, found it difficult to make the various German "auxiliaries" in Poland submit to its will.[188] This passive role did not sit well with some activists in Poland, and especially for Rudolf Wiesner. Briefly arrested in Poland, the JDP leader fled to Danzig. There, he continued his attempts to portray his indispensability to the Third Reich. Encouraged by the Gauleiter of Danzig, Albert Forster, Wiesner offered to play the role of a Polish Henlein, which meant in this case that he would try to mediate a possible compromise to avert war.[189] Wiesner, in conjunction with the special representative of the Foreign Ministry in Danzig, wrote a declaration of the injustices that had been done to the German minority. The VoMi's Lorenz was taken aback by this activism from below and demanded that the declaration not be published. Lorenz also let it be known that Hitler was not interested in using the German minority to solve the Polish problem and demanded that Wiesner proceed to Berlin where he could not cause any trouble. Gauleiter Forster protected Wiesner in this case, however, and he remained in Danzig.[190] These events reveal that German activists who claimed to be National Socialist were not necessarily obedient to state and party organizations in Germany. Minority client activism was driving events and forcing the intervention of their patrons in the Reich. The nominal allegiance to National Socialism, however, had also divided the Germans in Poland and made minority activists especially vulnerable to the twists and turns of Germany's foreign policy. During Wiesner's antics

---

186 Auswärtiges Amt, *Dokumente zur Vorgeschichte des Krieges,* document nos. 370, 371, 381, 414, and 415.

187 Auswärtiges Amt, *Dokumente zur Vorgeschichte des Krieges,* especially documents nos. 48–53, pp. 41–56. See also Loesch, "Polnische Ausrottungspolitik," 50–86.

188 Lumans, *Himmler's Auxiliaries,* 99.

189 Lumans, *Himmler's Auxiliaries,* 99.

190 "Der Sonderbeauftragte des Reichsaußenministers in Danzig (Veesenmayer) an das Auswärtige Amt," August 22, 1939, in *ADAP,* ser. D, vol. 7, document no. 172, pp. 151–152; "Vortragender Legationsrat Schliep (Pol. Abt.) an den Sonderbeauftragen des Reichsaußenministers in Danzig," August 22, 1939, ibid., document no. 182, p. 159; "Vermerk des Vortragenden Legationsrats Schliep (Pol. Abt.)," August 23, 1939, ibid., document no. 195, p. 173; "Der Sonderbeauftrage des Reichsaußenministers in Danzig an das Auswärtige Amt," August 23, 1939, ibid., document no. 196, pp. 173–174; cf. Lumans, *Himmler's Auxiliaries,* 99.

in Danzig, the German foreign minister, Joachim von Ribbentrop, was meeting with the Soviet leadership in Moscow. Although they sought to use National Socialism for their own ends, the German political leaders in Poland had themselves become instrumentalized in Hitler's path to war. The politics of irredentism had entered a new phase.

6

Lodzers into Germans? (1939–2000)

On September 1, 1939, Nazi Germany invaded Poland. The night before the attack, Polish military and civilian authorities arrested key German minority leaders. In the following days and weeks, Germans were rounded up and evacuated, and many were killed. One of them was Eugen Naumann, the former DV leader and longtime Sejm deputy in the 1920s. Although Nazi propaganda claimed that about 60,000 minority members had died in the first days of the war, the number was closer to 5,000.[1] The most well-known incident was the so-called Bromberger Blutsonntag (Bromberg Bloody Sunday) incident on September 3, 1939. Several hundred German civilians were killed in Bydgoszcz by retreating Polish troops, who believed that local Germans had fired on them.[2] Real and imagined Polish atrocities served as a pretext for German troops to massacre Polish prisoners of war and civilians, including many Jews.[3] Yet the so-called ethnic Germans also took a brutal toll on their neighbors as well. This chapter looks at how the regionalization processes discussed in previous chapters were transferred to the landscape of occupied Poland. It explores how the constructions of new hierarchies of Germanness had deadly implications for Poles and Jews. Finally, it follows the postwar attempts to unify the Germans in Poland once and for all.

---

1 Richard Blanke, *Orphans of Versailles: The Germans in Western Poland, 1918–1939* (Lexington: University Press of Kentucky, 1993); Doris L. Bergen, *War and Genocide: A Concise History of the Holocaust*, 2nd ed. (Lanham: Rowman & Littlefield, 2009), 107.
2 Hugo Rasmus, *Pommerellen-Westpreußen 1919–1939* (Munich: Herbig, 1989); Włodzimierz Jastrzębski, *Der Bromberger Blutsonntag – Legende und Wirklichkeit* (Poznań: Instytut Zachodni, 1990).
3 Alexander B. Rossino, *Hitler Strikes Poland: Blitzkrieg, Ideology and Atrocity* (Lawrence: University of Kansas Press, 2003), 191–235; Jochen Böhler, *Auftakt zum Vernichtungskrieg. Die Wehrmacht in Polen 1939* (Frankfurt/Main: Fischer Taschenbuch, 2006).

Figure 6.1. "Liberation" of ethnic Germans in Łódź in September 1939. *Source*: Bundesarchiv Bild 183-E10713.

FROM ŁÓDŹ TO LITZMANNSTADT

Many Germans enthusiastically greeted Reich troops when they entered the city (Figure 6.1). The conquest of Poland seemed to confirm Nazi plans for creating *Lebensraum* (living space) in the East. Yet the fate of the city with the largest number of Germans in Poland was initially unclear in September 1939. In the first few months of the war, various circles discussed how far east the Reich's border would extend. After the conquest of Poland, the historian Theodor Schieder worked with other scholars on redrawing the Reich's eastern border. His work at this time has often been considered the basis for the later Generalplan Ost of the SS.[4] Yet Schieder initially assumed that the new German border with Poland would run

---

4 Jörg Hackmann, "Deutsche Ostforschung und Geschichtswissenschaft," in *Deutsche Ostforschung und Polnische Westforschung im Spannungsfeld von Wissenschaft und Politik. Disziplinen im Vergleich*, ed. Jan M. Piskorski, Jörg Hackmann, and Rudolf Jaworski, 25–45 (Osnabrück: Fibre, 2002), 42; Ingo Haar, "German Ostforschung and Anti-Semitism," in *German Scholars and Ethnic Cleansing, 1919–1945*, ed. Ingo Haar and Michael Fahlbusch, 1–27 (New York: Berghahn Books, 2005), 14–15; Bergen, *War and Genocide*, 168. After the war, Theodor Schieder became an influential historian and served as president of the Association of Historians in Germany from 1967 to 1972. See Robert G. Moeller, *War Stories: The Search for a Usable Past in the Federal Republic of Germany* (Berkeley/Los Angeles: University of California Press, 2001), 56–57.

largely along the old 1914 border. He even contemplated using Germans from Łódź to resettle and re-Germanize the recovered territories in Poznania and Pomerelia.[5] Indeed, the annexation remained contested despite later attempts to justify these plans with the large German population in Poland.[6]

Michael Alberti notes that the division of Poland did not follow any racial logic or prewar planning.[7] Indeed, many Nazi officials doubted the utility of annexing Łódź directly to the Reich. On November 8, the day before the city's incorporation in the Reich, Propaganda Minister Joseph Goebbels wrote his concerns in his diary: "I am also not much enamoured of the proposal to turn Lodz into a German city. The place is no more than a rubbish-heap, inhabited by the dregs of the Poles and Jews."[8] Nine days later, Goebbels continued to believe that the completed annexation was a mistake: "The situation in Łódź is still topsy-turvy. The Jewish plague is gradually becoming intolerable. The various authorities seem to be exercising power against each other, rather than in co-operation. Why should this rubbish-heap, of all places, be intended to become a German city! Trying to Germanise Lodz is a real labor of Sisyphus. And we could have put the city to such good use as a dumping-ground."[9] The question of "Reich or Generalgouvernement" would plague Łódź administrators for several months more.[10] Despite the initial hesitation, however, Łódź remained in Reichsgau Wartheland. Figure 6.2 shows the administrative division of Poland during the Second World War.

As itself *the* model of a German city in the East, Łódź was now supposed to confirm the triumph of the Greater German idea and to forget its hybrid past. Claiming 750,000 inhabitants in 1941, it was the largest city

---

5 Götz Aly, "Rückwärtsgewandte Propheten – Bemerkungen in eigener Sache," in *Macht – Geist – Wahn. Kontinuitäten deutschen Denkens*, 153–183 (Berlin: Argon, 1997), 180; Angelika Ebbinghaus and Karl Heinz Roth, "Vorläufer des 'Generalplans Ost.' Eine Dokumentation über Theodor Schieders Polendenkschrift vom 7. Oktober 1939," *1999: Zeitschrift für Sozialgeschichte des 20. und 21. Jahrhunderts* 7, no. 1 (1992): 62–94, here 81, 83, 87–89.

6 On the ethnic argument for annexation made by Łódź's mayor, who also claimed that earlier German immigration had contributed to the city's American-like rapid development, see untitled text of interview (presumably end of 1940–beginning of 1941), USHMM, RG-05.008M, reel 1, folder 31, 117–126, here 124. Also in USHMM, RG-05.008M, reel 2, folder 72, 90ff.

7 Michael Alberti, *Die Verfolgung und Vernichtung der Juden im Reichsgau Wartheland 1939–1945* (Wiesbaden: Harrassowitz, 2006), 51.

8 Elke Fröhlich, ed., *Die Tagebücher von Joseph Goebbels*, vol. 1, no. 7 (Munich: Saur, 1998), 186. Translation from Fred Taylor, ed. and trans., *The Goebbels Diaries, 1939–1941* (London: Hamish Hamilton, 1982), 42–43. Goebbels spelled the name of the city as Lodz (without diacritical markings), not Lodsch, as was common for Germans at this time. Taylor kept this spelling in the translation.

9 Fröhlich, *Tagebücher von Joseph Goebbels*, 199. Translation from Taylor, *Goebbels Diaries*, 50–51.

10 Karl Marder, "Litzmannstadt," undated manuscript (presumably end of 1940), in USHMM, RG-05.008M, reel 1, folder 31, 113–115. Marder was mayor and city treasurer.

Occupied Poland in the Second World War

Source: Martin Broszat, *Nationalsozialistische Polenpolitik, 1939–1945*
(Stuttgart: Deutsche Verlags-Anstalt, 1961), unpaginated, c. page 200

Rights holder: Oldenbourg-Verlag

0	50	100	150 km
0	25	50	75	100 miles

Country and regional names have been translated into English, city and town names have
been generally left as spelled in the source map. Names listed for counties do not reflect
the official designations for *Kreise*.

Figure 6.2. Division of Poland in the Second World War. Note Łódź's proximity to the
border with the Generalgouvernement. Map reprinted with permission of Oldenbourg
Wissenschaftsverlag, Munich.

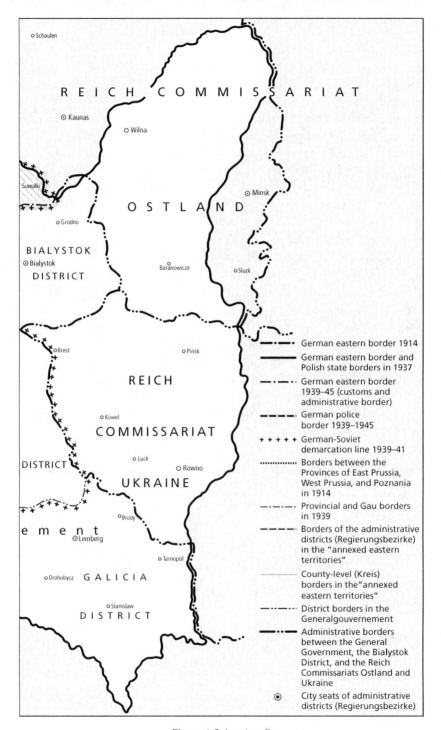

Figure 6.2 (*continued*)

in Reichsgau Wartheland and the sixth largest city in the Reich.[11] In April 1940, Łódź was renamed in honor of the German general who had successfully fought the Russians near the city during the First World War. The name Litzmannstadt emphasized the importance of that event in the German revival in Central Poland. The supposed discovery of the Germans in Central Poland by the Reich served as proof of pan-German thought and the realization of Volksgemeinschaft.[12] As the seat of important institutions belonging to the Volksdeutsche Mittelstelle, Łódź became a major center of Nazi Germany's ethnic reordering of the East.[13] One such institution was the Einwandererzentrale (Immigration Central Office, EWZ), which was responsible for "bringing home" Germans from the Baltic countries and from the parts of Poland (including Volhynia) that the USSR had recently annexed.[14]

This vast Germanization program had devastating consequences for those considered undesirable. The Umwandererzentrale (Migration Central Office) set up shop in Łódź in 1940 in order to take care of the resettlement of Poles and Jews. In 1940, 325,000 Poles were deported to the Generalgouvernement.[15] For many Jews, resettlement initially meant ghettoization.[16] Łódź was the site of the first ghetto in occupied Poland, which was eventually second only to Warsaw's in size.[17] Within a few months after Poland's defeat, one observer from the Deutsches Ausland-Institut noted in

---

11 Karl Marder, "Aus Lodsch wird Litzmannstadt," in *Der Osten des Warthelandes. Herausgegeben anläßlich der Heimatschau in Litzmannstadt*, ed. Hubert Müller, 264–278 (Stuttgart: Stähle & Friedel, 1941), here 264.

12 Paul Althaus, "Die Entdeckung des Deutschtums in Mittelpolen," in *Deutschtum im Aufbruch. Vom Volkstumskampf der Deutschen im östlichen Wartheland*, ed. Adolf Kargel and Eduard Kneifel (Leipzig: Hirzel, 1942), 191–197.

13 Valdis O. Lumans, *Himmler's Auxiliaries: The Volksdeutsche Mittelstelle and the German National Minorities of Europe, 1933–1945* (Chapel Hill: University of North Carolina Press, 1993), 255.

14 Stephan Döring, *Die Umsiedlung der Wolhyniendeutschen in den Jahren 1939 bis 1940* (Frankfurt/Main: Peter Lang, 2001), 81–85. For an account of the postwar fate of the EWZ files, see Astrid M. Eckert, *Kampf um die Akten. Die Westalliierten und die Rückgabe von deutschem Archivgut nach dem Zweiten Weltkrieg* (Stuttgart: Franz Steiner, 2004), 229–232.

15 Bergen, *War and Genocide*, 108.

16 There has been much written in recent years on the ghetto and Germanization plans in Łódź and the Reichsgau Wartheland: Markus Leniger, *Nationalsozialistische "Volkstumsarbeit" und Umsiedlungspolitik 1933–1945. Von der Minderheitenbetreuung zur Siedlerauslese* (Berlin: Frank & Timme, 2006); Andrea Löw, *Juden im Getto Litzmannstadt. Lebensbedingungen, Selbstwahrnehmung, Verhalten* (Göttingen: Wallstein, 2006); Phillip T. Rutherford, *Prelude to the Final Solution: The Nazi Program for Deporting Ethnic Poles, 1939–1941* (Lawrence: University Press of Kansas, 2007); Gordon Horwitz, *Ghettostadt: Łódź and the Making of a Nazi City* (Cambridge, MA: Belknap Press of Harvard University Press, 2008); Peter Klein, *Die "Gettoverwaltung Litzmannstadt" 1940 bis 1944. Eine Dienststelle im Spannungsfeld von Kommunalbürokratie und staatlicher Verfolgungspolitik* (Hamburg: Hamburger Ed., 2009).

17 Neils Gutschow, "Stadtplanung im Warthegau, 1939–1944," in *Der "Generalplan" Ost. Hauptlinien der nationalsozialistischen Planungs- und Vernichtungspolitik*, ed. Mechtild Rössler and Sabine Schleiermacher, 232–258 (Berlin: Akademie Verlag, 1993), here 240.

Łódź that the "Jew is as good as gone from street life."[18] The first killing center using gas was established in December 1941 in nearby Chełmno (Kulmhof).[19] Deportations from the ghetto began in 1942, and 44,000 Polish Jews and more than 10,000 non-Polish Jews were sent to their deaths by June of that year.[20]

The conquest and division of Poland also formally ended the Volksgruppe building project that had sought a common sense of Germanness across Poland. The Germans in Western Poland were partitioned when Reichs-gau Danzig-Westpreußen absorbed Bydgoszcz and Toruń (now once again Bromberg and Thorn), while Reichsgau Wartheland absorbed Poznania and made Poznań/Posen its capital.[21] German-speakers in Central Poland were also divided between the so-called Warthegau and the Generalgou-vernement. At the same time, however, the regional subgroups that had successfully thwarted the project to build a unified minority organization during the interwar period were themselves dismantled. Gero von Gersdorff, the DV's youth leader, dissolved the DV in 1940 and pronounced that the JDP–DV conflict had simply been one big misunderstanding between two National Socialist organizations.[22] Importantly, the Germans of Łódź and Poznania were both included in the Reichsgau Wartheland. The rhetoric of völkisch unity continued, but as in the interwar period the ties of the national community depended on a hierarchy of insiders and outsiders.

INTREPRETING GERMAN DIFFERENCES IN OCCUPIED POLAND

For Nazi authorities, local Germans, resettlers, and Reich Germans were to become the forerunners of a new and more radical struggle in formerly Polish territories. Yet how were the Germans who had lived in interwar Poland – especially those from Łódź – to fit into this concept of a Greater German Empire? What happened when Reich Germans came face to face with the Germans in Poland they had idealized for so long? As we have seen, neither Polish policies nor the common acceptance of Nazism did much to undermine the latent regional divisions within the German minority in Poland. For optimistic observers in Germany, however, the metamorphosis of the Germans in Poland into a Volksgruppe successfully proved Nazi

---

18 Hermann Rüdiger, DAI-Kommission, report "Nachträge zu Posen," March 11, 1940, in BA Koblenz, R57, folder 164, unpaginated.

19 Bergen, *War and Genocide*, 183.

20 Elizabeth R. Harvey, *Women and the Nazi East: Agents and Witnesses of Germanization* (New Haven/London: Yale University Press, 2003), 216.

21 Herbert S. Levine, "Local Authority and the SS State: The Conflict Over Population Policy in Danzig-West Prussia, 1939–1945," *Central European History* 2, no. 4 (1969): 331–355, here 348.

22 Blanke, *Orphans of Versailles*, 239; Theodor Bierschenk, *Die deutsche Volksgruppe in Polen, 1934–1939* (Würzburg: Holzner, 1954), 48.

racial precepts. The following appeared just a mere two months before the invasion in the Danzig-based journal *Der Deutsche im Osten*:

The greatest difference is undoubtedly . . . that the [Prussian] Germans, for which nationality and citizenship had been congruent up until then, had to undergo an intellectual transformation, while the Germandom in the other parts of Poland was already used to differentiating between duty to the state and duty to nationality. So it is understandable that the Germans in the different regions of Poland did not come to a mutual understanding right away, but only in the course of time. This process was not made any easier by the liberal thinking of the postwar years. Only the National Socialist Weltanschauung had allowed the unified direction and the völkisch purpose essentially to become reality *so that today we can speak of a German Volksgruppe in Poland.*[23]

The reality of war would soon dispel this myth for many, and contact with the ethnic Germans would allow hierarchies of Reichness and Germanness to reassert themselves during the war years.

Dr. Wilhelm Gradmann, an employee of the Deutsches Ausland-Institut in Stuttgart and an SS officer cadet, arrived in conquered Łódź in the autumn of 1939 to begin his new assignment as press and information officer at the Einwandererzentrale. In his additional position as head of the EWZ's Ethnic German Information Office, Dr. Gradmann answered questions regarding property rights, researched the whereabouts of missing relatives, and prepared "morale reports" about the resettlements. From his numerous tasks, the just thirty-year-old Gradmann believed that he had a better overview of the Germans in Poland than any other Reich administrator in Łódź.[24]

A historian by training, Gradmann wrote a report on the Germans in interwar Poland for the DAI. The introduction was titled "Five groups fully different from one another," and the report sketched the history of the Germans, dividing them into the regions of Poznania and the Corridor, Upper Silesia, Central Poland, Galicia, and Volhynia. According to Gradmann, enormous gulfs separated these groups. He described these differences in terms of national and cultural backwardness. Concerning the Germans in Łódź, Gradmann said that they were lukewarm in their concern for German nationality, adding that the term lodzerdeutsch had become a "buzzword for an indecisive völkisch attitude."[25] In his description of the Germans

---

23 G. Hübschmann, "Das Deutschtum in Polen. Einige Angaben über die historischen Grundlagen und die heutige Struktur der deutschen Volksgruppe im gegenwärtigen polnischen Staat," *Der Deutsche im Osten. Monatsschrift für Kultur, Politik und Unterhaltung* 2, no. 5 (July 1939): 93–96, here 94. Emphases in original.

24 Dr. W. Gradmann to Deutsches Ausland-Institut in Stuttgart, December 17, 1939, in BA Koblenz, R57 Neu, folder 627, 2.

25 Wilhelm Gradmann, "Das Deutschtum in Polen," circa December 1939, in BA Koblenz, R57 Neu, folder 627, 4–5, 7–8.

in Volhynia, Gradmann praised the biological qualities of the Germans, but he also complained about their lack of education, adding that many of their leaders could not read. In a reprise of more traditional views of the Eastern Polish Germans, Gradmann suggested that Germans from elsewhere in Poland could help raise the Volhynian Germans' economic and cultural level.[26] Yet Gradmann also managed to qualify these differences by emphasizing the overriding dominance of the community of blood within the German minority, especially among its political leaders:

The overview above shows how diverse Germandom in former Poland had been, which counted well over a million people in all its splinter groups. It shows that the unification of the leadership, which had to account for different needs, was not easy. Only the inseparable unity of common blood and common fate could overcome all difficulties and build bridges.[27]

Despite this last qualification, Gradmann's description seemed to concur with common Reich German perceptions during the 1920s and early 1930s and showed little appreciation for the Germans in the central and eastern parts of Poland, especially in Łódź. From his observations and especially from his negative reference to the term "Lodzer German," it would seem that the lodzermensch had never fully disappeared. Perhaps his contact with the Western Polish Germans and their prejudices – Gradmann had spent time in occupied Poznań before arriving in Łódź – had influenced his view. Probably the poorer surroundings in much of Łódź and perhaps the encounter with Polish Jews contributed to his aversion to Łódź.

Gradmann was soon criticized, however, for his politically incorrect views that focused on the differences rather than the commonalities of the Germans in Poland. A reader (identity unknown) at the DAI felt that Gradmann's report was too harsh. Throughout the report, the DAI reader edited statements and numbers to put the Polish Germans in a better light. He also crossed out the reference to a large number of German–Slavic mixed people (Mischvolk) in Upper Silesia and recommended that Gradmann should either not bring up the subject of the low cultural level of Volhynian Germans or to express it "more tactfully." The reader also criticized Gradmann's description of a weaker sense of national belonging among Germans in Central Poland: "[T]he depiction of estrangement of the Central Polish Germandom is no longer timely. It would probably be better to give a more restrained depiction." The DAI reader's position to the article underlined

26 Wilhelm Gradmann, "Das Deutschtum in Polen," circa December 1939, in BA Koblenz, R57 Neu, folder 627, 4–5, 7–8.
27 Wilhelm Gradmann, "Das Deutschtum in Polen," circa December 1939, in BA Koblenz, R57 Neu, folder 627, 8.

the current political need for suppressing differences among the Germans in Poland: "It is recommended not to emphasize so blatantly the differences between the various parts of the Volksgruppe. Precisely that could cast doubt upon the justification of our current activities."[28] The reaction indicates that Gradmann's comments had clearly touched a sensitive nerve. Gradmann essentially saw the German Volksgruppe in Poland as multiple and disparate national communities. This recognition, however, was no longer politically opportune: if the Germans in Poland had failed to become a unitary Volksgemeinschaft in twenty years as a minority in Poland, the project of molding a new Germandom in the annexed eastern territories might appear questionable at best and counterproductive at worst. As the criticism of Gradmann's report exemplifies, the transformation of Lodzers into Germans would be proclaimed whether it had happened or not.

Whether or not Gradmann ever saw the DAI criticisms remains unknown, but he quickly adjusted to the role expected of him. About one month later, Gradmann himself wrote a response to an article by Walter Kuhn, the Ostforscher from Bielsko/Bielitz and now a professor in Breslau. Gradmann suggested that Kuhn pay less attention to the inherited peculiarities of the Germans because a "melting and growing together of the different tribes is unconditionally necessary."[29] Indeed, the apparently low degree to which the Germans in interwar Poland had coalesced gave reason to reflect on how the wartime Germanization and settlement policies were to proceed. Although many advocated splitting the Germans from the East and mixing them with colonists from the Reich, Walter Kuhn and Kurt Lück advocated maintaining the German villages in self-contained units. Kuhn argued that dividing the biologically valuable eastern Germans would waste their natural talents, for they would adopt the bad habits of their more worldly western cousins, while also encountering discrimination:

In the case of the Germans from Eastern Poland, the situation is made more difficult by their persisting educational backwardness. They would be seen by their Western German fellow villagers as inferior, as simple-minded, naive, and backward East Europeans whose language lacks concepts and is filled with loan words, and many of them cannot read or write. In the context of the former Polish state, there was only very little possibility for an understanding between the Germans from Eastern Poland and the more advanced and better educated, if biologically weaker, Germans from Poznania-West Prussia.[30]

28 Author unknown, "Bemerkungen zum Artikel von Dr. W. Gradmann: 'Das Deutschtum in Polen,'" copy in BA Koblenz, R57 Neu, folder 627.
29 "Stellungnahme von SS-Anwärter Dr. W. Gradmann," January 22, 1940, copy in BA Koblenz, R57, folder 1386, 7.
30 "Bericht von Professor Dr. Kuhn, Breslau, über: III. Geschlossene oder zerstreute Ansiedlung der Deutschen aus Ostpolen," January 22, 1940, copy in BA Koblenz, R57, folder 1386, 11–14.

Thus, west-east distinctiveness had now become an issue in German colonization schemes, and the question of how far the German minority had come together during the interwar period was important to the planning.

Kuhn was undoubtedly a well-established authority on the Germans in Poland and had been one of the optimists in rehabilitating the Germans of Eastern Poland and in creating a unified Volksgemeinschaft. Yet the experience of the German minority in interwar Poland had shown him that the reconciliation of east with west was extremely difficult. Kuhn's more cautious approach thus did not go far enough for radicals and opportunists such as Gradmann, whom Michael Burleigh described as a "cog in the process of screening expatriates."[31] Although Gradmann agreed with Kuhn's assessment for the most part, he was not afraid to use old tropes in supporting his argument to break up the individual village units of the Volhynian German resettlers. Gradmann claimed, for example, that incest had already led to "feeble-mindedness" among many Galician German children.[32] This kind of conformist self-censorship and the reinterpretation of völkisch precepts became symptomatic for Nazi racial policies in the occupied East. As in the interwar period, political and ideological pressures heavily influenced how the Germans in (former) Poland were perceived. Regional and social differences were often simply ignored or given a new meaning that presupposed a natural – and transcendental – unity. As will be seen, however, the practice of Germanness in Poland actually reestablished west-to-east hierarchies, albeit in reconfigured form.

ERADICATING THE LODZERMENSCH

The project to create a new Germandom in the East was particularly evident and brutal in Łódź, where the amphibious lodzermensch was to be completely erased, both physically and historically, as the renaming of the city to Litzmannstadt also suggests. An exhibit celebrating the Germanization of the city resulted in a book called *Der Osten des Warthelandes* (Wartheland's East) in 1941. Both the exhibit and the book were prepared in cooperation with the Reich Propaganda Ministry.[33] As the showcase of the new German East, Łódź was to be an example of this purification of the German national body. Fritz Gissibl, who had once been an important figure in the

---

31 Michael Burleigh, *Germany Turns Eastwards: A Study of Ostforschung in the Third Reich* (London: Pan Macmillan, 2002), 178–179. Stephan Döring argues for a more influential role played by Gradmann. See *Die Umsiedlung der Wolhyniendeutschen*, 250.

32 "Stellungnahme von SS-Anwärter Dr. W. Gradmann," January 22, 1940, copy in BA Koblenz, R57, folder 1386, 15.

33 For proceeds from the exhibit, see Kassenbericht der Heimatschau per 23. April 1941, in USHMM, RG-05.008M, reel 1, folder 31, 130–132.

pro-Nazi movement in the United States and later served in the Reich Propaganda Ministry, wrote the introduction.[34] He stated that the purpose of
the exhibit and book was to disabuse the average German of his "fantasies"
about the new German East being frightening, Asiatic, and the birthplace
of the "Galician world Jewry." Gissibl noted that in the initial period of
the occupation, there had been the prevailing opinion that there was little
German influence in Łódź. However, the roughly 200,000 people counted
as German in the greater Litzmannstadt area had been not just the largest
German concentration in former Polish territories, but they also had an
able leader in Ludwig Wolff. Thus, Gissibl argued, great German cultural
achievements over the centuries gave the Reich "justifiable claim" to this
territory.[35] Another contribution in the book reminded the reader of the
"deeply rooted Germandom" and reiterated the claim that the Germans
in Łódź had grown to become the strongest German Volksgruppe (here
in its regional-tribal sense), both absolutely and relatively, in all of Poland.
This growth, the author noted, was in contrast to the mass emigration of
Germans elsewhere in Poland.[36] Filled with denigrating photos of Jews
and Poles, the book showed how Łódź had progressed from the cultural
hybridity and national ambiguity of the lodzermensch to the racial clarity
of the New Order. Especially the juxtaposition of photographs and their
captions is revealing: the "typical representative of the 'chosen people'"
stood across from a "German farmer" while a picture of shabbily clothed,
dark-looking boys labeled "Jewish offspring" was contrasted against blond,
smartly uniformed "Volksdeutsche Pimpfe"[37] (Figure 6.3 and Figure 6.4).
These photographs represented an attempt to extirpate all Polish and Jewish
influences by contrasting them against supposedly pure German qualities.
The construction of such differences could then justify or elide abuses,
including expropriation. In a separate article titled "Litzmannstadt – Center
of Resettlement," Wilhelm Gradmann complained that many confiscated
Jewish homes were "tasteless" and did not meet "German needs."[38]

Indeed, many German writers took the opportunity in wartime to reval-
idate the narrative of the German Volksgruppe in Poland. Especially the

---

34 On Fritz Gissibl's activities in the United States and Germany, see Cornelia Wilhelm, *Bewegung oder
    Verein? Nationalsozialistische Volkstumspolitik in den USA* (Stuttgart: Steiner, 1998), 128–130, 291.
35 Fritz Gissibl, "Der Osten des Warthelandes," in *Der Osten des Warthelandes*, 14–16.
36 [Horst] Markgraf, "Litzmannstadt und seine Wirtschaft. Rückblick auf 120 Jahre deutschen
    Gewerbeschaffens," in *Der Osten des Warthelandes*, 50–77, here 76–77.
37 "Pimpfe" was a term for boys in the Deutsches Jungvolk (German Young Volk), the subdivision of
    the Hitler Youth for boys between 10 and 14 years of age.
38 Wilhelm Gradmann, "Litzmannstadt – Mittelpunkt der Umsiedlung," *Deutschtum im Ausland* 25,
    nos. 1–2 (1942): 12–16, here 13.

Figure 6.3. Children of the past: photo depicting "Jew brood" in ghetto. *Source*: Hubert Müller, ed., *Der Osten des Warthelandes. Herausgegeben anläßlich der Heimatschau in Litzmannstadt* (Stuttgart: Stähle & Friedel, 1941), 308.

Figure 6.4. Children of the future: photo depicting Volksdeutsche Pimpfe of the Hitler Youth. *Source*: Hubert Müller, ed., *Der Osten des Warthelandes. Herausgegeben anläßlich der Heimatschau in Litzmannstadt* (Stuttgart: Stähle & Friedel, 1941), 309.

hardship experienced at the beginning of the war was to serve as a touchstone for the Germans from Poland. One example was Kurt Lück's collection of stories in *Marsch der Deutschen in Polen*, which described the internment and forced marches of German minority leaders at the outbreak of war. Germans from Poznania-Pomerelia (Kurt Lück, Hans Kohnert, Heinrich Weiss, Friedrich Swart, and Alfred Lattermann) as well as from Łódź (Horst Markgraf and Ludwig Wolff) recounted their experiences of hardship in September 1939, which often seemed to stand in for the entire two decades of Polish rule before their purported liberation.[39] There was one contribution to the collection on the Volhynian Germans, but the author remained anonymous. Labeled as a collective story ("told by Volhynian colonists"), it was probably written by the editor Kurt Lück.[40] Old habits of speaking for the Volhynian Germans died hard.

In such narratives, the Germans in interwar Poland increasingly appeared in the role of the hardened ethnic warrior on the frontline of the battle for Lebensraum, and the increasing racialization of categories such as ethnic Germans, Slavs, and Jews left less room for in-between entities such as the lodzermensch. For Reich Germans, Poles, and Jews alike, it seemed that the Germans in Central Poland had evolved from an apolitical and not-quite-German margin into the very pioneers of Germany's new colonial enterprise.[41] During the Second World War, a German pastor and writer in Poland construed the ability of the eastern Germans in Poland to speak multiple languages as a sign of natural German mastery over the local peoples.[42] This rediscovered hybridity no longer expressed growing Polonization or the contamination of the lodzermensch, but it now signaled the vital qualities necessary for colonizing the German East. Yet as in the interwar period, the practice of national community differed greatly from its discourse.

A PLACE IN THE NEW ORDER: INTRA-ETHNIC CLEAVAGES AND ETHNIC CLEANSING

As we have seen, the turn toward anti-Semitism in the politics of Łódź German activists came well before the arrival of German troops in 1939.

---

39 Kurt Lück, ed., *Marsch der Deutschen in Polen. Deutsche Volksgenossen im ehemaligen Polen berichten über Erlebnisse in den Septembertagen 1939* (Berlin: Grenze und Ausland, 1940).

40 "Von Wolhynien nach Bereza Kartuska. Erzählt von wolhynischen Kolonisten," in *Marsch der Deutschen in Polen*, 103–106.

41 Karl Weber, *Litzmannstadt. Geschichte und Probleme eines Wirtschaftszentrums im deutschen Osten* (Jena: Fischer, 1943), 30.

42 Eduard Kneifel, "Adolf Eichler – Ein Leben im Dienste des Deutschtums," in *Deutschtum im Aufbruch*, 11–32, here 25–26. See also Reichsführer-SS und Chef der Deutschen Polizei, Der Chef der Sicherheitspolizei und des SD, Amt III, "Meldungen aus dem Reich," March 27, 1940, in BA Berlin, R58, folder 149, 166–167.

Despite the often patronizing treatment of the ethnic Germans, there was no shortage of Łódź German participation in the machinery of oppression. More than 3,000 Germans from the Łódź area were involved in the short-lived but brutal Volksdeutscher Selbstschutz (ethnic German militia).[43] Because the citizenship status of many ethnic Germans remained unclear for the time being, they could not initially join the Wehrmacht. The SS and Waffen-SS, however, began an early recruitment among them.[44] The leader of the DVV, Ludwig Wolff, joined the SS at the rank of Obersturm-bannführer, equivalent to a lieutenant colonel. He received the golden party pin[45] and also served briefly as the Nazi Party's Kreisleiter for Łódź. Many others assisted in the administration of the Reichsgau Wartheland and the Generalgouvernement. There were of course many cases of ethnic Germans in occupied Poland who sought to help their Polish neighbors.[46] However, even as they did so, many of these same Germans participated in the New Order and supported the Reich German occupiers, or at least did little to undermine them. Indeed, the Polish and Jewish populations were especially fearful of the Central Polish "foksy" (Polish colloquial expression for Volksdeutsche), whose knowledge of Polish and local customs made them seem particularly dangerous and traitorous.[47]

The direct and indirect involvement of many Polish Germans in the murderous policies of the Nazis was a fateful development for the rest of the German population in Central Poland. In his *Dark Side of Democracy*, Michael Mann argues that borderland Germans were more inclined to be involved than their (other) Reich German counterparts in ethnic cleansing and made up one of the "core constituencies" of Nazi perpetrators.[48] His statistical analysis indicates that ethnic Germans in interwar Poland played a disproportionate role (if lower than other borderland groups) in wartime crimes against Poles and Jews. Mann concludes that these core

---

43 Christian Jansen and Arno Weckbecker, *Der "Volksdeutsche Selbstschutz" in Polen 1939/40* (Munich: Oldenbourg, 1992), here 72–77.

44 Michael Mann, *The Dark Side of Democracy: Explaining Ethnic Cleansing* (Cambridge/New York: Cambridge University Press, 2005), 226–227.

45 Albrecht, "Stimmung der Polen. Dienstreise nach Polen vom 11.10. bis 3.11.1939," in BA Koblenz, R57, folder 1050 (19 pages, here p. 15).

46 Jan Grabowski and Zbigniew R. Grabowski, "Germans in the Eyes of the Gestapo: The Ciechanów District, 1939–1945," *Contemporary European History* 13, no. 1 (2004): 21–43, here 31.

47 Jerzy Kochanowski: "Kto ty jesteś? Niemiec mały! Volksdeutsche: sprawa jest bardziej skomp-likowana niż myślimy!" *Polityka*, September 7, 2003, 64–66. According to one historian, the back and forth behavior of the local Germans reminded Poles of the foxtrot. See Georg W. Strobel, "Industriemetropole zwischen Orient und Okzident. Eine Hommage an die Vielvölkerstadt Lodz," in *Deutsch-Polnische Ansichten zur Literatur und Kultur. Jahrbuch 1992*, 31–59 (Darmstadt: Deutsches Polen-Institut; Wiesbaden: Harrassowitz, 1993), 49.

48 Mann, *Dark Side of Democracy*, 223–239.

constituencies from "lost territories or threatened borders" were "probably ideological killers."[49] Catherine Epstein's biography of Arthur Greiser lends context and credence to this thesis.[50] Mann's study does suggest that "other eastern ethnic Germans" (such as those in Łódź) were slightly more likely to participate in war crimes than those in lands lost to Poland after the First World War (such as Poznań).[51] According to Mann, Eastern European Germans were able to turn the table on Poles and Jews for real and perceived wrongs in the new situation. Bitterness and revenge were thus important motivations.[52]

Yet the participation of many Germans from Łódź seems to stand in contradiction to widespread depictions of the local population having been more resistant to nationalism or even being indifferent to nationality. Did the participation of local Germans happen despite or because of the city's association with the lodzermensch? To understand this process, we must also look at contingency and the wartime context. The killers' origins in the German-Polish borderlands is perhaps less an explanation in itself and more the starting point for understanding how the occupation radicalized cleavages – not just between Germans and Poles, but also between groups that were deemed somehow German. Borderland backgrounds may have been inherently deadly precisely because they also fostered a constellation of German insiders and outsiders that facilitated mass murder. The former Germans in Poland, as an essential building block in the Greater German Reich, had the opportunity in wartime to prove their Germanness anew.

Doris Bergen offers a framework for understanding how such German hierarchies worked in occupied Poland. Bergen argues that the notion of Volksdeutsche as deployed in wartime was to a large extent invented and that it fostered Nazi rule by incentivizing action against undesirable populations such as Jews. She states that "the tenuousness of the concept of Volksdeutsche encouraged anti-Semitism as a way of establishing German credentials."[53] Eric Steinhart describes a similar process in the occupied Soviet territories.[54] Several observers have noted how the continuing

---

49 Mann, *Dark Side of Democracy*, 239.
50 Catherine Epstein, *Model Nazi: Arthur Greiser and the Occupation of Western Poland* (Oxford/New York: Oxford University Press, 2010), 3–4.
51 Mann, *Dark Side of Democracy*, 224–225.   52 Mann, *Dark Side of Democracy*, 227.
53 Doris L. Bergen, "The Nazi Concept of 'Volksdeutsche' and the Exacerbation of Anti-Semitism in Eastern Europe, 1939–45," *Journal of Contemporary History* 29, no. 4 (1994): 569–582, here 570–571, 575. See also: Doris L. Bergen, "Tenuousness and Tenacity: The *Volksdeutschen* of Eastern Europe, World War II, and the Holocaust," in *The Heimat Abroad: The Boundaries of Germanness*, ed. Krista O'Donnell, Renate Bridenthal, and Nancy Reagin, 265–286 (Ann Arbor: University of Michigan Press, 2005), 269.
54 Eric C. Steinhart, "Policing the Boundaries of 'Germandom' in the East: SS Ethnic German Policy and Odessa's 'Volksdeutsche,' 1941–1944," *Central European History* 43, no. 1 (2010): 85–116.

second-class status of many Łódź Germans within the German in-group probably led to their participation in the occupation regime and in their radicalization. Georg W. Strobel, a German political scientist and historian originally from Łódź, describes the enthusiastic and compensatory attempt of many ethnic Germans to prove their loyalty to Nazi principles vis-à-vis the "arrogant," "know-it-all," and "tone-setting" behavior of the Reich Germans. Strobel attributes this behavior mainly to the lumpenproletariat and petite bourgeois elements among the ethnic Germans in Łódź.[55] Yet national marginalization could cut across class boundaries. Hence, the interplay of ideology *and* practice of national community was integral to the landscape of murder and plunder in occupied Poland.

THE HIERARCHY OF GERMANNESS IN PRACTICE

Despite the rhetoric of a pan-Geman community in the East, the occupation revealed deep rifts in the Volksgemeinschaft and exposed a familiar west-to-east hierarchy. Indeed, the relationship between German groups in interwar Poland, with the Western Polish Germans seeking to raise their eastern brethren, now became more complicated. In the pecking order of Germanness of occupied Poland, Reich Germans were on top and ethnic Germans below them. Germans from former Western Poland now found themselves grouped together with the other so-called Beutedeutsche (booty Germans) in Central and Eastern Poland. Having been Reich citizens at one time and then accustomed to a privileged role within the minority, the Western Polish Germans found that their residual citizenship counted for little now. The ethnic Germans were themselves were divided by the Deutsche Volksliste, a four-category hierarchical system designed to verify the Germanness of the often suspect ethnic Germans and to confer citizenship upon them.[56]

The Nazi administration themselves did little in practice to foster the integration of the Germans in occupied Poland. Especially the dissonance

---

55 Strobel, "Industriemetropole zwischen Orient und Okzident," 49–50.
56 On the Deutsche Volksliste, see Epstein, *Model Nazi*, 193–230; Isabel Heinemann, "Rasse, Siedlung, deutsches Blut": Das Rasse- und Siedlungshauptamt der SS und die rassenpolitische Neuordnung Europas (Göttingen: Wallstein, 2003), 260–282; Gerhard Wolf, "Deutsche Volksliste," in *Handbuch der völkischen Wissenschaften*, ed. Ingo Haar and Michael Fahlbusch, 129–135 (Munich: Saur, 2008); Alexa Stiller, "Grenzen des 'Deutschen': Nationalsozialistische Volkstumspolitik in Polen, Frankreich und Slowenien während des Zweiten Weltkriegs," in *Deutschsein als Grenzerfahrung. Minderheitenpolitik in Europa zwischen 1914 und 1950*, ed. Mathias Beer, Dietrich Beyrau, and Cornelia Rauh, 61–84 (Essen: Klartext, 2009). See also Diemut Majer, *"Fremdvölkische" im Dritten Reich. Ein Beitrag zur nationalsozialistischen Rechtssetzung und Rechtspraxis in Verwaltung und Justiz unter besonderer Berücksichtigung der eingegliederten Ostgebiete und des Generalgouvernements* (Boppard am Rhein: Boldt, 1981), 414–430.

among competing agencies and institutions in the newly won East made this goal more difficult to attain. The Gauleiter of Danzig-Westpreußen, Albert Forster, distrusted the Germans in Bromberg (Bydgoszcz), whom he feared had come under the influence of his SS rivals. He ignored these ethnic Germans when it came to handing out assignments to the Kreisleitung (district offices) and Gauleitung (provincial offices) and chose people from what had recently been the Free City of Danzig or from German-West Prussia.[57] This discrimination persisted despite labor shortages. As David Blackbourn notes, even the general trumpeting of the value of settling in the East (a so-called Ostrausch) could not convince enough qualified Reich Germans to serve in occupied Poland.[58] For many civil servants, the East was akin to a penal colony where their careers would end.[59] Once on the job, occupation authorities themselves curried a negative image of the Łódź Germans. A monthly report by the city administration for August 1940 noted that the local Germans desired better positions although they lacked a work ethic and performed poorly.[60] In a meeting with the staff of the Reich treasurer, Greiser discussed how years of oppression had warped the Łódź Germans and resettlers and how they should not be made equal with "other Germans." Suffering from an apparent "inferiority complex," these eastern Germans would still need a long time to learn their role as the leading stratum in occupied Poland.[61] With such attitudes, it is not surprising that few Germans from interwar Poland achieved high-ranking positions in the civil administration despite the labor shortage.[62]

During an inspection tour a half-year after the conquest of Poland, Hermann Rüdiger of the Deutsches Ausland-Institut listed the various forms of humiliation that the Łódź Germans had to endure, including not being served by various offices. He noted how one German dentist from the Reich flaunted his Reich German status in a newspaper announcement. He believed this degrading treatment by Reich Germans, often sarcastically

---

57 Levine, "Local Authority and the SS State," 348.
58 David Blackbourn, *The Conquest of Nature: Water, Landscape, and the Making of Modern Germany* (New York/London: Norton, 2006), 262–301.
59 Reichsführer-SS und Chef der Deutschen Polizei, Der Chef der Sicherheitspolizei und des SD, Amt III, "Meldungen aus dem Reich," Nr. 123 from September 12, 1940, in BA Berlin, R58 (RSHA), folder 154, 83; ibid., Nr. 133 from October 17, 1940, in BA Berlin, R58 (RSHA), folder 155, 111. For more on motivations, behavior, and attitudes of Reich German administrators, see David Furber, "Going East: Colonialism and German Life in Nazi-Occupied Poland," (Ph.D. dissertation, State University of New York, Buffalo, 2003).
60 Monatsbericht der Stadt Litzmannstadt, August 1940, in USHMM, RG-05.008M, reel 3, folder 138, 41.
61 Reichsamtsleiter Schieder, "Besuchs-Vermerk," January 11, 1940 (signed January 12, 1940), in BA Berlin, former BDC, Partei-Kanzlei: Arthur Greiser, 22.01.1897, Film D0160–89, 2862–2874.
62 Blanke, *Orphans of Versailles*, 239.

called Reichsgermanen by the locals, made the ethnic Germans take out their anger and inferiority complex on the Baltic German settlers, who themselves had not wanted to come to Łódź in the first place. Although Rüdiger bemoaned this lack of unity, he never doubted the basic hierarchy: Reich Germans were, after all, "absolutely indispensable" in the project to build Łódź anew.[63] Like Rüdiger, another DAI member reported that local Germans were often treated as Poles in the initial stages of the occupation: waiting rooms in Łódź were segregated between Reich Germans and Poles, but the ethnic Germans were not allowed to enter the Reich German rooms.[64]

The hierarchy of Germanness also informed and reflected perceived economic disparities.[65] Especially buying power highlighted differences between Reich and ethnic Germans. In part due to favorable exchange rates, Reich Germans traveling home often looked like Santa Claus because they could "hamster" so many goods while in Poland.[66] As a product of an ideological and economic compromise, Łódź was less than 30 kilometers from the Reich's border with the Generalgouvernement.[67] The nearby border hobbled economic life by cutting the city off from other towns and countryside to its east. This distortion of its trade networks led the government to set high prices in the city for foodstuffs and for wares.[68] Not surprisingly, many Reich Germans complained about the rent, prices, and lack of amenities.[69]

63 Hermann Rüdiger, DAI-Kommission, report "Nachträge zu Posen," March 11, 1940, in BA Koblenz, R57, folder 164, unpaginated. The use of the term "Reichsgermanen" also appears in Max Treger, *Lodz-Berlin 1914–1984. Ein Zeitdokument* (Frankfurt/Main: Autoren-Selbstverlag, 1985), 74. On DAI activities during the Second World War, see Ernst Ritter, *Das Deutsche Ausland-Institut in Stuttgart 1917–1945. Ein Beispiel Deutscher Volkstumsarbeit zwischen den Weltkriegen* (Wiesbaden: Franz Steiner, 1976), 136–147.

64 Albrecht, Stimmung der Polen, Dienstreise nach Polen vom 11.10. bis 3.11.1939, in BA Koblenz, R57, folder 1050 (19 pages, here p. 16).

65 Letter from Barbara to Heinrich, dated February 1940, in USHMM, RG-05.008M, reel 3, folder 139, 139–141.

66 Albrecht, Stimmung der Polen, Dienstreise nach Polen vom 11.10. bis 3.11.1939, in BA Koblenz, R57, folder 1050 (19 pages, here p. 19).

67 In several answers to questions posed by a journalist, Mayor Karl Marder noted the distance to be 20 km and discussed the many issues facing Litzmannstadt, including Germanization, smuggling, and the ghetto. Untitled text of interview (presumably end of 1940–beginning of 1941), USHMM, RG-05.008M, reel 1, folder 31, 117–126, here 117. Also in USHMM, RG-05.008M, reel 2, folder 72, 90ff. Alberti gives the distance to be about 20 km (*Die Verfolgung und Vernichtung der Juden*, 51). Friedrich Swart notes 30 km in *Diesseits und jenseits der Grenze. Das deutsche Genossenschaftswesen im Posener Land und das deutsch-polnische Verhältnis bis zum Ende des Zweiten Weltkrieges* (Leer: Rautenberg & Möckel, 1954), 154.

68 Karl Marder to SS-Ustuf. Huttenburg, June 4, 1940, with attachment "Tomaschow und Lodscher Wirtschaftsbereich," in USHMM, RG-05.008M, reel 1, folder 31, 16–19.

69 Letter from Barbara to Heinrich, dated February 1940, in USHMM, RG-05.008M, reel 3, folder 139, 139–141.

Reich Germans were especially wary of Łódź Germans, whom they suspected of holding back on goods.[70] Indeed, many believed that the local Germans were practically crypto-Poles who spoke Polish in public and favored Polish customers over Reich German ones.[71] Economic tensions revived older resentments against those in the west who appeared more privileged. Poznań's allocation of cheese, for example, was twice as large as Łódź, causing great consternation.[72] Reich Germans living in Łódź were beginning to feel what the periphery had to offer. The high turnover of Reich German civil servants was in part due to this disheartening economic situation, whereas others assumed the "tiredness of the east" was due to the poor quality of the human material being sent east, which also seemed to contribute to the solidarity of Poles and ethnic Germans.[73]

The local Germans often reacted with considerable resentment, not just against the Reich Germans but also against the Baltic German resettlers, who were often given higher positions at work. Resistance to work speed and procedures caused Baltic Germans to complain about the inability of local Łódź Germans to work properly. Moreover, they also grumbled about the lack of qualified ethnic German teachers in schools, who meted out harsh punishment on pupils.[74] The following saying already appeared in the first few months of the occupation and reflected this clash of German cultures:

> The Baltic [Germans] speak Russian,
> the ethnic Germans Polish,
> the Poles German,
> the Reich Germans are speechless.[75]

---

70 Statistisches Amt 011, Lagebericht am 5. April 1940, in USHMM, RG-05.008M, reel 3, folder 126, 154–157, here 154; Letters by Behr and Napp, included as attachments from Bürgermeister Karl Marder to Kreisleiter Ludwig Wolff, "Unterschiedliche Behandlung von Deutschen," January 4, 1941, in USHMM, RG-05.008M, reel 2, folder 72, 23–30.

71 Statistisches Amt 011, Lagebericht für den Februar 1940, dated March 3, 1940, in USHMM, RG-05.008M, reel 3, folder 126, 207; Statistisches Amt 011, Lagebericht am 5. April 1940, in USHMM, RG-05.008M, reel 3, folder 126, 154–157, here 154; Lagebericht für September 1940, dated October 1, 1940, in USHMM, RG-05.008M, reel 3, folder 126, 187.

72 Statistisches Amt 011 (presumably to Regierungspräsident in Litzmannstadt), Lagebericht für den Monat Mai 1940, dated May 30, 1940, in USHMM, RG-05.008M, reel 3, folder 126, 212.

73 Reichsführer-SS und Chef der Deutschen Polizei, Der Chef der Sicherheitspolizei und des SD, Amt III, "Meldungen aus dem Reich," Nr. 131, October 10, 1940, in BA Berlin, R58 (RSHA), folder 155, 60.

74 Statistisches Amt 011 (presumably to Regierungspräsident in Litzmannstadt), Lagebericht für den Februar 1940, March 3, 1940, in USHMM, RG-05.008M, reel 3, folder 126, 207.

75 Hermann Rüdiger, DAI-Kommission, report "Nachträge zu Posen," March 11, 1940, in BA Koblenz, R57, folder 164, unpaginated; translation from Epstein, *Model Nazi*, 176. See also Wilhelm Fielitz, *Das Stereotyp des wolhyniendeutschen Umsiedlers. Popularisierungen zwischen Sprachinselforschung und nationalsozialistischer Propaganda* (Marburg: N.G. Elwert, 2000), 20.

Similarly snide comments and backhanded remarks, especially by Reich Germans about the questionable Germanness of the ethnic Germans, became commonplace. In August 1940, the lord mayor (Oberbürger-meister) reported a noticeable drop in ethnic German morale in the face of discriminatory treatment. The local Germans even worried that they could face deportation to the old Reich territories for the purpose of their "political and character refinement."[76]

Although memoirs often recalled incidents of discrimination and demeaning treatment, it is important to not take such accounts at face value, for many Łódź Germans may have wanted to distance themselves from the Reich after the war. Still, the incidents described often show a hierarchy of Germanness that was demoralizing and hypocritical in the face of the loud proclamations of a Volksgemeinschaft. Max Treger, a Łódź German who found a job with the criminal police, recounted how some Reich Germans cursed the local Germans as "Pollacken."[77] He recalled an incident in the office in which Reich Germans were asked to sit on the right and ethnic Germans on the left. One person responded that "we are not second class people," and Treger added: "We are Germans not only on account of our nationality. Our grandfathers, fathers, and we have also proved for well over a hundred years that we are Germans."[78] Ethnic Germans could use the idea of nationality struggle and biological determin-ism to reassert their value within the Volksgemeinschaft, but their feelings of marginalization were clear.

West-to-east hierarchies of Germanness coincided with established ideas of masculinity. In good colonial fashion, Reich German men were often sexually aggressive toward ethnic German women.[79] In his memoirs, the renowned Polish-German translator Karl Dedecius noted how local German women tended to be swept off their feet by Reich German men, who were not like the everyday mortal men in Łódź: "They had a different demeanor: self-confident, decidedly manly, superior, and they were not just dashing, but also attractive. Only for a few girls did the uniform perhaps also play

---

76 Oberbürgermeister to Regierungspräsident in Litzmannstadt, "Lagebericht für Monat August 1940," dated September 7, 1940, in USHMM, RG-05.008M, reel 1, folder 32, 21–22; Statistisches Amt Litzmannstadt, Lagebericht am 1. September 1940, dated August 31, 1940, in USHMM, RG-05.008M, reel 3, folder 126, 181.

77 Treger, *Lodz-Berlin*, 74. "Pollacken" is a German derogatory word for Poles, similar to the term "polack" in English.

78 Treger, *Lodz-Berlin*, 72–78. Treger later notes that work went well in the Kripo between Reich and local Germans, and he owed his own success to his previous experience with "streetwise" Jews. There is no other mention of the fate of Łódź Jews.

79 Harvey, *Women and the Nazi East*, 212.

a role."[80] Yet the East, too, could be where relations between men and women might take forms different from those in the Reich. As Elizabeth Harvey has shown, Reich German women, who were recruited to teach ethnic Germans in occupied Poland, took on positions that gave them the feeling of considerable authority. Even in the city of Poznań, which had been under German control until 1920, school assistants from the Bund deutscher Mädel considered themselves to be more authentically German than their charges.[81] Those advisors who tried to impart German domesticity to the resettlers complained, for example, that the Galician Germans spoke Polish instead of German.[82] The sense of distinction was especially great as the war effort faltered, when Reich German women realized that they could only rely on themselves and not the ethnic Germans.[83]

Rather than uncovering a long-suppressed völkisch solidarity, the conquest of Poland recreated the west-east divide between Reich Germans and ethnic Germans and further fragmented the former Polish Germans as well. The interwar goal of minority leaders to form the widely extolled Volksgruppe now seemed more remote than ever. As shown previously, the outrage and emasculation felt by many ethnic Germans could take self-serving and brutal forms. The search for a new commonality by German activists in Poland after the war would stress the hardships under Nazi rule, the flight from Soviet armies, and the expulsions. Above all, however, they idealized their cooperation against the Polish state in the interwar period and downplayed regionalized political conflicts.

POLISH GERMANS IN THE FEDERAL REPUBLIC — A VOLKSGRUPPE AT LAST?

Nazi resettlement policies had diluted the interwar German communities in occupied Poland, and the Nazi defeat washed them away altogether. The Polish neighbors and administrators who returned during and after the war had little regard for individual circumstances and often punished the Germans collectively. While a great many fled or were expelled, thousands experienced captivity or forced labor in Polish internment and work camps. Others — especially women — faced various forms of enslavement in order

---

80 Karl Dedecius, *Ein Europäer aus Lodz. Erinnerungen* (Frankfurt/Main: Suhrkamp, 2006), here 112.
81 Harvey, *Women and the Nazi East*, 169, 208–210; see also Elizabeth R. Harvey, "'We Forgot All Jews and Poles': German Women and the 'Ethnic Struggle' in Nazi-Occupied Poland," *Contemporary European History* 10, no. 3 (2001): 447–461.
82 Nancy R. Reagin, "German *Brigadoon*? Domesticity and Metropolitan Perceptions of *Auslands-deutschen* in Southwest Africa and Eastern Europe," in *The Heimat Abroad*, 248–266, here 260.
83 Harvey, *Women and the Nazi East*, 266, 276–277.

to gain protection for themselves or their families. Rape and murder were common.[84]

In the shifting of territories at the end of the war, a new German minority was created in Poland's so-called recovered western territories. The Germans from interwar Poland, however, were largely removed and resettled throughout the two new Germanies. The East German government did not allow expellees to organize, but expellee organizations became a powerful political force in the Federal Republic. Although it may seem that the dream of creating a Volksgruppe of Germans *from* Poland could finally be fulfilled in the postwar period, those German expellees who had lived in interwar Poland continued to be divided organizationally in the West German political landscape. Germans from the Pomerelian Corridor joined Landsmannschaft Westpreußen, while the Germans from Upper Silesia and Teschen Silesia were integrated into Landsmannschaft Schlesien. Because both organizations were made up mainly of Germans who had lived in Reich territories during the interwar period, the demands for a return to the 1937 German borders dominated. Although these borders would have technically excluded the Germans from interwar Poland, the expellee organizations continued to insist on the "right to the homeland." The Sudeten Germans are an important but illustrative case of an expellee organization that did not base the claim to Heimat on a legalistic argument of the sanctity of Germany's 1937 borders but nonetheless had an extreme political position; their vocal position was due to Czechoslovakia's geographical proximity and the sheer numbers of expellees, concentrated especially in Bavaria. Maximalist elements in the expellee organizations influenced the Bund der Vertriebenen, which acted as an umbrella organization for the Landsmannschaften.[85] Yet revisionism and irredentism had also readjusted to the new political realities.

The Polish Germans from the former Reichsgau Wartheland did take a different path from the Sudeten Germans. The former Poseners and the Lodzers joined together in one organization, Landsmannschaft Weichsel-Warthe (LWW), named after the two rivers of Western and Central Poland (and incidentally the two rivers mentioned in the Polish national anthem).

84 Ingo Eser and Jerzy Kochanowski, *Polska Centralna. Województwo Śląskie*, vol. 2 of *Niemcy w Polsce 1945–1950. Wybór dokumentów*, ed. Włodzimierz Borodziej and Hans Lemberg (Warsaw: Neriton, 2000); Piotr Pytlakowski, "Naprzykrzyło się grzebać. Co się stało z Niemcami z Aleksandrowa Kujawskiego?" *Polityka*, January 27, 2001, 78–81; Piotr Pytlakowski, "Ciężar pamięci. Jak na Kujawach zabijano Niemców (c.d.)," *Polityka*, February 24, 2001, 64–66.

85 For a listing of the different constituent Landsmannschaften, see the website of the Bund der Vertriebenen: "Mitgliedsverbände," Bund der Vertriebenen, accessed August 10, 2006, http://www.bund-der-vertriebenen.de/derbdv/mitgliedsverbaende3.php3.

Because the LWW did not make any territorial claims, it has been considered a politically moderate organization in the expellee landscape.[86] In the 1970s, one of the LWW's more prominent members, the historian Richard Breyer, refused to endorse the demand for a return to the German borders of 1937, leading to bad blood with the Bund der Vertriebenen.[87] Although this position may appear to be reconciliatory, it was also clear that LWW expellees had little to gain from territorial demands. This political moderation, however, has also meant less potential for material benefit for its members. With fewer resources to mobilize, the LWW has appeared less dynamic than other expellee organizations. Not surprisingly, the LWW has remained one of the smallest and weakest of the member organizations in the Bund der Vertriebenen.[88] In 2006, for example, the LWW did not have its own Internet Web site, unlike those groups with territorial demands or stronger material claims, such as the Sudeten German organization. Still, one might argue that within the landscape of expellee organizations in the Federal Republic of Germany, the LWW played the role of the nationally ambiguous lodzermensch. Already in 1961, and before the first signs of thaw between the West German and Polish states, the LWW used the motto: "The Germans from Poland – Bridge of Understanding."[89] The political changes in Eastern Europe after 1989 gave new impetus to Landsmannschaft Weichsel-Warthe to celebrate itself as a mediator between Poland and Germany.[90] One of its publications, *Der Kulturwart*, carries the subtitle "Contributions to German-Polish Neighborliness."

Despite their postwar dispersal, German expellees from the territory of interwar Poland remained true to the "Volksgruppe paradigm": their political and scholarly organizations have focused on similarities rather than on differences.[91] True, many members of the various Landsmannschaften and especially the LWW (notably Ludwig Wolff) had been activists during

---

86 Jutta Faehndrich, "Erinnerungskultur und Umgang mit Vertreibung in Heimatbüchern deutschsprachiger Vertriebener," *Zeitschrift für Ostmitteleuropa-Forschung* 52, no. 2 (2003): 191–229.

87 Wolfgang Kessler, "Die Lodzer Deutschen nach 1945," in *Między Śląskiem a Wiedniem. Księga Jubileuszowa z okazji 60. urodzin prof. dr. hab. Krzysztofa A. Kuczyńskiego*, ed. Aleksander Kozłowski and Małgorzata Znyk, 329–337 (Płock: Wydawnictwo Naukowej Państwowej Wyższej Szkoły Zawodowej, 2008), here 332.

88 Kessler, "Die Lodzer Deutschen nach 1945," 332–333.

89 Ursula Brehmer, "Die Landsmannschaft Weichsel-Warthe in ihrem Wirken für Versöhnung und Verständigung mit den Polen," in *Polska Środkowa w niemieckich badaniach wschodnich. Historia i współczesność*, ed. Lucjan Meissner, 195–202 (Łódź: Ibidem, 1999), here 198.

90 See for example a recent publication by the LWW: Thora von Bonin, ed., *Von der Konfrontation zur Kooperation. 50 Jahre Landsmannschaft Weichsel-Warthe, Jahresdokumentation 1999 der Landsmannschaft Weichsel-Warthe* (Wiesbaden: Landsmannschaft Weichsel-Warthe, 2000).

91 See Joachim Rogall, "Einheit in Vielfalt der Deutschen aus Polen," in *Archive und Sammlungen der Deutschen aus Polen. Erlebte Geschichte, bewahrtes Kulturgut*, ed. Peter E. Nasarski (Berlin/Bonn: Landsmannschaft Weichsel-Warthe, 1992), 13–18; Wilfried Gerke, "Auf dem Wege zur Einheit.

the interwar period, and they continued after the war to talk the talk of minority unity. Moreover, the political alignments in interwar Polish regions had now lost their salience in the Federal Republic of Germany. Good postwar cooperation has been projected back into the interwar period, reinforcing the idea that a Volksgruppe had already existed then. In this sense, the LWW has continued to function as a minority organization, stressing the familiarity of being amongst those "of our kind."[92]

Even though the turf wars have disappeared, however, regional attitudes and antagonisms remain. Although the Posener Germans dominated the LWW in the early period, Central Polish Germans (such as Richard Breyer) were active members and scholars in the LWW. They continued to act as the Other, positive or otherwise, for their Western Polish counterparts. The former LWW president Gotthold Rhode (a Posener) mentioned how Peter Nasarski and other Lodzers in the LWW were more creative and organizationally talented. Rhode regurgitated the view common in the late 1930s that the Germans from Western Poland remained too dependent on the state for guidance, even in postwar Germany. In contrast, he argued that the grassroots work of the Lodzers, who were used to self-help, had been crucial to the success of the LWW.[93] Such old tropes of difference have been made harmless and humorous. The regionalisms of the interwar period now appear as folkloric anecdotes about dialects and dress.[94] In these ways, the Landsmannschaft Weichsel–Warthe preserved in stasis the divisions of the interwar period while no longer politicizing them. Reflecting interwar power relations, the LWW's press, mainly the *Jahrbuch Weichsel-Warthe* and *Der Kulturwart*, still contains relatively few contributions on Central Poland and Galicia.[95]

In 1950, the Johann Gottfried Herder Research Advisory Council created the Historisch-Landeskundliche Kommission für Posen und das Deutschtum in Polen, which was to serve as the scholarly mouthpiece for issues regarding the German minority in Poland. As with the LWW, there

Die Deutschen in Polen zwischen den Weltkriegen," *Germano-Polonica. Mitteilung zur Geschichte der Deutschen in Polen und der deutsch-polnischen Beziehungen* 2 (2002/2003): 10–17.

92 Fritz Weigelt, ed., *Von unserer Art. Vom Leben und Wirken deutscher Menschen im Raume von Weichsel und Warthe* (Wuppertal: Landsmannschaft Weichsel-Warthe, 1963).

93 Gotthold Rhode, "Lodzer Deutsche – Posener Deutsche. Keine wissenschaftliche Untersuchung, sondern eine Plauderei," in *Suche die Meinung. Karl Dedecius, dem Übersetzer und Mittler zum 65. Geburtstag*, ed. Elvira Grözinger and Andreas Lawaty, 237–256 (Wiesbaden: Harrassowitz, 1986), 249, 254.

94 This romanticized view of current cooperation can be compared to his recollection of his childhood experience of meeting German schoolchildren from Łódź. See Rhode, "Lodzer Deutsche – Posener Deutsche," 254–256.

95 Hans-Werner Rautenberg, "Geschichte und Gegenwart Mittelpolens in der Forschung des Herder-Instituts," in *Polska Środkowa w niemieckich badaniach wschodnich*, 71–89, here 84.

was a discernible dominance of the Posener faction. Although there were some authentic Lodzers such as Richard Breyer and Eugen Oskar Kossmann in the Herder Advisory Council, relatively few works devoted to the Central Polish Germans were produced by the commission. Personal animosities between Lodzers also hurt efforts to create a coherent view of Łódź and its German inhabitants.[96] The name change in 1997 to the Kommission für die Geschichte der Deutschen in Polen made little difference.[97] In the Federal Republic of Germany, historical research on the Germans in Central Poland remained largely outside of the university. The historian Wolfgang Kessler notes that even the more abundant work on Western Poland has been rather amateurish and motivated by personal interest, and the commission itself is run by volunteers because of the lack of funds.[98] Today, most of the research done on Germans in Central Poland is done in Poland.[99] More problematic in expellee politics and research has been the obsession with the wrongs done to the German population – in part a legacy of Ostforschung.[100] As Severin Gawlitta has argued, there was also a functionalist aspect to this focus on German heritage in Poland – it served to unify the very disparate groups that made up expellee groups such as the LWW.[101] As was often the case with expellee accounts, much of the war was erased except for the suffering the Germans themselves faced.[102] This view of the Germans in Poland perpetuated a marginal, even diminishing, Polish and Jewish presence. As Robert Moeller points out, Jews were often an "absent presence" in expellee literature, with their fate structuring how expellees would see themselves.[103] The expellees' nod to Łódź's multiethnic

---

96 Wolfgang Kessler, "Lodz nach Lodz. Beobachtungen zu Erinnerung und Gedächtnis der Deutschen aus Lodz nach 1945," in *Lodz jenseits von Fabriken, Wildwest und Provinz. Kulturwissenschaftliche Studien über die Deutschen in und aus den polnischen Gebieten*, eds. Stefan Dyroff, Krystyna Radziszewska, and Isabel Röskau-Rydel, 151–169 (Munich: Martin Meidenbauer, 2009), here 163.

97 Rautenberg, "Geschichte und Gegenwart Mittelpolens in der Forschung des Herder-Instituts," 79, 81–84.

98 Wolfgang Kessler, "Die Geschichte der Deutschen in Großpolen im Spiegel der deutschen Historiographie nach 1945," in *Doświadczenia przeszłości. Niemcy w Europie Środkowo-Wschodniej w historiografii po 1945 roku = Erfahrungen der Vergangenheit. Deutsche in Ostmitteleuropa in der Historiographie nach 1945*, ed. Jerzy Kłoczowski, Witold Matwiejczyk, and Eduard Mühle, 101–118 (Marburg: Herder-Institut; Lublin: Instytut Europy Środkowo-Wschodniej, 2000), here 104–106.

99 Wolfgang Kessler, "Volksgeschichte oder Regionalgeschichte? Grundlinien der deutschen historischen und heimatkundlichen Forschung über Zentralpolen," in *Polska Środkowa w niemieckich badaniach wschodnich*, 7–20, here 19.

100 Kessler, "Lodz nach Lodz," 155–156, 167.

101 Severin Gawlitta, "Zwischen politischer Legitimation und gesellschaftlicher Integration. Die 'Deutschen Kulturleistungen' in der Publizistik der Deutschen in und aus Mittelpolen 1914–1963," in *Lodz jenseits von Fabriken, Wildwest und Provinz*, 171–188, here 187–188.

102 Bergen, "Tenaciousness and Tenacity," 279.

103 Moeller, *War Stories*, 80, 127.

past in the postwar period was frequent, but it often remained embedded in a Germano-centric narrative.[104]

THE REDISCOVERY OF THE LODZERMENSCH

After the war, the marginal position of the lodzermensch in Polish narratives likewise reflected the physical loss of Łódź's German and Jewish populations. In communist Poland, the lodzermensch remained a symbol of foreign capitalist exploitation. The ideology of class struggle easily combined with traditional resentments against the urban middle class and with national antagonisms against Jews and Germans.[105] Since 1989, Poles and Germans alike have taken an interest in recovering and reinventing Łódź's multiethnic past, and the current revival of the lodzermensch is noticeable in the press and in scholarly works.[106] At the same time, a romanticization of the stereotype is discernible.[107] For various reasons, Łódź continues to be a city of ill-repute, but the lodzermensch itself is no longer associated with contaminated hybridity, but with a marketable multiculturalism and as a model of European reconciliation. Especially Karl Dedecius, the Polish-German translator who was born in Łódź in 1921, has been held up as the quintessential lodzermensch. He attended a Polish high school but served in the Wehrmacht; captured at Stalingrad, he ended up in West Germany after the war and translated Polish poetry at night while working for an insurance firm during the day. In 1980, he established the Deutsches Polen-Institut in Darmstadt and won the Peace Prize of the German Book Trade in 1990. Countless homages have portrayed this "European from Lodz" as instrumental in improving German-Polish relations.[108] A once-despised figure from the ethnic margins, the lodzermensch has been domesticated and assimilated by both Poles and Germans for new political paradigms.

---

104 For a classic example of this German-centric view, see Peter E. Nasarski, ed., *Lodz. Die Stadt der Völkerbegegnung im Wandel der Geschichte* (Cologne-Rodenkirchen: Liebig, 1978).

105 Bianka Pietrow-Ennker, "Ein Klischee lernt das Zwinkern. Der 'Lodzermensch' verkörpert eine Lebensweise, die in Lodz wieder modern wird," *Frankfurter Allgemeine Zeitung*, January 3, 2002, 48.

106 Paweł Samuś, ed., *Polacy–Niemcy–Żydzi w Łodzi w XIX-XX w. Sąsiedzi dalecy i bliscy* (Łódź: Ibidem, 1997); Krystyna Radziszewska, ed., *Niemieckimi śladami po "Ziemi Obiecanej"* (Łódź: Literatura, 1997); Jürgen Hensel, ed., *Polen, Deutsche und Juden in Lodz 1820–1939. Eine schwierige Nachbarschaft* (Osnabrück: Fibre, 1999); Thomas Roser, "Der Mythos vom gelobten Land. Das polnische Lodz galt einst als 'Manchester des Ostens' – und hegt jetzt die Hoffnung auf ein Comeback," *Frankfurter Rundschau*, April 12, 2002, 6; Pietrow-Ennker, "Ein Klischee lernt das Zwinkern," 48; see also various works by Thomas Fuchs and Krzysztof Woźniak.

107 An example of this romanticization can be found in the last paragraph of Krystyna Radziszewska, "Die Schulpolitik der Zweiten Polnischen Republik gegenüber der deutschen Minderheit am Beispiel der Stadt Lodz," *Germano-Polonica. Mitteilungen zur Geschichte der Deutschen in Polen und der deutsch-polnischen Beziehungen* 2 (2002/2003): 18–26.

108 This term appears as the title of Dedecius's autobiography, *Ein Europäer aus Lodz*.

Conclusion

After the Polish referendum for joining the European Union in June 2003, in which the majority voted yes despite a sizable anti-EU coalition, the Polish newsweekly *Polityka* noted a curious thing. In an article titled "The New Partition of Poland," it was shown that regional variations in voting behavior coincided with the historical borders of the partitions. The areas including Poznania, Pomerelia, and Upper Silesia had a markedly higher voter turnout than elsewhere in Poland – almost all the formerly Prussian Polish districts (*gminy*) registered more than 50 percent turnout, and in many it was as high as 70 percent. The author, a sociologist, attributed the difference to the Prussian heritage of the Poles in the region: their political culture could boast a longer history of public and democratic participation that stretched back to Imperial Germany.[1] The legacy of "practicing democracy" in the Wilhelmine period was not easy to eradicate even within the Polish population.[2]

The collusion of history and geography made itself felt in other ways as well. West of the traditional Prussian Polish regions of Poznania, Pomerelia, and eastern Upper Silesia were the so-called recovered lands (*ziemie odzyskane*), which Poland had acquired after the Second World War. The main cities in these regions are Wrocław (Breslau) in Lower Silesia and Szczecin (Stettin) in Pomerania. Here, in what had been Poland's Wild West in the postwar period, Poles were less apt to vote, but if they did, they voted overwhelmingly in favor of the EU. With the exception of the cities and Upper Silesia, the percentage of yes votes in the recovered territories

---

1 Jacek Żakowski, "Nowy rozbiór Polski. Granice rozbiorów pokrywają się z granicami poparcia dla Unii," *Polityka*, June 24, 2003, 32–33.
2 On German democratic culture before the First World War, see Margaret Lavinia Anderson, *Practicing Democracy: Elections and Political Culture in Imperial Germany* (Princeton: Princeton University Press, 2000), 426–429.

was even higher than in the traditional Prussian Polish regions (roughly 50 to 70 percent). The author offered the following explanation for this apparent paradox: the lower voter turnout was attributed to a backward eastern mentality of the Polish population, almost all of whom were expellees or their descendants from the eastern territories (*kresy*) lost by Poland after the Second World War. At the same time, he attributed the higher proportion of pro-EU votes to the migrant outlook of this newly settled population and their propensity to take risks. The author came to the conclusion that Poland, a country lacking substantial capital and large companies, was not necessarily uncompetitive in the European Union or on the world stage.[3] If the partitions continued to play a role in shaping Polish politics after eighty years, their impact on German minorities in interwar Poland had been even more immediate and divisive. In both cases, the fetishization of regional differences resulted in part from the frustration of not having overcome these cleavages within the national community.

This study sought to explain how variations of nationalism contributed to the persistence and dynamism of regional distinctiveness. While the territories lost to Poland remained a kind of lost limb for the Reich, old boundaries between Germany, Russia, and Austria were revived as phantom borders in their own right. Especially important was the strong interest of Reich authorities and civil groups in the Western Polish Germans, who were seen not just as lost ethnic brothers but also as former citizens. Likewise, these phantom Germans also claimed privileges vis-à-vis the German state and enjoyed a kind of Reich social membership. The relative neglect of the non-Prussian regions of Poland highlights Weimar Germany's largely etatist approach to the minority question. This distinction becomes even clearer when the distribution of Reich funds within Poland is examined. The considerable aid for the Germans in Western Poland was a show of solidarity for an older state community, not necessarily for an ethnic one.

Especially the differences in possible outcomes activated and exacerbated regional cleavages within the minority. The return-to-homeland politics of the Germans in Western Poland, their residual citizenship, and their compensatory Reichness came into conflict with the goals of building a unified minority in Poland. The revisionism of the Germans in Western Poland focused on their own regional chances for returning to the Reich. If the Germans in Western Poland successfully exited from the Polish state, however, the German activists in Central and Eastern Poland would have been almost certainly left behind and would have then been in a weaker

---

3 Żakowski, "Nowy rozbiór Polski," 32–33.

position than before. For the entire interwar period, these conflicting long-term interests between the borderland and the diaspora Germans could not be overcome.

The politics of territorial revision also deeply influenced the German minority in Poland by creating a regional constellation with centers and peripheries. German-speakers in non-Prussian Poland, having never been German citizens and not residing in the strategically important regions of Western Poland, were often seen as indifferent or even suspect to the German cause. A form of social racism that stigmatized the periphery as somehow less German underpinned this hierarchy of Germanness. In the 1920s and early 1930s, the constant stereotyping of the Łódź Germans as national renegades resulted in the ideological creation of an underclass within the supposed community of Germans in Poland. At the same time, the denigration of this periphery was essential for mobilizing the minority as a whole, for the lodzermensch was an awful warning of the cultural contamination that could result from too little resistance to a foreign environment. The supposedly asocial behavior of the Łódź Germans was all the more dangerous to the German minority because it coincided with the external threat represented by the Polish government and society. Although many peripheral Germans joined nationalist movements, the stigmatization and the growing sense of disenfranchisement fostered a sense of regional distinctiveness. At the same time, the clear dominance of the German leaders in the Western Polish regions hindered open conflict within the minority in the 1920s. Thus, the hierarchization of the German in-group was important for stabilizing minority politics in Poland.

The situational nature and tenuousness stability of this hierarchy became apparent in the early 1930s, however, when demographic and political changes reshuffled the deck of Germanness and undermined the privileged position of the Western Polish Germans. By strengthening the periphery vis-à-vis the center, the easternization of the minority meant a dispersal of power that slowly emancipated the Germans in Central and Eastern Poland from the tutelage of the Germans in Western Poland. The Jungdeutsche Partei from formerly Austrian Bielsko played the midwife in this process. Despite its ultimate failure to become the main party for the Germans in Poland, the JDP was itself proof of an energetic challenge emanating from non-Prussian Poland. Its constant vilification of the Western Polish-dominated minority system and its veneration of a Volksgemeinschaft that would give all regions a voice empowered Polish German leaders on the periphery. The raised expectations led to a political assertiveness, but it also led to an increased awareness of regional alignments and their persistence.

This book has demonstrated that the salience of place grew especially in hypernationalist settings. Nationhood was not merely transmitted from the center to the periphery, but the margins were constructing their own version(s) of what the nation should be. Ideological changes, instrumentalized by actors in the Reich and in Poland, were important in this process. Especially the reinterpretation of Germany's foreign policy objectives and the shift in privileging race over space resulted in the increased appreciation of the Germans in Łódź and Central Poland. By the late 1930s, a growing number of German authorities and nationalists considered the Łódź German to be a pure and savvy ethnic survivor. This reconsideration of what constituted being a good German allowed Central Polish German activists to rerank themselves within the hierarchy of regions. Politically active Germans in Central Poland on the ground rallied not behind the supraregional JDP, but behind their own regional party. Through these multiple challenges emanating from the East, the Germans in the Western Polish regions increasingly appeared weak and incapable of upholding German interests. Reich authorities demanded that Germans in Western Poland stop being irredentist in their outlook and become more like the Germans in Central Poland. The established hierarchy was undermined without creating a new one, however, and the exacerbated regional tensions resulted in a leadership dilemma that lasted until the end of the interwar period.

The common acceptance of Nazism by minority activists did little to lessen or transcend the latent regional divisions; it merely activated and dynamicized them further. Nazi discourse deepened the schisms within the minority precisely because its often egalitarian message promoted unrealistically high expectations of solidarity that conflicted with the political interests of regional leaders. Especially the concept of Volksgemeinschaft became a site of constant negotiation and power struggle, where competing notions of Germanness were legitimated and instrumentalized. It empowered peripheral groups and opened new space for them to make claims on national goods. German leaders in Poland did less adapting to National Socialism than the selective adopting of National Socialist tenets. They were able to synthesize prevailing ideological considerations with their own concrete interests, often in ways quite frustrating to their Reich caregivers. Even the most Nazi-oriented of minority activists who publicly advocated unifying the Germans in Poland ultimately found themselves to be stakeholders in the system of regional parties. When authorities in Germany sponsored and supported attempts at unification, their efforts failed or even backfired. Hardly dependent vassals of the German state, minority leaders enjoyed a relationship of give and take with state and party organizations in

Germany; each side exploited differences when opportune. In this way, the competing groups within the minority were also able to redefine what it meant to be German in the East – with all the fateful consequences in the Second World War.

The competition of regions in interwar Poland was influenced by the relationship of minority activists to their host state as well as to their purported ethnic homeland. These states, in turn, informed the kind of nationalism that the regional actors espoused. In contrast to the narrative of Volksgruppe and Volkstumskampf, Polish repression did not necessarily facilitate political unification or even solidarity within the German minority in Poland. Rather, the Polish government increasingly politicized existing organizational and personal rivalries, helping to cement regional alignments. Still, German minority leaders were not as powerless against the Polish state as they often claimed, and they took part in local and national politics with considerable success in the 1920s. In the honeymoon period after the 1934 German–Polish non-aggression pact, the increasing mobilization of Germans in Poland did not translate to more unity. As one German consul suggested, it was regrettable that these Germans enjoyed "too much freedom of opinion" in the Polish political system.[4] German minority activists enlisted Polish aid to muzzle their opponents, driving competing Nazi-oriented German parties to outdo one another in their proclamations of loyalty to Poland. The oft-pronounced national awakening of the Germans in Poland may have well happened, but the antagonists in the project for German unity were not necessarily the Poles.

This book has shown why the search for regional distinctiveness was so persistent among German national activists and how they used these discourses of difference. In interwar Poland, German minority activists insisted on presenting a united front, but they failed to do so not just vis-à-vis the Polish government but also to Reich authorities. By reframing the activity of the German parties in terms of their *regional interests* (and not a purported national self-defense vis-à-vis the Poles), this study has attempted to provide a nuanced picture of crosscutting loyalties within a national minority. By examining the origins, nature, and reproduction of territorial distinctiveness as well as their interplay with ethnic mobilization, we can better understand the radicalization and limits of Central European nationalisms in the twentieth century.

4 Richard Blanke, *Orphans of Versailles: The Germans in Western Poland, 1918–1939* (Lexington: University Press of Kentucky, 1993), 180.

Bibliography

Key to Archives and Collections

Archives in Poland

AAN   Archiwum Akt Nowych
(Central Archives of Modern Records in Warsaw)
Ministerstwo Spraw Wewnętrznych (MSW)
971   Wydział Narodowościowy – Komunikaty dzienne Wydziału
      Narodowościowego M.S.W. (1939)
1003 Wydział Narodowościowy – Korespondencja w sprawach organizacji i
      działalności "Deutscher Kultur- und Wirtschaftsbund" w Polsce
      (1931–1934)
1005 Wydział Narodowościowy – Materiały w sprawie organizacji i działalności
      "Jungdeutsche Partei" (1936–1939)

Ministerstwo Spraw Zagranicznych (MSZ)
2234 Mniejszość w Polsce. Raport, petycje, notatki, korespondencja, druki,
      wycinki prasowe (1930, 1931)
2238 Mniejszość niemiecka w Polsce. Działalność organizacji i szkolnictwa.
      Sprawozdania, notatki, korespondencja, wyrok przeciw NSDAP w Polsce
      (1936)
2348 Sprawozdania o ruchu mniejszościowym w Polsce: głównie komunikaty
      Ministerstwo Spraw Wewnętrznych (1934, 1935) [reports mostly from
      1936]
2352 Sprawozdania o ruchu mniejszościowym w Polsce: głównie komunikaty
      Ministerstwo Spraw Wewnętrznych (1938)

AP Bydgoszcz   Archiwum Państwowe w Bydgoszczy
(State Archive in Bydgoszcz)
Urząd Wojewódzki Pomorski
2788 Urząd Województwo Pomorza w Toruniu. Wydział Społeczno-Polityczny.
      Sprawy organizacji niemieckich w Polsce i na Pomorzu, 1933–1936

AP Katowice   Archiwum Państwowe w Katowicach
(State Archive in Katowice)
Dyrekcja Policji w Katowicach
310   Rat der Deutschen in Polen – Akta informacyjne
312   Deutscher Arbeitskreis-Niemieckie Koło Pracy – stow. zwykłe z siedzibą w
Katowicach
Policja Województwa Śląskiego 1922–1939
197   Niemieckie partie i stowarzyszenia: Informacje o działalności

AP Łódź   Archiwum Państwowe w Łodzi
(State Archive in Łódź)
Urząd Wojewódzki Łódzki
2507 a–p   Miesięczne sprawozdanie wojewody z ruchu zawodowego,
politycznego i narodowościowego, 1926–1939

AP Poznań   Archiwum Państwowe w Poznaniu
(State Archive in Poznań)
Urząd Wojewódzki Poznański
5569–5725   Sprawozdania z życia mniejszości narodowych, 1922/1939

Archives in Germany

PAAA   Politisches Archiv des Auswärtigen Amts
(Political Archive of the Federal Foreign Office, Bonn/Berlin)
Abteilung IV
Politik 12D Polen   Pressewesen: "Wolhynischer Bote," vols. 1–7, 1927–1928,
R82083–82089
Politik 25 Polen   Deutschtum im Ausland (Polen), vols. 1–37, 1920–1936,
R82180–82217

Abteilung IV-Geheimakten
Politik 25 Polen   Deutschtum im Ausland, vols. 1–9, 1920–1936,
R30860–30868

Abteilung V
Politik 25 Polen   Deutschtum in Polen, vols. 1–11, 1936–1941,
R104198–104208

Inland II Geheim
Geheime Verschlußsachen des Referats Kult. A, vols. 1–27 (220–226), 1935–1941

Botschaft Warschau
PI 2e   Tod des Marschalls Pilsudski, vol. 1, 1935–1936
PIII 9i   Olsagebiet, 1939

BA Berlin   Bundesarchiv Berlin
(Federal Archive in Berlin)
R58   Reichssicherheitshauptamt
Folder 149   Meldungen aus dem Reich, March 1–29, 1940

Folder 154   Meldungen aus dem Reich, September 2–30, 1940
Folder 155   Meldungen aus dem Reich, October 3–31, 1940

R8043   Deutsche Stiftung
Folder 940   Kongreßpolen 1927
              April 1927–March 1928
Folder 941   Kongreßpolen 1928, 1929, 1930
              April 1928–March 1931
Folder 942   Kongreßpolen 1931, 1932, 1933
              April 1931–September 1933
Folder 943   Kongreßpolen 1933–1937
              September 1933–March 1938 [pages 260–572, circa September
              1933 to November 1935, are on microfilm reel 62662]
Folder 944   Kongreßpolen 1938, 1939
              April 1938–February 1940
Folder 945   Wolhynien 1926, 1927
              December 1926–March 1938
Folder 946   Wolhynien 1928–1937
              August 1928–March 1938
Folder 947   Wolhynien 1938, 1939
              April 1938–December 1940

BDC   Former Berlin Document Center
SS-O und RS
Partei-Kanzlei

**BA Koblenz   Bundesarchiv Koblenz
                (Federal Archive in Koblenz)**
R57   Deutsches Ausland-Institut
0164   Reiseberichte Dr. Könekamp, Dr. Quiring, Dr. Rüdiger, Dr.
              Stumpp, Korrespondenz O.B. Strölin betr. Nachrichtenstelle
              Dokumentation, 1939–1942
1050   Länder-Berichte
1386   Reiseberichte

R57-Neu   Deutsches Ausland-Institut
0627   Tätigkeit des Dr. W. Gradmann bei der Einwandererzentralstelle
              Litzmannstadt
1093–21   Jungdeutsche Partei für Polen in Bielitz 1934–1937
1094–1   Deutsche Vereinigung, Landesverband Bromberg 1926–1938

**GStA   Geheimes Staatsarchiv Preußischer Kulturbesitz
          (Secret State Archives, Prussian Cultural Heritage)**
I HA   *Hauptabteilung I: Alte und neue Reposituren*
Rep. 77   Ministerium des Innern, Abteilung II – Ost-West Abteilung
Tit. 856   Dt.-poln. Angelegenheiten
31–33   Schutz der Deutschen in Polen, 3 vols., 1919–1933
253   Weiterzahlung von Reichs- und staatlichen Mitteln in den
              abgetrennten Gebieten, 1919–1927

317	Auslanddeutschtum – Zeitungsausschnitte, 1.5.29 bis 30.4.33
325	Unterdrückung Deutscher in Polen – Zeitungsausschnitte, 1929–1932
610	Verfolgung der deutschen Organisationen in Polen, 1923–1933
752	Auseinandersetzungen innerhalb der deutschen Minderheit in Polen, Zeitungsausschnitte, 30.8.33 bis 31.3.35
753	Auseinandersetzungen innerhalb der deutschen Minderheit in Polen – Zeitungsausschnitte, 1.4.35 bis 31.10.35

Tit. 4032	Minderheitenprobleme und Minderheiten in Deutschland
15	Deutschtum im Auslande (Minderheitenfragen), 18.10.24–31.12.29

Archives in the United States

USHMM	**United States Holocaust Memorial Museum**
RG-05.008M	Stadtverwaltung Litzmannstadt
Reel 1	Folder 31 Berichte über den Aufbau von Litzmannstadt (Bürgermeister und Stadtkammerer), 1940–1944
Reel 1	Folder 32 Handakten für den Bürgermeister (Gettoverwaltung), 1940–1943
Reel 2	Folder 72 Abschriften des Schriftverkehrs (Vorzimmer Stadtdirektor), 1941
Reel 3	Folder 126 Lageberichte der Stadtämter (Haupt- und Organisationsamt, Statistisches Amt), 1940–1944
Reel 3	Folder 138 Monatsberichte der Stadt Litzmannstadt, 1940
Reel 3	Folder 139 Vierteljahresberichte und Prüfungsberichte (Haupt- und Organisationsamt), 1940–1943

Periodicals

Bielitz-Bialer Deutsche Zeitung
Deutsche Blätter in Polen
Deutsche Monatshefte in Polen
Deutscher Volksbote
Freie Presse
Jomsburg. Völker und Staaten im Osten und Norden Europas
Sprawy Narodowościowe
Vergangenheit und Gegenwart
Der Volksfreund

Published Sources

ADAP = Auswärtiges Amt (Federal Republic of Germany). *Akten zur deutschen auswärtigen Politik, 1918–45.* Göttingen: Vandenhoeck & Ruprecht, c. 1966–1982. Series A (1918–1925); series B (1925–1933); series C (1933–1936); series D (1937–1945).

Fröhlich, Elke, ed. *Die Tagebücher von Joseph Goebbels.* Vol. 1, no. 7. Munich: Saur, 1998.

Jacobsen, Hans-Adolf, ed. *Hans Steinacher, Bundesleiter des VDA 1933–1937. Erinnerungen und Dokumente.* Boppard am Rhein: Boldt, 1970.

Jaworski, Rudolf, Marian Wojciechowski, Mathias Niendorf, and Przemysław Hauser, eds. *Deutsche und Polen zwischen den Kriegen. Minderheitenstatus und "Volkstumskampf" im Grenzgebiet. Amtliche Berichterstattung aus beiden Ländern, 1920–1939.* 2 vols. Munich: Saur, 1997.

Taylor, Fred, ed. and trans. *The Goebbels Diaries, 1939–1941.* London: Hamish Hamilton, 1982.

Publications before 1945

Auswärtiges Amt (Deutsches Reich). *Dokumente zur Vorgeschichte des Krieges.* Berlin: Carl Heymanns, 1939.

————. *Urkunden zur letzten Phase der deutsch-polnischen Krise.* Berlin: Reichsdruckerei, 1939.

Althaus, Paul. "Die Entdeckung des Deutschtums im ehemaligen Mittelpolen." In *Deutschtum im Aufbruch. Vom Volkstumskampf der Deutschen im östlichen Wartheland,* edited by Adolf Kargel and Eduard Kneifel, 191–197. Leipzig: S. Hirzel, 1942.

Bahr, Richard. *Volk jenseits der Grenzen. Geschichte und Problematik der deutschen Minderheiten.* 2nd ed. Hamburg: Hanseatische Verlagsanstalt, 1933.

Bartkiewicz, Zygmunt. *Złe miasto. Obrazy z 1907 roku.* Warsaw: Nakł. Jana Czempińskiego, 1911.

————. *Trzy opowieści.* Warsaw: Dom Książki Polskiej, 1930.

Behrens, Eduard von. "Das Deutschtum in Kongreßpolen." In "Vom Deutschtum in Kongreßpolen I." Special issue, *Deutsche Blätter in Polen* 1, no. 5 (1924): 199–203.

Beyer, Hans Joachim. "Mittelpolen in der neueren deutschen Volksgeschichte." *Vergangenheit und Gegenwart* 29, nos. 9-10 (1939): 510–524.

Boehm, Max Hildebert. *Europa Irredenta. Eine Einführung in das Nationalitätenproblem der Gegenwart.* Berlin: Reimar Hobbing, 1923.

————. *Die deutschen Grenzlande.* Berlin: Reimar Hobbing, 1925.

————. *Grenzdeutsch–Großdeutsch. Vortrag anläßlich der Hauptausschußtagung des V.D.A. im November 1924.* Dresden: Verein für das Deutschtum im Ausland, 1925.

Boehm, Max Hildebert and Karl C. von Loesch, eds. *Der befreite Osten.* Berlin: Hofmeyer, 1943.

Borse, D. "Der Deutsche Schul- und Bildungsverein zu Lodz." *Deutsche Blätter in Polen* 8, nos. 8-9 (1931): 470–471.

Breyer, Albert. "Neuerscheinungen im Deutschen Schrifttum Mittelpolens (1925–1930)." *Deutsche Blätter in Polen* 8, no. 4 (1931): 227–230.

————. "Das Deutschtum in Mittelpolen. Bemerkungen zu der anliegenden Karte." *Jomsburg. Völker und Staaten im Osten und Norden Europas* 2 (1938): 74–77.

Burchard, Walther Th. "Vom kommenden ständischen Aufbau der deutschen Minderheit in Polen." *Deutsche Blätter in Polen* 2, no. 2 (1925): 66–72.

————. "Weichselkolonisten." *Deutsche Blätter in Polen* 2, no. 5 (1925): 278–295.

Eichler, Adolf. *Das Deutschtum in Kongreßpolen.* Stuttgart: Ausland und Heimat Verlags-Aktiengesellschaft, 1921.

————. "Die nationale Selbstbehauptung der Lodzer Deutschen." In "Vom Deutschtum in Kongreßpolen I." Special issue, *Deutsche Blätter in Polen* 1, no. 5 (1924): 193–198.

En Plattdütscher [pseud.]. "Die Weichselkolonisten." In "Vom Deutschtum in Kongreßpolen I." Special issue, *Deutsche Blätter in Polen* 1, no. 5 (1924): 203–205.

Gissibl, Fritz. "Der Osten des Warthelandes." In *Der Osten des Warthelandes. Herausgegeben anläßlich der Heimatschau in Litzmannstadt*, edited by Hubert Müller, 14–16. Stuttgart: Stähle & Friedel, 1941.

Gorski, Stefan. *Łódź Spółczesna. Obrazki i szkice publicystyczne.* Łódź: Księg. Narodowa, 1904.

Gostyński, Karol. "Zarys historii politycznej Niemców w województwach zachodnich po wojnie." In "Problem niemiecki na Ziemiach Zachodnich." Special issue, *Strażnica Zachodnia* 12, nos. 1–2 (1933): 45–81.

———. "Przewrót Hitlerowski w Niemczech i Niemcy w Polsce (Część pierwsza)." *Sprawy Narodowościowe* 10, nos. 1–2, (1936): 22–39.

———. "Przewrót Hitlerowski w Niemczech i Niemcy w Polsce (Dokończenie)." *Sprawy Narodowościowe* 10, no. 3 (1936): 197–222.

Gradmann, Wilhelm. "Litzmannstadt – Mittelpunkt der Umsiedlung." *Deutschtum im Ausland* 25, nos. 1-2 (1942): 12–16.

Hansen, Ernst. *Polens Drang nach dem Westen*. Berlin: Koehler, 1927.

Heidelck, Friedrich. "Die Stellung des Deutschtums in Polen. Kritische Untersuchungen zu Zygmunt Stoliński. *Die deutsche Minderheit in Polen." Deutsche Blätter in Polen* 6, no. 2 (1929): 49–104.

———. *Die deutschen Ansiedlungen in Westpreußen und Posen in den ersten zwölf Jahren der polnischen Herrschaft.* Breslau: Priebatsch, 1934.

Heiss, Friedrich, and A. Hillen Ziegfeld. *Deutschland und der Korridor.* Berlin: Volk und Reich Verlag, 1933.

Jungdeutsche Partei für Polen, ed. *Reden und Berichte vom Parteitag 1934.* 2nd ed. Bielsko: Jungdeutsche Partei für Polen, 1934.

Kammel, Richard [Gottfried Martin, pseud.]. *"Brennende Wunden." Tatsachenbericht über die Notlage der evangelischen Deutschen in Polen.* Berlin: Eckart, 1931.

Karasek, Alfred, and Kurt Lück, eds. *Die deutschen Siedlungen in Wolhynien. Geschichte, Volkskunde, Lebensfragen.* Leipzig: Hirzel, 1931.

Karge, Fritz. "Die Geschichte des deutschen Ostraums im Unterricht der Mittelstufe. Eine Längsschnittdarstellung." *Vergangenheit und Gegenwart* 28, no. 2 (1938): 79–94.

Kargel, Adolf, and Eduard Kneifel. *Deutschtum im Aufbruch. Vom Volkstumskampf der Deutschen im östlichen Wartheland.* Leipzig: Hirzel, 1942.

Kauder, Viktor. "Vorwort." In *Die deutschen Siedlungen in Wolhynien. Geschichte, Volkskunde, Lebensfragen*, edited by Alfred Karasek and Kurt Lück. Leipzig: Hirzel, 1931.

———. "Blick in die Zeit." *Deutsche Monatshefte in Polen* 1 (11), no. 1 (1934): 1–4.

———. "Grundlagen volksdeutscher Politik in Polen." *Deutsche Monatshefte in Polen* 1 (11), no. 3 (1934): 75–78.

———. "Mutterland und Auslanddeutschtum." *Deutsche Monatshefte in Polen* 2 (12), no. 3 (1935): 79–84.

———. *Das Deutschtum in Posen und Pommerellen.* Vol. 3 of *Das Deutschtum in Polen. Ein Bildband*, edited by Viktor Kauder. Leipzig: Hirzel, 1937.

———. *Das Deutschtum in Ostpolen.* Vol. 5 of *Das Deutschtum in Polen. Ein Bildband*, edited by Viktor Kauder. Leipzig: Hirzel, 1939.

Keyser, Erich. "Der Deutschtumsverlust in Westpreußen 1918–1939." *Ostdeutsche Wissenschaft* 8 (1961): 63–79.

Kneifel, Eduard. "Adolf Eichler – Ein Leben im Dienste des Deutschtums." In *Deutschtum im Aufbruch. Vom Volkstumskampf der Deutschen im östlichen Wartheland*, edited by Adolf Kargel and Eduard Kneifel, 11–32. Leipzig: Hirzel, 1942.

Kohnert, Hans. *Dr. Kohnert spricht. Zwei Reden an die Delegierten der Deutschen Vereinigung.* Bydgoszcz: Deutsche Vereinigung, 1936.

Kohnert, Hans, and Gero von Gersdorff, eds. *Wille zur Einheit. Reden und Aufsätze. Eine Schrift der Deutschen Vereinigung.* Bydgoszcz: Deutsche Vereinigung, 1937.

Kossmann, Eugen Oskar. "Deutsche auf Lodzer Boden." *Deutsche Monatshefte in Polen* 2 (12), nos. 1–2 (1936): 58–76.

Krajna, Franciszek. *Katalog Prasowy PARa. Rocznik IX 1934–35.* Poznań: Polska Agencja Reklamy, 1934–1935.

Kuhn, Walter. "Versuch einer Naturgeschichte der deutschen Sprachinsel." *Deutsche Blätter in Polen* 3, no. 2 (February 1926): 65–140.

———. "Kirche und Schule." *Deutsche Blätter in Polen* 3, nos. 11-12 (1926): 613–629.

———. "Wege und Ziele ostlanddeutscher Heimatforschung." *Deutsche Blätter in Polen* 3, no. 7 (1926): 368–380.

——— [Andreas Mückler, pseud.]. *Das Deutschtum Kongreßpolens. Eine Statistisch-Kritische Studie.* Leipzig/Vienna: Franz Deuticke, 1927.

———. "Statistik der Volksbildung bei den Deutschen Wolhyniens." In *Die deutschen Siedlungen in Wolhynien. Geschichte, Volkskunde, Lebensfragen*, edited by Alfred Karasek and Kurt Lück, 32–41. Leipzig: Hirzel, 1931.

———. "Das Deutschtum in Kongreßpolen und Ungarn. Ein sprachinselkundlicher Vergleich." *Deutsche Monatshefte in Polen* 1, no. 1 (1934): 5–14.

Lattermann, Alfred. "Deutsche Forschung im ehemaligen Polen 1919–1939." In *Deutsche Ostforschung. Ergebnisse und Aufgaben seit dem ersten Weltkrieg*, edited by Hermann Aubin, Otto Brunner, Wolfgang Kohte, and Johannes Papritz, 461–487. Leipzig: Hirzel, 1943.

Loesch, Karl C. von. "Polnische Ausrottungspolitik." In *Der befreite Osten*, edited by Max Hildebert Boehm and Karl C. von Loesch, 50–86. Berlin: Hofmeyer, 1943.

Lück, Kurt. "Das Deutschtum innerhalb der Bevölkerung Wolhyniens." *Deutsche Blätter in Polen* 3, nos. 11–12 (1926): 521–529.

———. "Um die Reinheit unserer Muttersprache." In *Die deutschen Siedlungen in Wolhynien. Geschichte, Volkskunde, Lebensfragen*, edited by Alfred Karasek and Kurt Lück, 45–48. Leipzig: Hirzel, 1931.

———. "Deutsches Wesen im Spiegel der polnischen Literatur und Volksüberlieferung." *Deutsche Monatshefte in Polen* 2 (12), no. 8 (1936): 307–318.

———, ed. *Marsch der Deutschen in Polen. Deutsche Volksgenossen im ehemaligen Polen berichten über Erlebnisse in den Septembertagen 1939.* Berlin: Grenze und Ausland, 1940.

Marder, Karl. "Aus Lodsch wird Litzmannstadt." In *Der Osten des Warthelandes. Herausgegeben anläßlich der Heimatschau in Litzmannstadt*, edited by Hubert Müller, 264–278. Stuttgart: Stähle & Friedel, 1941.

Markgraf, [Horst]. "Litzmannstadt und seine Wirtschaft. Rückblick auf 120 Jahre deutschen Gewerbeschaffens." In *Der Osten des Warthelandes. Herausgegeben anläßlich der Heimatschau in Litzmannstadt,* edited by Hubert Müller, 50–77. Stuttgart: Stähle & Friedel, 1941.

Męclewski, Edmund. *Walka graniczna trwa.* Poznań: Gospodarka Zachodnia, 1939.

Monens, Erich. "Wir Deutschen in Polen. Ein Querschnitt durch die rechtlichen und moralischen Grundlagen unseres Volkskörpers, seine Nöte und Kämpfe." *Deutsche Blätter in Polen* 3, no. 1 (1926): 23–42.

Müller, Hubert, ed. *Der Osten des Warthelandes. Herausgegeben anläßlich der Heimatschau in Litzmannstadt.* Stuttgart: Stähle & Friedel, 1941.

Oberländer, Theodor. "Die wirtschaftliche Notlage der früher preußischen Provinzen Posen und Westpreußen." *Jomsburg. Völker und Staaten im Osten und Norden Europas* 1 (1937): 143–54.

Papen, Franz von. *Volksdeutscher Durchbruch. Aufrufe und Bekenntnisse zur gesamtdeutschen Verbundenheit.* Berlin: VDA, 1934.

Penck, Albrecht. "Deutscher Volks- und Kulturboden." In *Volk unter Völkern,* edited by Karl C. von Loesch and A. Hillen Ziegfeld, 62–73. Breslau: Hirt, 1925.

Rauschning, Hermann. "Zur Einführung." In "Vom Deutschtum in Kongreßpolen I." Special issue, *Deutsche Blätter in Polen* 1, no. 5 (1924): 190–193.

———. *Die Entdeutschung Westpreussens und Posens. Zehn Jahre polnischer Politik.* Berlin: Reimar Hobbing, 1930.

Reiners, Johann. "Von der Struktur des Deutschtums in Polen." In "Ständischer Aufbau." Special issue, *Deutsche Blätter in Polen* 2, no. 1 (January 1925): 18–34.

Schacht, Horand Horsa. *Du mußt volksdeutsch sein!* Dortmund: Crüwell, 1935.

Smogorzewski, Kazimierz. "Czy dziejowy zwrot w stosunkach polskoniemieckich?" *Strażnica Zachodnia* 12, no. 4 (1933): 447–477.

Spitzer, Erich. *Wir schmieden die Zukunft. Der Kampf der "Jungdeutschen Partei" in Posen-Pommerellen.* Bydgoszcz: Geschäftsstelle Bromberg der JDP, 1935.

Stoliński, Zygmunt. *Liczba i rozmieszczenie Niemców w Polsce.* Warsaw: Wydawnictwo Instytutu Badań Spraw Narodowościowych, 1927.

———. *Die deutsche Minderheit in Polen.* Warsaw: Instytut Badań Spraw Narodowościowych, 1928.

T.R. "Innere Zerrissenheit." In "Vom Deutschtum in Kongreßpolen II." Special issue, *Deutsche Blätter in Polen* 2, no. 3 (1925): 109–113.

Volz, Wilhelm, ed. *Der ostdeutsche Volksboden. Aufsätze zu den Fragen des Ostens.* Breslau: Hirt, 1926.

"Von Wolhynien nach Bereza Kartuska. Erzählt von wolhynischen Kolonisten." In *Marsch der Deutschen in Polen. Deutsche Volksgenossen im ehemaligen Polen berichten über Erlebnisse in den Septembertagen 1939,* edited by Kurt Lück, 103–106. Berlin: Grenze und Ausland, 1940.

Weber, Karl. *Litzmannstadt. Geschichte und Probleme eines Wirtschaftszentrums im deutschen Osten.* Jena: Fischer, 1943.

Wertheimer, Fritz. *Von deutschen Parteien und Parteiführern im Ausland.* 2nd ed. Berlin: Zentral-Verlag, 1930.

Winiewicz, Józef. *Mobilizacja sił niemieckich w Polsce.* Warsaw: Polityka, 1939.

Wolff, Ludwig. "Der Volkstumskampf des Deutschtums im Osten des Warthe-landes." In *Der Osten des Warthelandes. Herausgegeben anläßlich der Heimatschau in Litzmannstadt*, edited by Hubert Müller. Stuttgart: Stähle & Friedel, 1941.

Publications after 1945

Alberti, Michael. *Die Verfolgung und Vernichtung der Juden im Reichsgau Wartheland 1939–1945*. Wiesbaden: Harrassowitz, 2006.

Alexander, Manfred. "Oberschlesien im 20. Jahrhundert – eine mißverstandene Region." *Geschichte und Gesellschaft* 30, no. 3 (2004): 465–489.

Aly, Götz. "Rückwärtsgewandte Propheten – Bemerkungen in eigener Sache." In *Macht–Geist–Wahn. Kontinuitäten deutschen Denkens*, 153–183. Berlin: Argon, 1997.

Ambrosio, Thomas. "Irredentism: Self-Determination and Interstate War." In *International Law and the Rise of Nations. The State System and the Challenge of Ethnic Groups*, edited by Robert J. Beck and Thomas Ambrosio, 284–312. New York/London: Chatham House, 2002.

Anderson, Benedict. *Imagined Communities: Reflections on the Origins and Spread of Nationalism*. London/New York: Verso, 2006.

Anderson, Margaret Lavinia. *Practicing Democracy: Elections and Political Culture in Imperial Germany*. Princeton: Princeton University Press, 2000.

Applegate, Celia. *A Nation of Provincials: The German Idea of Heimat*. Berkeley: University of California Press, 1990.

————. "A Europe of Regions: Reflections on the Historiography of Sub-National Places in Modern Times." *American Historical Review* (1999): 1157–1182.

Arnold, Georg. *Gustav Stresemann und die Problematik der deutschen Ostgrenzen*. Peter Lang: Frankfurt/Main, 2000.

Baechler, Christian. *Gustave Stresemann (1878–1929). De l'impérialisme à la sécurité collective*. Strasbourg: Presses Universitaires de Strasbourg, 1996.

Balling, Mads Ole. *Von Reval bis Bukarest. Statistisch-Biographisches Handbuch der Parlamentarier der deutschen Minderheiten in Ostmittel- und Südosteuropa 1919–1945*. 2 vols. Copenhagen: Dokumentation Verlag, 1991.

Bamberger-Stemmann, Sabine. *Der Europäische Nationalitätenkongreß 1925 bis 1938. Nationale Minderheiten zwischen Lobbyistentum und Großmatinteressen*. Marburg: Verlag Herder-Institut, 2000.

Berdahl, Daphne. *Where the World Ended: Re-Unification and Identity in the German Borderland*. Berkeley: University of California Press, 1999.

Bergen, Doris L. "The Nazi Concept of 'Volksdeutsche' and the Exacerbation of Anti-Semitism in Eastern Europe, 1939–45." *Journal of Contemporary History* 29, no. 4 (1994): 569–582.

————. "Tenuousness and Tenacity: The *Volksdeutschen* of Eastern Europe, World War II, and the Holocaust." In *The Heimat Abroad: The Boundaries of Germanness*, ed. Krista O'Donnell, Renate Bridenthal, and Nancy Reagin, 265–286. Ann Arbor: University of Michigan Press, 2005.

————. *War and Genocide. A Concise History of the Holocaust*. 2nd ed. Lanham: Rowman & Littlefield, 2009.

Bessel, Richard. *Germany after the First World War*. Oxford: Clarendon Press, 1993.

Bierschenk, Theodor. *Die deutsche Volksgruppe in Polen, 1934–1939.* Würzburg: Holzner, 1954.

———. "In Memoriam Rudolf Wiesner." In *Heimat Wolhynien*, edited by Alfred Cammann, 42–43. Marburg/Lahn: N.G. Elwert, 1988.

Birken, Lawrence. "Völkisch Nationalism in Perspective." *The History Teacher* 27, no. 2 (1994): 133–143.

Bjork, James E. *Neither German nor Pole: Catholicism and National Indifference in a Central European Borderland.* Ann Arbor: University of Michigan Press, 2009.

Blachetta-Madajczyk, Petra. *Klassenkampf oder Nation? Deutsche Sozialdemokratie in Polen 1918–1939.* Düsseldorf: Droste, 1997.

Blackbourn, David. *The Conquest of Nature: Water, Landscape, and the Making of Modern Germany.* New York/London: Norton, 2006.

Blanke, Richard. *Orphans of Versailles: The Germans in Western Poland, 1918–1939.* Lexington: University Press of Kentucky, 1993.

Böhler, Jochen. *Auftakt zum Vernichtungskrieg. Die Wehrmacht in Polen 1939.* Frankfurt/Main: Fischer Taschenbuch, 2006.

Bonin, Thora von, ed. *Von der Konfrontation zur Kooperation. 50 Jahre Landsmannschaft Weichsel-Warthe, Jahresdokumentation 1999 der Landsmannschaft Weichsel-Warthe.* Wiesbaden: Landsmannschaft Weichsel-Warthe, 2000.

Boockmann, Hartmut. "Deutsche Geschichte ist mehr als rhein-donauländische Heimatkunde. Die ostdeutsche Geschichte wird in der Bundesrepublik zuwenig erforscht." *Frankfurter Allgemeine Zeitung*, May 22, 1989, 12.

———. *Ostpreussen und Westpreussen. Deutsche Geschichte im Osten Europas.* Berlin: Siedler, 1992.

Boysen, Jens. "Der Geist des Grenzlands. Ideologische Positionen deutscher und polnischer Meinungsführer in Posen und Westpreußen vor und nach dem Ersten Weltkrieg." In *Die Geschichte Polens und Deutschlands im 19. und 20. Jahrhundert. Ausgewählte Beiträge*, edited by Markus Krzoska and Peter Tokarski, 104–123. Osnabrück: Fibre, 1998.

Brehmer, Ursula. "Die Landsmannschaft Weichsel-Warthe in ihrem Wirken für Versöhnung und Verständigung mit den Polen." In *Polska Środkowa w niemieckich badaniach wschodnich. Historia i współczesność*, edited by Lucjan Meissner, 195–202. Łódź: Ibidem, 1999.

Breuer, Stefan. *Ordnungen der Ungleichheit – die deutsche Rechte im Widerstreit ihrer Ideen 1871–1945.* Darmstadt: Wissenschaftliche Buchgesellschaft, 2001.

———. *Die Völkischen in Deutschland. Kaiserreich und Weimarer Republik.* Darmstadt: Wissenschaftliche Buchgesellschaft, 2008.

Breuilly, John. "The National Idea in Modern German History." In *The State of Germany. The National Idea in the Making, Unmaking, and Remaking of a Modern Nation-State*, edited by John Breuilly, 1–28. New York: Longman, 1992.

———. *Nationalism and the State.* Manchester: Manchester University Press, 1993.

Breyer, Richard. *Das Deutsche Reich und Polen, 1932–1937. Außenpolitik und Volksgruppenfragen.* Würzburg: Holzner, 1955.

———. "Der 'Lodzer Mensch' – Legende und Wirklichkeit." In *Lodz. Die Stadt der Völkerbegegnung im Wandel der Geschichte*, edited by Peter E. Nasarski, 74–75. Cologne-Rodenkirchen: Liebig, 1978.

Breyer, Richard, and Peter E. Nasarski. *Erfahrung und Zeugnis der Deutschen aus Polen.* Berlin/Bonn: Westkreuz, 1987.

Breyer, Richard, Peter E. Nasarski, and Janusz Piekalkiewicz. *Nachbarn seit tausend Jahren. Deutsche und Polen in Bildern und Dokumenten.* Mainz: Hase & Koehler, 1976.

Broszat, Martin. "Die völkische Ideologie und der Nationalsozialismus." *Deutsche Rundschau* 84, no. 1 (1958): 53–68.

———. "'Jungdeutsche Partei' und 'Deutsche Vereinigung' in Posen-Pommerellen." *Gutachten des Instituts für Zeitgeschichte* 1 (1958): 404–407.

———. *Nationalsozialistische Polenpolitik, 1939–1945.* Stuttgart: Deutsche Verlags-Anstalt, 1961.

———. *Zweihundert Jahre deutsche Polenpolitik.* Frankfurt/Main: Suhrkamp, 1972.

Brubaker, Rogers. *Nationalism Reframed: Nationhood and the National Question in the New Europe.* Cambridge/New York: Cambridge University Press, 1996.

———. "Ethnicity Without Groups." *Archives européennes de sociologie* 43, no. 2 (2002): 163–189.

———. "Neither Individualism nor 'Groupism': A Reply to Craig Calhoun." *Ethnicities* 3 (2003): 553–557.

———. "The 'Diaspora' Diaspora." *Ethnic and Racial Studies* 28, no. 1 (2005): 1–19.

Brubaker, Rogers, and Frederick Cooper. "Beyond Identity." *Theory and Society* 29 (2000): 1–47.

Bryant, Chad. "Either German or Czech: Fixing Nationality in Bohemia and Moravia, 1939–1946." *Slavic Review* 61, no. 4 (2002): 683–706.

———. *Prague in Black: Nazi Rule and Czech Nationalism.* Cambridge: Harvard University Press, 2007.

Bund der Vertriebenen. "Mitgliedsverbände." Accessed August 10, 2006. http://www.bund-der-vertriebenen.de/derbdv/mitgliedsverbaende3.php3.

Burkert, Martin. *Die Ostwissenschaften im Dritten Reich. Teil 1: Zwischen Verbot und Duldung. Die schwierige Gratwanderung der Ostwissenschaften zwischen 1933 und 1939.* Wiesbaden: Harrassowitz, 2000.

Burleigh, Michael. *Germany Turns Eastwards: A Study of Ostforschung in the Third Reich.* Cambridge/New York: Cambridge University Press, 1988.

Centre Marc Bloch. "Phantomgrenzen in Ostmitteleuropa." Accessed March 11, 2012. http://phantomgrenzen.eu.

Chazan, Naomi. "Introduction." In *Irredentism and International Politics*, edited by Naomi Chazan, 1–8. Boulder: Lynne Rienner Publishers, 1991.

Chickering, Roger. *We Men Who Feel Most German: A Cultural Study of the Pan-German League, 1886–1914.* Boston: Allen & Unwin, 1984.

Clavin, Patricia. "Defining Transnationalism." *Contemporary European History* 14, no. 4 (2005): 421–439.

Confino, Alon. *The Nation as a Local Metaphor: Württemberg, Imperial Germany, and National Memory, 1871–1918.* Chapel Hill: University of North Carolina Press, 1997.

Connelly, John. "The Uses of Volksgemeinschaft: Letters to the NSDAP Kreisleitung Eisenach, 1939–1940." *Journal of Modern History* 68, no. 4 (1996): 899–930.

———. "Nazis and Slavs: From Racial Theory to Racist Practice." *Central European History* 32, no. 1 (1999): 1–33.

Conze, Werner. "Nationalstaat oder Mitteleuropa? Die Deutschen des Reiches und die Nationalitätenfragen Ostmitteleuropas im Ersten Weltkrieg." In *Deutschland und Europa. Historische Studien zur Völker- und Staatenordnung des Abendlandes, Festschrift für Hans Rothfels*, edited by Werner Conze, 201–230. Düsseldorf: Droste, 1951.

Cygański, Mirosław. *Mniejszość niemiecka w Polsce centralnej w latach 1919–1939*. Łódź: Wydawnictwo Łódzkie, 1962.

Dedecius, Karl. *Ein Europäer aus Lodz. Erinnerungen*. Frankfurt/Main: Suhrkamp, 2006.

Dehmer, Maria. "Die deutsche Minderheit in Lodz nach dem Ersten Weltkrieg bis zum Ende der Ära Pilsudski (1920–1931). Die Schulpolitik anhand ihrer Darstellung in der *Neuen Lodzer Zeitung*." M.A. thesis, University of Konstanz, 1999.

Döring, Stephan. *Die Umsiedlung der Wolhyniendeutschen in den Jahren 1939 bis 1940*. Frankfurt/Main: Peter Lang, 2001.

Drożdowski, Marian Marek. "The National Minorities in Poland 1918–1939." *Acta Poloniae historica* 22 (1970): 226–251.

Drummond, Elizabeth A. "From 'verloren gehen' to 'verloren bleiben': Changing German Discourses on Nation and Nationalism in Poznania." In *The Germans and the East*, edited by Charles W. Ingrao and Franz A.J. Szabo, 226–240. West Lafayette: Purdue University Press, 2008.

Dyroff, Stefan, Krystyna Radziszewska, and Isabel Röskau-Rydel, eds. *Lodz jenseits von Fabriken, Wildwest und Provinz. Kulturwissenschaftliche Studien über die Deutschen in und aus den polnischen Gebieten*. Munich: Martin Meidenbauer, 2009.

Ebbinghaus, Angelika, and Karl Heinz Roth. "Vorläufer des 'Generalplans Ost.' Eine Dokumentation über Theodor Schieders Polendenkschrift vom 7. Oktober 1939." *1999: Zeitschrift für Sozialgeschichte des 20. und 21. Jahrhunderts* 7, no. 1 (1992): 62–94.

Eckert, Astrid M. *Kampf um die Akten. Die Westallierten und die Rückgabe von Deutschem Archivgut nach dem Zweiten Weltkrieg*. Stuttgart: Franz Steiner, 2004.

Engel, David. "Lwów, 1918: The Transmutation of a Symbol and its Legacy in the Holocaust." In *Contested Memories: Poles and Jews during the Holocaust and its Aftermath*, edited by Joshua D. Zimmerman, 32–44. New Brunswick/London: Rutgers University Press, 2003.

Enssle, Manfred Joachim. *Stresemann's Territorial Revisionism. Germany, Belgium, and the Eupen-Malmédy Question 1919–1929*. Wiesbaden: Steiner, 1980.

Epstein, Catherine. *Model Nazi: Arthur Greiser and the Occupation of Western Poland*. Oxford/New York: Oxford University Press, 2010.

Eser, Ingo. *"Volk, Staat, Gott!" Die deutsche Minderheit in Polen und ihr Schulwesen 1918–1939*. Wiesbaden: Harrassowitz, 2010.

Eser, Ingo, and Jerzy Kochanowski, eds. *Polska Centralna. Województwo Śląskie*. Vol. 2 of *Niemcy w Polsce 1945–1950. Wybór dokumentów*, edited by Włodzimierz Borodziej and Hans Lemberg. Warsaw: Neriton, 2000.

Faehndrich, Jutta. "Erinnerungskultur und Umgang mit Vertreibung in Heimatbüchern deutschsprachiger Vertriebener." *Zeitschrift für Ostmitteleuropa-Forschung* 52, no. 2 (2003): 191–229.

Fahlbusch, Michael. *Wissenschaft im Dienst der nationalsozialistischen Politik? Die "Volksdeutschen Forschungsgemeinschaften" von 1931–1945.* Baden-Baden: Nomos Verlagsgesellschaft, 1999.

Falęcki, Tomasz. "Niemcy w Łodzi i Niemcy w województwie śląskim w okresie międzywojennym. Wzajemne powiązania oraz podobieństwa i różnice pod względem społeczno-ekonomicznym i świadomościowym." In *Niemcy w Łodzi do 1939 roku,* edited by Marian Wilk, 74–88. Łódź: Uniwersytet Łódzki, 1996.

Fałowski, Janusz. *Parlamentarzyści mniejszości niemieckiej w Drugiej Rzeczypospolitej.* Częstochowa: Wydawnictwo Wyższej Szkoły Pedagogicznej w Częstochowie, 2000.

Fiedor, Karol. "'Die blutende Grenze' – hasłem pruskiego nacjonalizmu." In *Górny Śląsk po podziale w 1922 roku. Co Polska, a co Niemcy dały mieszkańcom tej ziemi?* edited by Maria Wanda Wanatowicz, Zbigniew Kapała, and Wiesław Lesiuk, 103–121. Bytom: Uniwerstytet Śląski w Katowicach, 1997.

Fielitz, Wilhelm. *Das Stereotyp des wolhyniendeutschen Umsiedlers. Popularisierungen zwischen Sprachinselforschung und nationalsozialistischer Propaganda.* Marburg: N.G. Elwert, 2000.

———. "Volkslied und Volksliedsammlung zwischen den Weltkriegen in Wolhynien." *Germano-Polonica. Mitteilungen zur Geschichte der Deutschen in Polen und der deutsch-polnischen Beziehungen* 3 (2003): 17–24.

Fink, Carole. "Defender of Minorities: Germany in the League of Nations, 1926–1933." *Central European History* 5, no. 4 (1972): 330–357.

———. "Stresemann's Minority Policies, 1924–29." *Journal of Contemporary History* 14, no. 3 (1979): 403–422.

———. "The Weimar Republic and its Minderheitenpolitik: Challenge to a Democracy." *German Politics and Society* 14, no. 1 (1996): 80–95.

Fischer, Fritz. *Griff nach der Weltmacht. Die Kriegszielpolitik des kaiserlichen Deutschland 1914/18.* Düsseldorf: Droste, 1967.

Fischer, Peter. *Die deutsche Publizistik als Faktor der deutsch-polnischen Beziehungen 1919–1939.* Wiesbaden: Harrassowitz, 1991.

Föllmer, Moritz. "The Problem of National Solidarity in Interwar Germany." *German History* 23, no. 2 (2005): 202–231.

Föllmer, Moritz, and Rüdiger Graf, eds. *Die "Krise" der Weimarer Republik. Zur Kritik eines Deutungsmusters.* Frankfurt/Main: Campus, 2005.

Frysztacki, Krzysztof. ed. *Polacy, Ślązacy, Niemcy. Studia nad stosunkami społeczno-kulturowymi na Śląsku Opolskim.* Cracow: Universitas, 1998.

Furber, David. "Going East: Colonialism and German Life in Nazi-Occupied Poland." Ph.D. dissertation, State University of New York, Buffalo, 2003.

Gawlitta, Severin. "Zwischen politischer Legitimation und gesellschaftlicher Integration. Die 'Deutschen Kulturleistungen' in der Publizistik der Deutschen in und aus Mittelpolen 1914–1963." In *Lodz jenseits von Fabriken, Wildwest und Provinz. Kulturwissenschaftliche Studien über die Deutschen in und aus den polnischen Gebieten,* edited by Stefan Dyroff, Krystyna Radziszewska, and Isabel Röskau-Rydel, 171–188. Munich: Martin Meidenbauer, 2009.

Gerke, Wilfried. "Auf dem Wege zur Einheit. Die Deutschen in Polen zwischen den Weltkriegen." *Germano-Polonica. Mitteilung zur Geschichte der Deutschen in Polen und der deutsch-polnischen Beziehungen* 2 (2002/2003).

Gierlak, Maria. "Deutsche Presse in Polen 1919–1939. Forschungsstand, -postulate und -desiderate." In *Grenzdiskurse. Zeitungen deutschsprachiger Minderheiten und ihr Feuilleton in Mitteleuropa bis 1939*, edited by Sibylle Schönborn, 67–80. Essen: Klartext, 2009.

Gosewinkel, Dieter. *Einbürgern und Ausschließen. Die Nationalisierung der Staatsangehörigkeit vom Deutschen Bund bis zur Bundesrepublik Deutschland.* Göttingen: Vandenhoeck & Ruprecht, 2001.

Grabowski, Jan, and Zbigniew R. Grabowski. "Germans in the Eyes of the Gestapo: The Ciechanów District, 1939–1945." *Contemporary European History* 13, no. 1 (2004): 21–43.

Green, Abigail. *Fatherlands: State-Building and Nationhood in Nineteenth-Century Germany.* Cambridge/New York: Cambridge University Press, 2001.

Grünberg, Karol. *Nazi-Front Schlesien. Niemieckie organizacje polityczne w województwie śląskim w latach 1933–1939.* Katowice: Wydawnictwo Śląsk, 1963.

————. *Niemcy i ich organizacje polityczne w Polsce międzywojennej.* Warsaw: Wiedza Powszechna, 1970.

Gutschow, Niels. "Stadtplanung im Warthegau, 1939–1944." In *Der "Generalplan" Ost. Hauptlinien der nationalsozialistischen Planungs- und Vernichtungspolitik*, edited by Mechtild Rössler and Sabine Schleiermacher, 232–258. Berlin: Akademie Verlag, 1993.

Haar, Ingo. *Historiker im Nationalsozialismus. Deutsche Geschichtswissenschaft und der "Volkstumskampf" im Osten.* Göttingen: Vandenhoeck & Ruprecht, 2000.

————. "German Ostforschung and Anti-Semitism." In *German Scholars and Ethnic Cleansing, 1919–1945*, edited by Ingo Haar and Michael Fahlbusch, 1–27. New York: Berghahn Books, 2005.

————. "Vom 'Volksgruppen-Paradigma' bis zum 'Recht auf Heimat': Exklusion und Inklusion als Deutungsmuster in den Diskursen über Zwangsmigrationen vor und nach 1945." In *Die "Volksdeutschen" in Polen, Frankreich, Ungarn und der Tschechoslowakei. Mythos und Realität*, edited by Jerzy Kochanowski and Maike Sach, 17–39. Osnabrück: Fibre, 2006.

Haar, Ingo, and Michael Fahlbusch, eds. *German Scholars and Ethnic Cleansing, 1919–1945.* New York: Berghahn Books, 2005.

Hackmann, Jörg. "Deutsche Ostforschung und Geschichtswissenschaft." In *Deutsche Ostforschung und Polnische Westforschung im Spannungsfeld von Wissenschaft und Politik. Disziplinen im Vergleich*, edited by Jan M. Piskorski, Jörg Hackmann, and Rudolf Jaworski, 25–45. Osnabrück: Fibre, 2002.

Hagen, William W. *Germans, Poles, and Jews: The Nationality Conflict in the Prussian East, 1772–1914.* Chicago: University of Chicago Press, 1980.

————. "The Moral Economy of Ethnic Violence: The Pogrom in Lwów, November 1918." *Geschichte und Gesellschaft* 31, no. 2 (2005): 203–226.

Hardin, Russell. *One for All: The Logic of Group Conflict.* Princeton: Princeton University Press, 1995.

Hartung, Günter. "Völkische Ideologie," in *Handbuch zur "Völkischen Bewegung" 1871–1918*, edited by Uwe Puschner, Walter Schmitz, and Justus H. Ulbricht, 22–41. Munich: Saur, 1996.

Harvey, Elizabeth R. "Pilgrimages to the 'Bleeding Border': Gender and Rituals of Nationalist Protest in Germany, 1919–39." *Women's History Review* 9, no. 2 (2000): 201–229.

————. "'We Forgot All Jews and Poles': German Women and the 'Ethnic Struggle' in Nazi-Occupied Poland." *Contemporary European History* 10, no. 3 (2001): 447–461.

————. *Women and the Nazi East: Agents and Witnesses of Germanization.* New Haven/London: Yale University Press, 2003.

Haupt, Heinz-Gerhard, Michael G. Müller, and Stuart J. Woolf. "Introduction." In *Regional and National Identities in Europe in the XIXth and XXth Centuries = Les identités régionales et nationales en Europe aux XIXe et XXe siècles,* edited by Heinz-Gerhard Haupt, Michael G. Müller, and Stuart Woolf. The Hague/London/Boston: Kluwer Law International, 1998.

Hauser, Przemysław. "The German Minority in Poland in the Years 1918–1939. Reflections in the State of Research and Interpretation, Proposals for Further Research." *Polish Western Affairs* 32, no. 2 (1991): 13–38.

————. "Die deutsche Minderheit in den Wojewodschaften Posen und Pommerellen 1919–1939." In *Deutsche und Polen zwischen den Kriegen. Minderheitenstatus und "Volkstumskampf" im Grenzgebiet. Amtliche Berichterstattung aus beiden Ländern, 1920–1939,* edited by Rudolf Jaworski, Marian Wojciechowski, Mathias Niendorf, and Przemysław Hauser, vol. 1, 273–282. Munich: Saur, 1997.

————. *Mniejszość niemiecka na Pomorzu w okresie międzywojennym.* Poznań: Wydawnictwo Naukowe UAM, 1998.

————. "Kolonista niemiecki na ziemiach polskich w okresie rozbiorów (Uwagi i refleksje na temat funkcjonowania mitu oraz rzeczywistości)." In *Niemieccy osadnicy w Królestwie Polskim 1815–1915,* edited by Wiesław Caban, 225–242. Kielce: Wyższa Szkoła Pedagogiczna, 1999.

Hechter, Michael. *Containing Nationalism.* Oxford: Oxford University Press, 2000.

Heike, Otto. *Das Deutschtum in Polen, 1918–1939.* Bonn: self-published, 1955.

————. *Das deutsche Schulwesen in Mittelpolen. Ein Kapitel mühsamer Abwehr staatlichen Unrechts.* Dortmund: Ostdeutsche Forschungsstelle im Lande Nordrhein-Westfalen, 1963.

————. *Die deutsche Arbeiterbewegung in Polen, 1835–1945.* Dortmund: Ostdeutsche Forschungsstelle im Lande Nordrhein-Westfalen, 1969.

————. *Die deutsche Minderheit in Polen bis 1939. Ihr Leben und Wirken, kulturell, gesellschaftlich, politisch. Eine historisch-dokumentarische Analyse.* Leverkusen: self-published, 1985.

Hein, Heidi. "Der Piłsudski-Kult in der Woiwodschaft Schlesien. Ein Mittel zur politischen Integration?" In *Dzieje Śląska w XX w. w świetle badań młodych historyków z Polski, Czech i Niemiec,* edited by Krzysztof Ruchniewicz, 102–113. Wrocław: Instytut Historyczny Uniwersytetu Wrocławskiego, 1998.

————. "Die Piłsudski-Feiern in der *Kattowitzer Zeitung* und dem *Oberschlesischen Kurier.* Ein Beitrag zum Piłsudski-Bild und zur Rezeption des Piłsudski-Kultes der deutschen Minderheit in der Wojewodschaft Schlesien (1926–1939)." In *Die Geschichte Polens und Deutschlands im 19. und 20. Jahrhundert. Ausgewählte Beiträge,* edited by Markus Krzoska and Peter Tokarski, 124–141. Osnabrück: Fibre, 1998.

————. *Der Piłsudski-Kult und seine Bedeutung für den polnischen Staat 1926–1939.* Marburg: Herder-Institut, 2002.

Heinemann, Isabel. "Rasse, Siedlung, deutsches Blut": Das Rasse- und Siedlungshauptamt der SS und die rassenpolitische Neuordnung Europas. Göttingen: Wallstein, 2003.

Henke, Herbert. "Heimat in Topcza – Familienschicksal und Lebenslauf." In *Heimat Wolhynien*, edited by Alfred Cammann, 65–102. Marburg/Lahn: N.G. Elwert, 1988.

Hensel, Jürgen, ed. *Polen, Deutsche und Juden in Lodz 1820–1939. Eine schwierige Nachbarschaft*, edited by Jürgen Heyde. Osnabrück: Fibre, 1999.

Herb, Guntram Henrik. *Under the Map of Germany: Nationalism and Propaganda 1918–1945.* London/New York: Routledge, 1997.

————. "Von der Grenzrevision zur Expansion. Territorialkonzepte in der Weimarer Republik." In *Welt-Räume. Geschichte, Geographie und Globalisierung seit 1900*, edited by Iris Schröder and Sabine Höhler, 175–203. Frankfurt/Main: Campus, 2005.

Hering, Rainer. *Konstruierte Nation. Der Alldeutsche Verband 1890 bis 1939.* Hamburg: Christians, 2003.

Hiden, John W. "The Weimar Republic and the Problem of the Auslandsdeutsche." *Journal of Contemporary History* 12 (1977): 273–289.

Hillgruber, Andreas. "'Revisionismus' – Kontinuität und Wandel in der Außenpolitik der Weimarer Republik." *Historische Zeitschrift* 237 (1983): 597–621.

Hirschman, Albert O. *Exit, Voice, and Loyalty: Responses to Decline in Firms, Organizations, and States.* Cambridge: Harvard University Press, 1970.

Hochman, Erin Regina. "Staging the Nation, Staging Democracy: The Politics of Commemoration in Germany and Austria, 1918-1933/34." Ph.D. dissertation, University of Toronto, 2010.

Hoensch, Jörg K. *Geschichte Polens.* Stuttgart: Eugen Ulmer, 1998.

Hoffmann, Christhard, Werner Bergmann, and Helmut Walser Smith, eds. *Exclusionary Violence: Antisemitic Riots in Modern German History.* Ann Arbor: The University of Michigan Press, 2002.

Hofmann, Andreas R. "Die vergessene Okkupation. Lodz im Ersten Weltkrieg." In *Deutsche–Juden–Polen. Geschichte einer wechselvollen Beziehung im 20. Jahrhundert. Festschrift für Hubert Schneider*, edited by Andrea Löw, Kerstin Robusch, and Stefanie Walter, 59–78. Frankfurt/Main: Campus, 2004.

Höltje, Christian. *Die Weimarer Republik und das Ostlocarno-Problem, 1919–34.* Würzburg: Holzner, 1958.

Horowitz, Donald L. *Ethnic Groups in Conflict.* Berkeley: University of California Press, 1985.

————. *The Deadly Ethnic Riot.* Berkeley: University of California Press, 2001.

Horwitz, Gordon. *Ghettostadt: Łódź and the Making of a Nazi City.* Cambridge: Belknap Press of Harvard University Press, 2008.

Iggers, Georg G. "Foreword." In *German Scholars and Ethnic Cleansing, 1919–1945*, edited by Ingo Haar and Michael Fahlbusch, vii–xviii. New York: Berghahn Books, 2005.

Ingrao, Charles W., and Franz A.J. Szabo, eds. *The Germans and the East.* West Lafayette: Purdue University Press, 2008.

Jacobsen, Hans-Adolf. *Nationalsozialistische Außenpolitik, 1933–1938.* Frankfurt/Main: A. Metzner, 1968.

———, ed. *Hans Steinacher, Bundesleiter des VDA 1933–1937. Erinnerungen und Dokumente.* Boppard am Rhein: Boldt, 1970.

Jansen, Christian, and Arno Weckbecker. *Der "Volksdeutsche Selbstschutz" in Polen 1939/40.* Munich: Oldenbourg, 1992.

Jastrzębski, Włodzimierz. *Der Bromberger Blutsonntag – Legende und Wirklichkeit.* Poznań: Instytut Zachodni, 1990.

Jaworski, Rudolf. "Der auslandsdeutsche Gedanke in der Weimarer Republik." *Annali dell'Instituto storico-germanico in Trento* 4 (1978): 369–386.

Jaworski, Rudolf, Christian Lübke, and Michael G. Müller. *Eine kleine Geschichte Polens.* Frankfurt/Main: Suhrkamp, 2000.

Judson, Pieter. "When Is a Diaspora Not a Diaspora? Rethinking Nation-Centered Narratives about Germans in Habsburg East Central Europe." In *The Heimat Abroad: The Boundaries of Germanness,* edited by Krista O'Donnell, Renate Bridenthal, and Nancy Reagin, 219–247. Ann Arbor: University of Michigan Press, 2005.

———. *Guardians of the Nation: Activists on the Language Frontiers of Imperial Austria.* Cambridge: Harvard University Press, 2006.

Kargel, Adolf. "Das Lodzer deutsche Schulwesen im Zeitraffer. Von seinen Anfängen bis zu seiner Auflösung." In *Das Lodzer Deutsche Gymnasium. Im Spannungsfeld zwischen Schicksal und Erbe, 1906–1981,* edited by Peter E. Nasarski, 11–18. Berlin/Bonn: Westkreuz, 1981.

Keipert, Maria, and Peter Grupp (Auswärtiges Amt, Historischer Dienst), eds. *Biographisches Handbuch des deutschen Auswärtigen Dienstes 1871–1945,* vol. 1: A–F. Paderborn: Ferdinand Schöningh, 2000.

———. *Biographisches Handbuch des deutschen Auswärtigen Dienstes 1871–1945,* vol. 2: G–K. Paderborn: Ferdinand Schöningh, 2005.

———. *Biographisches Handbuch des deutschen Auswärtigen Dienstes 1871–1945,* vol. 3: L–R. Paderborn: Ferdinand Schöningh, 2008.

Kenney, Padraic. *Rebuilding Poland: Workers and Communists, 1945–1950.* Ithaca/London: Cornell University Press, 1997.

Kershaw, Ian. *Der NS-Staat. Geschichtsinterpretationen und Kontroversen im Überblick.* Reinbek bei Hamburg: Rowohlt Taschenbuch, 1994.

———. "Working Towards the Führer," in *Stalinism and Nazism: Dictatorships in Comparison,* eds. Ian Kershaw and Moshe Lewin, 88–106. Cambridge/New York: Cambridge University Press, 1997.

Kessler, Wolfgang. "Volksgeschichte oder Regionalgeschichte? Grundlinien der deutschen historischen und heimatkundlichen Forschung über Zentralpolen." In *Polska Środkowa w niemieckich badaniach wschodnich. Historia i współczesność,* edited by Lucjan Meissner, 7–20. Łódź: Ibidem, 1999.

———. "Die Deutschen im polnischen Westwolhynien (1921–1939/40) in der historischen Forschung." *Nordost-Archiv* 9, no. 2 (2000): 449–457.

———. "Die Geschichte der Deutschen in Großpolen im Spiegel der deutschen Historiographie nach 1945." In *Doświadczenia przeszłości. Niemcy w Europie Środkowo-Wschodniej w historiografii po 1945 roku = Erfahrungen der Vergangenheit. Deutsche in Ostmitteleuropa in der Historiographie nach 1945,* edited by

Jerzy Kłoczowski, Witold Matwiejczyk, and Eduard Mühle, 101–118. Marburg: Herder-Institut; Lublin: Instytut Europy Środkowo-Wschodniej, 2000.

———. "Die 'Ostforschung' und die Deutschen in Polen." *Nordost-Archiv* 9, no. 2 (2000): 379–411.

———. "Die Lodzer Deutschen nach 1945." In *Między Śląskiem a Wiedniem. Księga Jubileuszowa z okazji 60. urodzin prof. dr. hab. Krzysztofa A. Kuczyńskiego*, edited by Aleksander Kozłowski and Małgorzata Znyk, 329–337. Płock: Wydawnictwo Naukowej Państwowej Wyższej Szkoły Zawodowej, 2008.

———. "Lodz nach Lodz. Beobachtungen zu Erinnerung und Gedächtnis der Deutschen aus Lodz nach 1945." In *Lodz jenseits von Fabriken, Wildwest und Provinz. Kulturwissenschaftliche Studien über die Deutschen in und aus den polnischen Gebieten*, edited by Stefan Dyroff, Krystyna Radziszewska, and Isabel Röskau-Rydel, 151–169. Munich: Martin Meidenbauer, 2009.

King, Jeremy. "The Nationalization of East Central Europe: Ethnicism, Ethnicity, and Beyond." In *Staging the Past: The Politics of Commemoration in Habsburg Central Europe, 1848 to the Present*, edited by Maria Bucur and Nancy M. Wingfield, 112–152. West Lafayette: Purdue University Press, 2001.

———. *Budweisers into Czechs and Germans: A Local History of Bohemian Politics, 1848–1948*. Princeton: Princeton University Press, 2002.

Klein, Michael B. *Zwischen Reich und Region. Identitätsstrukturen im Deutschen Kaiserreich (1871–1918)*. Stuttgart: Franz Steiner, 2005.

Klein, Peter. *Die "Gettoverwaltung Litzmannstadt" 1940 bis 1944. Eine Dienststelle im Spannungsfeld von Kommunalbürokratie und staatlicher Verfolgungspolitik*. Hamburg: Hamburger Ed., 2009.

Kochanowski, Jerzy. "Kto ty jesteś? Niemiec mały! Volksdeutsche: sprawa jest bardziej skomplikowana niż myślimy!" *Polityka*, September 7, 2003, 64–66.

Kochanowski, Jerzy, and Maike Sach, eds. *Die "Volksdeutschen" in Polen, Frankreich, Ungarn und der Tschechoslowakei. Mythos und Realität*. Osnabrück: Fibre, 2006.

Kolb, Eberhard. *Gustav Stresemann*. Munich: C.H. Beck, 2003.

Komjathy, Anthony Tihamer, and Rebecca Stockwell. *German Minorities and the Third Reich: Ethnic Germans of East Central Europe Between the Wars*. New York: Holmes & Meier, 1980.

Kontje, Todd. *German Orientalisms*. Ann Arbor: University of Michigan Press, 2004.

Koonz, Claudia. *The Nazi Conscience*. Cambridge: Belknap Press of Harvard University Press, 2003.

Kopp, Kristin Leigh. "Contesting Borders: German Colonial Discourse and the Polish Eastern Territories." Ph.D. Dissertation, University of California, Berkeley, 2001.

Korzec, Paweł. "Der Block der Nationalen Minderheiten im Parlamentarismus Polens des Jahres 1922." *Zeitschrift für Ostforschung* 24, no. 2 (1975): 193–220.

———. "Der zweite Block der nationalen Minderheiten im Parlamentarismus Polens 1927–28." *Zeitschrift für Ostforschung* 26, no. 1 (1977): 76–116.

Kosmala, Beate. "Lodzer Juden und Deutsche im Jahr 1933. Die Rezeption der nationalsozialistischen Machtübernahme in Deutschland und ihre Wirkung auf das Verhältnis von jüdischer und deutscher Minderheit." In *Polen, Deutsche und*

Juden in Lodz 1820–1939. Eine schwierige Nachbarschaft, edited by Jürgen Hensel, 237–245. Osnabrück: Fibre, 1999.

————. *Juden und Deutsche im polnischen Haus. Tomaszów Mazowiecki 1914–1939.* Berlin: Metropol, 2001.

Kossert, Andreas. "'Promised Land'? Urban Myth and the Shaping of Modernity in Manchester and Lodz." In *The Politics of Urban Space.* Vol. 2 of *Imagining the City*, edited by Christian Emden, Catherine Keen, and David Midgley, 169–192. Oxford/Bern: Peter Lang, 2006.

Kossmann, Eugen Oskar. *Es begann in Polen. Erinnerungen eines Diplomaten und Ostforschers.* Lüneburg: Nordostdeutsches Kulturwerk, 1989.

Kotowski, Albert S. *Polens Politik gegenüber seiner deutschen Minderheit, 1919–1939.* Wiesbaden: Harrassowitz, 1998.

————. "Die deutsche Minderheit in Polen 1919–1939/45. Forschungsstand und -desiderata." *Nordost-Archiv* 9, no. 2 (2000): 483–506.

————. *Hitlers Bewegung im Urteil der polnischen Nationaldemokratie.* Wiesbaden: Harrassowitz, 2000.

Kracht, Klaus Große. *Die zankende Zunft. Historische Kontroversen in Deutschland nach 1945.* Göttingen: Vandenhoeck & Ruprecht, 2005.

Krekeler, Norbert Friedrich. *Revisionsanspruch und geheime Ostpolitik der Weimarer Republik. Die Subventionierung der deutschen Minderheit in Polen.* Stuttgart: Deutsche Verlags-Anstalt, 1973.

Kruck, Alfred. *Geschichte des Alldeutschen Verbandes 1890–1939.* Wiesbaden: Steiner, 1954.

Krüger, Peter. *Die Außenpolitik der Republik von Weimar.* Darmstadt: Wissenschaftliche Buchgesellschaft, 1985.

————. "The European East and Weimar Germany." In *Germany and the European East in the Twentieth Century*, edited by Eduard Mühle, 7–27. Oxford/New York: Berg, 2003.

Krzoska, Markus. "Tagungsbericht: Die Erforschung der Geschichte der Deutschen in Polen. Stand und Zukunftsperspektiven." Conference of the Kommission für die Geschichte der Deutschen in Polen e.V. from May 29 to 31, 1999, in Mainz, report dated November 1, 1999. Accessed August 10, 2006. http://hsozkult. geschichte.hu-berlin.de/BEITRAG/TAGBER/polen.htm.

Kuhn, Walter. "Das Deutschtum in Polen und sein Schicksal in Kriegs- und Nachkriegszeit." In *Osteuropa Handbuch Polen*, edited by Werner Markert, 138–164. Cologne: Böhlau, 1959.

Kühne, Thomas. "Historische Wahlforschung in der Erweiterung." In *Modernisierung und Region im wilhelminischen Deutschland. Wahlen, Wahlrecht und Politische Kultur*, edited by Simone Lässig, Karl Heinrich Pohl, and James N. Retallack, 39–67. Bielefeld: Verlag für Regionalgeschichte, 1995.

Kurcz, Zbigniew. *Mniejszość niemiecka w Polsce.* Wrocław: Wydawnictwo Uniwersytetu Wrocławskiego, 1995.

Lakeberg, Beata. "Identitätsfragen in der deutschen Minderheitenpresse während der ersten Jahre der Zweiten Polnischen Republik." In *Grenzdiskurse. Zeitungen deutschsprachiger Minderheiten und ihr Feuilleton in Mitteleuropa bis 1939*, edited by Sibylle Schönborn, 81–93. Essen: Klartext, 2009.

———. *Die deutsche Minderheitenpresse in Polen 1918–1939 und ihr Polen- und Juden-bild.* Frankfurt/Main: Peter Lang, 2010.

Lehfeldt, Walburg. *Gut Lehfelde. Eine deutsche Geschichte, 1932–1950 (Wie konnte das geschehen?).* Wiesbaden: Limes, 1986.

Leniger, Markus. *Nationalsozialistische "Volkstumsarbeit" und Umsiedlungspolitik 1933–1945. Von der Minderheitenbetreuung zur Siedlerauslese.* Berlin: Frank & Timme, 2006.

Leśniewski, Andrzej, ed. *Irredentism and Provocation: A Contribution to the History of the German Minority in Poland.* Poznań: Wydawnictwo Zachodnie, 1960.

Levine, Herbert S. "Local Authority and the SS State: The Conflict Over Population Policy in Danzig-West Prussia, 1939–1945." *Central European History 2,* no. 4 (1969): 331–355.

Liulevicius, Vejas Gabriel. *War Land on the Eastern Front. Culture, National Identity and German Occupation in World War I.* Cambridge/New York: Cambridge University Press, 2000.

———. *The German Myth of the East: 1800 to the Present.* Oxford: Oxford University Press, 2009.

Lorenz, Torsten. "Międzychód optiert. Behördenpolitik, Migration und Wandel in einem westpolnischen Landkreis." In *Preußens Osten – Polens Westen. Das Zerbrechen einer Nachbarschaft,* edited by Helga Schultz, 145–181. Berlin: Berlin Verlag Arno Spitz, 2001.

———. *Von Birnbaum nach Międzychód. Bürgergesellschaft und Nationalitätenkampf in Großpolen bis zum Zweiten Weltkrieg.* Berlin: Berliner Wissenschafts-Verlag, 2005.

Löw, Andrea. *Juden im Getto Litzmannstadt. Lebensbedingungen, Selbstwahrnehmung, Verhalten.* Göttingen: Wallstein, 2006.

Lüdtke, Alf, ed. *Alltagsgeschichte. Zur Rekonstruktion historischer Erfahrungen und Lebensweisen.* Frankfurt/Main: Campus, 1989.

———. *Eigen-Sinn. Fabrikalltag, Arbeitererfahrungen und Politik vom Kaiserreich bis in den Faschismus.* Hamburg: Ergebnisse-Verlag, 1993.

Lumans, Valdis O. *Himmler's Auxiliaries: The Volksdeutsche Mittelstelle and the German National Minorities of Europe, 1933–1945.* Chapel Hill: University of North Carolina Press, 1993.

Luther, Rudolf. *Blau oder Braun? Der Volksbund für das Deutschtum im Ausland (VDA) im NS-Staat 1933–1937.* Neumünster: Wachholtz, 1999.

Luther, Tammo. *Volkstumspolitik des deutschen Reiches 1933–1938. Die Ausland-deutschen im Spannungsfeld zwischen Traditionalisten und Nationalsozialisten.* Stuttgart: Franz Steiner, 2004.

Macmillan, Margaret. *Paris 1919: Six Months That Changed the World.* New York: Random House, 2003.

Maier, Charles. *Dissolution: The Crisis of Communism and the End of East Germany.* Princeton: Princeton University Press, 1997.

Majer, Diemut. *"Fremdvölkische" im Dritten Reich. Ein Beitrag zur nationalsozia-listischen Rechtssetzung und Rechtspraxis in Verwaltung und Justiz unter beson-derer Berücksichtigung der eingegliederten Ostgebiete und des Generalgouvernements.* Boppard am Rhein: Boldt, 1981.

Mann, Michael. *The Dark Side of Democracy: Explaining Ethnic Cleansing.* Cambridge/New York: Cambridge University Press, 2005.

Matelski, Dariusz. *Mniejszość niemiecka w Wielkopolsce w latach 1919–1939*. Poznań: Wydawnictwo Naukowe UAM, 1997.

———. *Niemcy w Polsce w XX wieku*. Warsaw/Poznań: Wydawnictwo Naukowe PWN, 1999.

Megerle, Klaus. "Danzig, Korridor und Oberschlesien. Zur deutschen Revisionspolitik gegenüber Polen in der Locarnodiplomatie." *Jahrbuch für die Geschichte Mittel- und Ostdeutschlands* 25 (1976): 145–178.

Mendelsohn, Ezra. "Jewish Historiography on Polish Jewry in the Interwar Period." *Polin: Studies in Polish Jewry* 8 (1994): 3–13.

Meyer, Henry Cord. *Drang nach Osten. Fortunes of a Slogan-Concept in German-Slavic Relations*. Bern: Peter Lang, 1996.

Moeller, Robert G. *War Stories: The Search for a Usable Past in the Federal Republic of Germany*. Berkeley: University of California Press, 2001.

Mühle, Eduard. "Institutionelle Grundlegung und wissenschaftliche Programmatik der westdeutschen Beschäftigung mit 'deutscher Geschichte' im östlichen Mitteleuropa (1945–1959)." In *Doświadczenia przeszłości. Niemcy w Europie Środkowo-Wschodniej w historiografii po 1945 roku = Erfahrungen der Vergangenheit. Deutsche in Ostmitteleuropa in der Historiographie nach 1945*, edited by Jerzy Kłoczowski, Witold Matwiejczyk, and Eduard Mühle, 25–66. Marburg: Herder-Institut; Lublin: Instytut Europy Środkowo-Wschodniej, 2000.

———. "The Mental Map of German Ostforschung." In *Germany and the European East in the Twentieth Century*, edited by Eduard Mühle, 107–130. Oxford/New York: Berg, 2003.

Müller, Sven Oliver. "Die umstrittene nationale Gemeinschaft. Nationalismus als Konfliktphänomen." In *Politische Kollektive. Die Konstruktion nationaler, rassischer und ethnischer Gemeinschaften*, edited by Ulrike Jureit, 122–143. Münster: Westfälisches Dampfboot, 2001.

Münz, Rainer, and Rainer Ohliger. "Auslandsdeutsche." In *Deutsche Erinnerungsorte I*, edited by Etienne François and Hagen Schulze, 370–388. Munich: Beck, 2001.

Murphy, Alexander B. "Regions as Social Constructs: The Gap between Theory and Practice." *Progress in Human Geography* 15, no. 1 (1991): 33–35.

Murphy, David Thomas. *The Heroic Earth: Geopolitical Thought in Weimar Germany, 1918–1933*. Kent/London: The Kent State University Press, 1997.

Nasarski, Peter E., ed. *Lodz. Die Stadt der Völkerbegegnung im Wandel der Geschichte*. Cologne-Rodenkirchen: Liebig, 1978.

Nelson, Robert L., ed. *Germans, Poland, and Colonial Expansion to the East*. New York: Palgrave Macmillan, 2009.

Neumann, Iver B. *Uses of the Other: "The East" in European Identity Formation*. Minneapolis: University of Minnesota Press, 1999.

Niendorf, Mathias. "Deutsche und Polen in Pommerellen von 1920 bis 1945. Rollenerwartungen und Realität." *Nordost-Archiv* 6, no. 2 (1997): 687–728.

———. *Minderheiten an der Grenze. Deutsche und Polen in den Kreisen Flatow (Złotów) und Zempelburg (Sępólno Krajeńskie) 1900–1939*. Wiesbaden: Harrassowitz, 1997.

Nordblom, Pia. *Für Glaube und Volkstum. Die katholische Wochenzeitung "Der Deutsche in Polen" (1934–1939) in der Auseinandersetzung mit dem Nationalsozialismus*. Paderborn: Ferdinand Schöningh, 2000.

O'Donnell, Krista, Renate Bridenthal, and Nancy Reagin, eds. *The Heimat Abroad: The Boundaries of Germanness*. Ann Arbor: University of Michigan Press, 2005.

Orłowski, Hubert. "'Polnische Wirtschaft': The History and Function of the Stereotype." *Polish Western Affairs* 32, no. 2 (1991): 107–128.

———. "Polnische Wirtschaft": In *Deutsche und Polen. Hundert Schlüsselbegriffe*, edited by Ewa Kobylińska, Andreas Lawaty, and Rüdiger Stephan, 515–522. Munich: Piper, 1992.

———. *"Polnische Wirtschaft": Zum deutschen Polendiskurs der Neuzeit*. Wiesbaden: Harrassowitz, 1996.

Pease, Neal. *Rome's Most Faithful Daughter: The Catholic Church and Independent Poland, 1914–1939*. Athens: Ohio University Press, 2009.

Peters, Michael. "Alldeutscher Verband (ADV) (1891–1939)." *Historisches Lexikon Bayerns*. Accessed August 10, 2006. http://www.historisches-lexikon-bayerns. de/artikel/artikel_44184.

Peukert, Detlev. *Weimar Republic: The Crisis of Classical Modernity*, translated by Richard Deveson. New York: Hill and Wang, 1993.

Pieper, Helmut. *Die Minderheitenfrage und das Deutsche Reich 1919–1933/34*. Hamburg: Institut für Internationale Angelegenheiten der Universität Hamburg, 1974.

Pietrow-Ennker, Bianka. "Auf dem Weg zur Bürgergesellschaft. Modernisierungsprozesse in Lodz (1820–1914)." In *Polen, Deutsche und Juden in Lodz 1820–1939. Eine schwierige Nachbarschaft*, edited by Jürgen Hensel, 103–129. Osnabrück: Fibre, 1999.

———. "Ein Klischee lernt das Zwinkern. Der 'Lodzermensch' verkörpert eine Lebensweise, die in Łódź wieder modern wird." *Frankfurter Allgemeine Zeitung*, January 3, 2002, 48.

Pietsch, Martina. *Zwischen Verachtung und Verehrung. Marschall Józef Piłsudski im Spiegel der deutschen Presse 1926–1935*. Cologne/Weimar/Vienna: Böhlau, 1995.

Pinwinkler, Alexander. "Walter Kuhn (1903–1983) und der Bielitzer 'Wandervogel e.V.' Historisch-volkskundliche 'Sprachinselforschung' zwischen völkischem Pathos und politischer Indienstnahme." *Zeitschrift für Volkskunde* 105 (2009): 29–52.

Piskorski, Jan M. "Polish *myśl zachodnia* and German *Ostforschung*: An Attempt at a Comparison." In *German Scholars and Ethnic Cleansing, 1919–1945*, edited by Ingo Haar, and Michael Fahlbusch, 260–271. New York: Berghahn Books, 2005.

Piskorski, Jan M., Jörg Hackmann, and Rudolf Jaworski, eds. *Deutsche Ostforschung und Polnische Westforschung im Spannungsfeld von Wissenschaft und Politik. Disziplinen im Vergleich*. Osnabrück: Fibre, 2002.

Pohl, Karl Heinrich. "Der 'Kronprinzenbrief' Gustav Stresemanns vom September 1925 – Ein Beispiel für wissenschaftliche Quelleninterpretation auf der Oberstufe des Gymnasiums." *Geschichtsdidaktik* 8 (1983): 152–163.

———, ed. *Politiker und Bürger. Gustav Stresemann und seine Zeit*. Göttingen: Vandenhoeck & Ruprecht, 2002.

Polcuch, Valentin. "Wie ein Schmonzeslied zum Schlager wurde." In *Lodz. Die Stadt der Völkerbegegnung im Wandel der Geschichte*, edited by Peter E. Nasarski, 78. Cologne-Rodenkirchen: Liebig, 1978.

————. "'Theo, wir fahr'n nach Lodz.' Ein Schlager im Wandel der Geschichte." In *Lodz – "Gelobtes Land": Von deutscher Tuchmachersiedlung zur Textilmetropole im Osten. Dokumente und Erinnerungen,* edited by Peter E. Nasarski, 11–12. Berlin/Bonn: Westkreuz, 1988.

Pryt, Karina. *Befohlene Freundschaft. Die deutsch-polnischen Kulturbeziehungen 1934– 1939.* Osnabrück: Fibre, 2010.

Puś, Wiesław. "Die Berufs- und Sozialstruktur der wichtigsten ethnischen Gruppen in Lodz und ihre Entwicklung in den Jahren 1820–1914." In *Polen, Deutsche und Juden in Lodz 1820–1939. Eine schwierige Nachbarschaft,* edited by Jürgen Hensel, 33–43. Osnabrück: Fibre, 1999.

Pytlakowski, Piotr. "Naprzykrzyło się grzebać. Co się stało z Niemcami z Aleksandrowa Kujawskiego?" *Polityka,* January 27, 2001, 78–81.

————. "Ciężar pamięci. Jak na Kujawach zabijano Niemców (c.d.)." *Polityka,* February 24, 2001, 64–66.

Pytlas, Stefan. "Problemy asymilacji i polonizacji społeczności niemieckiej w Łodzi do 1914 r." In *Niemcy w Łodzi do 1939 roku,* edited by Marian Wilk, 13–20. Łódź: Uniwersytet Łódzki, 1996.

Radziszewska, Krystyna, ed. *Niemieckimi śladami po "Ziemi Obiecanej."* Łódź: Literatura, 1997.

————. "Die Schulpolitik der Zweiten Polnischen Republik gegenüber der deutschen Minderheit am Beispiel der Stadt Lodz." *Germano-Polonica. Mitteilungen zur Geschichte der Deutschen in Polen und der deutsch-polnischen Beziehungen,* no. 2 (2002/2003): 18–26.

Raitz von Frentz, Christian. *A Lesson Forgotten. Minority Protection Under the League of Nations: The Case of the German Minority in Poland, 1920–1934.* New York: St. Martin's Press, 1999.

Rasmus, Hugo. *Pommerellen-Westpreußen 1919–1939.* Munich/Berlin: Herbig, 1989.

Rautenberg, Hans-Werner. "Geschichte und Gegenwart Mittelpolens in der Forschung des Herder-Instituts." In *Polska Środkowa w niemieckich badaniach wschodnich. Historia i współczesność,* edited by Lucjan Meissner, 71–89. Łódź: Ibidem, 1999.

Reagin, Nancy R. "Recent Work on German National Identity: Regional? Imperial? Gendered? Imaginary?" *Central European History* 37, no. 2 (2004): 273–289.

————. "German *Brigadoon*? Domesticity and Metropolitan Perceptions of *Auslandsdeutschen* in Southwest Africa and Eastern Europe." In *The Heimat Abroad: The Boundaries of Germanness,* ed. Krista O'Donnell, Renate Bridenthal, and Nancy Reagin, 248–266. Ann Arbor: University of Michigan Press, 2005.

Reinecke, Christiane. "Krisenkalkulationen. Demographische Krisenszenarien und statistische Expertise in der Weimarer Republik." In *Die "Krise" der Weimarer Republik. Zur Kritik eines Deutungsmusters,* edited by Moritz Föllmer and Rüdiger Graf, 209–240. Frankfurt/Main: Campus, 2005.

Rhode, Gotthold. "Das Deutschtum in Posen und Pommerellen in der Zeit der Weimarer Republik." In *Die deutschen Ostgebiete zur Zeit der Weimarer Republik,* 88–132. Cologne/Graz: Böhlau, 1966.

————. "Lodzer Deutsche – Posener Deutsche. Keine wissenschaftliche Untersuchung, sondern eine Plauderei." In *Suche die Meinung. Karl Dedecius, dem*

Übersetzer und Mittler zum 65. Geburtstag, edited by Elvira Grözinger and Andreas Lawaty, 237–256. Wiesbaden: Harrassowitz, 1986.

Riekhoff, Harald von. *German-Polish Relations, 1918–1933*. Baltimore: The Johns Hopkins University Press, 1971.

Ritter, Ernst. *Das Deutsche Ausland-Institut in Stuttgart 1917–1945. Ein Beispiel Deutscher Volkstumsarbeit zwischen den Weltkriegen*. Wiesbaden: Franz Steiner, 1976.

Rogall, Joachim. "Einheit in Vielfalt der Deutschen aus Polen." In *Archive und Sammlungen der Deutschen aus Polen. Erlebte Geschichte, bewahrtes Kulturgut*, edited by Peter E. Nasarski, 13–18. Berlin/Bonn: Landsmannschaft Weichsel-Warthe, 1992.

———. *Die Deutschen im Posener Land und in Mittelpolen*. Munich: Langen Müller, 1993.

Rosen, Hans Freiherr von. *Wolhynienfahrt 1926*. Siegen: Selbstverlag der J.G. Herder-Bibliothek Siegerland e.V., 1982.

Rosenthal, Harry K. *German and Pole: National Conflict and Modern Myth*. Gainesville: University Presses of Florida, 1976.

Roser, Thomas. "Der Mythos vom gelobten Land. Das polnische Lodz galt einst als 'Manchester des Ostens' – und hegt jetzt die Hoffnung auf ein Comeback." *Frankfurter Rundschau*, April 12, 2002, 6.

Rossino, Alexander B. *Hitler Strikes Poland: Blitzkrieg, Ideology and Atrocity*. Lawrence: University of Kansas Press, 2003.

Roth, Karl Heinz. "Heydrichs Professor. Historiographie des 'Volkstums' und der Massenvernichtungen: Der Fall Hans Joachim Beyer." In *Geschichtsschreibung als Legitimationswissenschaft 1918–1945*, edited by Peter Schöttler, 262–342. Frankfurt/Main: Suhrkamp Taschenbuch, 1999.

Rutherford, Phillip T. *Prelude to the Final Solution: The Nazi Program for Deporting Ethnic Poles, 1939–1941*. Lawrence: University Press of Kansas, 2007.

Safran, William. "Diasporas in Modern Societies: Myth of Homeland and Return." *Diaspora* 1, no. 1 (1991): 83–99.

Sahlins, Peter. *Boundaries: The Making of France and Spain in the Pyrenees*. Berkeley: University of California Press, 1989.

Salewski, Michael. "Das Weimarer Revisionssyndrom." *Aus Politik und Zeitgeschichte* 30, no. 2 (1976): 14–25.

Sammartino, Annemarie. "Culture, Belonging, and the Law: Naturalization in the Weimar Republic." In *Citizenship and National Identity in Twentieth-Century Germany*, edited by Geoff Eley and Jan Palmowski, 57–72. Stanford: Stanford University Press, 2008.

———. *The Impossible Border: Germany and the East, 1914–1922*. Ithaca: Cornell University Press, 2010.

Samuś, Paweł. "Lodz. Heimatstadt von Polen, Deutschen und Juden." In *Polen, Deutsche und Juden in Lodz 1820–1939. Eine schwierige Nachbarschaft*, edited by Jürgen Hensel, 13–32. Osnabrück: Fibre, 1999.

———, ed. *Polacy–Niemcy–Żydzi w Łodzi w XIX–XX w. Sąsiedzi dalecy i bliscy*. Łódź: Ibidem, 1997.

Schot, Bastiaan. *Nation oder Staat? Deutschland und der Minderheitenschutz. Zur Völkerbundpolitik der Stresemann-Ära*. Marburg/Lahn: Verlag Herder-Institut, 1988.

Schöttler, Peter, ed. *Geschichtsschreibung als Legitimationswissenschaft 1918–1945.* Frankfurt/Main: Suhrkamp Taschenbuch, 1999.

Schulze, Hagen. "Versailles." In *Deutsche Erinnerungsorte I*, edited by Etienne François and Hagen Schulze, 407–421. Munich: Beck, 2001.

Serrier, Thomas. "'Deutsche Kulturarbeit in der Ostmark.' Der Mythos vom deutschen Vorrang und die Grenzproblematik in der Provinz Posen (1871–1914)." In *Die Nationalisierung von Grenzen. Zur Konstruktion nationaler Identität in sprachlich gemischten Grenzregionen*, edited by Michael G. Müller and Rolf Petri, 13–33. Marburg: Verlag Herder-Institut, 2002.

Sheehan, James J. "What is German History?" *Journal of Modern History* 53, no. 1 (March 1981): 1–23.

Smelser, Ronald M. *The Sudeten Problem, 1933–1938: Volkstumspolitik and the Formulation of Nazi Foreign Policy.* Middleton: Wesleyan University Press, 1975.

Smith, Helmut Walser. *The Butcher's Tale: Murder and Anti-Semitism in a German Town.* New York/London: Norton, 2002.

Smogorzewska, Małgorzata. *Posłowie i Senatorowie Rzeczypospolitej 1919–1939. Słownik biograficzny.* Vol. 2: E-J. Warsaw: Wydawnictwo Sejmowe, 2000.

Sontheimer, Kurt. *Antidemokratisches Denken in der Weimarer Republik. Die politischen Ideen des deutschen Nationalismus zwischen 1918 und 1933.* Munich: Nymphenburger Verlagshandlung, 1962.

Spickermann, Roland. "The Elections Cartel in Regierungsbezirk Bromberg (Bydgoszcz), 1898–1903: Ethnic Rivalry, Agrarianism, and 'Practicing Democracy.'" *Central European History* 37, no. 1 (2004): 91–114.

Steinhart, Eric C. "Policing the Boundaries of 'Germandom' in the East: SS Ethnic German Policy and Odessa's 'Volksdeutsche,' 1941–1944." *Central European History* 43, no. 1 (2010): 85–116.

Steinweis, Alan E. *Studying the Jew: Scholarly Antisemitism in Nazi Germany.* Cambridge: Harvard University Press, 2006.

Stiller, Alexa. "Grenzen des 'Deutschen': Nationalsozialistische Volkstumspolitik in Polen, Frankreich und Slowenien während des Zweiten Weltkriegs." In *Deutschsein als Grenzerfahrung. Minderheitenpolitik in Europa zwischen 1914 und 1950*, edited by Mathias Beer, Dietrich Beyrau, and Cornelia Rauh, 61–84. Essen: Klartext, 2009.

Storm, Eric. "Regionalism in History, 1890–1945: The Culturalist Approach." *European History Quarterly* 33, no. 2 (2003): 251–265.

Strobel, Georg W. "Industriemetropole zwischen Orient und Okzident. Eine Hommage an die Vielvölkerstadt Lodz." *Deutsch-Polnische Ansichten zur Literatur und Kultur. Jahrbuch 1992*, 31–59. Darmstadt: Deutsches Polen-Institut; Wiesbaden: Harrassowitz, 1993.

———. "Das multinationale Lodz, die Textilmetropole Polens, als Produkt von Migration und Kapitalwanderung." In *Wanderungen und Kulturaustausch im östlichen Mitteleuropa. Forschungen zum ausgehenden Mittelalter und zur jüngeren Neuzeit*, edited by Hans-Werner Rautenberg, 163–223. Munich: Oldenbourg, 2006.

Struve, Kai, and Philipp Ther, eds. *Die Grenzen der Nationen. Identitätenwandel in Oberschlesien in der Neuzeit.* Marburg: Verlag Herder-Institut, 2002.

Suval, Stanley. "Overcoming Kleindeutschland: The Politics of Historical Myth-making in the Weimar Republic." *Central European History* 2, no. 4 (1969): 312–330.

Swart, Friedrich. *Diesseits und jenseits der Grenze. Das deutsche Genossenschaftswesen im Posener Land und das deutsch-polnische Verhältnis bis zum Ende des Zweiten Weltkrieges.* Leer: Rautenberg & Möckel, 1954.

Swart, Friedrich, and Richard Breyer. "Die deutsche Volksgruppe im polnischen Staat." In *Das östliche Deutschland. Ein Handbuch*, edited by Göttinger Arbeitskreis, 477–526. Würzburg: Holzner, 1959.

Szmeja, Maria. *Niemcy? Polacy? Ślązacy! Rodzimi mieszkańcy Opolszczyzny w świetle analiz socjologicznych.* Cracow: Universitas, 2000.

Tacke, Charlotte. *Denkmal im sozialen Raum. Nationale Symbole in Deutschland und Frankreich im 19. Jahrhundert.* Göttingen: Vandenhoeck & Ruprecht, 1995.

Ther, Philipp. "Deutsche Geschichte als imperiale Geschichte. Polen, slawophone Minderheiten und das Kaiserreich als kontinentales Empire." In *Das Kaiserreich transnational. Deutschland in der Welt 1871–1914*, edited by Sebastian Conrad and Jürgen Osterhammel, 129–158. Göttingen: Vandenhoeck & Ruprecht, 2004.

Threde, Walther, and Peter E. Nasarski. *Polen und sein preußischer Streifen, 1919–1939. Die deutsche Volksgruppe in Posen und Pommerellen.* Berlin/Bonn: Westkreuz, 1983.

Thum, Gregor, ed. *Traumland Osten. Deutsche Bilder vom östlichen Europa im 20. Jahrhundert.* Göttingen: Vandenhoeck & Ruprecht, 2006.

———. "Mythische Landschaften. Das Bild vom 'deutschen Osten' und die Zäsuren des 20. Jahrhunderts." In *Traumland Osten. Deutsche Bilder vom östlichen Europa im 20. Jahrhundert*, edited by Gregor Thum, 181–211. Göttingen: Vandenhoeck & Ruprecht, 2006.

Todorova, Maria. "The Balkans: From Discovery to Invention." *Slavic Review* 53, no. 2 (1994): 453–482.

Tomaszewski, Jerzy. "Jews in Łódź in 1931 According to Statistics." *Polin. A Journal of Polish-Jewish Studies* 6 (1990): 173–200.

Treger, Max. *Lodz–Berlin 1914–1984. Ein Zeitdokument.* Frankfurt/Main: Autoren-Selbstverlag, 1985.

Walicki, Jacek. "Żydzi i Niemcy w samorządzie Łodzi lat 1917–1939." In *Polacy–Niemcy–Żydzi*, edited by Paweł Samuś, 359–376. Łódź: Ibidem, 1997.

Wehler, Hans-Ulrich. "Nationalsozialismus und Historiker," in *Deutsche Historiker im Nationalsozialismus*, edited by Winfried Schulze and Otto Gerhard Oexle, 306–339. Frankfurt/Main: Fischer Taschenbuch, 1999.

Weichlein, Siegfried. *Nation und Region. Integrationsprozesse im Bismarckreich.* Düsseldorf: Droste, 2004.

Weigelt, Fritz, ed. *Von unserer Art. Vom Leben und Wirken deutscher Menschen im Raume von Weichsel und Warthe.* Wuppertal: Landsmannschaft Weichsel-Warthe, 1963.

Weinberg, Gerhard L. *Germany, Hitler, and World War II: Essays in Modern German and World History.* Cambridge/New York: Cambridge University Press, 1995.

Weitz, Eric. "Racial Politics Without the Concept of Race: Reevaluating Soviet Ethnic and National Purges." *Slavic Review* 61, no. 1 (2002): 1–29.

Wierzchosławski, Szczepan. "Społeczeństwo Prus Zachodnich wobec administracji Pruskiej (1815–1914)." In *Toruń i Pomorze pod władzą pruską. Materiały konferencji z 10–11 grudnia 1993 r. w Toruniu*, edited by Szczepan Wierzchosławski, 63–76. Toruń: Towarzystwo Naukowe w Toruniu, 1995.

Wildt, Michael. Generation der Unbedingten. *Das Führungskorps des Reichssicherheitshauptamtes*. Hamburg: Hamburger Edition, HIS Verlag, 2002.

Wilhelm, Cornelia. *Bewegung oder Verein? Nationalsozialistische Volkstumspolitik in den USA*. Stuttgart: Steiner, 1998.

Wippermann, Wolfgang. *Der deutsche "Drang nach Osten." Ideologie und Wirklichkeit eines politischen Schlagwortes*. Darmstadt: Wissenschaftliche Buchgesellschaft, 1981.

―――. *Die Deutschen und der Osten. Feindbild und Traumland*. Darmstadt: Primus, 2007.

Wojciechowski, Marian. "Die deutsche Minderheit in Polen (1920–1939)." In *Deutsche und Polen zwischen den Kriegen. Minderheitenstatus und "Volkstumskampf" im Grenzgebiet. Amtliche Berichterstattung aus beiden Ländern, 1920–1939*, edited by Rudolf Jaworski, Marian Wojciechowski, Mathias Niendorf, and Przemysław Hauser, vol. 1, 1–26. Munich: Saur, 1997.

Wojciechowski, Mieczysław. "Mniejszość niemiecka w Toruniu w latach 1920–1939." In *Mniejszości narodowe i wyznaniowe w Toruniu w XIX i XX wieku*, edited by Mieczysław Wojciechowski, 59–80. Toruń: Uniwersytet Mikołaja Kopernika, 1993.

Wolf, Gerhard. "Deutsche Volksliste." In *Handbuch der völkischen Wissenschaften*, edited by Ingo Haar and Michael Fahlbusch, 129–135. Munich: Saur, 2008.

Wolff, Stefan. *Disputed Territories: The Transnational Dynamics of Ethnic Conflict Settlement*. New York/Oxford: Berghahn Books, 2003.

Woźniak, Krzysztof. "Spory o genezę Łodzi przemysłowej w pracach historycznych autorów polskich, niemieckich i żydowskich." In *Polacy–Niemcy–Żydzi w Łodzi w XIX–XX w. Sąsiedzi dalecy i bliscy*, edited by Paweł Samuś, 9–26. Łódź: Ibidem, 1997.

―――. "Forschungsstand und Forschungsdesiderata zur Geschichte der Deutschen in Mittelpolen." *Nordost-Archiv* 9, no. 2 (2000): 413–427.

Wright, Jonathan. Review of *Gustave Stresemann (1878–1929). De l'impérialisme à la sécurité collective*, by Christian Baechler. *German History* 16, no. 1 (1998): 107–108.

―――. *Gustav Stresemann. Weimar's Greatest Statesman*. Oxford: Oxford University Press, 2004.

Wróbel, Janusz. "Between Co-Existence and Hostility: A Contribution to the Problem of National Antagonisms in Łódź in the Inter-War Period." *Polin. A Journal of Polish-Jewish Studies* 6 (1990): 201–206.

Wrzesiński, Wojciech. *Sąsiad, czy wróg? Ze studiów nad kształtowaniem się obraz Niemca w Polsce w latach 1795–1939*. Wrocław: Wydawnictwo Uniwersytetu Wrocławskiego, 1992.

―――, ed. *Twórcy polskiej myśli zachodniej*. Olsztyn: Ośrodek Badań Naukowych, 1996.

Wynot, Edward D. "The Polish Germans, 1919–1939: National Minority in a Multinational State." *The Polish Review* 17, no. 1 (1972): 22–64.

Wysocka, Barbara. *Regionalizm wielkopolski w II Rzeczypospolitej 1919–1939.* Poznań: Uniwersytet im. Adama Mickiewicza, 1981.

Yuval-Davis, Nira. "Women, Citizenship and Difference." *Feminist Review* 57 (1997): 4–21.

Zahra, Tara. *Kidnapped Souls: National Indifference and the Battle for Children in the Bohemian Lands, 1900–1948.* Ithaca: Cornell University Press, 2008.

―――. "Imagined Noncommunities: National Indifference as a Category of Analysis." *Slavic Review* 69, no. 1 (Spring 2010): 93–119.

Żakowski, Jacek. "Nowy rozbiór Polski. Granice rozbiorów pokrywają się z granicami poparcia dla Unii." *Polityka*, June 24, 2003, 32–33.

Zientara, Benedykt. "Zum Problem des geschichtlichen Terminus 'Drang nach Osten.'" In *Preußen, Deutschland, Polen im Urteil polnischer Historiker. Millenium Germano-Polonicum,* edited by Lothar Dralle. Berlin: Historische Kommission zu Berlin, 1983.

Index